NETWORK AND SYSTEM SECURITY

SECOND EDITION

Edited by

JOHN R. VACCA

ELSEVIER

AMSTERDAM • BOSTON • HEIDELBERG • LONDON
NEW YORK • OXFORD • PARIS • SAN DIEGO
SAN FRANCISCO • SYDNEY • TOKYO
Syngress is an imprint of Elsevier

SYNGRESS.

Publisher: Steven Elliot
Senior Developmental Editor: Nathaniel McFadden
Editorial Project Manager: Lindsay Lawrence
Project Manager: Mohanambal Natarajan
Designer: Matthew Limbert

Syngress is an imprint of Elsevier
225 Wyman Street, Waltham, MA 02451, USA

Second Edition 2014

Notice
No responsibility is assumed by the publisher for any injury and/or damage to persons or property as a matter of products liability, negligence or otherwise, or from any use or operation of any methods, products, instructions or ideas contained in the material herein. Because of rapid advances in the medical sciences, in particular, independent verification of diagnoses and drug dosages should be made

Library of Congress Cataloging-in-Publication Data
A catalog record for this book is available from the Library of Congress

British Library Cataloguing in Publication Data
A catalogue record for this book is available from the British Library

For information on all **Syngress** publications,
visit our website at store.elsevier.com/Syngress

ISBN: 978-0-12-416689-9

Printed and bound in USA

14 15 16 17 18   10 9 8 7 6 5 4 3 2 1

Working together
to grow libraries in
developing countries

ELSEVIER   Book Aid International

www.elsevier.com • www.bookaid.org

This book is dedicated to my wife Bee.

Contents

Acknowledgements

There are many people whose efforts on this book have contributed to its successful completion. I owe each a debt of gratitude and want to take this opportunity to offer my sincere thanks.

A very special thanks to my publisher, Steve Elliot, without whose continued interest and support this book would not have been possible. Senior development editor Nate McFadden provided staunch support and encouragement when it was most needed. Thanks to my production project manager, Mohanambal Natarajan, whose fine work and attention to detail has been invaluable. Thanks also to my marketing manager, Todd Conly, whose efforts on this book have been greatly appreciated.

Finally, thanks to all the other people at Morgan Kaufmann Publishers/Elsevier Science & Technology Books, whose many talents and skills are essential to a finished book.

Thanks to my wife, Bee Vacca, for her love, her help, and her understanding of my long work hours. Finally, I wish to thank all the following authors who contributed chapters that were necessary for the completion of this book: Gerald Beuchelt, Erdal Cayirci, Tom Chen, Hongbing Cheng, Scott Ellis, Cem Gurkok, Almantas Kakareka, Thomas La Porta, Peng Liu, Bill Mansoor, Pramod Pandya, Chunming Rong, Mario Santana, Jesse Walker, Michael West, Liang Yan, Gansen Zhao.

About the Editor

John Vacca is an information technology consultant, professional writer, editor, reviewer and internationally-known, best-selling author based in Pomeroy, Ohio. Since 1982, John has authored 73 books (some of his most recent books include):

- **Computer and Information Security Handbook, 2E** (*Publisher:* Morgan Kaufmann (an imprint of Elsevier Inc.) (May 31, 2013))
- **Identity Theft (Cybersafety)** (*Publisher:* Chelsea House Pub (April 1, 2012)
- **System Forensics, Investigation, And Response** (*Publisher:* Jones & Bartlett Learning (September 24, 2010)
- **Managing Information Security** (*Publisher:* Syngress (an imprint of Elsevier Inc.) (March 29, 2010))
- **Network and Systems Security** (*Publisher:* Syngress (an imprint of Elsevier Inc.) (March 29, 2010))
- **Computer and Information Security Handbook, 1E** (*Publisher:* Morgan Kaufmann (an imprint of Elsevier Inc.) (June 2, 2009))
- **Biometric Technologies and Verification Systems** (*Publisher:* Elsevier Science & Technology Books (March 16, 2007))
- **Practical Internet Security** (Hardcover): (*Publisher:* Springer (October 18, 2006))
- **Optical Networking Best Practices Handbook** (Hardcover): (*Publisher:* Wiley-Interscience (November 28, 2006))
- **Guide to Wireless Network Security** (*Publisher:* Springer (August 19, 2006)
- **Computer Forensics: Computer Crime Scene Investigation (With CD-ROM), 2nd Edition** (*Publisher:* Charles River Media (May 26, 2005)

and, more than 600 articles in the areas of advanced storage, computer security and aerospace technology (copies of articles and books are available upon request). John was also a configuration management specialist, computer specialist, and the computer security official (CSO) for NASA's space station program (Freedom) and the International Space Station Program, from 1988 until his retirement from NASA in 1995. In addition, John is also an independent online book reviewer. Finally, John was one of the security consultants for the MGM movie titled: "AntiTrust," which was released on January 12, 2001. A detailed copy of my author bio can be viewed at URL: http://www.johnvacca.com. John can be reached at: john2164@windstream.net.

Contributors

Almantas Kakareka, CISSP, GSNA, GSEC, CEH **(Chapter 1)**, CTO, Demyo, Inc., Sunny Isles Beach, Florida 33160

Michael A. West (Chapter 2), *Senior technical writer, Truestone Maritime Operations* Martinez, California 94553

Tom Chen (Chapter 3), Professor, Swansea University, Singleton Park, SA2 8PP, Wales, United Kingdom

Cem Gurkok (Chapter 4), Threat Intelligence Development Manager, Terremark Worldwide, Inc., **Miami, Florida 33131**

Gerald Beuchelt (Chapter 5), Principal Software Systems Engineer, Bedford, MA 01803

Mario Santana (Chapter 6), Consultant, Terremark, **Miami, Florida 33131**

Jesse Walker (Chapter 7), Principal Engineer, Intel Corporation, Hillsboro, Oregon 97124

Bill Mansoor (Chapter 8), Information Security Analyst III, Information Security Office County of Riverside, Viejo, California 92692

Pramod Pandya (Chapter 9), Professor, Department of Information Systems and Decision Sciences, California State University, Fullerton, California 92834

Chunming Rong (Chapter 10), Professor, Ph.D., Chair of Computer Science Section, Faculty of Science and Technology, University of Stavanger, N-4036 Stavanger, Norway

Erdal Cayirci, Professor (Chapters 10, 12), Professor, University of Stavanger, N-4036 Stavanger, Norway

Hongbing Cheng (Chapters 10, 12), Professor, *University of Stavanger, Norway*

Liang Yan (Chapters 10, 12), Professor, *University of Stavanger, Norway*

Gansen Zhao (Chapters 10, 12), Professor, South China Normal University, Guangzhou 510631, P.R. China

Thomas F. LaPorta (Chapter 11), Department of Computer Science and Engineering, The Pennsylvania State University, University Park, Pennsylvania 16802

Peng Liu (Chapter 11), Director, Cyber Security Lab, College of Information Sciences and Technology, The Pennsylvania State University, University Park, Pennsylvania 16802

Chunming Rong (Chapter 12), Professor, Ph.D., Chair of Computer Science Section, Faculty of Science and Technology, University of Stavanger, N-4036 Stavanger, Norway

Scott R. Ellis, EnCE, RCA (Chapter 13), Manager, Infrastructure Engineering Team, *kCura*, Chicago, IL 60604

Introduction

Organizations today are linking their systems across enterprise-wide networks and virtual private networks (VPNs), as well as increasing their exposure to customers, competitors, browsers and hackers on the Internet. According to industry analysts, NAC is now the "Holy Grail" of network security; but, NAC isn't the sole contributor to the booming security market. According to industry analysts, hackers are inventing new ways to attack corporate networks, and vendors are just as quickly devising ways to protect against them. Those innovations will continue to push the security market higher.

First, there's a real need for enterprise-class security for handheld devices, especially wireless client devices, such as Wi-Fi VoIP handsets. Second, as the next step in perimeter security, network IPS is beginning to make the transition from niche security technology to core network infrastructure. And, finally, enterprises are fed up with viruses, spyware and malware, and are willing to make significant investments to put a stop to them. Industry analysts have identified the following trends in the burgeoning security market:

- Software, hardware appliances and security routers are the preferred security for most respondents and will continue to be through 2014. Secure routers show the most growth.
- Fifty-three percent of respondents have purchased wireless LAN security products, while 34% said they will buy or are considering buying WLAN security.

- The need to block viruses and the fear of hackers are prompting respondents to buy security products and services en masse.
- Increased service reliability is the most important payback respondents expect from managed security service. Respondents also thought organizations should focus on core competencies, have access to more advanced technology and have access to better expertise.

In this book, you will learn how to analyze risks to your networks and the steps needed to select and deploy the appropriate countermeasures to reduce your exposure to physical and network threats. This book will enhance the skills and knowledge of practitioners and IT professionals who need to identify and counter some fundamental security risks and requirements. Practitioners and IT professionals will learn some advanced network security skills pertaining to network threat identification and prevention. They will also examine Internet security threats and measures (audit trails IP sniffing/spoofing etc. . . .) and learn how to implement advanced security policies and procedures. In addition, in this book, you will also learn how to:

1. Secure UNIX and Linux systems from internal and external threats
2. Establish authenticated access to local and remote resources
3. Avoid potential security loopholes by limiting super user privileges
4. Protect UNIX file systems

5. Configure tools and utilities to minimize exposure and detect intrusions
6. Tackle security problems by swapping out insecure software components
7. Add tools and services to increase security
8. Create, document and test continuity arrangements for your organization
9. Perform a risk assessment and Business Impact Assessment (BIA) to identify vulnerabilities
10. Select and deploy an alternate site for continuity of mission-critical activities
11. Identify appropriate strategies to recover the infrastructure and processes
12. Test and maintain an effective recovery plan in a rapidly changing technology environment
13. Detect and respond to vulnerabilities that put your organization at risk using scanners
14. Employ real-world exploits and evaluate their effect on your systems
15. Analyze the results of vulnerability scans
16. Assess vulnerability alerts and advisories
17. Build a firewall to protect your network
18. Install and configure proxy-based and stateful-filtering firewalls
19. Provide access to HTTP and FTP services on the Internet
20. Implement publicly accessible servers without compromising security
21. Protect internal IP addresses with NAT and deploy a secure DNS architecture
22. Identify security threats to your data and IT infrastructure
23. Recognize appropriate technology to deploy against these threats
24. Adapt your organization's information security policy to operational requirements and assess compliance
25. Effectively communicate information security issues

In addition, you will also gain the skills needed to secure your UNIX and Linux platforms. You will learn to use tools and utilities to assess vulnerabilities, detect configurations that threaten information assurance and provide effective access controls.

You will also learn to identify vulnerabilities and implement appropriate countermeasures to prevent and mitigate threats to your mission-critical processes. You will learn techniques for creating a business continuity plan (BCP) and the methodology for building an infrastructure that supports its effective implementation.

Knowledge of vulnerability assessment and hacking techniques allows you to detect vulnerabilities before your networks are attacked. In this book, you will learn to configure and use vulnerability scanners to detect weaknesses and prevent network exploitation. You will also acquire the knowledge to assess the risk to your enterprise from an array of vulnerabilities and to minimize your exposure to costly threats.

ORGANIZATION OF THIS BOOK

The book is composed of 13 contributed chapters by leading experts in their fields:

Contributor **Almantas Kakareka** (Chapter 1, "Detecting System Intrusions") describes the characteristics of the DSI technologies and provides recommendations for designing, implementing, configuring, securing, monitoring, and maintaining them. Detecting system intrusions is the process of monitoring the events occurring in a computer system or network and analyzing them for signs of possible incidents, which are violations or imminent threats of violation of computer security policies, acceptable use policies, or standard security practices.

The detection of system intrusions (DSIs) is primarily focused on identifying possible incidents, logging information about them, attempting to stop them, and reporting them to security administrators. In addition, organizations use the DSIs for other purposes, such as identifying problems with security policies, documenting existing threats, and deterring individuals from violating security policies.

The DSIs have become a necessary addition to the security infrastructure of nearly every organization. In addition, the DSIs typically record information related to observed events, notify security administrators of important observed events, and produce reports.

Many of the DSIs can also respond to a detected threat by attempting to prevent it from succeeding. They use several response techniques, which involve the DSIs stopping the attack itself, changing the security environment (reconfiguring a firewall), or changing the attack's content. This chapter describes the characteristics of the DSI technologies and provides recommendations for designing, implementing, configuring, securing, monitoring, and maintaining them.

Next, contributor Michael West (Chapter 2, "Preventing System Intrusions") discusses how to prevent system intrusions, where an unauthorized-penetration of a computer in your enterprise occurs or an address in your assigned domain. The moment you establish an active Web presence, you put a target on your company's back. And like the hapless insect that lands in the spider's web, your company's size determines the size of the disturbance you create on the Web—and how quickly you're noticed by the bad

guys. How attractive you are as prey is usually directly proportionate to what you have to offer a predator. If yours is an ecommerce site whose business thrives on credit card or other financial information or a company with valuable secrets to steal, your "juiciness" quotient goes up; you have more of value there to steal. And if your business is new and your Web presence is recent, the assumption could be made that perhaps you're not yet a seasoned veteran in the nuances of cyber warfare and, thus, are more vulnerable to an intrusion.

Unfortunately for you, many of those who seek to penetrate your network defenses are educated, motivated, and quite brilliant at developing faster and more efficient methods of quietly sneaking around your perimeter, checking for the smallest of openings. Most IT professionals know that an enterprise's firewall is ceaselessly being probed for weaknesses and vulnerabilities by crackers from every corner of the globe. Anyone who follows news about software understands that seemingly every few months, word comes out about a new, exploitable opening in an operating system or application. It's widely understood that no one—not the most savvy network administrator or the programmer who wrote the software—can possibly find and close all the holes in today's increasingly complex software.

Bugs exist in applications, operating systems, server processes (daemons), and clients. System configurations can also be exploited, such as not changing the default administrator's password or accepting default system settings, or unintentionally leaving a hole open by configuring the machine to run in a nonsecure mode. Even Transmission Control Protocol/Internet Protocol (TCP/IP), the foundation on which all Internet traffic operates, can be exploited, since the protocol was designed before the threat of hacking was really widespread. Therefore, it contains design flaws that can allow, for example, a cracker to easily alter IP data.

Once the word gets out that a new and exploitable opening exists in an application (and word *will* get out), crackers around the world start scanning sites on the Internet searching for any and all sites that have that particular opening. Making your job even harder is the fact that many openings into your network can be caused by your employees. Casual surfing of porn sites can expose the network to all kinds of nasty bugs and malicious code, merely by an employee visiting the site. The problem is that, to users, it might not seem like such a big deal. They either don't realize or don't care that they're leaving the network wide open to intrusion.

Preventing network intrusions is no easy task. Like cops on the street—usually outnumbered and under equipped compared to the bad guys—you face an enemy with determination, skill, training, and a frightening array of increasingly sophisticated tools for hacking their way through your best defenses. And, no matter how good your defenses are today, it's only a matter of time before a tool is developed that can penetrate them. If you know that ahead of time, you'll be much more inclined to keep a watchful eye for what "they" have and what you can use to defeat them.

Your best weapon is a logical, thoughtful, and nimble approach to network security. You have to be nimble—to evolve and grow with changes in technology, never being content to keep things as they are because "Hey, they're working just fine." Today's "just fine" will be tomorrow's "What the hell happened?"

Stay informed. There is no shortage of information available to you in the form of white papers, seminars, contract security specialists, and online resources, all dealing with various aspects of network security.

Have a good, solid, comprehensive, yet easy-to-understand network security policy in place. The very process of developing one will get all involved parties thinking about how to best secure your network while addressing user needs. When it comes to your users, you simply can't over-educate them where network security awareness is concerned. The more they know, the better equipped they'll be to act as allies against, rather than accomplices of, the hoards of crackers looking to steal, damage, hobble, or completely cripple your network.

Do your research and invest in good, multipurpose network security systems. Select systems that are easy to install and implement, are adaptable and quickly configurable, can be customized to suit your needs of today as well as tomorrow, and are supported by companies that keep pace with current trends in cracker technology.

Then, contributor Tom Chen (Chapter 3, "Guarding Against Network Intrusions") continues by showing how to guard against network intrusions, by understanding the variety of attacks from exploits to malware to social engineering. Virtually all computers today are connected to the Internet through dialup, broadband, Ethernet, or wireless technologies. The reason for this Internet ubiquity is simple: Applications depending on the network, such as email, Web, remote login, instant messaging, and VoIP, have become essential to the computing experience. Unfortunately, the Internet exposes computer users to risks from a wide variety of possible attacks. Users have much to lose—their privacy, valuable data, control of their computers, and possibly theft of their identities. The network enables attacks to be carried out remotely, with relative anonymity and low risk of traceability.

The nature of network intrusions has evolved over the years. A few years ago, a major concern was fast worms such as Code Red, Nimda, Slammer, and Sobig. More recently, concerns shifted to spyware, Trojan horses, and botnets. Although these other threats still continue to be major problems, the Web has become the primary vector for stealthy attacks today.

Contributor Cem Gurkok (Chapter 4, "Securing Cloud Computing Systems") discusses how to prevent system intrusions and where an unauthorized penetration of a computer in your enterprise or an address in your assigned domain can occur. Cloud computing is a method of delivering computing resources.

Cloud computing services ranging from data storage and processing to software, such as customer relationship management systems, are now available instantly and on demand. In times of financial and economic hardship, this new low cost of ownership model for computing has gotten lots of attention and is seeing increasing global investment.

Generally speaking, cloud computing provides implementation agility, lower capital expenditure, location independence, resource pooling, broad network access, reliability, scalability, elasticity, and ease of maintenance. While in most cases cloud computing can improve security due to ease of management, the provider's lack of knowledge and experience can jeopardize customer environments. This chapter aims to discuss various cloud computing environments and methods to make them more secure for hosting companies and their customers.

Next, contributor Gerald Beuchelt (Chapter 5, "UNIX and Linux Security") discusses how to scan for vulnerabilities;

reduce denial-of-service (DoS) attacks; deploy firewalls to control network traffic; and, build network firewalls. When **Unix** was first booted on a PDP-8 computer at Bell Labs, it already had a basic notion of user isolation, separation of kernel and user memory space, and process security. It was originally conceived as a multiuser system, and as such, security could not be added on as an afterthought. In this respect, **Unix** was different from a whole class of computing machinery that had been targeted at single-user environments.

The examples in this chapter refer to the Solaris operating system and Debian-based Linux distributions, a commercial and a community developed operating system. Solaris is freely available in open source and binary distributions. It derives directly from AT&T System V R4.2 or higher, and is one of the few operating systems that can legally be called **Unix**. It is distributed by Sun Microsystems, but there are independent distributions built on top of the open source version of Solaris.

Then, contributor **Mario Santana (Chapter 6, "Eliminating The Security Weakness of Linux and UNIX Operating Systems")** presents an introduction to securing UNIX in general and Linux in particular, providing some historical context and describing some fundamental aspects of the secure operating system architecture. Linux and other Unix-like operating systems are prevalent on the Internet for a number of reasons.

As an operating system designed to be flexible and robust, Unix lends itself to providing a wide array of host- and network-based services. Unix also has a rich culture from its long history as a fundamental part of computing research in industry and academia.

Unix and related operating systems play a key role as platforms for delivering the key services that make the Internet possible. For these reasons, it is important that information security practitioners understand fundamental Unix concepts in support of practical knowledge of how Unix systems might be securely operated.

This chapter is an introduction to Unix in general and to Linux in particular, presenting some historical context and describing some fundamental aspects of the operating system architecture. Considerations for hardening Unix deployments will be contemplated from net- work-centric, host-based, and systems management perspectives. Finally, proactive considerations are presented to identify security weaknesses to correct them and to deal effectively with security breaches when they do occur.

Contributor Jesse Walker (Chapter 7, "Internet Security") continues by showing you how cryptography can be used to address some of the security issues besetting communications protocols. The Internet, and all its accompanying complications, has become integral to our lives. The security problems besetting the Internet are legendary and have been daily annoyances to many users. Given the Net's broad impact on our lives and the widespread security issues associated with, it is worthwhile understanding what can be done to improve the immunity of our communications from attack.

The Internet can serve as a laboratory for studying network security issues; indeed, we can use it to study nearly every kind of security issue. Walker will pursue only a modest set of questions related to this theme. The goal of this chapter is to understand how cryptography can be used to address some of the security issues besetting communications protocols. To do so, it will be helpful to first understand the Internet architecture. After that, he will

survey the types of attacks that are possible against communications. With this background he will be in a position to understand how cryptography can be used to preserve the confidentiality and integrity of messages.

Walker's goal is modest. It is only to describe the network architecture and its cryptographic-based security mechanisms sufficiently to understand some of the major issues confronting security systems designers and to appreciate some of the major design decisions they have to make to address these issues.

This chapter also examines how cryptography is used on the Internet to secure protocols. It reviews the architecture of the Internet protocol suite, as even what security means is a function of the underlying system architecture. Next, it reviews the Dolev-Yao model, which describes the threats to which network communications are exposed. In particular, all levels of network protocols are completely exposed to eavesdropping and manipulation by an attacker, so using cryptography properly is a first-class requirement to derive any benefit from its use. Walker also shows you that effective security mechanisms to protect session-oriented and session establishment protocols are different, although they can share many cryptographic primitives. Cryptography can be very successful at protecting messages on the Internet, but doing so requires pre-existing, long-lived relationships. How to build secure open communities is still an open problem; it is probably intractable because a solution would imply the elimination of conflict between human beings who do not know each other.

Then, contributor Bill Mansoor (Chapter 8, "Intranet Security") covers internal security strategies and tactics; external security strategies and tactics;

network access security; and, Kerberos. Thus, the onus of preventing embarrassing security gaffes falls squarely on the shoulders of IT security chiefs (CISOs and security officers). These CISOs, are sometimes hobbled by unclear mandates from government regulators and lack of sufficient budgeting to tackle the mandates.

It is true that the level of Internet hyperconnectivity among generation X and Y users has mushroomed lately, and the network periphery that we used to take for granted as a security shield has been diminished, to a large extent, because of the explosive growth of social networking and the resulting connectivity boom. However, with the various new types of incoming application traffic (VoIP, SIP, and XML traffic) to their networks, security administrators need to stay on their toes and deal with these new protocols by implementing newer tools and technology. One recent example of new technology is the application-level firewall for connecting outside vendors to intranets (also known as an XML firewall, placed within a DMZ) that protects the intranet from malformed XML and SOAP message exploits coming from outside sourced applications.

So, with the myriad security issues facing intranets today, most IT shops are still well equipped to defend themselves if they assess risks and, most important, train their employees regarding data security practices on an ongoing basis. The problems with threat mitigation remain largely a matter of meeting gaps in procedural controls rather than technical measures. Trained and security-aware employees are the biggest deterrent to data thefts and security breaches.

Contributor Dr. Pramod Pandya (Chapter 9, "Local Area Network Security,") continues by discussing network design and security deployment; and,

ongoing management and auditing. Securing available resources on any corporate or academic data network is of paramount importance because most of these networks connect to the Internet for commercial or research activities. Therefore, the network is under attack from hackers on a continual basis, so network security technologies are ever evolving and playing catch-up with hackers. Around 20 years ago the number of potential users was small and the scope of any activity on the network was limited to local networks only. As the Internet expanded in its reach across national boundaries and as the number of users increased, potential risk to the network grew exponentially. Over the past 10 years, ecommerce-related activities such as online shopping, banking, stock trading, and social networking have permeated extensively, creating a dilemma for both service providers and their potential clients, as to who is a trusted service provider and a trusted client on the network. Of course, this being a daunting task for security professionals, they have needed to design security policies appropriate for both the servers and their clients. The security policy must be a factor in the clients' level of access to the resources. So, in whom do we place trust, and how much trust?

Securing network systems is an ongoing process in which new threats arise all the time. Consequently, firewalls, NIDS, and intrusion prevention systems are continuously evolving technologies. In this chapter, Pandya's focus has been and will be wired networks. However, as wireless data networks proliferate and seamlessly connect to the cellular voice networks, the risk of attacks on the wired networks is growing exponentially.

In addition, the responsibility for the design and implementation of network security, should be headed by the chief information officer (CIO) of the enterprise network. The CIO has a pool of network administrators and legal advisers to help with this task. The network administrators define the placing of the network access controls, and the legal advisors underline the consequences and liabilities in the event of network security breaches. We have seen cases of customer records such as credit card numbers, Social Security numbers, and personal information being stolen. The frequency of these reports have been on the increase in the past years, and consequently this has led to a discussion on the merits of encryption of stored data. One of the most quoted legal requirements on the part of any business, whether small or big, is the protection of consumer data under the Health Insurance Portability and Accountability Act (HIPAA), which restricts disclosure of health-related data and personal information.

Next, contributors Chunming Rong, Erdal Cayirci, Gansen Zhao, Hongbing Cheng and Laing Yan (Chapter 10, "Wireless Network Security") present an overview of wireless network security technology; how to- design wireless network security, plan for wireless network security; install and deploy wireless network security, and maintain wireless network security; information warfare countermeasures: the wireless network security solution; and, wireless network security solutions and future directions. With the rapid development of technology in wireless communication and microchips, wireless technology has been widely used in various application areas. The proliferation of wireless devices and wireless networks in the past decade shows the widespread of wireless technology.

Wireless networks is a general term to refer to various types of networks that are wireless, meaning that they communicate without the need of wire lines. Wireless networks can be broadly categorized into two classes based on the structures of the networks: wireless ad hoc networks and cellular networks. The main difference between these two network classes is whether a fixed infrastructure is present.

Three of the well-known cellular networks are the GSM network, the CDMA network, and the 802.11 wireless LAN. The GSM network and the CDMA network are the main network technologies that support modern mobile communication, with most of the mobile phones and mobile networks that are built based on these two wireless networking technologies and their variants. As cellular networks required fixed infrastructures to support the communication between mobile nodes, deployment of the fixed infrastructures is essential. Further, cellular networks require serious and careful topology design of the fixed infrastructures before deployment, because the network topologies of the fixed infrastructures are mostly static and will have a great impact on network performance and network coverage.

Then, contributors Peng Liu and Thomas F. LaPorta (Chapter 11, "Cellular Network Security"), address the security of the cellular network; educate readers on the current state of security of the network and its vulnerabilities; outline the cellular network specific attack taxonomy, also called *three dimensional attack taxonomy*; discuss the vulnerability assessment tools for cellular networks; and, provides insights as to why the network is so vulnerable, and why securing it can prevent communication outages during emergencies.

In recent years, cellular networks have become open public networks to which end subscribers have direct access. This has greatly increased the threats to the cellular network. Though cellular networks have vastly advanced in their performance abilities, the security of these networks still remains highly outdated. As a result, they are one of the most insecure networks today—so much so that using simple off-the-shelf equipment, any adversary can cause major network outages affecting millions of subscribers.

In this chapter, Liu and LaPorta, address the security of the cellular network. They educate readers on the current state of security of the network and its vulnerabilities. They also outline the cellular network specific attack taxonomy, also called the *three-dimensional attack taxonomy*. They then discuss the vulnerability assessment tools for cellular networks. Finally, they provide insights as to why the network is so vulnerable and why securing it can prevent communication outages during emergencies.

Cellular networks are high-speed, high-capacity voice and data communication networks with enhanced multimedia and seamless roaming capabilities for supporting cellular devices. With the increase in popularity of cellular devices, these networks are used for more than just entertainment and phone calls. They have become the primary means of communication for finance-sensitive business transactions, lifesaving emergencies, and life-/mission-critical services such as E-911. Today these networks have become the lifeline of communications.

A breakdown in the cellular network has many adverse effects, ranging from huge economic losses due to financial transaction disruptions; loss of life due to loss of phone calls made to emergency workers; and communication outages during emergencies such as the September 11, 2001, attacks. Therefore, it is a high priority for the cellular network to function accurately.

It must be noted that it is not difficult for unscrupulous elements to break into the cellular network and cause outages. The major reason for this is that cellular networks were not designed with security in mind. They evolved from the old-fashioned telephone networks that were built for performance. To this day, the cellular network has numerous well-known and unsecured vulnerabilities providing access to adversaries. Another feature of cellular networks is network relationships (also called *dependencies*) that cause certain types of errors to propagate to other network locations as a result of regular network activity. Such propagation can be very disruptive to the network, and in turn it can affect subscribers. Finally, Internet connectivity to the cellular network is another major contributor to the cellular network's vulnerability because it gives Internet users direct access to cellular network vulnerabilities from their homes.

To ensure that adversaries do not access the network and cause breakdowns, a high level of security must be maintained in the cellular network. However, though great efforts have been made to improve the cellular network in terms of support for new and innovative services, greater number of subscribers, higher speed, and larger bandwidth, very little has been done to update the security of the cellular network. Accordingly, these networks have become highly attractive targets to adversaries, not only because of their lack of security but also due to the ease with which these networks can be exploited to affect millions of subscribers.

In this chapter, the contributors analyze the security of cellular networks. Toward understanding the security issues in cellular networks, the rest of the chapter is organized as follows. They present a comprehensive overview of cellular networks with a goal of providing a fundamental understanding of their functioning.

Next, they present the current state of cellular network security through an in-depth discussion on cellular network vulnerabilities and possible attacks. In addition, they present the cellular network specific attack taxonomy. Finally, they present a review of current cellular network vulnerability assessment techniques and conclude with a discussion.

Next to the Internet, the cellular network is the most highly used communication network. It is also the most vulnerable, with inadequate security measures making it a most attractive target to adversaries that want to cause communication outages during emergencies. As the cellular network is moving in the direction of the Internet, becoming an amalgamation of several types of diverse networks, more attention must be paid to securing these networks. A push from government agencies requiring mandatory security standards for operating cellular networks would be just the momentum needed to securing these networks.

Of all the attacks discussed in this chapter, cascading attacks have the most potential to stealthily cause major network disoperation. At present there is no standardized scheme to protect from such attacks. EndSec is a good solution for protecting from cascading attacks, since it requires every data item to be signed by the source service node. Because service nodes are unlikely to corrupt data items they are to be accounted for by their signatures, the possibility of cascading attacks is greatly reduced. EndSec has the added advantage of providing end-to-end security for all types of signaling messages. Hence, standardizing EndSec and mandating its deployment would be a good step toward securing the network.

Both Internet and PSTN connectivity are the open gateways that adversaries can use to gain access and attack the network. Because the PSTN's security is not going to be improved, at least its gateway to the core network must be adequately secured. Likewise, since neither the Internet's design nor security will to be changed to suit the cellular network, at least its gateways to the core network must be adequately secured.

So, because the cellular network is an amalgamation of many diverse networks, it has too many vulnerable points. Hence, the future design of the network must be planned to reduce the number of vulnerable networks points and reduce the number of service nodes that participate in servicing the subscriber, thereby reducing the number of points from which an adversary may attack.

Contributors Chunming Rong, Erdal Cayirci, Gansen Zhao, Hongbing Cheng and Laing Yan (Chapter 12, "RFID Security") describe the RFID tags and RFID reader and back-end database in detail. Radio frequency identification (RFID) systems use RFID tags to annotate and identify objects. When objects are processed, an RFID reader is used to read information from the tags attached to the objects. The information will then be used with the data stored in the back-end databases to support the handling of business transactions. Generally, an RFID system consists of three basic components: RFID tags, RFID readers, and a back-end database.

- *RFID tags or RFID transponders.* These are the data carriers attached to objects. A typical RFID tag contains information about the attached object, such as an identifier (ID) of the object and other related properties of the object that may help to identify and describe it.
- *The RFID reader or the RFID transceiver.* These devices can read information from

tags and may write information into tags if the tags are rewritable.

- *Back-end database*. This is the data repository responsible for the management of data related to the tags and business transactions, such as ID, object properties, reading locations, reading time, and so on.

Finally, contributor Scott R. Ellis (Chapter 13, "Optical Wireless Network Security") focuses on free space optics (FSO) and the security that has been developed to protect its transmissions, as well as an overview of the basic technology. Optical wireless systems provide a high degree of physical security if only because the signals are difficult to intercept. They typically take place high above ground. This, in and of itself, helps protect it from tampering and intrusion. Furthermore, optical wireless networking transmissions occur on the physical, or layer 1, level.

Optical and copper cables are far more vulnerable to unauthorized access. The level of difficulty of interception of optical wireless signals that using narrow beam technology makes this form of network communication the most appealing choice for establishing communications between remote locations.

This chapter focuses on free space optics (FSO) and the security that has been developed to protect its transmission, and presents an overview of the basic technology. Security of communications is thought of primarily as having to do with the security of the data itself.

Of secondary, yet no less important, interest is the physical security. Tapping into communication links that traverse public space is very difficult to detect, and cabling and fiber are very vulnerable once they leave the building and enter basements, attics, tunnels, and other untended locations.

The topic of optical wireless security is one of physical security. On the physical layer, it is one of the most secure forms of communication. On a higher level, at the protocol level, technologies such as AES128 or 256 encryption provide excellent security and can be implemented with optical systems in the same manner as any other system, there are no special considerations.

John R. Vacca
Editor-in-Chief

Detecting System Intrusions

Almantas Kakareka, CISSP, GSNA, GSEC, CEH

Demyo, Inc.

1. INTRODUCTION

First things first: Detecting system intrusion is not the same as Intrusion Detection System/Intrusion Prevention System (IDS/IPS). We want to detect system intrusion once attackers pass all defensive technologies in the company (such as IDS/IPS mentioned above), full-packet capture devices with analysts behind them, firewalls, physical security guards, and all other preventive technologies and techniques. Many preventative technologies are using blacklisting [1] most of the time, and thus that's why they fail. Blacklisting is allowing everything by default and forbidding something that is considered to be malicious. So, for the attacker, it is a challenge to find yet another way to bypass the filter. It is so much harder to circumvent a whitelisting system.

2. MONITORING KEY FILES IN THE SYSTEM

What are key files on the server? In the Linux machine it will be /etc/passwd, /etc/shadow, just to mention a few. Let's take a look at an example of /etc/shadow file below:

```
# cat /etc/shadow

root:$6$0Fny79f/$LC5hcqZXNYKachPKheRh5WkeTpa/
zO3y8OX3EUHrFkrFQAdLUTKwGjLPSdZ9uhwJQ9GmChLvbhPRbPw71DTg90:15231:0:99999:7:::
daemon:x:15204:0:99999:7:::
bin:x:15204:0:99999:7:::
sys:x:15204:0:99999:7:::
www-data:15204:0:99999:7:::
<snip>

pulse:j:15204:0:99999:7:::
rtkit:j:15204:0:99999:7:::
```

```
festival:j:15204:0:99999:7:::
postgres:!:15204:0:99999:7:::
apache:$6$LqrWIgqp$jdq1exB2GiBFgLL9kDlDkks30azWBJ1/mDU.to84mHn6nmzUzV7iHiMXK7rVm8.
plMmaNKg9Yyu7ryw00r5VX.:15452:0:99999:7:::
```

What is wrong with the preceding file? If you take a look at users listed in this file, you will notice that an apache user has a hash value attached to it. Typically, apache service never has any hash associated with it. If there is a hash for a use in this file, that means this user has a password associated with it and is able to log in via Secure Shell (SSH). What happens here is that a hacker made a brand-new account and is trying to camouflage it with a valid system user/process.

One of the ways to monitor changes in the file system is to implement LoggedFS. This particular file system logs everything that happens inside the file system. It is easily configurable via Extensible Markup Language (XML) files to fit your needs [2]. An example of a LoggedFS configuration file is as follows:

```
<?xml version = "1.0" encoding = "UTF-8"?>
<loggedFS logEnabled = "true" printProcessName = "true">
  <includes>
    <include extension = ".j" uid = "j" action = ".j" retname = ".j"/>
  </includes>
  <excludes>
    <exclude extension = ".j\.bak$" uid = "j" action = ".j" retname = "SUCCESS"/>
    <exclude extension = ".j" uid = "1000" action = ".j" retname = "FAILURE"/>
    <exclude extension = ".j" uid = "j" action = "getattr" retname = ".j"/>
  </excludes>
</loggedFS>
```

The preceding configuration can be used to log everything except if it concerns a *.bak file, or if the uid is 1000, or if the operation is getattr.

Files Integrity

File integrity monitoring (FIM) is an internal control or process that performs the act of validating the integrity of the operating system and application software files using a verification method between the current file state and the known, good baseline. This comparison method often involves calculating a known cryptographic checksum of the file's original baseline and comparing that with the calculated checksum of the current state of the file. Other file attributes can also be used to monitor integrity.

Generally, the act of performing file integrity monitoring is automated, using internal controls such as an application or a process. Such monitoring can be performed randomly, at a defined polling interval, or in real time.

3. SECURITY OBJECTIVES

Changes to configurations, files, and file attributes across the IT infrastructure are common; but hidden within a large volume of daily changes can be the few that impact the file or configuration integrity. These changes can also reduce security posture and in some cases may be leading indicators of a breach in progress. Values monitored for unexpected changes to files or configuration items include:

- Credentials
- Privileges and security settings
- Content
- Core attributes and size
- Hash values
- Configuration values

Many open-source and commercial software products are available that perform file integrity monitoring:

- CimTrak
- OSSEC
- Samhain
- Tripwire
- Qualys
- nCircle
- Verisys
- AIDE [3]

An nCircle file integrity monitor panel is shown in Figure 1.1.

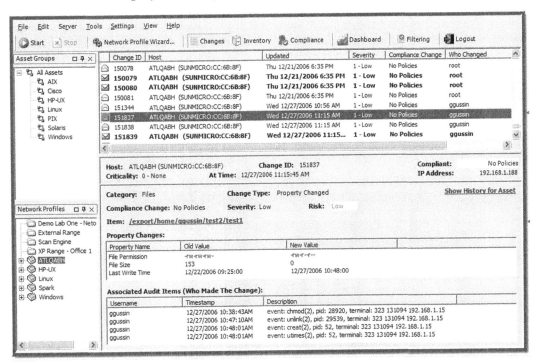

FIGURE 1.1   nCircle file integrity monitor panel.

There Is Something Very Wrong Here

One bit or one symbol in the output may make the difference between war and peace, friend and foe, compromised and clean system. Let's take a look at the example that is shown in Figure 1.2: What appears to be wrong with this screenshot?

For those who don't see the wrong symbol here, I will give you a hint. It is a command to list files in the directory; switch −h is for listing output in human readable format (megabytes will be megabytes and gigabytes will be gigabytes, not 1 073 741 824 bytes). Switch −l makes a list of files, once again to be easily readable by humans. Now, we are coming to the main piece of information here: Switch −a output will include directory entries whose names begin with a dot (.). A common hacker's technique is to hide within legitimate file names or within somewhat legitimate names. In this case, the hacker has a directory on the system, which is named '. ' ; this is the main issue here. In normal output, you should see one single dotted directory; in this case, we see two single dotted directories, which should raise big red flags for you. A change to this hidden directory is made by issuing command cd '. '. Just make sure there is a space after dot.

So, that's why we want to use ls −hal with switch 'a' all the time: because we want to see hidden directories and hidden files. It is pretty common to have these hidden directories in common places, such as: /root, /var/www, /home, and others.

Additional Accounts on the System

Every account on the system should be accounted for. If there are accounts whose source nobody knows, that may mean the system is compromised. Sometimes, IT administrators forget to disable old accounts for people who have left the company; some of these accounts may be active for months and even years. This is an unnecessary risk that is introduced by poor IT administrators' management. A good practice is to disable an employee's account before the exit interview. After a compromise, hackers may create a new account on the server and try to mimic some legitimate accounts that should exist. An example of additional account Distributed Brokered Networking (DBNET) is shown in Figure 1.3.

Timestamps

A timestamp is a sequence of characters or encoded information that identifies when a certain event occurred, usually giving date and time of day; it is sometimes accurate to a small

```
[root@vps www]# ls -hal
total 32K
drwxr-xr-x  8 root root 4.0K Feb 27 16:51 .
drwxr-xr-x  2 root root 4.0K Feb 27 16:51 .
drwxr-xr-x 18 root root 4.0K Feb 17 13:25 ..
drwxr-xr-x  2 root root 4.0K Feb 13 17:33 cgi-bin
drwxr-xr-x  2 root root 4.0K Feb 27 16:51 demyo.com
drwxr-xr-x  3 root root 4.0K Feb 17 13:25 error
drwxr-xr-x  5 root root 4.0K Feb 17 13:47 html
drwxr-xr-x  3 root root 4.0K Feb 17 13:25 icons
[root@vps www]#
```

FIGURE 1.2   The wrong symbol.

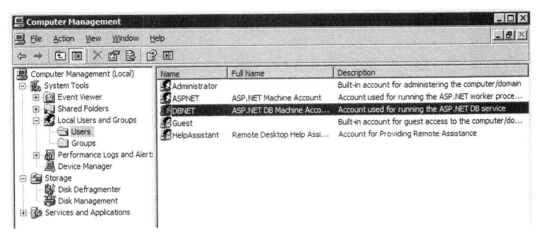

FIGURE 1.3   Additional account DBNET.

fraction of a second. The term is derived from the rubber stamps that were used in nineteenth-century offices to stamp the current date and time (in ink) on paper documents and to record when the document was received. A common example of this type of time-stamp is a postmark on a letter. However, in modern times, usage of the term has expanded to refer to the digital date and time the information was attached to digital data. For example, computer files contain timestamps that tell when the file was last modified; digital cameras add timestamps to the pictures they take, recording the date and time the picture was taken.

A timestamp is the time an event is recorded by a computer, not the time of the event itself. In many cases, the difference may be inconsequential: The time at which an event is recorded by a timestamp (entered into a log file) should be close to the time of the event.

The sequential numbering of events is sometimes called timestamping. The practice of recording timestamps in a consistent manner along with the actual data is called time-stamping. This data is usually presented in a consistent format, allowing for the easy comparison of two different records and tracking progress over time.

Timestamps are typically used for logging events or in a sequence of events (SOE), in which case each event in the log or SOE is marked with a timestamp. In file systems, the timestamp may mean the stored date/time when a file is created or modified.

Let's say you have a lot of folders and executable files in the C:/Windows/System32 directory. All of them pretty much match operating system (OS) installation date and time, but there is one folder that does not match OS installation time. Could there be a problem? This executable might be just some additional software that was installed later on the system, or it also might be malware hiding in this directory. Windows malware just loves this folder! The folder shown in Figure 1.4 was modified in a different month from all the others.

Hidden Files and Directories

A hidden file is not normally visible when examining the contents of the directory in which it resides. Likewise, a hidden directory is normally invisible when examining the contents of the directory in which it resides.

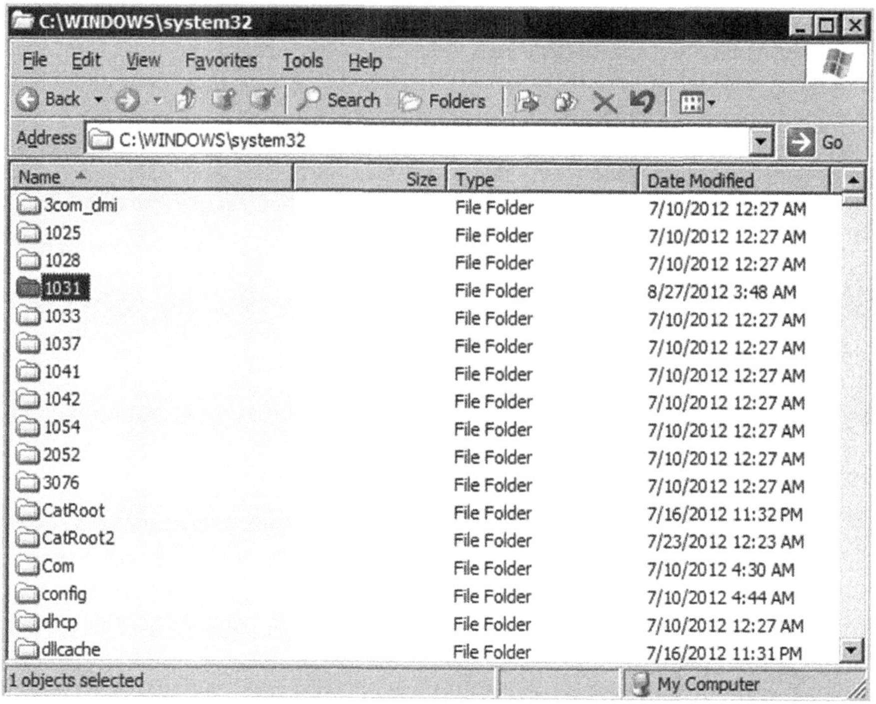

FIGURE 1.4   Folder modification.

A file is a named collection of related information that appears to the user as a single, contiguous block of data and that is retained in storage. Storage refers to computer devices or media that can retain data for relatively long periods of time (years or decades), such as hard disk drives (HDDs), Compact Disk—Read Only Memory (CDROMs), and magnetic tape; this contrasts with memory, which retains data only as long as the data is in use or the memory is connected to a power supply.

A directory (also sometimes referred to as a folder) can be conveniently viewed as a container for files and other directories. In Linux and other Unix-like operating systems, a directory is merely a special type of file that associates file names with a collection of metadata (data about the files). Likewise, a link is a special type of file that points to another file (which can be a directory). Thus, it is somewhat redundant to use phrases such as hidden files and directories; however, they are descriptive and convenient, and thus they are frequently used. More precise terms are hidden file system objects and hidden items.

Hidden items on Unix-like operating systems are easily distinguishable from regular (nonhidden) items because their names are prefixed by a period (a dot). In Unix-like operating systems, periods can appear anywhere within the name of a file, directory, or link, and they can appear as many times as desired. However, usually, the only time that they have special significance is when they are used to indicate a hidden file or directory.

In the Microsoft Windows operating systems, whether or not a file system object is hidden is an attribute of the item, along with such things as whether the file is read-only and a system file (a file that is critical to the operation of the operating system). Changing the visibility of such items is accomplished using a multistep procedure.

Unix-like operating systems provide a larger set of attributes for file system objects than do the Microsoft Windows operating systems, including a system of permissions, which control which user(s) have access to each such object for reading, writing and executing. However, whether or not objects are hidden is not among the attributes. Rather, it is merely a superficial property that is easily changed by adding or removing a period from the beginning of the object name.

Many operating systems and application programs routinely hide objects in order to reduce the chances of users accidentally damaging or deleting critical system and configuration files. Hiding objects can also be useful for reducing visual clutter in directories, thereby making it easier for users to locate desired files and subdirectories.

Another reason to hide file system objects is to make them invisible to casual snoopers. Although it is very easy to make hidden files and directories visible, the great majority of computer users are not even aware that such files and directories exist (nor need they be) [4].

4. 0DAY ATTACKS

About 90 percent of all successful compromises are made via known flaws, so 0day attacks are not that common. A zero-day attack or threat is an attack that exploits a previously unknown vulnerability in a computer application, meaning that the attack occurs on "day zero" of awareness of the vulnerability. This means that the developers have had zero days to address and patch the vulnerability. 0day exploits (actual software that uses a security hole to carry out an attack) are used or shared by attackers before the developer of the target software knows about the vulnerability.

Attack Vectors

Malware writers are able to exploit zero-day vulnerabilities through several different attack vectors. Web browsers are a particular target because of their widespread distribution and usage. Attackers can also send email attachments, which exploit vulnerabilities in the application opening the attachment. Exploits that take advantage of common file types are listed in databases such as United States Computer Emergency Readiness (US-CERT). Malware can be engineered to take advantage of these file-type exploits to compromise attacked systems or steal confidential data such as banking passwords and personal identity information.

Vulnerability Window

Zero-day attacks occur during the vulnerability window that exists in the time between when vulnerability is first exploited and when software developers start to develop and publish a counter to that threat. For viruses, Trojans, and other zero-day attacks, the vulnerability window typically follows this time line:

- The developer creates software containing an unknown vulnerability.
- The attacker finds the vulnerability before the developer does.
- The attacker writes and distributes an exploit while the vulnerability is not known to the developer.
- The developer becomes aware of the vulnerability and starts developing a fix.

Measuring the length of the vulnerability window can be difficult, as attackers do not announce when the vulnerability was first discovered. Developers may not want to distribute data for commercial or security reasons. They also may not know if the vulnerability is being exploited when they fix it, and so they may not record the vulnerability as a zero-day attack. However, it can be easily shown that this window can be several years long. For example, in 2008, Microsoft confirmed vulnerability in Internet Explorer, which affected some versions that were released in 2001. The date the vulnerability was first found by an attacker is not known; however, the vulnerability window in this case could have been up to seven years.

Discovery

A special type of vulnerability management process focuses on finding and eliminating zero-day weaknesses. This unknown vulnerability management life cycle is a security and quality assurance process that aims to ensure the security and robustness of both in-house and third-party software products by finding and fixing unknown (zero-day) vulnerabilities. The unknown vulnerability management process consists of four phases: analyze, test, report, and mitigate.

- Analyze: This phase focuses on attack surface analysis.
- Test: This phase focuses on fuzz testing the identified attack vectors.
- Report: This phase focuses on reproduction of the found issues to developers.
- Mitigate: This phase looks at the protective measures explained below.

Protection

Zero-day protection is the ability to provide protection against zero-day exploits. Zero-day attacks can also remain undetected after they are launched.

Many techniques exist to limit the effectiveness of zero-day memory corruption vulnerabilities, such as buffer overflows. These protection mechanisms exist in contemporary operating systems such as Windows 7, Microsoft Windows Vista, Apple's Mac OS X, recent Oracle Solaris, Linux and possibly other Unix and Unix-like environments; Microsoft Windows XP Service Pack 2 includes limited protection against generic memory corruption vulnerabilities. Desktop and server protection software also exists to mitigate zero-day buffer overflow vulnerabilities.

"Multiple layers" provides service-agnostic protection and is the first line of defense should an exploit in any one layer be discovered. An example of this for a particular service is implementing access control lists in the service itself, restricting network access to it via local server firewalling (IP tables), and then protecting the entire network with a hardware firewall. All three layers provide redundant protection in case a compromise in any one of them occurs.

The use of port knocking or single-packet authorization daemons may provide effective protection against zero-day exploits in network services. However, these techniques are not suitable for environments with a large number of users.

Whitelisting effectively protects against zeroday threats. Whitelisting will only allow known good applications to access a system, and so, any new or unknown exploits are not allowed access. Although whitelisting is effective against zero-day attacks, an application "known" to be good can in fact have vulnerabilities that were missed in testing. To bolster its protection capability, it is often combined with other methods of protection such as a host-based intrusion-prevention system or a blacklist of virus definitions, and it can some-times be quite restrictive to the user. Also, keeping the computer's software up to date is very important, and it does help.

Users need to be careful when clicking on links or opening email attachments with images or PDF files from unknown users. This is how many cyber criminals deceive users, by pretending they are something they are not and gaining the user's trust. In addition, sites should be utilized with Secure Socket Layer (SSL), which secures the information being passed between the user and the visited site.

Ethics

Differing views surround the collection and use of zero-day vulnerability informa-tion. Many computer security vendors perform research on zero-day vulnerabilities in order to better understand the nature of vulnerabilities and their exploitation by individuals, computer worms, and viruses. Alternatively, some vendors purchase vul-nerabilities to augment their research capacity. While selling and buying these vulner-abilities is not technically illegal in most parts of the world, there is much controversy over the method of disclosure. A recent German decision to include Article 6 of the Convention on Cybercrime and the European Union (EU) Framework Decision on Attacks against Information Systems may make selling or even manufacturing vulner-abilities illegal.

Most formal efforts follow some form of disclosure guidelines or the more recent Office of Information Systems (OIS) Guidelines for Security Vulnerability Reporting and Response. In general, these rules forbid the public disclosure of vulnerabilities without notification to the developer and adequate time to produce a patch.

5. GOOD KNOWN STATE

When attackers compromise a system, what is the very first thing they do? They install different backdoors and as many as possible. So, if some backdoor was found on the sys-tem and it was deleted, it does not mean the system is clean. It is much safer to restore the system to a good known state; typically it is done via OS reinstallation. Big companies typically have a gold image for their systems. They use a gold image to quickly wipe any infected machine and reinstall OS with all of its updates, and software at once. On Linux systems, the software called System Imager is capable of doing many Linux installations at once.

System Imager is software that makes the installation of Linux to numerous similar machines relatively easy. It makes software distribution, configuration, and operating system updates easy, and it can also be used for content distribution [5].

Monitoring Running Processes in the System

What is wrong with the running process list in the following Linux system, as shown in Figure 1.5?

The process ./httpd should catch a security professional's eye. Dot slash at the beginning indicates it was launched locally from the directory. Processes on the servers typically are not launched locally from their directories. The attacker has launched a process and is trying to hide by renaming his software to legitimate-looking software typically found on the server.

Files with Weird Names

Malware frequently makes weird-looking file names. An example of this is shown in the Windows Task Manager screen in Figure 1.6.

```
root@bt:~/. # ps aux
USER      PID %CPU %MEM  VSZ  RSS TTY    STAT START  TIME COMMAND
root        1 0.0 0.3 2844 1604 ?      Ss  Apr15  0:01 /sbin/init
root        2 0.0 0.0    0    0 ?     S   Apr15  0:00 [kthreadd]
<snip>
root    10962 0.0 0.0 2740  476 ?      S<  09:33  0:00 udevd --daemon
root    11550 0.0 0.0    0    0 ?     S   11:13  0:00 [kworker/0:2]
root    11567 0.0 0.0    0    0 ?     S<  11:15  0:00 [hci0]
root    11619 0.0 0.0    0    0 ?     S   11:18  0:00 [kworker/0:1]
root    11654 0.0 0.0    0    0 ?     S   11:23  0:00 [kworker/0:0]
root    11664 5.3 6.1 36092 31360 pts/1  S   11:24  0:00 ./httpd
root    11665 0.0 0.2 2764 1052 pts/1  R+  11:24  0:00 ps aux
root    12015 0.0 1.7 34800 8736 ?      S   Apr16  0:00 /usr/lib/notification-daemon/notification-daemon
```

FIGURE 1.5   The running process list.

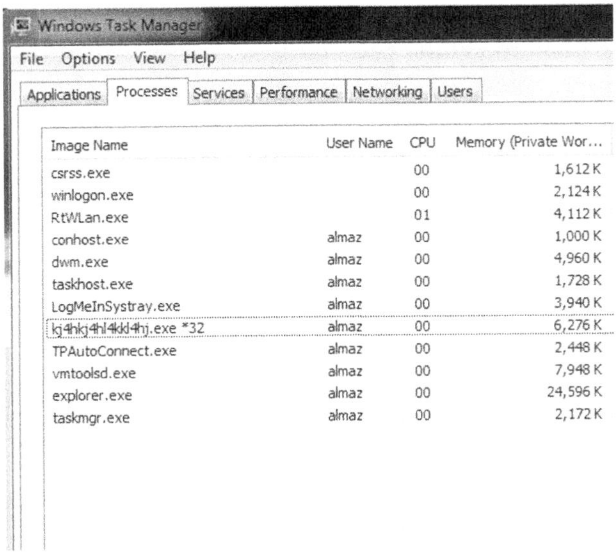

FIGURE 1.6   Strange file names.

The file: kj4hkj4hl4kkl4hj.exe shown in Figure 1.6 is running in memory. This should be a first indicator that something funky is going on in the system. Windows updates create random named temporary folders and should not be confused with malware.

6. ROOTKITS

A rootkit is a stealthy type of malicious software designed to hide the existence of certain processes or programs from normal methods of detection, and enables continued privileged access to a computer. The term *rootkit* is a concatenation of the word "root" (the traditional name of the privileged account on Unix operating systems) and the word "kit" (which refers to the software components that implement the tool). The term *rootkit* has negative connotations through its association with malware.

Rootkit installation can be automated, or an attacker can install it once they've obtained root or Administrator access. Obtaining this access is either a result of a direct attack on a system (exploiting a known vulnerability), or by having obtained a password (either by cracking, privilege escalation, or through social engineering). Once installed, it becomes possible to hide the intrusion as well as to maintain privileged access. Like any software, they can have a good purpose or a malicious purpose. The key is the root/administrator access. Full control over a system means that existing software can be modified, including software that might otherwise be used to detect or circumvent it.

Rootkit detection is difficult because a rootkit may be able to subvert the software that is intended to find it. Detection methods include using an alternative and trusted operating system, behavioral-based methods, signature scanning, difference scanning, and memory dump analysis. Removal can be complicated or practically impossible, especially in cases where the rootkit resides in the kernel; reinstallation of the operating system may be the only available solution to the problem. When dealing with firmware rootkits, removal may require hardware replacement or specialized equipment.

Kernel-Level Rootkits

Kernel-mode rootkits run with the highest operating system privileges (Ring 0) by adding code or replacing portions of the core operating system, including both the kernel and associated device drivers. Most operating systems support kernel-mode device drivers, which execute with the same privileges as the operating system itself. As such, many kernel-mode rootkits are developed as device drivers or loadable modules, such as loadable kernel modules in Linux or device drivers in Microsoft Windows. This class of rootkit has unrestricted security access but is more difficult to write. The complexity makes bugs common, and any bugs in code operating at the kernel level may seriously impact system stability, leading to the discovery of the rootkit. One of the first widely known kernel rootkits was developed for Windows NT 4.0 and released in the *Phrack* magazine in 1999 [6].

Kernel rootkits can be especially difficult to detect and remove because they operate at the same security level as the operating system itself and are thus able to intercept or subvert the most trusted operating system operations. Any software, such as antivirus software, running on the compromised system is equally vulnerable. In this situation, no part of the system can be trusted.

A rootkit can modify data structures in the Windows kernel using a method known as direct kernel object modification (DKOM). This method can hook kernel functions in the System Service Descriptor Table (SSDT), or modify the gates between user mode and kernel mode, in order to cloak itself. Similarly for the Linux operating system, a rootkit can modify the system call table to subvert kernel functionality. It's not uncommon for a rootkit to create a hidden, encrypted file system in which it can hide other malware or original copies of files it has infected.

Operating systems are evolving to counter the threat of kernel-mode rootkits. For example, 64-bit editions of Microsoft Windows now implement mandatory signing of all kernel-level drivers in order to make it more difficult for untrusted code to execute with the highest privileges in a system.

Userland Rootkits

User-mode rootkits run in ring 3, along with other applications as user, rather than low-level system processes. They have a number of possible installation vectors to intercept and modify the standard behavior of application programming interfaces (APIs). Some inject a dynamically linked library (such as a .dll file on Windows, or a .dylib file on Mac OS X) into other processes and are thereby able to execute inside any target process to spoof it; others with sufficient privileges simply overwrite the memory of a target application. Injection mechanisms include:

- Use of vendor-supplied application extensions. For example, Windows Explorer has public interfaces that allow third parties to extend its functionality.
- Interception of messages

- Debuggers
- Exploitation of security vulnerabilities
- Function hooking or patching of commonly used APIs, for example, to mask a running process or file that resides on a file system

Rootkit Detection

There are a lot of software for rootkit searches that are meant to be run on a live system. One of many examples would be the software "rootkit hunter".

7. LOW HANGING FRUIT

Do you have to run faster than a cheetah? Not necessarily. You just have to be running faster than your friend, so he will be eaten and not you. Do your systems have to be as secure as Pentagon computers with a myriad of controls? Not necessarily. Your system has to be more secure than your neighbor's, and hopefully you will avoid trouble. Here are some other techniques to deter intrusions:

- Deterring intrusions by snow flaking (no two snowflakes are the same, so it takes more time to analyze a particular system in order to gain access, making them useless to be scanned with automatic tools). An example would be to move an SSH port from default TCP/22 to TCP/31234. Some determined hacker will find out pretty soon, but it will be an extra step for a script kiddie.
- Low hanging fruit is attacked most of the time by simply ignoring the pings to the host. This will deter some hackers (as there are many more systems that reply to ping), and it takes less time to detect those live IPs and scan them for vulnerabilities [7].

8. ANTIVIRUS SOFTWARE

The biggest fear for malware is the antivirus (AV) engine on the system. An antivirus can detect attack, but it might be too late already. AV is based on signatures in the files. Hackers bypass signature detection by encrypting their executables in unique ways. Every executable is encrypted in a unique way; AV engines are always losing ground because they are late arrivals in the detection game. If your AV engine fires, that means that the malware managed to slip by your IDS/IPS solution into the network and/or system.

9. HOMEGROWN INTRUSION DETECTION

In order to defeat a hacker, you have to think like a hacker. Let's take a look at what a robots.txt file looks like in a Web server. This file sits in the root of a Web page (for example, www.mywebpage.com/robots.txt); provides information to search engines of what should be cached and what should be skipped; shows how frequent crawling has to be done, and so on. Let's say you have sensitive files in a directory called "reports." This directory can be excluded from search engine crawlers and will not end up in search results. Other files and directories such as /private/, /adminpanel/, /phpmyadmin/ should be excluded from the search engine results. This technique looks great so far, but an experienced attacker will take a look at robots.txt file below and see what you don't want him to know!

Incorrect robots.txt implementation	Correct robots.txt implementation
Disallow: /adminpanel/ Disallow: /phpmyadmin/ Disallow: /backup/ Disallow: /uploads/	Move all sensitive directories into one directory called for example /private/ and disallow this directory: Disallow: /private/

A little customized robots.txt file would look like the following:

```
User-Agent: *

Disallow: /private/

Allow: /

User-Agent: hacker

Disallow: /please/go/to/an/easier/target/
```

It would give the attacker some clue that this is probably not the easiest target, and hopefully he or she will move to an easier one. Needless to say, it will not prevent a targeted attack [8]. So, if you have somebody trying to access a nonexisting directory "/please/go/to/an/easier/target/" on the server, it should give you a clue as to who is interested in your Web site.

10. FULL-PACKET CAPTURE DEVICES

Sometimes it is easier to detect intrusion on the wire by monitoring ingress and egress traffic. We have to be aware of out-of-band communications—for example, communication that comes to the corporate network via Global System for Mobile Communications (GSM) signals. These communications do not go through border routers of the company and thus cannot be inspected via this technology.

Packet capture appliance is a standalone device that performs packet capture. Although packet capture appliances may be deployed anywhere on a network, most are commonly placed at the entrances to the network (the Internet connections) and in front of critical equipment, such as servers containing sensitive information.

In general, packet capture appliances capture and record all network packets in full (both header and payload); however, some appliances may be configured to capture a subset of a network's traffic based on user-definable filters. For many applications, especially network forensics and incident response, it is critical to conduct full-packet capture, though filtered packet capture may be used at times for specific, limited information-gathering purposes.

Deployment

The network data that a packet capture appliance captures depends on where and how the appliance is installed on a network. There are two options for deploying packet capture appliances on a network. One option is to connect the appliance to the Switch Port Analyzer (SPAN) port (port mirroring) on a network switch or router. A second option is to connect the appliance inline, so that network activity along a network route traverses the appliance (similar in configuration to a network tap, but the information is captured and stored by the packet capture appliance rather than passing on to another device). When connected via a SPAN port, the packet capture appliance may receive and record all Ethernet/IP activity for all of the ports of the switch or router.

When connected inline, the packet capture appliance captures only the network traffic traveling between two points—that is, traffic that passes through the cable to which the packet capture appliance is connected. There are also two general approaches to deploying packet capture appliances: centralized and decentralized.

Centralized

With a centralized approach, one high-capacity, high-speed packet capture appliance connects to the data-aggregation point. The advantage of a centralized approach is that with one appliance, you gain visibility over the network's entire traffic. This approach, however, creates a single point of failure that is a very attractive target for hackers; additionally, one would have to reengineer the network to bring traffic to the appliance, and this approach typically involves high costs.

Decentralized

With a decentralized approach, you place multiple appliances around the network, starting at the point(s) of entry and proceeding downstream to deeper network segments, such as workgroups. The advantages include: no network reconfiguration required; ease of deployment; multiple vantage points for incident response investigations; scalability; no single point of failure—if one fails, you have the others; if combined with electronic invisibility, this approach practically eliminates the danger of unauthorized access by hackers; and low cost. The disadvantage is the potential increased maintenance of multiple appliances.

In the past, packet capture appliances were sparingly deployed, oftenonly at the point of entry into a network. Packet capture appliances can now be deployed more effectively at various points around the network. When conducting incident response, the ability to see the network data flow from various vantage points is indispensable in reducing the time to resolution and narrowing down which parts of the network ultimately were affected. By placing packet capture appliances at the entry point and in front of each workgroup, following the path of a particular transmission deeper into the network would be simplified and much quicker. Additionally, the appliances placed in front of the workgroups would show intranet transmissions that the appliance located at the entry point would not be able to capture.

Capacity

Packet capture appliances come with capacities ranging from 500 Gigabytes (GB) to 32 Terabytes (TB) and more. Only a few organizations with extremely high network usage would have use for the upper ranges of capacities. Most organizations would be well served with capacities from 1 TB to 4 TB.

A good rule of thumb when choosing capacity is to allow 1 GB per day for heavy users, down to 1 GB per month for regular users. For a typical office of 20 people with average usage, 1 TB would be sufficient for about one to four years.

Features: Filtered versus Full-Packet Capture

Full-packet capture appliances capture and record all Ethernet/IP activity, while filtered packet capture appliances capture only a subset of traffic, based on a set of user-definable filters, such as IP address, MAC address, or protocol. Unless you use the packet capture appliance for a very specific purpose (narrow purpose covered by the filter parameters), it is generally best to use full-packet capture appliances or otherwise risk missing the vital data. Particularly, when using a packet capture for network forensics or cyber security purposes, it is paramount to capture everything because any packet not captured on the spot is a packet that is gone forever. It is impossible to know ahead of time the specific characteristics of the packets or transmissions needed, especially in the case of an advanced persistent threat (APT). APTs and other hacking techniques rely on the success of network administrators not knowing how they work and thus not having solutions in place to counteract them. Most APT attacks originate from Russia and China.

Encrypted versus Unencrypted Storage

Some packet capture appliances encrypt the captured data before saving it to disk, while others do not. Considering the breadth of information that travels on a network or Internet connection (and that at least a portion of it could be considered sensitive), encryption is a good idea for most situations as a measure to keep the captured data secure. Encryption is also a critical element of authentication of data for the purposes of data/network forensics.

Sustained Capture Speed versus Peak Capture Speed

The sustained captured speed is the rate at which a packet capture appliance can capture and record packets without interruption or error over a long period of time. This is different from the peak capture rate, which is the highest speed at which a packet capture appliance can capture and record packets. The peak capture speed can only be maintained for a short period of time, until the appliance's buffers fill up and it starts losing packets. Many packet capture appliances share the same peak capture speed of 1 Gigabytes per Second (Gbps), but actual sustained speeds vary significantly from model to model.

Permanent versus Overwritable Storage

A packet capture appliance with permanent storage is ideal for network forensics and permanent record-keeping purposes because the data captured cannot be overwritten, altered, or deleted. The only drawback of permanent storage is that eventually the appliance becomes full and requires replacement. Packet capture appliances with overwritable storage are easier to manage because once they reach capacity, they will start overwriting the oldest captured data with the new; however, network administrators run the risk of losing important capture data when it gets overwritten. In general, packet capture appliances with overwrite capabilities are useful for simple monitoring or testing purposes, for which a permanent record is not necessary. Permanent recording is a must for network forensics information gathering.

Data Security

Since packet capture appliances capture and store a large amount of data on network activity (including files, emails, and other communications), they could, in themselves, become attractive targets for hacking. A packet capture appliance deployed for any length of time should incorporate security features to protect the recorded network data from access by unauthorized parties. If deploying a packet capture appliance introduces too many additional concerns about security, the cost of securing it may outweigh the benefits. The best approach would be for the packet capture appliance to have built-in security features. These security features may include encryption, or methods to "hide" the appliance's presence on the network. For example, some packet capture appliances feature "electronic invisibility," that is, having a stealthy network profile by not requiring or using IP or MAC addresses.

Although on the face of it, connecting a packet capture appliance via a SPAN port appears to make it more secure, the packet capture appliance would ultimately still have to be connected to the network in order to allow management and data retrieval. Though not accessible via the SPAN link, the appliance would be accessible via the management link.

Despite the benefits, a packet capture appliance's remote access feature presents a security issue that could make the appliance vulnerable. Packet capture appliances that allow remote access should have a robust system in place to protect it against unauthorized access. One way to accomplish this is to incorporate a manual disable, such as a switch or toggle that allows the user to physically disable remote access. This simple solution is very effective, as it is doubtful that a hacker would have an easy time gaining physical access to the appliance in order to flip a switch.

A final consideration is physical security. All the network security features in the world are moot if someone is simply able to steal the packet capture appliance or make a copy of it and have ready access to the data stored on it. Encryption is one of the best ways to address this concern, though some packet capture appliances also feature tamperproof enclosures.

11. OUT-OF-BAND ATTACK VECTORS

What is the weakest link in any corporation? The answer is people. People fall into social engineering attacks; people bring "forgotten" Universal Serial Bus (USB) sticks and

CDs from bathrooms/parking lots and plug them into their computers just out of curiosity. People bring their own devices from home and connect to corporate networks. BYOD or Bring Your Own Device is a big pain for IT administrators to manage. It also introduces additional risk because an employee's own devices might already be backdoored or infected, and by connecting these devices to the corporate network, employees are introducing a new risk. A social engineering attack with a lost CD is shown in Figure 1.7.

A Demyo plug is a full-blown Linux-based OS with many penetration testing tools preinstalled. It looks like an innocent power surge/split, but it has a Wireless Fidelity (Wi-Fi), Bluetooth, and GSM 3 g modem installed inside. Once connected to the power outlet, it immediately calls back home via GSM 3 g modem and establishes a connection. Once connected, penetration testers can use it as a jump box to do further penetration testing inside the local area network (LAN) of the corporation [9]. The Demyo plug is shown in Figure 1.8.

How do you prevent employees from bringing their "lost CDs" and "lost USB sticks" from parking lots and plugging them into their machines? A strong policy should be in place that disallows connecting nonapproved hardware to workstations. It is not enough to just write a policy and consider the job done. Policy has to be enforced, and most

FIGURE 1.7   A social engineering attack with a lost CD.

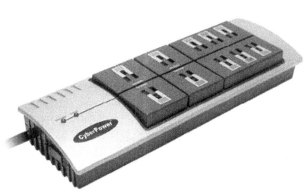

FIGURE 1.8   The Demyo plug.

importantly, policy has to be understood by employees. There is no way that rules can be followed if they are not understood. Another way to minimize risk is to provide security awareness training to employees, explaining typical social engineering attacks and how not to fall for them.

12. SECURITY AWARENESS TRAINING

Security awareness is the knowledge and attitude members of an organization possess regarding the protection of the physical and, especially, information assets of that organization. Many organizations require formal security awareness training for all workers when they join the organization and periodically thereafter (usually annually). Topics covered in security awareness training include the following:

- The nature of sensitive material and physical assets that they may come in contact with, such as trade secrets, privacy concerns, and government classified information
- Employee and contractor responsibilities in handling sensitive information, including the review of employee nondisclosure agreements
- Requirements for proper handling of sensitive material in physical form, which includes marking, transmission, storage, and destruction
- Proper methods for protecting sensitive information on computer systems, including password policy and use of the two-factor authentication
- Other computer security concerns, including malware, phishing, and social engineering
- Workplace security, including building access, wearing of security badges, reporting of incidents, and forbidden articles
- Consequences of failure to properly protect information, including the potential loss of employment, economic consequences to the firm, damage to individuals whose private records are divulged, and possible civil and criminal penalties

Being security aware means that you understand that there is the potential for some people to deliberately or accidentally steal, damage, or misuse the data that is stored within a company's computer system and throughout its organization. Therefore, it would be prudent to support the assets of the institution (information, physical, and personal) by trying to stop that from happening.

According to the European Network and Information Security Agency, "Awareness of the risks and available safeguards is the first line of defense for the security of information systems and networks." The focus of Security Awareness consultancy should be to achieve a long-term shift in the attitude of employees towards security, while promoting a cultural and behavioral change within an organization. Security policies should be viewed as key enablers for the organization, not as a series of rules restricting the efficient working of your business.

13. DATA CORRELATION

Data correlation is a technique used in information security to put all the pieces together and come up with some meaningful information. For example, if you see Linux system SSH

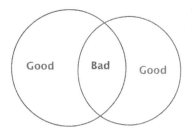

FIGURE 1.9   The combination of two good things can create one bad thing.

connections coming in all day long, and after watching someone log in 200 times there is a successful login: What does it tell you? It should be a good starting point to suggest that a brute force attack is going on. All technologies help to find out intrusions; however, technologies do not find intrusions, people do. Appliances and sensors are typically good about finding bad events, but good events can combine into bad ones as well. Let's look at a simple scenario in which a human makes a determination about compromise:

Let's say there is a company with many employees who travel a lot around the globe. The company is doing a good job by implementing various control systems and logging systems; this company also uses Radio Frequency Identification (RFID) enabled cards for its employees in order to track who is coming and leaving its offices. All data is collected and pushed to the Security Information and Event Management (SIEM) engine to correlate events and logs. One morning two seemingly good events come into SIEM. The first event is user John's virtual private network (VPN) connection being established from overseas to the corporate office. The second event is user John's RFID badge being scanned at the entrance to the corporate office. Well, both events are pretty standard and are harmless when taken separately, but when combined, they reveal something weird. How can user John VPN in from overseas and get a physical entrance to the office at the same time? The answer is one of two: Either the VPN credentials have been compromised, or his employee card is being used by someone else to enter the office. Figure 1.9 shows how two good things can create one bad thing when combined.

14. SIEM

Security Information and Event Management (SIEM) solutions are a combination of the formerly disparate product categories of SIM (security information management) and SEM (security event manager). SIEM technology provides real-time analysis of security alerts generated by network hardware and applications. SIEM solutions come as software, appliances, or managed services, and they are also used to log security data and generate reports for compliance purposes.

The acronyms SEM, SIM, and SIEM have been used interchangeably, though there are differences in meaning and product capabilities. The segment of security management that deals with real-time monitoring, correlation of events, notifications, and console views is commonly known as Security Event Management (SEM). The second area provides long-term storage, analysis, and reporting of log data and is known as Security Information Management (SIM).

The term *Security Information Event Management* (SIEM) describes the product capabilities of gathering, analyzing, and presenting information from network and security devices; identity and access management applications; vulnerability management and policy compliance tools; operating system, database and application logs; and external threat data. A key focus is to monitor and help manage user and service privileges, directory services, and other system configuration changes, as well as providing log auditing and review and incident response. The following are a list of SIEM capabilities:

- *Data Aggregation*: SIEM/LM (log management) solutions aggregate data from many sources, including network, security, servers, databases, and applications, providing the ability to consolidate monitored data to help avoid missing crucial events.
- *Correlation*: Looks for common attributes and links events together into meaningful bundles. This technology provides the ability to perform a variety of correlation techniques to integrate different sources, in order to turn data into useful information.
- *Alerting*: The automated analysis of correlated events and production of alerts, to notify recipients of immediate issues.
- *Dashboards*: SIEM/LM tools take event data and turn it into informational charts to assist in seeing patterns or identifying activity that is not forming a standard pattern.
- *Compliance*: SIEM applications can be employed to automate the gathering of compliance data, producing reports that adapt to existing security, governance, and auditing processes.
- *Retention*: SIEM/SIM solutions employ long-term storage of historical data to facilitate the correlation of data over time and to provide the retention necessary for compliance requirements.

15. OTHER WEIRD STUFF ON THE SYSTEM

What are the other symptoms of possible system compromises? Following are some examples:

- Log files are missing completely. Why are there no log files? Script kiddies delete logs, whereas hackers modify them by taking out only their IP addresses, their commands, and manipulations with the system.
- Network interface is in a promiscuous mode: In computer networking, promiscuous mode is a mode for a wired network interface controller (NIC) or wireless network interface controller (WNIC) that causes the controller to pass all traffic it receives to the central processing unit (CPU), rather than passing only the frames that the controller is intended to receive. This mode is normally used for packet sniffing that takes place on a router or on a computer connected to a hub (instead of a switch) or that is part of a wireless local area network (WLAN). The mode is also required for bridged networking for hardware virtualization.

In IEEE 802 networks such as Ethernet, token ring, IEEE 802.11, and FDDI, each frame includes a destination Media Access Control address (MAC address). In nonpromiscuous mode, when an NIC receives a frame, it normally drops it unless the frame is addressed to that NIC's MAC address or is a broadcast or multicast frame. In promiscuous mode, however, the card allows all frames through, thus allowing the computer to read frames intended for other machines or network devices.

Many operating systems require super user privileges to enable promiscuous mode. In a nonrouting node, promiscuous mode can generally only monitor traffic to and from other nodes within the same broadcast domain (for Ethernet and IEEE 802.11) or ring (for token ring or Fiber-Optic Data Distribution Interface (FDDI)). Computers attached to the same network hub satisfy this requirement, which is why network switches are used to combat malicious use of promiscuous mode. A router may monitor all traffic that it routes.

Promiscuous mode is often used to diagnose network connectivity issues. There are programs that make use of this feature to show the user all the data being transferred over the network. Some protocols like File Transfer Protocol (FTP), Telnet transfer data, passwords in clear text without encryption, and network scanners can see this data. Therefore, computer users are encouraged to stay away from insecure protocols like Telnet and use more secure ones such as secure shell (SSH).

16. DETECTION

As promiscuous mode can be used in a malicious way to sniff on a network, one might be interested in detecting network devices that are in a promiscuous mode. In promiscuous mode, some software might send responses to frames, even though they were addressed to another machine. However, experienced sniffers can prevent this (using carefully designed firewall settings).

An example of the preceding is sending a ping (Internet Control Message Protocol (ICMP) echo request) with the wrong Media Access Control (MAC) address, but the right IP address. If an adapter is operating in normal mode, it will drop this frame, and the IP stack never sees or responds to it. If the adapter is in promiscuous mode, the frame will be passed on, and the IP stack on the machine (to which a MAC address has no meaning) will respond, as it would to any other ping. The sniffer can prevent this by configuring his firewall to block ICMP traffic:

- Immutable files on the system that cannot be deleted can be found with the lsattr command. lsattr is a command-line program for listing the attributes on a Linux second extended file system. It is also a command to display attributes of devices on an Advanced Interactive eXecutive (AIX) operating system. Some malware puts a + i flag on its own executable, so you cannot delete it, even if you are a root.
- Mysterious open ports and services: All open ports and running services should be accounted for. For example, if there is a service running, but it's not clear what it does or why it is running, an investigation should be launched [10].

Finally, let's briefly look at the most common way to classify the detection of system intrusions (DSIs). Classification of the DSIs is to group them by information source. Some of the DSIs analyze network packets, captured from network backbones or LAN segments, in order to find attackers. Other DSIs analyze information sources generated by the operating system or application software for signs of intrusion.

17. NETWORK-BASED DETECTION OF SYSTEM INTRUSIONS (DSIS)

The majority of the commercial detection of system intrusions are network-based. These DSIs detect attacks by capturing and analyzing network packets. By listening on a network segment or switch, one network-based DSI can monitor the network traffic that is affecting multiple hosts connected to the network segment, thereby protecting those hosts.

Network-based DSIs often consist of a set of single-purpose sensors or hosts placed at various points in a network. These units monitor network traffic, performing local analysis of that traffic and reporting attacks to a central management console. As the sensors are limited to running the DSIs, they can be more easily secured against attack. Many of these sensors are designed to run in stealth mode, in order to make it more difficult for an attacker to determine their presence and location.

In addition, the following high-level checklist (see checklist: An Agenda for Action of the Advantages and Disadvantages of Network-Based DSIs) addresses the advantages and disadvantages of how the network-based DSIs monitor network traffic for particular network segments or devices, and analyzes network, transport, and application protocols to identify suspicious activity. The network-based DSI components are similar to other types of DSI technologies, except for the sensors. A network-based DSI sensor monitors and analyzes network activity on one or more network segments. Sensors are available in two formats: appliance-based sensors, which are comprised of specialized hardware and software optimized for DSI sensor use; and software-only sensors, which can be installed onto hosts that meet certain specifications.

AN AGENDA FOR ACTION OF THE ADVANTAGES AND DISADVANTAGES OF NETWORK-BASED DSIS ACTIVITIES

The following high-level checklist displays the advantages and disadvantages of how the network-based DSIs monitor network traffic for particular network segments (check all tasks completed):

Advantages

_____1. Install network-based DSIs so that they can monitor a large network.

_____2. Deploy network-based DSIs so that they have little impact on an existing network.

_____3. Make sure that the network-based DSIs listen in on a network wire without interfering with the normal operation of a network.

_____4. Retrofit a network to include network-based DSIs with minimal effort.

_____5. Make the network-based DSIs very secure against attack and invisible to attackers.

Disadvantages

_____6. Do your network-based DSIs have difficulty processing all packets in a large or busy network and, therefore, fail to recognize an attack launched during periods of high traffic?

_____7. Do your vendors implement DSIs completely in hardware, which is much faster?

_____8. Do your vendors analyze packets quickly, which forces them to both detect fewer attacks and also detect attacks with as little computing resource as possible, which can reduce detection effectiveness?

_____9. Is it true that many of the advantages of network-based DSIs don't apply to more modern switch-based networks?

_____10. Do switches subdivide networks into many small segments (usually one fast Ethernet wire per host) and provide dedicated links between hosts serviced by the same switch?

_____11. Do most switches that do not provide universal monitoring ports limit the monitoring range of a network-based DSIs sensor to a single host?

_____12. Do most switches that provide monitoring ports cause the single port to not mirror all traffic traversing the switch?

_____13. Is it true that network-based DSIs cannot analyze encrypted information?

_____14. Is the problem of not being able to analyze encrypted information increasing, as more organizations (and attackers) use virtual private networks?

_____15. Is it true that most network-based DSIs cannot tell whether or not an attack was successful, and that they can only discern that an attack was initiated?

_____16. Is it true that after a network-based DSIs detects an attack administrators must manually investigate each attacked host to determine whether it was indeed penetrated?

_____17. Do some network-based DSIs have problems dealing with network-based attacks that involve fragmenting packets?

_____18. Do malformed packets cause the DSIs to become unstable and crash?

18. SUMMARY

As we outlined earlier, there are many ways to detect system intrusions and many ways to hide them. What is the proper way to analyze suspect systems then? The proper sequence is as follows:

1. Memory dump and analysis: Hackers are getting smart these days; they stay in the memory as long as possible. Why? Because they know forensics will be done on the HDD itself; but if they stay in memory, it requires a better skill to do memory analysis. Some companies just pull the plug from the power and network, and do HDD forensics analysis. This is wrong because as soon as you pull the power plug, half of the goodies are gone.

2. Selective HDD files analysis (we make the HDD image first, and work from the copy). Depending on the machine role on the network, doing a full-blown forensic analysis might be an overkill. In some situations, a partial forensic examination is enough.
3. A full HDD analysis is needed (we make the HDD image first and work from the copy).

Finally, let's move on to the real interactive part of this chapter: review questions/exercises, hands-on projects, case projects, and optional team case project. The answers and/or solutions by chapter can be found in the Online Instructor's Solutions Manual.

CHAPTER REVIEW QUESTIONS/EXERCISES

True/False

1. True or False? One of the ways to monitor changes in the file system is to implement LoggedFS.
2. True or False? File integrity monitoring (FIM) is an internal control or process that performs the act of validating the integrity of the operating system and application software files using a verification method between the current file state and the known, good baseline.
3. True or False? A timestamp is a sequence of characters or encoded information identifying when a certain event occurred, usually giving date and time of day, sometimes accurate to a small fraction of a second.
4. True or False? A hidden file is normally visible when examining the contents of the directory in which it resides.
5. True or False? About 90 percent of all successful compromises are made via known flaws, so 0day attacks are common.

Multiple Choice

1. Values monitored for unexpected changes to files or configuration items include the following, except which one?
   A. Credentials.
   B. Cannot be understood.
   C. Privileges and security settings.
   D. Content.
   E. Core attributes and size.
2. What phase focuses on attack surface analysis?
   A. Analyze.
   B. Test.
   C. Report.

    D. Mitigate.

    E. Cipher.

3. Injection mechanisms include the following, except which one:

    A. Use of vendor-supplied application extensions.

    B. Interception of messages.

    C. Buggers.

    D. Exploitation of security vulnerabilities.

    E. Function hooking or patching of commonly used APIs.

4. What describes the product capabilities of gathering, analyzing, and presenting information from network and security devices; identity and access management applications; vulnerability management and policy compliance tools; operating system, database, and application logs; and external threat data?

    A. Security Information Event Management.

    B. Security Information Management.

    C. Security Event Management.

    D. Security Management Information.

    E. Security Event Information.

5. What is it called when SIEM/LM tools take event data and turn it into informational charts to assist in seeing patterns, or identifying activity that is not forming a standard pattern?

    A. Compliance.

    B. Retention.

    C. Dashboards.

    D. Alerting.

    E. Correlation.

EXERCISE

Problem

Which of the following attributes suggests that the packets below have been crafted?

00:03:21.680333   216.164.222.250.1186 > us.us.us.44.8080: S 2410044679:2410044679 (0) win 512

00:03:21.810732   216.164.222.250.1189 > us.us.us.50.8080: S 2410044679:2410044679 (0) win 512

Hands-On Projects

Project

What is the most likely reason for choosing to use HEAD requests instead of GET requests when scanning for the presence of vulnerable Web-based applications?

Case Projects

Problem

What is the LEAST effective indicator that the attacker's source address is not spoofed?

Optional Team Case Project

Problem

What is the most likely explanation for "arp info overwritten" messages on a BSD-based system?

References

[1] B. Schneier, Whitelisting vs. Blacklisting. <https://www.schneier.com/blog/archives/2011/01/whitelisting_vs.html>, January 28, 2011.
[2] LoggedFS. <http://loggedfs.sourceforge.net/>.
[3] AIDE. <http://aide.sourceforge.net/>.
[4] Hidden files. <http://www.linfo.org/hidden_file.html>.
[5] SystemImager. <http://sourceforge.net/projects/systemimager/>.
[6] Phrack. <http://phrack.org./>.
[7] What is vulnerability. <http://bit.ly/PFCWCh>.
[8] Targeted attack. <http://bit.ly/MTjLVv>.
[9] Demyo plug. <http://www.demyo.com>.
[10] Intrusion Detection. <http://bit.ly/OCB7UU>.

2

Preventing System Intrusions

Michael West

Senior Technical Writer, Truestone Maritime Operations

There's a war raging across the globe, and you're right in the middle of it. But while this war doesn't include gunfire and mass carnage, its effects can be thoroughly devastating nonetheless. This war is being waged in cyberspace by people bent on stealing the heart and soul of your business, your company's plans and secrets, or worse, your client names and their financial information.

So how bad is it? Just what are you up against?

Imagine this: You're in charge of security for an advanced movie screening. You've been hired and assigned the daunting task of keeping the advanced screening from being copied and turned into a bootleg version available overseas or on the Web. So how do you make sure that doesn't happen (how many times have we heard about this scenario or seen it in the movies)?

First, you might start by controlling access to the theater itself, allowing only the holders of very tightly controlled tickets into the screening. You post a couple of personnel at the door who carefully check every ticket against a list to verify the identity of both the ticket holder and their numbered ticket. Your goal is clear: restrict the viewers and, hopefully, reduce the possibility of someone entering with a counterfeit ticket. But what about the back stage door? While you're busy watching the front door, someone could simply sneak in the back. So, you secure that door and post a guard. But what about the ventilation system (the ventilation system is a favorite Hollywood scenario—remember Tom Cruise in *Mission Impossible*)? So, you secure that too. You also secure the projection room.

Did you think about a ticket holder coming into the theater with a digital recording device? Or a recording device surreptitiously planted just outside the projection room before anyone even entered. Or, worse, someone who rigged up a digital recording system that captures the movie from *inside* the projector and feeds it directly to their computer?

The point is this: No matter how diligent you are at securing your network, there are always people waiting just outside who are just as motivated to steal what you're trying to protect as you are trying to keep them from stealing it. You put up a wall; they use a

Network and System Security
DOI: http://dx.doi.org/10.1016/B978-0-12-416689-9.00002-2

back door. You secure the back door; they come in through a window. You secure the windows; they sneak in through the ventilation system. You secure the ventilation system; they simply bypass the physical security measures and go straight for your users, turning them into unwitting thieves. And so on and so on.

There's a very delicate balance between the need to keep your network secured and allowing user access. Users may be your company's lifeblood, but they are simultaneously your greatest and most necessary asset, and your weakest link.

It almost sounds like an impossible task, doesn't it? It's easy to see how it might seem that way when a casual Internet search reveals no shortage of sites selling hacking tools. In some cases, the hacking tools were written for—and marketed to—those not schooled in programming languages.

When I wrote this chapter three years ago, the cyber world was a very different place. Back then, crackers were simply stealing credit card numbers and financial data (for example, in January, hackers penetrated the customer database for online shoe store giant Zappos and stole names, email addresses, shipping addresses, phone numbers, and the last four digits of credit card numbers for over 24 million customers), siphoning corporate proprietary information (also known as industrial espionage), and defacing Web sites.

In today's world, crackers twice took control of an American satellite called Terra Eos, not just interrupting data flow, but taking full control of the satellite's guidance systems. They literally could have given the satellite commands to start a de-orbit burn.[1] And there's no shortage of some very simple and readily accessible software tools that allow crackers to sit nearby, say, in a coffee shop and wirelessly follow your Web browsing, steal your passwords, or even assume your identity.

Now, who do you think could pull off a feat like that? Most likely, it's not your neighbor's kid or the cyberpunk with just enough skill to randomly deface Web sites. Many experts believe this effort was well funded, most likely with government sponsorship. The Chinese military believes that attacking the communications links between ground stations and orbiting satellites is a legitimate strategy at the outset of any conflict. If that's the case, then a government-sponsored attack is a frightening prospect.

The moment you established an active Web presence, you put a target on your company's back. And like the hapless insect that lands in the spider's web, your company's size determines the size of the disturbance you create on the Web—and how quickly you're noticed by the bad guys. How attractive you are as prey is usually directly proportionate to what you have to offer a predator. If yours is an e-commerce site whose business thrives on credit card or other financial information or a company with valuable secrets to steal, your "juiciness" quotient goes up; you have more of value there to steal. And if your business is new and your Web presence is recent, the assumption could be made that perhaps you're not yet a seasoned veteran in the nuances of cyber warfare and, thus, are more vulnerable to an intrusion.

Unfortunately for you, many of those who seek to penetrate your network defenses are educated, highly motivated, and quite brilliant at developing faster and more efficient

1. ABC News, November 16, 2011.

methods of quietly sneaking around your perimeter, checking for the smallest of openings. Most IT professionals know that an enterprise's firewall is relentlessly being probed for weaknesses and vulnerabilities by crackers from every corner of the globe. Anyone who follows news about software understands that seemingly every few months, word comes out about a new, exploitable opening in an operating system or application. It's widely understood that no one—not the most savvy network administrator, or the programmer who wrote the software—can possibly find and close all the holes in today's increasingly complex software.

Despite the increased sophistication of today's software applications, bugs and holes exist in those applications, as well as in operating systems, server processes (daemons), and client applications. System configurations can be easily exploited, especially if you don't change the default administrator's password, or if you simply accept default system settings, or unintentionally leave a gaping hole open by configuring the machine to run in a nonsecure mode. Even Transmission Control Protocol/Internet Protocol (TCP/IP), the foundation on which all Internet traffic operates, can be exploited, since the protocol was designed before the threat of hacking was really widespread. Therefore it contains design flaws that can allow, for example, a cracker to easily alter IP data.

Once the word gets out that a new and exploitable opening exists in an application (and word *will* get out), crackers around the world start scanning sites on the Internet searching for any and all sites that have that particular opening.

Making your job even harder is the fact that many of the openings into your network are caused by your employees. Casual surfing of online shopping sites, porn sites, and even banking sites can expose your network to all kinds of nasty bugs and malicious code, simply because an employee visited the site. The problem is that, to users, it might not seem like such a big deal. They either don't realize that they're leaving the network wide open to intrusion, or they don't care.

1. SO, WHAT IS AN INTRUSION?

A network intrusion is an unauthorized penetration of your enterprise's network, or an individual machine address in your assigned domain. Intrusions can be passive (in which the penetration is gained stealthily and without detection) or active (in which changes to network resources are effected). Intrusions can come from outside your network structure or inside (an employee, a customer, or business partner). Some intrusions are simply meant to let you know the intruder was there by defacing your Web site with various kinds of messages or crude images. Others are more malicious, seeking to extract critical information on either a one-time basis or as an ongoing parasitic relationship that continues to siphon off data until it's discovered. Some intruders implant carefully crafted code, such as Trojan-type malicious software (malware), designed to steal passwords, record keystrokes, or open an application's "back door."

Still worse, some high-end crackers can set up phony Web sites that exactly mimic your company's site, and surreptitiously redirect your unaware users away from your site to theirs (known as a "man in the browser attack"). Others will embed themselves into your network like a tick, quietly siphoning off data until found and rendered inert.

An attacker can get into your system physically (by gaining physical access to a restricted machine's hard drive and/or BIOS), externally (by attacking your Web servers or finding a way to bypass your firewall), or internally (your own users, customers, or partners).

2. SOBERING NUMBERS

So how often do these intrusions and data thefts occur? The estimates are staggering: In August of 2009, InfoTech Spotlight reported that "cybercrime costs organizations an average of $3.8 million per year,"[2] and there are thousands of new, fake phishing[3] Web sites set up online every day. The *APWG Phishing Activity Trends Report* for the first half of 2011 shows that even though unique phishing reports are down 35 percent (from an all-time high of 40,621 in August of 2009), data-stealing Trojan malware reached an all-time high in the first half of 2011 and comprised almost *half* of all detected malware. And from January to June of 2011, the number of new malware samples hit a whopping 11,777,775—an increase of 13 percent from the second half of 2010![4]

A March 2010 report by Security Management revealed that the most common Internet fraud complaints are from people whose identities have been compromised.[5] On two occasions, I myself have been the victim of a stolen credit-card number. In one case, a purchase was made at a jewelry store in Texas, and in the other, the purchases were made at a grocery store in the Philippines.

The Federal Bureau of Investigation (FBI) reports receiving over 330,000 identity theft reports, with losses estimated at over $560 million. And McAfee reports estimate business losses topped $1 trillion!Sadly, this number is likely to climb; 72 percent of newly detected malware are Trojans capable of stealing user information.

Not surprisingly, financial services are still the hardest hit and most frequently targeted sector, and account for almost half of all industry attacks. In the first half of 2011, new and more malevolent types of "Crimeware" (software specifically designed to steal customer information such as credit-card data, Social Security numbers, and customers' financial Web site credentials) appeared. Patrik Runald, senior manager of Security Research at Websense, has stated: "With cybercrime being an industry generating hundreds of millions of dollars for the bad guys, it's clear that this is a trend we will see for a long time."[6]

Unfortunately, the United States continues to host the highest number of infected phishing sites: Nearly 60 percent of all malware-infected URLs comes from the United States.

In today's cyber battlefield, attacks are specifically targeting one organization as a prelude to attacking and penetrating others. And if you're an enterprise's IT professional, you

2. Bright Hub, "Cyber Crime Costs / Cyber Crime Losses," September 13, 2010.

3. Phishing is an attempt to steal user information (e.g., usernames, passwords, credit-card information, etc.) by disguising phony Web sites as legitimate ones the user may be accustomed to accessing.

4. Panda Security, PandaLabs.

5. "Uptick in Cybercrime Cost Victims Big in 2009, FBI Report Says," *Security Management*, March 15, 2010.

6. APWG Phishing Activity Trends Report.

need to make a fundamental shift in mind-set away from trying to build the most impressive defenses that money can buy to thinking seriously about defense and detection. The reality is, you have to assume you have been or soon will be compromised.

Even the big boys in cybersecurity aren't immune. In March of 2010, RSA was among hundreds of major companies compromised in a massive, coordinated cyber attack. The attackers penetrated RSA's formidable defenses and made off with information that RSA said could "reduce the effectiveness" of its widely used SecurID authentication system. In what the cyber security industry refers to as an "advanced persistent threat," the crackers used the information they stole from RSA to attack defense contractor Lockheed Martin.[7]

Whatever the goal of the intrusion—fun, greed, bragging rights, or data theft — the end result will be the same: Someone discovered and exploited a weakness in your network security, and until you discover that weakness—the intrusion entry point—it will continue to be an open door into your environment.

So, just who's out there looking to break into your network?

3. KNOW YOUR ENEMY: HACKERS VERSUS CRACKERS

An entire community of people—experts in programming and computer networking and those who thrive on solving complex problems—have been around since the earliest days of computing. The term *hacker* originated from the members of this culture, and they are quick to point out that it was hackers who built and make the Internet run, and hackers who created the Unix operating system. Hackers see themselves as members of a community that builds things and makes them work. And to those in their culture, the term *cracker* is a badge of honor.

Ask a traditional hacker about people who sneak into computer systems to steal data or cause havoc, and he'll most likely correct you by telling you those people aren't true hackers. (In the cracker community, the term for these types is *cracker*, and the two labels aren't synonymous.) So, to not offend traditional hackers, I'll use the term *crackers* and focus on them and their efforts.

From the lone-wolf cracker seeking peer recognition to the disgruntled former employee out for revenge or the deep pockets and seemingly unlimited resources of a hostile government bent on taking down wealthy capitalists, crackers are out there in force, looking to find the chink in your system's defensive armor.

The crackers' specialty—or in some cases, their mission in life—is to seek out and exploit the vulnerabilities of an individual computer or network for their own purposes. Crackers' intentions are normally malicious and/or criminal in nature. They have, at their disposal, a vast library of information designed to help them hone their tactics, skills, and knowledge, and they can tap into the almost unlimited experience of other crackers through a community of like-minded individuals sharing information across underground networks.

They usually begin this life learning the most basic of skills: software programming. The ability to write code that can make a computer do what they want is seductive in and

7. CNNMoney, February 28, 2012.

of itself. As they learn more and more about programming, they also expand their knowledge of operating systems and, as a natural course of progression, operating systems' weaknesses. They also quickly learn that, to expand the scope and type of their illicit handiwork, they need to learn HTML—the code that allows them to create phony Web pages that lure unsuspecting users into revealing important financial or personal data.

There are vast underground organizations to which these new crackers can turn for information. They hold meetings, write papers, and develop tools that they pass along to each other. Each new acquaintance they meet fortifies their skill set and gives them the training to branch out to more and more sophisticated techniques. Once they gain a certain level of proficiency, they begin their trade in earnest.

They start off simply by researching potential target firms on the Internet (an invaluable source for all kinds of corporate network related information). Once a target has been identified, they might quietly tiptoe around, probing for old forgotten back doors and operating system vulnerabilities. As starting points for launching an attack, they can simply and innocuously run basic DNS queries that can provide IP addresses (or ranges of IP addresses). They might sit back and listen to inbound and/or outbound traffic, record IP addresses, and test for weaknesses by pinging various devices or users.

To breach your network, a cracker starts by creating a chain of exploited systems in which each successful takeover sets the stage for the next. The easiest systems to exploit are those in our homes: Most home users do little to secure their systems from outside intrusions. And a good cracker can implant malware so deeply in a home computer that the owner never knows it's there. Then, when they're asleep or away, the malware takes control of the home computer and starts sending out newly mutated versions to another compromised system. In this way, there are so many compromised systems between them and the intrusion that it sends investigators down long, twisted paths that can include dozens, if not hundreds, of unwittingly compromised systems. Once your network is breached, they can surreptitiously implant password cracking or recording applications, keystroke recorders, or other malware designed to keep their unauthorized connection alive—and profitable. From there, they sit back and siphon off whatever they deem most valuable.

The cracker wants to act like a cyber-ninja, sneaking up to and penetrating your network without leaving any trace of the incursion. Some more seasoned crackers can put multiple layers of machines, many hijacked, between them and your network to hide their activity. Like standing in a room full of mirrors, the attack appears to be coming from so many locations you can't pick out the real from the ghost. And before you realize what they've done, they've up and disappeared like smoke in the wind.

4. MOTIVES

Though the goal is the same—to penetrate your network defenses—crackers' motives are often different. In some cases, a network intrusion could be done from the inside by a disgruntled employee looking to hurt the organization or steal company secrets for profit.

There are large groups of crackers working diligently to steal credit-card information that they then turn around and make available for sale. They want a quick grab and dash—take what they want and leave. Their cousins are the network parasites—those who quietly breach your network, then sit there siphoning off data.

A new and very disturbing trend is the discovery that certain governments have been funding digital attacks on network resources of both federal and corporate systems. Various agencies from the U.S. Department of Defense to the governments of New Zealand, France, and Germany have reported attacks originating from unidentified Chinese hacking groups. It should be noted that the Chinese government denies any involvement, and there is no evidence that it is or was involved.

5. THE CRACKERS' TOOLS OF THE TRADE

Over the years, the tools available to crackers have become increasingly more sophisticated. How sophisticated?

Most security software products available today have three basic methods of spotting malicious software. First, it scans all incoming data traffic for traces of known malware (pulling malware characteristics from a source database). Then, it looks for any kind of suspicious activity (e.g., vulnerable processes unexpectedly activating or running too long, unusual activity during normally dormant periods, etc.). And finally, the security software checks for indications of information leaving from abnormal paths or processes.

Recently, however, a relatively new and extremely malicious malware program called Zeus has appeared. Designed specifically to steal financial information, Zeus can defeat the above methods by not only sitting discreetly and quietly—not drawing attention to itselfbut also by changing its appearance tens of thousands of times per day. But its most insidious characteristic is that it siphons data off from an infected system using your browser. Called a "man in the browser attack," Zeus implants itself in your browser, settling in between you and a legitimate Web site (say, the site for the financial institution that manages your IRA), and very capably altering what you see to the point at which you really can't tell the difference. Not knowing the difference, you confidently enter your most important financial details, which Zeus siphons off and sends to someone else. New Zeus updates come out regularly, and, once released, it can take weeks for its new characteristics to become known by security software companies.

Our "Unsecured" Wireless World

Do you think much about the time you spend using a coffee shop's free Wi-Fi signal to surf, check your email, or update your Facebook page? Probably not. But today, the person sitting next to you quietly sipping her coffee and working away on her laptop can now sit back and watch what Web sites you've visited, then assume your identity and log on to the sites you visited. How? A free program called Firesheep can grab from your Web browser the cookies[8] for each site you visit. That cookie contains identifying

---

8. Cookies are bits of software code sent to your browser by Web sites. They can be used for authentication, session identification, preferences, shopping cart contents, and so on.

information about your computer, and site settings for each site you visit plus your customized private information for that site. Once Firesheep grabs that cookie, a malicious user can use it to log on to sites as you, and can, in some cases, gain full access to your account.

You may be asking yourself "So what does this have to do with my network?" If the unsuspecting user is wirelessly completing a sales transaction or bank transfer when software like Firesheep snatches the browser cookie, the cracker can log back into your site as the compromised user and drain your account.

In years past, only the most experienced and savvy crackers with expensive tools and plenty of time could do much damage to secured networks. But like a professional thief with custom-made lock picks, crackers today can obtain a frightening array of tools to covertly test your network for weak spots. Their tools range from simple password-stealing malware and keystroke recorders (loggers) to methods of implanting sophisticated parasitic software strings that copy data streams coming in from customers who want to perform an e-commerce transaction with your company. Some of the more widely used tools include these:

- *Wireless sniffers.* Not only can these devices locate wireless signals within a certain range, they can siphon off the data being transmitted over the signals. With the rise in popularity and use of remote wireless devices, this practice is increasingly responsible for the loss of critical data and represents a significant headache for IT departments.
- *Packet sniffers.* Once implanted in a network data stream, these tools passively analyze data packets moving into and out of a network interface, and utilities capture data packets passing through a network interface.
- *Port scanners.* A good analogy for these utilities is a thief casing a neighborhood, looking for an open or unlocked door. These utilities send out successive, sequential connection requests to a target system's ports to see which one responds or is open to the request. Some port scanners allow the cracker to slow the rate of port scanning—sending connection requests over a longer period of time—so the intrusion attempt is less likely to be noticed. The usual targets of these devices are old, forgotten "back doors," or ports inadvertently left unguarded after network modifications.
- *Port knocking.* Sometimes network administrators create a secret backdoor method of getting through firewall-protected ports—a secret knock that enables them to quickly access the network. Port-knocking tools find these unprotected entries and implant a Trojan horse that listens to network traffic for evidence of that secret knock.
- *Keystroke loggers.* These are spyware utilities planted on vulnerable systems that record a user's keystrokes. Obviously, when someone can sit back and record every keystroke a user makes, it doesn't take long to obtain things like usernames, passwords, and ID numbers.
- *Remote administration tools.* Programs embedded on an unsuspecting user's system that allow the cracker to take control of that system.
- *Network scanners.* Explore networks to see the number and kind of host systems on a network, the services available, the host's operating system, and the type of packet filtering or firewalls being used.

- *Password crackers.* These sniff networks for data streams associated with passwords, then employ a brute-force method of peeling away any encryption layers protecting those passwords.

6. BOTS

Three years ago, bots were an emerging threat. Now , organized cyber criminals have begun to create and sell kits on the open market that inexperienced nonprogramming crackers can use to create their own botnets. It offers a wide variety of easy to use (or pre-programmed) modules that specifically target the most lucrative technologies. It includes a management console that can control every infected system and interrogate bot-infected machines. If desired, Zeus kit modules are available that can allow the user to create viruses that mutate every time they're implanted in a new host system.

So what are bots? Bots, also known as an Internet bots, Web robots, or WWW robots, are small software applications running automated tasks over the Internet. Usually, they run simple tasks that a human would otherwise have to perform, but at a much faster rate. When used maliciously, they are a virus, surreptitiously implanted in large numbers of unprotected computers (usually those found in homes), hijacking them (without the owners' knowledge) and turning them into slaves to do the cracker's bidding. These compromised computers, known as *bots*, are linked in vast and usually untraceable networks called *botnets*. Botnets are designed to operate in such a way that instructions come from a central PC and are rapidly shared among other botted computers in the network. Newer botnets are now using a "peer-to-peer" method that, because they lack a central identifiable point of control, makes it difficult if not impossible for law enforcement agencies to pinpoint. And because they often cross international boundaries into countries without the means (or will) to investigate and shut them down, they can grow with alarming speed. They can be so lucrative that they've now become the cracker's tool of choice.

There are all kinds of bots; there are bots that harvest email addresses (spambots), viruses and worms, filename modifiers, bots to buy up large numbers of concert seats, and bots that work together in botnets, or coordinated attacks on networked computers.

Botnets exist largely because of the number of users who fail to observe basic principles of computer security—installed and/or up-to-date antivirus software, regular scans for suspicious code, and so on—and thereby become unwitting accomplices. Once taken over and "botted," their machines are turned into channels through which large volumes of unwanted spam or malicious code can be quickly distributed. Current estimates are that, of the 800 million computers on the Internet, up to 40 percent are bots controlled by cyber thieves who are using them to spread new viruses, send out unwanted spam email, overwhelm Web sites in denial-of-service (DoS) attacks, or siphon off sensitive user data from banking or shopping Web sites that look and act like legitimate sites with which customers have previously done business.

Bot controllers, also called *herders*, can also make money by leasing their networks to others who need a large and untraceable means of sending out massive amounts of advertisements but don't have the financial or technical resources to create their own networks. Making matters worse is the fact that botnet technology is available on the Internet for less than $100, which makes it relatively easy to get started in what can be a very lucrative business.

7. SYMPTOMS OF INTRUSIONS

As stated earlier, merely being on the Web puts a target on your back. It's only a matter of time before you experience your first attack. It could be something as innocent looking as several failed login attempts or as obvious as an attacker having defaced your Web site or crippled your network. It's important that you go into this knowing you're vulnerable.

Crackers are going to first look for known weaknesses in the operating system (OS) or any applications you are using. Next, they would start probing, looking for holes, open ports, or forgotten back doors—faults in your security posture that can quickly or easily be exploited.

Arguably one of the most common symptoms of an intrusion—either attempted or successful—is repeated signs that someone is trying to take advantage of your organization's own security systems, and the tools you use to keep watch for suspicious network activity may actually be used against you quite effectively. Tools such as network security and file integrity scanners, which can be invaluable in helping you conduct ongoing assessments of your network's vulnerability, are also available and can be used by crackers looking for a way in.

Large numbers of unsuccessful login attempts are also a good indicator that your system has been targeted. The best penetration-testing tools can be configured with attempt thresholds that, when exceeded, will trigger an alert. They can passively distinguish between legitimate and suspicious activity of a repetitive nature, monitor the time intervals between activities (alerting when the number exceeds the threshold you set), and build a database of signatures seen multiple times over a given period.

The "human element" (your users) is a constant factor in your network operations. Users will frequently enter a mistyped response but usually correct the error on the next try. However, a sequence of mistyped commands or incorrect login responses (with attempts to recover or reuse them) can be a signs of brute-force intrusion attempts.

Packet inconsistencies—direction (inbound or outbound), originating address or location, and session characteristics (ingoing sessions vs. outgoing sessions)—can also be good indicators of an attack. If a packet has an unusual source or has been addressed to an abnormal port—say, an inconsistent service request—it could be a sign of random system scanning. Packets coming from the outside that have local network addresses that request services on the inside can be a sign that IP spoofing is being attempted.

Sometimes odd or unexpected system behavior is itself a sign. Though this is sometimes difficult to track, you should be aware of activity such as changes to system clocks, servers going down or server processes inexplicably stopping (with system restart attempts), system resource issues (such as unusually high CPU activity or overflows in file systems), audit logs behaving in strange ways (decreasing in size without administrator intervention), or unexpected user access to resources. You should investigate any and all unusual activity at regular times on given days, heavy system use (possible denial of service (DoS) attack) or CPU use (brute-force password-cracking attempts).

8. WHAT CAN YOU DO?

It goes without saying that the most secure network—the one that has the least chance of being compromised—is the one that has no direct connection to the outside world. But that's hardly a practical solution, since the whole reason you have a Web presence is to do business. And in the game of Internet commerce, your biggest concern isn't the sheep coming in but the wolves dressed like sheep coming in with them. So, how do you strike an acceptable balance between keeping your network intrusion free and keeping it accessible at the same time?

As your company's network administrator, you walk a fine line between network security and user needs. You have to have a good defensive posture that still allows for access. Users and customers can be both the lifeblood of your business and its greatest potential source of infection. Furthermore, if your business thrives on allowing users access, you have no choice but to let them in. It seems like a monumentally difficult task at best.

Like a castle, imposing but stationary, every defensive measure you put up will eventually be compromised by the legions of very motivated thieves looking to get in. It's a game of move/countermove: You adjust, they adapt. So you have to start with defenses that can quickly and effectively adapt and change as the outside threats adapt.

First and foremost, you need to make sure that your perimeter defenses are as strong as they can be, and that means keeping up with the rapidly evolving threats around you. The days of relying solely on a firewall that simply does firewall functions are gone; today's crackers have figured out how to bypass the firewall by exploiting weaknesses in applications themselves. Simply being reactive to hits and intrusions isn't a very good option either; that's like standing there waiting for someone to hit you before deciding what to do rather than seeing the oncoming punch and moving out of its way or blocking it. You need to be flexible in your approach to the newest technologies, constantly auditing your defenses to ensure that your network's defensive armor can meet the latest threat. You have to have a very dynamic and effective policy of constantly monitoring for suspicious activities that, when discovered, can be quickly dealt with so that someone doesn't slip something past without your noticing it. Once that happens, it's too late.

Next, and this is also a crucial ingredient for network administrators: You have to educate your users. No matter how good a job you've done at tightening up your network security processes and systems, you still have to deal with the weakest link in your armor—your users. It doesn't do any good to have bulletproof processes in place if they're so difficult to manage that users work around them to avoid the difficulty, or if they're so loosely configured that a casually surfing user who visits an infected site will pass that infection along to your network. The degree of difficulty in securing your network increases dramatically as the number of users goes up.

User education becomes particularly important where mobile computing is concerned. Losing a device, using it in a place (or manner) in which prying eyes can see passwords or data, awareness of hacking tools specifically designed to sniff wireless signals for data, and logging on to unsecured networks are all potential problem areas with which users need to be familiar.

A relatively new tool is the intrusion detection system, or IDS. IDSs merge their deep packet scanning with a firewall's blocking can filtering capabilities. A good IDS and not only detect intrusion attempts, but also stop the attack before it does any damage.

One type of IDS, known as an inline IDS, can sit between your network's outside interface and your most critical systems. They essentially inspect every data packet headed for those critical systems, sniffing and "tasting" them, then scrubbing out the ones that have suspicious characteristics.

Another type of IDS is based on an application firewall scheme. These types of IDSs sit on all protected servers and are configured to protect specific applications. They are designed to "learn" every aspect of an application—how it interacts with users and the Internet, how the application's features play with each other, and what "customizable" features the application has that may require more detailed configuration—then create a rule for dealing with those aspects. This last point reveals a drawback of application-based IDSs: In order for them to protect all aspects of the application, it has to "know" every aspect of the application. The only way you can configure the IDS to protect every one of the application's functions is to let it "learn" the functions by exercising them. It can't develop a protection rule for a feature with which it's unfamiliar. So thorough testing is needed, or the IDS may miss a particular vulnerability. And if you update the protected application, you'll need to exercise its features again to ensure the IDS knows what it's supposed to protect.

You can also set up a decoy—sort of the "sacrificial lamb"—as bait. Also known as "honey pots," these userless networks are specifically set up to draw in an attacker and gain valuable data on the methods, tools, and any new malware they might be using.

Know Today's Network Needs

The traditional approach to network security engineering has been to try to erect preventative measures—firewalls—to protect the infrastructure from intrusion. The firewall acts like a filter, catching anything that seems suspicious and keeping everything behind it as sterile as possible. However, though firewalls are good, they typically don't do much in the way of identifying compromised applications that use network resources. And with the speed of evolution seen in the area of penetration tools, an approach designed simply to prevent attacks will be less and less effective.

Today's computing environment is no longer confined to the office, as it used to be. Though there are still fixed systems inside the firewall, ever more sophisticated remote and mobile devices are making their way into the workforce. This influx of mobile computing has expanded the traditional boundaries of the network to farther and farther reaches and requires a different way of thinking about network security requirements.

Your network's endpoint or perimeter is mutating—expanding beyond its historical boundaries. Until recently, that endpoint was the user, either a desktop system or laptop, and it was relatively easy to secure those devices. To use a metaphor: The difference between endpoints of early network design and those of today is like the difference between the battles of World War II and the current war on terror. In the World War II battles there were very clearly defined "front lines"—one side controlled by the

Allied powers, the other by the Axis. Today, the war on terror has no such front lines and is fought in multiple areas with different techniques and strategies that are customized for each combat theater.

With today's explosion of remote users and mobile computing, your network's endpoint is no longer as clearly defined as it once was, and it is evolving at a very rapid pace. For this reason, your network's physical perimeter can no longer be seen as your best "last line of defense," even though having a robust perimeter security system is still a critical part of your overall security policy.

Any policy you develop should be organized in such a way as to take advantage of the strength of your unified threat management (UTM) system. Firewalls, antivirus, and intrusion detection systems (IDSs), for example, work by trying to block all currently known threats—the "blacklist" approach. But the threats evolve more quickly than the UTM systems can, so it almost always ends up being an "after the fact" game of catch-up. Perhaps a better, and more easily managed, policy is to specifically state which devices are allowed access and which applications are allowed to run in your network's applications. This "whitelist" approach helps reduce the amount of time and energy needed to keep up with the rapidly evolving pace of threat sophistication, because you're specifying what gets in versus what you have to keep out.

Any UTM system you employ should provide the means of doing two things: specify which applications and devices are allowed and offer a policy-based approach to managing those applications and devices. It should allow you to secure your critical resources against unauthorized data extraction (or data leakage), offer protection from the most persistent threats (viruses, malware, and spyware), and evolve with the ever-changing spectrum of devices and applications designed to penetrate your outer defenses.

So, what's the best strategy for integrating these new remote endpoints? First, you have to realize that these new remote, mobile technologies are becoming increasingly ubiquitous and aren't going away anytime soon. In fact, they most likely represent the future of computing. As these devices gain in sophistication and function, they are unchaining end users from their desks and, for some businesses, are indispensable tools. iPhones, Blackberries, Palm Treos, and other smart phones and devices now have the capability to interface with corporate email systems, access networks, run enterprise-level applications, and do full-featured remote computing. As such, they also now carry an increased risk for network administrators due to loss or theft (especially if the device is unprotected by a robust authentication method) and unauthorized interception of their wireless signals from which data can be siphoned off.

To cope with the inherent risks, you engage an effective security policy for dealing with these devices: Under what conditions can they be used, how many of your users need to employ them, what levels and types of access will they have, and how will they be authenticated?

Solutions are available for adding strong authentication to users seeking access via wireless LANs. Tokens, either of the hardware or software variety, are used to identify the user to an authentication server for verification of their credentials. For example, SafeNet's SafeWord can handle incoming access requests from a wireless access point and, if the user is authenticated, pass them into the network.

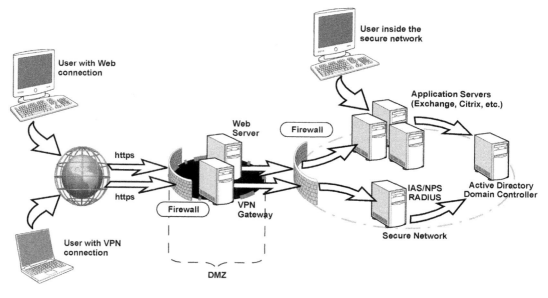

FIGURE 2.1   Network diagram.

Key among the steps you take to secure your network while allowing mobile computing is to fully educate the users of such technology. They need to understand, in no uncertain terms, the risks to your network (and ultimately to the company in general) represented by their mobile devices, and they also need to be aware that their mindfulness of both the device's physical and electronic security is an absolute necessity.

Network Security Best Practices

So, how do you either clean and tighten up your existing network, or design a new one that can stand up to the inevitable onslaught of attacks? Let's look at some basics. Consider the diagram shown in Figure 2.1.

Figure 2.1 shows what could be a typical network layout. Users outside the DMZ approach the network via a secure (HTTPS) Web or VPN connection. They are authenticated by the perimeter firewall and handed off to either a Web server or a virtual private network (VPN) gateway. If allowed to pass, they can then access resources inside the network.

If you're the administrator of an organization that has only, say, a couple dozen users with whom to contend, your task (and the illustration layout) will be relatively easy to manage. But if you have to manage several hundred (or several thousand) users, the complexity of your task increases by an order of magnitude. That makes a good security policy an absolute necessity.

9. SECURITY POLICIES

Like the tedious prep work before painting a room, organizations need a good, detailed, and well-written security policy. Not something that should be rushed through "just to get it done," your security policy should be well thought out; in other words, the "devil is in the details." Your security policy is designed to get everyone involved with your network "thinking along the same lines."

The policy is almost always a work in progress. It must evolve with technology, especially those technologies aimed at surreptitiously getting into your system. The threats will continue to evolve, as will the systems designed to hold them at bay.

A good security policy isn't always a single document; rather, it is a conglomeration of policies that address specific areas, such as computer and network use, forms of authentication, email policies, remote/mobile technology use, and Web surfing policies. It should be written in such a way that, while comprehensive, it can be easily understood by those it affects. Along those lines, your policy doesn't have to be overly complex. If you hand new employees something that resembles *War and Peace* in size and tell them they're responsible for knowing its content, you can expect to have continued problems maintaining good network security awareness. Keep it simple.

First, you need to draft some policies that define your network and its basic architecture. A good place to start is by asking the following questions:

- What kinds of resources need to be protected (user financial or medical data, credit-card information, etc.)?
- How many users will be accessing the network on the inside (employees, contractors, etc.)?
- Will there need to be access only at certain times or on a 24/7 basis (and across multiple time zones and/or internationally)?
- What kind of budget do I have?
- Will remote users be accessing the network, and if so, how many?
- Will there be remote sites in geographically distant locations (requiring a failsafe mechanism, such as replication, to keep data synched across the network)?

Next, you should spell out responsibilities for security requirements, communicate your expectations to your users (one of the weakest links in any security policy), and lay out the role(s) for your network administrator. It should list policies for activities such as Web surfing, downloading, local and remote access, and types of authentication. You should address issues such as adding users, assigning privileges, dealing with lost tokens or compromised passwords, and under what circumstances you will remove users from the access database.

You should establish a security team (sometimes referred to as a "tiger team") whose responsibility it will be to create security policies that are practical, workable, and sustainable. They should come up with the best plan for implementing these policies in a way that addresses both network resource protection and user friendliness. They should develop plans for responding to threats as well as schedules for updating equipment and software. And there should be a very clear policy for handling changes to overall network security—the types of connections through your firewall that will and will not be allowed. This is especially important because you don't want an unauthorized user gaining access, reaching into your network, and simply taking files or data.

10. RISK ANALYSIS

You should have some kind of risk analysis done to determine, as near as possible, the risks you face with the kind of operations you conduct (e-commerce, classified/proprietary information handling, partner access, or the like). Depending on the determined risk, you might need to rethink your original network design. Although a simple extranet/intranet setup with mid-level firewall protection might be okay for a small business that doesn't have much to steal, that obviously won't work for a company that deals with user financial data or proprietary/classified information. In that case, what might be needed is a tiered system in which you have a "corporate side" (on which things such as email, intranet access, and regular Internet access are handled) and a separate, secure network not connected to the Internet or corporate side. These networks can only be accessed by a user on a physical machine, and data can only be moved to them by "sneaker-net" physical media (scanned for viruses before opening). These networks can be used for data systems such as test or lab machines (on which, for example, new software builds are done and must be more tightly controlled, to prevent inadvertent corruption of the corporate side), or networks on which the storage or processing of proprietary, business-critical, or classified information are handled. In Department of Defense parlance, these are sometimes referred to as *red nets* or *black nets*.

Vulnerability Testing

Your security policy should include regular vulnerability testing. Some very good vulnerability testing tools, such as WebInspect, Acunetix, GFI LANguard, Nessus, HFNetChk, and Tripwire, allow you to conduct your own security testing. Furthermore, there are third-party companies with the most advanced suite of testing tools available that can be contracted to scan your network for open and/or accessible ports, weaknesses in firewalls, and Web site vulnerability.

Audits

You should also factor in regular, detailed audits of all activities, with emphasis on those that seem to be near or outside established norms. For example, audits that reveal high rates of data exchanges after normal business hours, when that kind of traffic would not normally be expected, is something that should be investigated. Perhaps, after checking, you'll find that it's nothing more than an employee downloading music or video files. But the point is that your audit system saw the increase in traffic and determined it to be a simple Internet use policy violation rather than someone siphoning off more critical data.

There should be clearly established rules for dealing with security, use, and/or policy violations as well as attempted or actual intrusions. Trying to figure out what to do after the intrusion is too late. And if an intrusion does occur, there should be a clear-cut system for determining the extent of damage; isolation of the exploited application, port, or machine; and a rapid response to closing the hole against further incursions.

Recovery

Your plan should also address the issue of recovery after an attack has occurred. You need to address issues such as how the network will be reconfigured to close off the exploited opening. This might take some time, since the entry point might not be immediately discernible. There has to be an estimate of damage—what was taken or compromised, was malicious code implanted somewhere, and, if so, how to most efficiently extract it and clean the affected system. In the case of a virus in a company's email system, the ability to send and receive email could be halted for days while infected systems are rebuilt. And there will have to be discussions about how to reconstruct the network if the attack decimated files and systems.

This will most likely involve more than simply reinstalling machines from archived backups. Because the compromise will most likely affect normal business operations, the need to expedite the recovery will hamper efforts to fully analyze just what happened.

This is the main reason for preemptively writing a disaster recovery plan and making sure that all departments are represented in its drafting. However, like the network security policy itself, the disaster recovery plan will also be a work in progress that should be reviewed regularly to ensure that it meets the current needs. Things such as new threat notifications, software patches and updates, vulnerability assessments, new application rollouts, and employee turnover all have to be addressed.

11. TOOLS OF YOUR TRADE

Although the tools available to people seeking unauthorized entry into your domain are impressive, you also have a wide variety of tools to help keep them out. Before implementing a network security strategy, however, you must be acutely aware of the specific needs of those who will be using your resources.

Simple antispyware and antispam tools aren't enough. In today's rapidly changing software environment, strong security requires penetration shielding, threat signature recognition, autonomous reaction to identified threats, and the ability to upgrade your tools as the need arises.

The following section describes some of the more common tools you should consider adding to your arsenal.

Intrusion Detection Systems (IDSs)

As discussed earlier in the chapter, it's no longer good enough to have solid defenses. You also need to know when you've been penetrated—and the sooner, the better.

Statistics paint a dismal picture. According to Verizon's threat report, less than 5 percent of cybersecurity breaches are detected within hours of the assault, and 80 percent weren't found for weeks, or months.[9] Bret Hartman, RSA's chief technology officer said, in a recent interview, that there's a new "shift in the level of paranoia to assume that you're always in a state of partial compromise."

A good IDS detects unauthorized intrusions using one of three types of models: anomaly-based, signature-based, and hybrid detection.

- Anomaly-based systems learn what's "normal" for a given network environment, so that they can quickly detect the "abnormal."
- Signature-based systems look for slight variations, or signatures, of suspicious network activity;
- Hybrid detection systems are currently in development which compensate for weaknesses of both anomaly and signature-based systems by combining the best of both.

Firewalls

Your first line of defense should be a good firewall, or better yet, a system that effectively incorporates several security features in one. Secure Firewall (formerly Sidewinder) from Secure Computing is one of the strongest and most secure firewall products available, and as of this writing it has never been successfully hacked. It is trusted and used by government and defense agencies. Secure Firewall combines the five most necessary security systems—firewall, antivirus/spyware/spam, VPN, application filtering, and intrusion prevention/detection systems—into a single appliance.

Intrusion Prevention Systems

A good *intrusion prevention system* (IPS) is a vast improvement over a basic firewall in that it can, among other things, be configured with policies that allow it to make autonomous decisions as to how to deal with application-level threats as well as simple IP address or port-level attacks.

IPS products respond directly to incoming threats in a variety of ways, from automatically dropping (extracting) suspicious packets (while still allowing legitimate ones to pass) to, in some cases, placing an intruder into a "quarantine" file. IPS, like an application layer firewall, can be considered another form of access control in that it can make pass/fail decisions on application content.

For an IPS to be effective, it must also be very good at discriminating between a real threat signature and one that looks like but isn't one (false positive). Once a signature interpreted to be an intrusion is detected, the system must quickly notify the administrator so that the appropriate evasive action can be taken. The following are types of IPS.

9. CNNMoney Tech, February 28, 2012.

- *Network-based.* Network-based IPSs create a series of choke points in the enterprise that detect suspected intrusion attempt activity. Placed inline at their needed locations, they invisibly monitor network traffic for known attack signatures that they then block.
- *Host-based.* These systems don't reside on the network per se but rather on servers and individual machines. They quietly monitor activities and requests from applications, weeding out actions deemed prohibited in nature. These systems are often very good at identifying post-decryption entry attempts.
- *Content-based.* These IPSs scan network packets, looking for signatures of content that is unknown or unrecognized or that has been explicitly labeled threatening in nature.
- *Rate-based.* These IPSs look for activity that falls outside the range of normal levels, such as activity that seems to be related to password cracking and brute-force penetration attempts, for example.

When searching for a good IPS, look for one that provides, at minimum:

- Robust protection for your applications, host systems, and individual network elements against exploitation of vulnerability-based threats as "single-bullet attacks," Trojan horses, worms, botnets, and surreptitious creation of "back doors" in your network.
- Protection against threats that exploit vulnerabilities in specific applications such as Web services, mail, DNS, SQL, and any Voice over IP (VoIP) services.
- Detection and elimination of spyware, phishing, and anonymizers (tools that hide a source computer's identifying information so that Internet activity can be undertaken surreptitiously).
- Protection against brute-force and DoS attacks, application scanning, and flooding.
- A regular method of updating threat lists and signatures.

Application Firewalls

Application firewalls (AFs) are sometimes confused with IPSs in that they can perform IPS-like functions. But an AF is specifically designed to limit or deny an application's level of access to a system's OS—in other words, closing any openings into a computer's OS to deny the execution of harmful code within an OS's structure. AFs work by looking at applications themselves, monitoring the kind of data flow from an application for suspicious or administrator-blocked content from specific Web sites, application-specific viruses, and any attempt to exploit an identified weakness in an application's architecture. Though AF systems can conduct intrusion prevention duties, they typically employ proxies to handle firewall access control and focus on traditional firewall-type functions. Application firewalls can detect the signatures of recognized threats and block them before they can infect the network.

Windows' version of an application firewall, called Data Execution Prevention (DEP), prevents the execution of any code that uses system services in such a way that could be deemed harmful to data or virtual memory (VM). It does this by considering RAM data as nonexecutable—in essence, refusing to run new code coming from the data-only area of RAM, since any harmful or malicious code seeking to damage existing data would have to run from this area.

The Macintosh Operating System (MacOS) also includes a built-in application firewall as a standard feature. The user can configure it to employ two-layer protection in which installing network-aware applications will result in an OS-generated warning that prompts for user authorization of network access. If authorized, MacOS will digitally sign the application in such a way that subsequent application activity will not prompt for further authorization. Updates invalidate the original certificate, and the user will have to revalidate before the application can run again.

The Linux OS has, for example, an application firewall called AppArmor that allows the administrator to create and link to every application a security policy that restricts its access capabilities.

Access Control Systems

Access control systems (ACSs) rely on administrator-defined rules that allow or restrict user access to protected network resources. These access rules can, for example, require strong user authentication such as tokens or biometric devices to prove the identity of users requesting access. They can also restrict access to various network services based on time of day or group need.

Some ACS products allow for the creation of an *access control list* (ACL), which is a set of rules that define security policy. These ACLs contain one or more *access control entries* (ACEs), which are the actual rule definitions themselves. These rules can restrict access by specific user, time of day, IP address, function (department, management level, etc.), or specific system from which a logon or access attempt is being made.

A good example of an ACS is SafeWord by Aladdin Knowledge Systems. SafeWord is considered a two-factor authentication system in that it uses what the user knows (such as a personal identification number, or PIN) and what the user has (such as a one-time passcode, or OTP, token) to strongly authenticate users requesting network access. SafeWord allows administrators to design customized access rules and restrictions to network resources, applications, and information.

In this scheme, the tokens are a key component. The token's internal cryptographic key algorithm is made "known" to an authentication server when the token's file is imported into a central database.

When the token is assigned to a user, its serial number is linked to that user in the user's record. On making an access request, the authentication server prompts the user to enter a username and the OTP generated by the token. If a PIN was also assigned to that user, she must either prepend or append that PIN to the token-generated passcode. As long as the authentication server receives what it expects, the user is granted whatever access privileges she was assigned.

Unified Threat Management

The latest trend to emerge in the network intrusion prevention arena is referred to as *unified threat management*, or UTM. UTM systems are multilayered and incorporate several security technologies into a single platform, often in the form of a plug-in appliance. UTM products can provide such diverse capabilities as antivirus, VPN, firewall services, and antispam as well as intrusion prevention.

The biggest advantages of a UTM system are its ease of operation and configuration and the fact that its security features can be quickly updated to meet rapidly evolving threats.

Sidewinder by Secure Computing is a UTM system that was designed to be flexible, easily and quickly adaptable, and easy to manage. It incorporates firewall, VPN, trusted source, IPS, antispam and antivirus, URL filtering, SSL decryption, and auditing/reporting.

Other UTM systems include Symantec's Enterprise Firewall and Gateway Security Enterprise Firewall Appliance, Fortinet, LokTek's AIRlok Firewall Appliance, and SonicWall's NSA 240 UTM Appliance, to name a few.

12. CONTROLLING USER ACCESS

Traditionally users—also known as employees—have been the weakest link in a company's defensive armor. Though necessary to the organization, they can be a nightmare waiting to happen to your network. How do you let them work within the network while controlling their access to resources? You have to make sure your system of user authentication knows who your users are.

Authentication, Authorization, and Accounting

Authentication is simply proving that a user's identity claim is valid and authentic. Authentication requires some form of "proof of identity." In network technologies, physical proof (such as a driver's license or other photo ID) cannot be employed, so you have to get something else from a user. That typically means having the user respond to a challenge to provide genuine credentials at the time he or she requests access.

For our purposes, credentials can be something the user knows, something the user has, or something they are. Once they provide authentication, there also has to be authorization, or permission to enter. Finally, you want to have some record of users' entry into your network—username, time of entry, and resources. That is the accounting side of the process.

What the User Knows

Users know a great many details about their own lives—birthdays, anniversaries, first cars, their spouse's name—and many will try to use these nuggets of information as a simple form of authentication. What they don't realize is just how insecure those pieces of information are.

In network technologies, these pieces of information are often used as fixed passwords and PINs because they're easy to remember. Unless some strict guidelines are established on what form a password or PIN can take (for example, a minimum number of characters or a mixture of letters and numbers), a password will offer little to no real security.

Unfortunately, to hold down costs, some organizations allow users to set their own passwords and PINs as credentials, then rely on a simple challenge-response mechanism in which these weak credentials are provided to gain access. Adding to the loss of security is the fact that not only are the fixed passwords far too easy to guess, but because the user already has too much to remember, she writes them down somewhere near the computer she uses (often in some "cryptic" scheme to make it more difficult to guess). To increase the effectiveness of any security system, that system needs to require a much stronger form of authentication.

What the User Has

The most secure means of identifying users is by a combination of (1) a hardware device in their possession that is "known" to an authentication server in your network, coupled with (2) what they know. A whole host of devices available today—tokens, smart cards, biometric devices—are designed to more positively identify a user. Since a good token is the most secure of these options, let us focus on them here.

Tokens

A *token* is a device that employs an encrypted key for which the encryption algorithm—the method of generating an encrypted password—is known to a network's authentication server. There are both software and hardware tokens. The software tokens can be installed on a user's desktop system, in the cellular phone, or on the smart phone. The hardware tokens come in a variety of form factors, some with a single button that both turns the token on and displays its internally generated passcode; others have a more elaborate numerical keypad for PIN input. If lost or stolen, tokens can easily be removed from the system, quickly rendering them completely ineffective. And the passcodes they generate are of the "one-time-passcode," or OTP, variety, meaning that a generated passcode expires once it's been used and cannot be used again for a subsequent logon attempt.

Tokens are either programmed onsite with token programming software or offsite at the time they are ordered from their vendor. During programming, functions such as a token's cryptographic key, password length, whether a PIN is required, and whether it generates passwords based on internal clock timing or user PIN input are written into the token's memory. When programming is complete, a file containing this information and the token's serial number are imported into the authentication server so that the token's characteristics are known.

A token is assigned to a user by linking its serial number to the user's record, stored in the system database. When a user logs onto the network and needs access to, say, her email, she is presented with some challenge that she must answer using her assigned token.

Tokens operate in one of three ways: time synchronous, event synchronous, or challenge-response (also known as asynchronous).

Time Synchronous

In time synchronous operations, the token's internal clock is synched with the network's clock. Each time the token's button is pressed, it generates a passcode in hash form, based on its internal timekeeping. As long as the token's clock is synched with the network clock, the passcodes are accepted. In some cases (for example, when the token hasn't been used for some time or its battery dies), the token gets out of synch with the system and needs to be resynched before it can be used again.

Event Synchronous

In event synchronous operations, the server maintains an ordered passcode sequence and determines which passcode is valid based on the current location in that sequence.

Challenge-Response

In challenge-response, a challenge, prompting for username, is issued to the user by the authentication server at the time of access request. Once the user's name is entered, the authentication server checks to see what form of authentication is assigned to that user and issues a challenge back to the user. The user inputs the challenge into the token, then enters the token's generated response to the challenge. As long as the authentication server receives what it expected, authentication is successful and access is granted.

The User is Authenticated, but is She/He Authorized?

Authorization is independent of authentication. A user can be permitted entry into the network but not be authorized to access a resource. You don't want an employee having access to HR information or a corporate partner getting access to confidential or proprietary information.

Authorization requires a set of rules that dictate the resources to which a user will have access. These permissions are established in your security policy.

Accounting

Say that our user has been granted access to the requested resource. But you want (or in some cases are required to have) the ability to call up and view activity logs to see who got into what resource. This information is mandated for organizations that deal with user financial or medical information or DoD classified information or that go through annual inspections to maintain certification for international operations.

Accounting refers to the recording, logging, and archiving of all server activity, especially activity related to access attempts and whether they were successful. This information should be written into audit logs that are stored and available any time you want or need to view them. The audit logs should contain, at minimum, the following information:

- The user's identity
- The date and time of the request
- Whether the request passed authentication and was granted

Any network security system you put into place should store, or archive, these logs for a specified period of time and allow you to determine for how long these archives will be maintained before they start to age out of the system.

Keeping Current

One of the best ways to stay ahead is to not fall behind in the first place. New systems with increasing sophistication are being developed all the time. They can incorporate a more intelligent and autonomous process in the way the system handles a detected threat, a faster and more easily accomplished method for updating threat files, and configuration flexibility that allows for very precise customization of access rules, authentication requirements, user role assignment, and how tightly it can protect specific applications.

Register for newsletters, attend seminars and network security shows, read white papers, and, if needed, contract the services of network security specialists. The point is, you shouldn't go cheap on network security. The price you pay to keep ahead will be far less than the price you pay to recover from a security breach or attack.

Finally, let's briefly look at how host-based IPS agents offer various intrusion prevention capabilities. The following describes common intrusion prevention capabilities.

13. INTRUSION PREVENTION CAPABILITIES

As previously mentioned, host-based IPS agents offer various intrusion prevention capabilities. Because the capabilities vary based on the detection techniques used by each product, the following activities (see checklist: An Agenda for Action for Intrusion Prevention Activities") describe the capabilities by detection technique.

AN AGENDA FOR ACTION FOR INTRUSION PREVENTION ACTIVITIES

From the organizational perspective, preventing intrusions includes the following key activities (check all tasks completed):

_____1. **Code Analysis:** The code analysis techniques can prevent code from being executed, including malware and unauthorized applications.

_____2. **Network Traffic Analysis:** This can stop incoming network traffic from being processed by the host and outgoing network traffic from exiting it.

_____3. **Network Traffic Filtering:** Working as a host-based firewall, this can stop unauthorized access and acceptable use policy violations (use of inappropriate external services).

_____4. **Filesystem Monitoring:** This can prevent files from being accessed, modified, replaced, or deleted, which could stop malware installation, including Trojan horses and rootkits, as well as

---

other attacks involving inappropriate file access.

_____5. **Removable Media Restriction:** Some products can enforce restrictions on the use of removable media, both Universal Serial Bus (USB-based (flash drive)) and traditional (CD). This can prevent malware or other unwanted files from being transferred to a host and can also stop sensitive files from being copied from the host to removable media.

_____6. **Audiovisual Device Monitoring:** A few host-based IPS products can detect when a host's audiovisual devices, such as microphones, cameras, or IP-based phones, are activated or used. This could indicate that the host has been compromised by an attacker.

_____7. **Host Hardening:** Some host-based intrusion detection and prevention systems (IDPSs) can automatically harden hosts on an ongoing basis. For example, if an application is reconfigured, causing a particular security function to be disabled, the IDPS could detect this and enable the security function.

_____8. **Process Status Monitoring:** Some products monitor the status of processes or services running on a host, and if they detect that one has stopped, they restart it automatically. Some products can also monitor the status of security programs such as antivirus software.

_____9. **Network Traffic Sanitization:** Some agents, particularly those deployed on appliances, can sanitize the network traffic that they monitor. For example, an appliance-based agent could act as a proxy and rebuild each request and response that is directed through it. This can be effective at neutralizing certain unusual activity, particularly in packet headers and application protocol headers.

14. SUMMARY

This chapter has made it very apparent that preventing network intrusions is no easy task. Like cops on the street—usually outnumbered and underequipped compared to the bad guys—you face enemies with determination, skill, training, and a frightening array of increasingly sophisticated tools for hacking their way through your best defenses. And no matter how good your defenses are today, it's only a matter of time before a tool is developed that can penetrate them. If you know that ahead of time, you'll be much more inclined to keep a watchful eye for what "they" have and what you can use to defeat them.

Your best weapon is a logical, thoughtful, and nimble approach to network security. You have to be nimble—to evolve and grow with changes in technology, never being content to keep things as they are because "Hey, they're working just fine." Well, today's "just fine" will be tomorrow's "What the hell happened?"

Stay informed. There is no shortage of information available to you in the form of white papers, seminars, contract security specialists, and online resources, all dealing with various aspects of network security.

Invest in a good intrusion detection system. You want to know, as soon as possible, that a breach has occurred, what was stolen, and, if possible, where it went.

Have a good, solid, comprehensive, yet easy-to-understand network security policy in place. The very process of developing one will get all involved parties thinking about how to best secure your network while addressing user needs. When it comes to your users, you simply can't overeducate them where network security awareness is concerned. The more they know, the better equipped they'll be to act as allies against, rather than accomplices of, the hordes of crackers looking to steal, damage, hobble, or completely cripple your network.

Do your research and invest in good, multipurpose network security systems. Select systems that are easy to install and implement, are adaptable and quickly configurable, can be customized to suit your needs of today as well as tomorrow, and are supported by companies that keep pace with current trends in cracker technology.

Finally, let's move on to the real interactive part of this chapter: review questions/exercises, hands-on projects, case projects and optional team case project. The answers and/or solutions by chapter can be found in the Online Instructor's Solutions Manual.

CHAPTER REVIEW QUESTIONS/EXERCISES

True/False

1. True or False? A network intrusion is an authorized penetration of your enterprise's network, or an individual machine address in your assigned domain.
2. True or False? In some cases, a network intrusion could be done from the inside by a disgruntled employee looking to hurt the organization or steal company secrets for profit.
3. True or False? Most security software products available today have two basic methods of spotting malicious software.
4. True or False? Crackers are going to first look for known strengths in the operating system (OS) or any applications you are using.
5. True or False? Finding a device, using it in a place (or manner) in which prying eyes can see passwords or data, awareness of hacking tools specifically designed to sniff wireless signals for data, and logging on to unsecured networks, are all potential problem areas with which users need to be familiar.

Multiple Choice

1. Which devices can locate wireless signals within a certain range, where they can siphon off the data being transmitted over the signals?
   A. Wireless sniffers.
   B. Packet sniffers.

C. Port scanners.

D. Port knocking.

E. Keystroke loggers.

2. You can expect to have continued problems maintaining good network security awareness. Keep it simple. You need to draft some policies that define your network and its basic architecture. A good place to start is by asking the following questions, except which one?

A. What kinds of resources need to be protected (user financial or medical data, credit-card information, etc.)?

B. How many users will be accessing the network on the inside (employees, contractors, etc.)?

C. Will there need to be access only at certain times or on a 24/7 basis (and across multiple time zones and/or internationally)?

D. What kind of budget do I have?

E. Will internal users be accessing the network, and if so, how many?

3. A good IDS detects unauthorized intrusions using three types of models:

A. Anomaly-based.

B. Signature-based.

C. Network-based.

D. Hybrid detection.

E. Host-based.

4. For an IPS to be effective, it must also be very good at discriminating between a real threat signature and one that looks like but isn't one (false positive). Once a signature interpreted to be an intrusion is detected, the system must quickly notify the administrator so that the appropriate evasive action can be taken. The following are types of IPS, except one:

A. Network-based.

B. Rate-based.

C. Host-based.

D. Backdoor-based.

E. Content-based.

5. The latest trend to emerge in the network intrusion prevention arena is referred to as:

A. antivirus.

B. unified threat management.

C. VPN.

D. firewall services.

E. antispam.

EXERCISE

Problem

Determine how an information system could prevent nonprivileged users from circumventing intrusion prevention capabilities.

Hands-On Projects

Project

To safeguard its intellectual property and business, a pharmaceutical company had to keep pace with an increasingly sophisticated threat landscape of malware and viruses, as well as complex security legislation across its multiple sites. Please describe what type of intrusion prevention capabilities/services the company implemented.

Case Projects

Problem

A large medical center sought a powerful security solution that could continuously protect its high-throughput network without compromising network performance. It also required a healthy network: one that is safe from hackers, worms, viruses, and spyware, that can compromise the performance of the medical's life-critical applications or the federally mandated confidentiality of its medical records. In addition, the security system needed to be cost-effective and interoperate transparently with the medical center's multivendor infrastructure. In this case project, how would an intrusion prevention system (IPS) provide the pervasive and proactive protection that the medical center required?

Optional Team Case Project

Problem

With so much at stake, companies of all sizes are taking a closer look at intrusion prevention systems (IPSs) security solutions. In order to sift through the claims and separate the intrusion prevention contenders from the pretenders, the companies need to ask potential vendors a number of obvious basic questions first. Please list the basic IPS questions that a company might ask their vendors?

Guarding Against Network Intrusions

Thomas M. Chen* and Patrick J. Walsh†

*Swansea University, †eSoft Inc.

Virtually all computers today are connected to the Internet through dialup, broadband, Ethernet, or wireless technologies. The reason for ubiquitous Internet connectivity is simple: Applications depending on the network, such as email, Web, remote login, instant messaging, social networking, and VoIP, have become essential to everyday computing. Unfortunately, the Internet exposes computer users to risks from a wide variety of possible threats. Users have much to lose—their privacy, valuable data, control of their computers, and possibly theft of their identities. The network enables attacks to be carried out remotely from anywhere in the world, with relative anonymity and low risk of traceability.

The nature of network intrusions has evolved over the years. A few years ago, a major concern was fast worms such as Code Red, Nimda, Slammer, and Sobig. More recently, concerns have shifted to spyware, Trojan horses, and botnets. Although these other threats = continue to be major problems, the Web has become the primary vector for stealthy attacks today.[1]

1. TRADITIONAL RECONNAISSANCE AND ATTACKS

Traditionally, attack methods follow sequential steps analogous to physical attacks, as shown in Figure 3.1: reconnaissance; compromise; and cover-up.[2] Here we are only addressing attacks directed at a specific target host. Some other types of attacks, such as worms or malicious Web sites, are not directed at specific targets. Instead, they attempt

1. Marc Fossi et al., *Symantec Global Internet Security Threat Report*, Volume 16, 2010, available at www.symantec.com (date of access: March 1, 2012).

2. Ed Skoudis, *Counter Hack Reloaded: A Step-by-Step Guide to Computer Attacks and Effective Defenses*, 2nd ed., Prentice Hall, 2006.

Network and System Security
DOI: http://dx.doi.org/10.1016/B978-0-12-416689-9.00003-4

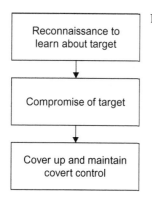

FIGURE 3.1   Steps in directed attacks.

to hit as many targets as quickly as possible without caring about who or what the targets are.

In the first step of a directed attack, the attacker performs reconnaissance to learn as much as possible about the chosen target before carrying out an actual attack. A thorough reconnaissance can lead to a more effective attack because the target's weaknesses can be discovered. One might expect the reconnaissance phase to possibly tip off the target about an impending attack, but scans and probes are going on constantly in the "background noise" of Internet traffic, so systems administrators might ignore attack probes as too troublesome to investigate.

Through pings and traceroutes, an attacker can discover IP addresses and map the network around the target. Pings are ICMP echo request and echo reply messages that verify a host's IP address and availability. Traceroute is a network mapping utility that takes advantage of the time-to-live (TTL) field in IP packets. It sends out packets with TTL = 1, then TTL = 2, and so on. When the packets expire, the routers along the packets' path report that the packets have been discarded, returning ICMP "time exceeded" messages and thereby allowing the traceroute utility to learn the IP addresses of routers at a distance of one hop, two hops, and so on.

Port scans can reveal open ports. Normally, a host might be expected to have certain well-known ports open, such as TCP port 80 (HTTP), TCP port 21 (FTP), TCP port 23 (Telnet), or TCP port 25 (SMTP). A host might also happen to have open ports in the higher range. For example, port 12345 is the default port used by the Netbus remote access Trojan horse, or port 31337 is the default port used by the Back Orifice remote access Trojan horse. Discovery of ports indicating previous malware infections could obviously help an attacker considerably.

In addition to discovering open ports, the popular NMAP scanner (www.insecure.org/nmap) can discover the operating system running on a target. NMAP uses a large set of heuristic rules to identify an operating system based on a target's responses to carefully crafted TCP/IP probes. The basic idea is that different operating systems will make different responses to probes to open TCP/UDP ports and malformed TCP/IP packets. Knowledge of a target's operating system can help an attacker identify vulnerabilities and find effective exploits.

Vulnerability scanning tests a target for the presence of vulnerabilities. Vulnerability scanners such as SATAN, SARA, SAINT, and Nessus typically contain a database of known vulnerabilities that is used to craft probes to a chosen target. The popular Nessus tool (www.nessus.org) has an extensible plug-in architecture to add checks for backdoors, misconfiguration errors, default accounts and passwords, and other types of vulnerabilities.

In the second step of a directed attack, the attacker attempts to compromise the target through one or more methods. Password attacks are common because passwords might be based on common words or names and are guessable by a dictionary attack, although computer systems today have better password policies that forbid easily guessable passwords. If an attacker can obtain the password file from the target, numerous password-cracking tools are available to carry out a brute-force password attack. In addition, computers and networking equipment often ship with default accounts and passwords intended to help systems administrators set up the equipment. These default accounts and passwords are easy to find on the Web (for example, www.phenoelit-us. org/dpl/dpl.html). Occasionally, users might neglect to change or delete the default accounts, offering intruders an easy way to access the target.

Another common attack method is an exploit attack code written to take advantage of a specific vulnerability.[3] Many types of software, including operating systems and applications, have vulnerabilities. Symantec discovered 6253 vulnerabilities in 2010, or 17 vulnerabilities per day on average.[4] Vulnerabilities are published by several organizations such as CERT and MITRE, as well as vendors such as Microsoft, through security bulletins. MITRE maintains a database of publicly known vulnerabilities identified by common vulnerabilities and exposures (CVE) numbers. The severity of vulnerabilities is reflected in the industry-standard common vulnerability scoring system (CVSS). In the first half of 2011, Microsoft observed that 44 percent of vulnerabilities were highly severe, 49 percent were medium-severe, and 7 percent were low-severe.[5] Furthermore, about 45 percent of vulnerabilities were easily exploitable.

Historically, buffer overflows have been the most common type of vulnerability.[6] They have been popular because buffer overflow exploits can often be carried out remotely and lead to complete compromise of a target. The problem arises when a program has allocated a fixed amount of memory space (such as in the stack) for storing data but receives more data than expected. If the vulnerability exists, the extra data will overwrite adjacent parts of memory, which could mess up other variables or pointers. If the extra data is random, the computer might crash or act unpredictably. However, if an attacker crafts the

3. S. McClure, J. Scambray, and G. Kutz, *Hacking Exposed*, 3rd ed., McGraw-Hill, 2001.

4. Marc Fossi et al., *Symantec Global Internet Security Threat Report*, Volume 16, 2010, available at www.symantec.com (date of access: March 1, 2012).

5. Joe Faulhaber et al., *Microsoft Security Intelligence Report*, Volume 11, available at www.microsoft.com (date of access: March 1, 2012).

6. J. Foster, V. Osipov, and N. Bhalla, *Buffer Overflow Attacks: Detect, Exploit, Prevent*, Syngress Publishing, 2005.

extra data carefully, the buffer overflow could overwrite adjacent memory in a way that benefits the attacker. For instance, an attacker might overwrite the return pointer in a stack, causing the program control to jump to malicious code inserted by the attacker.

An effective buffer overflow exploit requires technical knowledge of the computer architecture and operating system, but once the exploit code is written, it can be reused. Buffer overflows can be prevented by the programmer or compiler performing bounds checking or during runtime. Although C/C++ has received a good deal of blame as a programming language for not having built-in checking that data written to arrays stays within bounds, buffer overflow vulnerabilities appear in a wide variety of other programs, too.

Structured Query Language (SQL) injection is a type of vulnerability relevant to Web servers with a database backend.[7] SQL is an internationally standardized interactive and programming language for querying data and managing databases. Many commercial database products support SQL, sometimes with proprietary extensions. Web applications often take user input (usually from a Web form) and pass the input into an SQL statement. An SQL injection vulnerability can arise if user input is not properly filtered for string literal escape characters, which can allow an attacker to craft input that is interpreted as embedded SQL statements and thereby manipulate the application running on the database.

Servers have been attacked and compromised by toolkits designed to automate customized attacks. For example, the MPack toolkit emerged in early 2007 and is sold commercially in Russia, along with technical support and regular software updates. It is loaded into a malicious or compromised Web site. When a visitor goes to the site, a malicious code is launched through an iframe (inline frame) within the HTML code. It can launch various exploits, expandable through modules, for vulnerabilities in Web browsers and client software.

Metasploit (www.metasploit.com) is a popular Perl-based tool for developing and using exploits with an easy-to-use Web or command-line interface. Different exploits can be written and loaded into Metasploit and then directed at a chosen target. Exploits can be bundled with a payload (the code to run on a compromised target) selected from a collection of payloads. The tool also contains utilities to experiment with new vulnerabilities and help automate the development of new exploits.

Although exploits are commonplace, not all attacks require an exploit. *Social engineering* refers to types of attacks that take advantage of human nature to compromise a target, typically through deceit. A common social engineering attack is *phishing*, used in identity theft.[8] Phishing starts with a lure, usually a spam message that appears to be from a legitimate bank or e-commerce business. The message attempts to provoke the reader into visiting a fraudulent Web site pretending to be a legitimate business. These fraudulent sites are often set up by automated phishing toolkits that spoof legitimate sites of various brands, including

7 D. Litchfield, *SQL Server Security*, McGraw-Hill Osborne, 2003.

8. Markus Jakobsson and Steven Meyers, eds., *Phishing and Countermeasures: Understanding the Increasing Problem of Electronic Identity Theft*, Wiley-Interscience, 2006.

the graphics of those brands. The fraudulent site might even have links to the legitimate Web site, to appear more valid. Victims are thus tricked into submitting valuable personal information such as account numbers, passwords, and Social Security numbers.

Other common examples of social engineering are spam messages that entice the reader into opening an email attachment. Most people know by now that attachments could be dangerous, perhaps containing a virus or spyware, even if they appear to be innocent at first glance. But if the message is sufficiently convincing, such as appearing to originate from an acquaintance, even wary users might be tricked into opening an attachment. Social engineering attacks can be simple but effective because they target people and bypass technological defenses.

The third step of traditional directed attacks involves cover-up of evidence of the compromise and establishment of covert control. After a successful attack, intruders want to maintain remote control and evade detection. Remote control can be maintained if the attacker has managed to install any of a number of types of malicious software: a backdoor such as Netcat; a remote access Trojan such as BO2K or SubSeven; or a bot, usually listening for remote instructions on an Internet relay chat (IRC) channel, such as phatbot.

Intruders obviously prefer to evade detection after a successful compromise, because detection will lead the victim to take remedial actions to harden or disinfect the target. Intruders might change the system logs on the target, which will likely contain evidence of their attack. In Windows, the main event logs are secevent.evt, sysevent. evt, and appevent.evt. A systems administrator looking for evidence of intrusions would look in these files with the built-in Windows Event Viewer or a third-party log viewer. An intelligent intruder would not delete the logs but would selectively delete information in the logs to hide signs of malicious actions.

A *rootkit* is a stealthy type of malicious software (*malware*) designed to hide the existence of certain processes or programs from normal methods of detection.[9] Rootkits essentially alter the target's operating system, perhaps by changing drivers or dynamic link libraries (DLLs) and possibly at the kernel level. An example is the kernel-mode FU rootkit that manipulates kernel memory in Windows 2000, XP, and 2003. It consists of a device driver, msdirectx.sys, that might be mistaken for Microsoft's DirectX tool. The rootkit can hide certain events and processes and change the privileges of running processes.

If an intruder has installed malware for covert control, he will want to conceal the communications between himself and the compromised target from discovery by network-based *intrusion detection systems* (IDSs). Intrusion detection systems are designed to listen to network traffic and look for signs of suspicious activities. Several concealment methods are used in practice. *Tunneling* is a commonly used method to place packets of one protocol into the payload of another packet. The "exterior" packet serves a vehicle to carry and deliver the "interior" packet intact. Though the protocol of the exterior packet is easily understood by an IDS, the interior protocol can be any number of possibilities and hence difficult to interpret.

9. Greg Hoglund and Jamie Butler, *Rootkits: Subverting the Windows Kernel*, Addison-Wesley Professional, 2005.

Encryption is another obvious concealment method. Encryption relies on the secrecy of an encryption key shared between the intruder and the compromised target. The encryption key is used to mathematically scramble the communications into a form that is unreadable without the key to decrypt it. Encryption ensures secrecy in practical terms but does not guarantee perfect security. Encryption keys can be guessed, but the time to guess the correct key increases exponentially with the key length. Long keys combined with an algorithm for periodically changing keys can ensure that encrypted communications will be difficult to break within a reasonable time.

Fragmentation of IP packets is another means to conceal the contents of messages from IDSs, which often do not bother to reassemble fragments. IP packets may normally be fragmented into smaller packets anywhere along a route and reassembled at the destination. An IDS can become confused with a flood of fragments, bogus fragments, or deliberately overlapping fragments.

2. MALICIOUS SOFTWARE

Malicious software, or malware, continues to be an enormous problem for Internet users because of its variety and prevalence and the level of danger it presents.[10,11,12] It is important to realize that malware can take many forms. A large class of malware is *infectious*, which includes viruses and worms. Viruses and worms are self-replicating, meaning that they spread from host to host by making copies of themselves. Viruses are pieces of code attached to a normal file or program. When the program is run, the virus code is executed and copies itself to (or infects) another file or program. It is often said that viruses need a human action to spread, whereas worms are standalone automated programs. Worms look for vulnerable targets across the network and transfer a copy of themselves if a target is successfully compromised.

Historically, several worms have become well known and stimulated concerns over the possibility of a fast epidemic infecting Internet-connected hosts before defenses could stop it. The 1988 Robert Morris Jr. worm infected thousands of Unix hosts, at the time a significant portion of the Arpanet (the predecessor to the Internet). The 1999 Melissa worm infected Microsoft Word documents and emailed itself to addresses found in a victim's Outlook address book. Melissa demonstrated that email could be a very effective vector for malware distribution, and many subsequent worms have continued to use email, such as the 2000 Love Letter worm. In the 2001–2004 interval, several fast worms appeared, notably Code Red, Nimda, Klez, SQL Slammer/Sapphire, Blaster, Sobig, and MyDoom.

An important feature of viruses and worms is their capability to carry a *payload*— malicious code that is executed on a compromised host. The payload can be virtually anything. For instance, SQL Slammer/Sapphire had no payload, whereas Code Red

---

10. David Harley and David Slade, *Viruses Revealed*, McGraw-Hill, 2001.

11. Ed Skoudis, *Malware: Fighting Malicious Code*, Prentice Hall PTR, 2004.

12. Peter Szor, *The Art of Computer Virus Research and Defense*, Addison-Wesley, 2005.

carried an agent to perform a denial-of-service (DoS) attack on certain fixed addresses. The Chernobyl or CIH virus had one of the most destructive payloads, attempting to over-write critical system files and the system BIOS that is needed for a computer to boot up. Worms are sometimes used to deliver other malware, such as bots, in their payload. They are popular delivery vehicles because of their ability to spread by themselves and carry anything in their payload.

Members of a second large class of malware are characterized by attempts to conceal themselves. This class includes Trojan horses and rootkits. Worms are not particularly stealthy (unless they are designed to be) because they are typically indiscriminate in their attacks. They probe potential targets in the hope of compromising many targets quickly. Indeed, fast-spreading worms are relatively easy to detect because of the network conges-tion caused by their probes.

Stealth is an important feature for malware because the critical problem for antivirus software is obviously detection of malware. Trojan horses are a type of malware that appears to perform a useful function but hides a malicious function. Thus, the presence of the Trojan horse might not be concealed, but functionality is not fully revealed. For example, a video codec could offer to play certain types of video but also covertly steal the user's data in the background. In the second half of 2007, Microsoft reported a dramatic increase of 300 percent% in the number of Trojan downloaders and droppers, small programs to facilitate downloading more malware later.[4]

Rootkits are essentially modifications to the operating system to hide the presence of files or processes from normal means of detection. Rootkits are often installed as drivers or kernel modules. A highly publicized example was the extended copy protection (XCP) software included in some Sony BMG audio CDs in 2005, to prevent music copying. The software was installed automatically on Windows PCs when a CD was played. Made by a company called First 4 Internet, XCP unfortunately contained a hidden rootkit component that patched the operating system to prevent it from displaying any processes, Registry entries, or files with names beginning with sys. Although the intention of XCP was not malicious, there was concern that the rootkit could be used by malware writers to conceal malware.

A third important class of malware is designed for remote control. This class includes remote access Trojans (RATs) and bots. Instead of *remote access Trojan*, RAT is sometimes interpreted as *remote administration tool* because it can be used for legitimate purposes by sys-tems administrators. Either way, RAT refers to a type of software usually consisting of server and client parts designed to enable covert communications with a remote controller. The cli-ent part is installed on a victim host and mainly listens for instructions from the server part, located at the controller. Notorious examples include Back Orifice, Netbus, and Sub7.

Bots are remote-control programs installed covertly on innocent hosts.[13] Bots are typi-cally programmed to listen to IRC channels for instructions from a "bot herder." All bots under control of the same bot herder form a botnet. Botnets have been known to be rented out for purposes of sending spam or launching a distributed DoS (DDoS) attack.[14] The power of a botnet is proportional to its size, but exact sizes have been difficult to discover.

13. Craig Schiller et al., *Botnets: The Killer Web App*, Syngress Publishing, 2007.

14. David Dittrich, "Distributed Denial of Service (DDoS) Attacks/Tools," available at http://staff. washington.edu/dittrich/misc/ddos/ (date of access: July 1, 2008).

One of the most publicized bots is the Storm worm, which has various aliases. Storm was launched in January 2007 as spam with a Trojan horse attachment. As a botnet, Storm has shown unusual resilience by working in a distributed peer-to-peer manner without centralized control. Each compromised host connects to a small subset of the entire botnet. Each infected host shares lists of other infected hosts, but no single host has a full list of the entire botnet. The size of the Storm botnet has been estimated at more than 1 million compromised hosts, but an exact size has been impossible to determine because of the many bot variants and active measures to avoid detection. Its creators have been persistent in continually updating its lures with current events and evolving tactics to spread and avoid detection.

Another major class of malware is designed for data theft. This class includes keyloggers and spyware. A keylogger can be a Trojan horse or other form of malware. It is designed to record a user's keystrokes and perhaps report them to a remote attacker. Keyloggers are planted by criminals on unsuspecting hosts to steal passwords and other valuable personal information. It has also been rumored that the Federal Bureau of Investigation (FBI) has used a keylogger called Magic Lantern.

As the name implies, *spyware* is stealthy software designed to monitor and report user activities for the purposes of learning personal information without the user's knowledge or consent. Surveys have found that spyware is widely prevalent on consumer PCs, usually without knowledge of the owners. Adware is viewed by some as a mildly objectionable form of spyware that spies on Web browsing behavior to target online advertisements to a user's apparent interests. More objectionable forms of spyware are more invasive of privacy and raise other objections related to stealthy installation, interference with normal Web browsing, and difficulty of removal.

Spyware can be installed in a number of stealthy ways: disguised as a Trojan horse, bundled with a legitimate software program, delivered in the payload of a worm or virus, or downloaded through deception. For instance, a deceptive Web site might pop up a window appearing to be a standard Windows dialog box, but clicking any button will cause spyware to be downloaded. Another issue is that spyware might or might not display an end-user license agreement (EULA) before installation. If an EULA is displayed, the mention of spyware is typically unnoticeable or difficult to find.

More pernicious forms of spyware can change computer settings, reset homepages, and redirect the browser to unwanted sites. For example, the notorious CoolWebSearch changed homepages to Coolwebsearch.com, rewrote search engine results, and altered host files, and some variants added links to pornographic and gambling sites to the browser's bookmarks.

Lures and "Pull" Attacks

Traditional network attacks can be viewed as an "active" approach in which the attacker takes the initiative of a series of actions directed at a target. Attackers face the risk of revealing their malicious intentions through these actions. For instance, port scanning, password guessing, or exploit attempts can be readily detected by an IDS as suspicious activities. Sending malware through email can only be seen as an attempted attack.

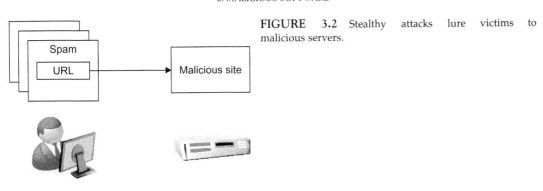

FIGURE 3.2 Stealthy attacks lure victims to malicious servers.

Security researchers have observed a trend away from direct attacks toward stealthier attacks that wait for victims to visit malicious Web sites, as shown in Figure 3.2.[15] The Web has become the primary vector for infecting computers, in large part because email has become better secured. Sophos discovers a new malicious Webpage every 14 seconds, on average.[16]

Web-based attacks have significant advantages for attackers. First, they are stealthier and not as "noisy" as active attacks, making it easier to continue undetected for a longer time. Second, Web servers have the intelligence to be stealthy. For instance, Web servers have been found that serve up an attack only once per IP address and otherwise serve up legitimate content. The malicious server remembers the IP addresses of visitors. Thus, a visitor will be attacked only once, which makes the attack harder to detect. Third, a Web server can serve up different attacks, depending on the visitor's operating system and browser.

As mentioned earlier, a common type of attack carried out through the Web is phishing. A phishing site is typically disguised as a legitimate financial organization or e-commerce business. During the month of June 2011, the Anti-Phishing Working Group found 28,148 new unique phishing sites hijacking 310 brands (www.antiphishing.org).

Another type of Web-based attack is a malicious site that attempts to download malware through a visitor's browser, called a *drive-by download*. A Web page usually loads a malicious script by means of an iframe (inline frame). It has been reported that most drive-by downloads are hosted on legitimate sites that have been compromised. For example, in June 2007 more than 10,000 legitimate Italian Web sites were discovered to be compromised with malicious code loaded through iframes. Many other legitimate sites are regularly compromised.

Drive-by downloading through a legitimate site holds certain appeal for attackers. First, most users will be reluctant to visit suspicious and potentially malicious sites but will not hesitate to visit legitimate sites in the belief that they are always safe. Even wary Web surfers may be caught off-guard. Second, the vast majority of Web servers run Apache

15. Joel Scambray, Mike Shema, and Caleb Sima, *Hacking Exposed Web Applications*, 2nd ed., McGraw-Hill, 2006.

16. Sophos, "Security Threat Report 2012," available at http://www.sophos.com/medialibrary/PDFs/other/SophosSecurityThreatReport2012.pdf (date of access: March 1, 2012).

(approximately 50 percent) or Microsoft IIS (approximately 40 percent), both of which have vulnerabilities that can be exploited by attackers. Moreover, servers with database applications could be vulnerable to SQL injection attacks. Third, if a legitimate site is compromised with an iframe, the malicious code might go unnoticed by the site owner for some time.

Pull-based attacks pose one challenge to attackers: They must somehow attract visitors to the malicious site, while avoiding detection by security researchers. One obvious option is to send out lures in spam. Lures have been disguised as email from the Internal Revenue Service, a security update from Microsoft, or a greeting card. The email attempts to entice the reader to visit a link. On one hand, lures are easier to get through spam filters because they only contain links and not attachments. It is easier for spam filters to detect malware attachments than to determine whether links in email are malicious. On the other hand, spam filters are easily capable of extracting and following links from spam. The greater challenge is to determine whether the linked site is malicious.

3. DEFENSE IN DEPTH

Most security experts would agree that perfect network security is impossible to achieve and that any single defense can always be overcome by an attacker with sufficient resources and motivation. The basic idea behind the *defense-in-depth strategy* is to hinder the attacker as much as possible with multiple layers of defense, even though each layer might be surmountable. More valuable assets should be protected behind more layers of defense. The combination of multiple layers increases the cost for the attacker to be successful, and the cost is proportional to the value of the protected assets. Moreover, a combination of multiple layers will be more effective against unpredictable attacks than will a single defense optimized for a particular type of attack.

The cost for the attacker could be in terms of additional time, effort, or equipment. For instance, by delaying an attacker, an organization would increase the chances of detecting and reacting to an attack in progress. The increased costs to an attacker could deter some attempts if the costs are believed to outweigh the possible gain from a successful attack.

Defense in depth is sometimes said to involve people, technology, and operations. Trained security people should be responsible for securing facilities and information assurance. However, every computer user in an organization should be made aware of security policies and practices. Every Internet user at home should be aware of safe practices (such as avoiding opening email attachments or clicking suspicious links) and the benefits of appropriate protection (antivirus software, firewalls).

A variety of technological measures can be used for layers of protection. These should include firewalls, IDSs, routers with ACLs, antivirus software, access control, spam filters, and so on. These topics are discussed in more depth later in this chapter.

The term *operations* refers to all preventive and reactive activities required to maintain security. Preventive activities include vulnerability assessments, software patching, system hardening (closing unnecessary ports), and access controls. Reactive activities should detect malicious activities and react by blocking attacks, isolating valuable resources, or tracing the intruder.

Protection of valuable assets can be a more complicated decision than simply considering the value of the assets. Organizations often perform a risk assessment to determine the value of assets, possible threats, likelihood of threats, and possible impact of threats. Valuable assets facing unlikely threats or threats with low impact might not need much protection. Clearly, assets of high value facing likely threats or high-impact threats merit the strongest defenses. Organizations usually have their own risk management process for identifying risks and deciding how to allocate a security budget to protect valuable assets under risk.

4. PREVENTIVE MEASURES

Most computer users are aware that Internet connectivity comes with security risks. It would be reasonable to take precautions to minimize exposure to attacks. Fortunately, several options are available to computer users to fortify their systems to reduce risks.

Access Control

In computer security, *access control* refers to mechanisms to allow users to perform functions up to their authorized level and restrict users from performing unauthorized functions.[17] Access control includes:

- Authentication of users
- Authorization of their privileges
- Auditing to monitor and record user actions

All computer users will be familiar with some type of access control.

Authentication, the process of verifying a user's identity, is typically based on one or more of these factors:

- Something the user knows, such as a password or PIN
- Something the user has, such as a smart card or token
- Something personal about the user, such as a fingerprint, retinal pattern, or other biometric identifier

Use of a single factor, even if multiple pieces of evidence are offered, is considered weak authentication. A combination of two factors, such as a password and a fingerprint, called *two-factor* (or *multifactor*) *authentication*, is considered strong authentication.

Authorization is the process of determining what an authenticated user can do. Most operating systems have an established set of permissions related to read, write, or execute access. For example, an ordinary user might have permission to read a certain file but not write to it, whereas a root or superuser will have full privileges to do anything.

17. B. Carroll, Cisco Access Control Security: AAA Administration Services, Cisco Press, 2004.

Auditing is necessary to ensure that users are accountable. Computer systems record actions in the system in audit trails and logs. For security purposes, they are invaluable forensic tools to re-create and analyze incidents. For instance, a user attempting numerous failed logins might be seen as an intruder.

Vulnerability Testing and Patching

As mentioned earlier, vulnerabilities are weaknesses in software that might be used to compromise a computer. Vulnerable software includes all types of operating systems and application programs. New vulnerabilities are being discovered constantly in different ways. New vulnerabilities discovered by security researchers are usually reported confidentially to the vendor, which is given time to study the vulnerability and develop a path. Of all vulnerabilities disclosed in 2007, 50 percent could be corrected through vendor patches.[18] When ready, the vendor will publish the vulnerability, hopefully along with a patch.

It has been argued that publication of vulnerabilities will help attackers. Although this might be true, publication also fosters awareness within the entire community. Systems administrators will be able to evaluate their systems and take appropriate precautions. One might expect systems administrators to know the configuration of computers on their network, but in large organizations, it would be difficult to keep track of possible configuration changes made by users. Vulnerability testing offers a simple way to learn about the configuration of computers on a network.

Vulnerability testing is an exercise to probe systems for known vulnerabilities. It requires a database of known vulnerabilities, a packet generator, and test routines to generate a sequence of packets to test for a particular vulnerability. If a vulnerability is found and a software patch is available, that host should be patched.

Penetration testing is a closely related idea but takes it further. Penetration testing simulates the actions of a hypothetical attacker to attempt to compromise hosts. The goal is, again, to learn about weaknesses in the network so that they can be remedied.

Closing Ports

Transport layer protocols, namely, Transmission Control Protocol (TCP) and User Datagram Protocol (UDP), identify applications communicating with each other by means of port numbers. Port numbers 1 to 1023 are well known and assigned by the Internet Assigned Numbers Authority (IANA) to standardized services running with root privileges. For example, Web servers listen on TCP port 80 for client requests. Port numbers 1024 to 49151 are used by various applications with ordinary user privileges. Port numbers above 49151 are used dynamically by applications.

It is good practice to close ports that are unnecessary, because attackers can use open ports, particularly those in the higher range. For instance, the Sub7 Trojan horse is known

18. IBM Internet Security Systems, *X-Force 2007 Trend Statistics*, January 2008 (date of access: July 1, 2008).

to use port 27374 by default, and Netbus uses port 12345. Closing ports does not by itself guarantee the safety of a host, however. Some hosts need to keep TCP port 80 open for HyperText Transfer Protocol (HTTP), but attacks can still be carried out through that port.

Firewalls

When most people think of network security, firewalls are one of the first things to come to mind. Firewalls are a means of perimeter security protecting an internal network from external threats. A firewall selectively allows or blocks incoming and outgoing traffic. Firewalls can be standalone network devices located at the entry to a private network or personal firewall programs running on PCs. An organization's firewall protects the internal community; a personal firewall can be customized to an individual's needs.

Firewalls can provide separation and isolation among various network zones, namely, the public Internet, private intranets, and a demilitarized zone (DMZ), as shown in Figure 3.3. The semiprotected DMZ typically includes public services provided by a private organization. Public servers need some protection from the public Internet, so they usually sit behind a firewall. This firewall cannot be completely restrictive because the public servers must be externally accessible. Another firewall typically sits between the DMZ and private internal network because the internal network needs additional protection.

There are various types of firewalls: packet-filtering firewalls, stateful firewalls, and proxy firewalls. In any case, the effectiveness of a firewall depends on the configuration of its rules. Properly written rules require detailed knowledge of network protocols. Unfortunately, some firewalls are improperly configured through neglect or lack of training.

Packet-filtering firewalls analyze packets in both directions and either permit or deny passage based on a set of rules. Rules typically examine port numbers, protocols, IP addresses, and other attributes of packet headers. There is no attempt to relate multiple packets with a flow or stream. The firewall is stateless, retaining no memory of one packet to the next.

Stateful firewalls overcome the limitation of packet-filtering firewalls by recognizing packets belonging to the same flow or connection and keeping track of the connection state. They work at the network layer and recognize the legitimacy of sessions.

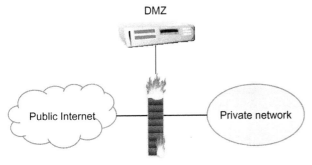

FIGURE 3.3 A firewall isolating various network zones.

Proxy firewalls are also called application-level firewalls because they process up to the application layer. They recognize certain applications and can detect whether an undesirable protocol is using a nonstandard port or an application layer protocol is being abused. They protect an internal network by serving as primary gateways to proxy connections from the internal network to the public Internet. They could have some impact on network performance due to the nature of the analysis.

Firewalls are essential elements of an overall defensive strategy but have the drawback that they only protect the perimeter. They are useless if an intruder has a way to bypass the perimeter. They are also useless against insider threats originating within a private network.

Antivirus and Antispyware Tools

The proliferation of malware prompts the need for antivirus software.[19] Antivirus software is developed to detect the presence of malware, identify its nature, remove the malware (disinfect the host), and protect a host from future infections. Detection should ideally minimize false positives (false alarms) and false negatives (missed malware) at the same time. Antivirus software faces a number of difficult challenges:

- Malware tactics are sophisticated and constantly evolving.
- Even the operating system on infected hosts cannot be trusted.
- Malware can exist entirely in memory without affecting files.
- Malware can attack antivirus processes.
- The processing load for antivirus software cannot degrade computer performance such that users become annoyed and turn the antivirus software off.

One of the simplest tasks performed by antivirus software is file scanning. This process compares the bytes in files with known signatures that are byte patterns indicative of a known malware. It represents the general approach of signature-based detection. When new malware is captured, it is analyzed for unique characteristics that can be described in a signature. The new signature is distributed as updates to antivirus programs. Antivirus looks for the signature during file scanning, and if a match is found, the signature identifies the malware specifically. There are major drawbacks to this method, however: New signatures require time to develop and test; users must keep their signature files up to date; and new malware without a known signature may escape detection.

Behavior-based detection is a complementary approach. Instead of addressing what malware is, behavior-based detection looks at what malware tries to do. In other words, anything attempting a risky action will come under suspicion. This approach overcomes the limitations of signature-based detection and could find new malware without a signature, just from its behavior. However, the approach can be difficult in practice. First, we must define what is suspicious behavior, or conversely, what is normal behavior. This definition often relies on heuristic rules developed by security experts, because normal

19. Peter Szor, *The Art of Computer Virus Research and Defense*, Addison-Wesley, 2005.

behavior is difficult to define precisely. Second, it might be possible to *discern* suspicious behavior, but it is much more difficult to *determine* malicious behavior, because malicious intention must be inferred. When behavior-based detection flags suspicious behavior, more follow-up investigation is usually needed to better understand the threat risk.

The ability of malware to change or disguise appearances can defeat file scanning. However, regardless of its form, malware must ultimately perform its mission. Thus, an opportunity will always arise to detect malware from its behavior if it is given a chance to execute. Antivirus software will monitor system events, such as hard-disk access, to look for actions that might pose a threat to the host. Events are monitored by intercepting calls to operating system functions.

Although monitoring system events is a step beyond file scanning, malicious programs are running in the host execution environment and could pose a risk to the host. The idea of emulation is to execute suspected code within an isolated environment, presenting the appearance of the computer resources to the code, and to look for actions symptomatic of malware.

Virtualization takes emulation a step further and executes suspected code within a real operating system. A number of virtual operating systems can run above the host operating system. Malware can corrupt a virtual operating system, but for safety reasons a virtual operating system has limited access to the host operating system. A "sandbox" isolates the virtual environment from tampering with the host environment, unless a specific action is requested and permitted. In contrast, emulation does not offer an operating system to suspected code; the code is allowed to execute step by step, but in a controlled and restricted way, just to discover what it will attempt to do.

Antispyware software can be viewed as a specialized class of antivirus software. Somewhat unlike traditional viruses, spyware can be particularly pernicious in making a vast number of changes throughout the hard drive and system files. Infected systems tend to have a large number of installed spyware programs, possibly including certain cookies (pieces of text planted by Web sites in the browser as a means of keeping them in memory).

Spam Filtering

Every Internet user is familiar with spam email. There is no consensus on an exact definition of spam, but most people would agree that spam is unsolicited, sent in bulk, and commercial in nature. There is also consensus that the vast majority of email is spam. Spam continues to be a problem because a small fraction of recipients do respond to these messages. Even though the fraction is small, the revenue generated is enough to make spam profitable because it costs little to send spam in bulk. In particular, a large botnet can generate an enormous amount of spam quickly.

Users of popular Webmail services such as Yahoo! and Hotmail are attractive targets for spam because their addresses might be easy to guess. In addition, spammers harvest email addresses from various sources: Web sites, newsgroups, online directories, data-stealing viruses, and so on. Spammers might also purchase lists of addresses from companies that are willing to sell customer information.

Spam is more than an inconvenience for users and a waste of network resources. Spam is a popular vehicle to distribute malware and lures to malicious Web sites. It is the first step in phishing attacks.

Spam filters work at an enterprise level and a personal level. At the enterprise level, mail gateways can protect an entire organization by scanning incoming messages for malware and blocking messages from suspicious or fake senders. A concern at the enterprise level is the rate of false positives, which are legitimate messages mistaken for spam. Users may become upset if their legitimate mail is blocked. Fortunately, spam filters are typically customizable, and the rate of false positives can be made very low. Additional spam filtering at the personal level can customize filtering even further, to account for individual preferences.

Various spam-filtering techniques are embodied in many commercial and free spam filters, such as DSPAM and SpamAssassin, to name two. Bayesian filtering is one of the more popular techniques.[20] First, an incoming message is parsed into tokens, which are single words or word combinations from the message's header and body. Second, probabilities are assigned to tokens through a training process. The filter looks at a set of known spam messages compared to a set of known legitimate messages and calculates token probabilities based on Bayes' theorem (from probability theory). Intuitively, a word such as *Viagra* would appear more often in spam, and therefore the appearance of a Viagra token would increase the probability of that message being classified as spam.

The probability calculated for a message is compared to a chosen threshold; if the probability is higher, the message is classified as spam. The threshold is chosen to balance the rates of false positives and false negatives (missed spam) in some desired way. An attractive feature of Bayesian filtering is that its probabilities will adapt to new spam tactics, given continual feedback, that is, correction of false positives and false negatives by the user.

It is easy to see why spammers have attacked Bayesian filters by attempting to influence the probabilities of tokens. For example, spammers have tried filling messages with large amounts of legitimate text (e.g., drawn from classic literature) or random innocuous words. The presence of legitimate tokens tends to decrease a message's score because they are evidence counted toward the legitimacy of the message.

Spammers are continually trying new ways to get through spam filters. At the same time, security companies respond by adapting their technologies.

Honeypots

The basic idea of a *honeypot* is to learn about attacker techniques by attracting attacks to a seemingly vulnerable host.[21] It is essentially a forensics tool rather than a line of defense. A honeypot could be used to gain valuable information about attack methods used

---

20. J. Zdziarski, *Ending Spam: Bayesian Content Filtering and the Art of Statistical Language Classification*, No Starch Press, 2005.

21. The Honeynet Project, *Know Your Enemy: Learning about Security Threats*, 2nd ed., Addison-Wesley, 2004.

elsewhere or imminent attacks before they happen. Honeypots are used routinely in research and production environments.

A honeypot has more special requirements than a regular PC. First, a honeypot should not be used for legitimate services or traffic. Consequently, every activity seen by the honeypot will be illegitimate. Even though honeypots typically record little data compared to IDS, for instance, their data has little "noise," whereas the bulk of IDS data is typically uninteresting from a security point of view.

Second, a honeypot should have comprehensive and reliable capabilities for monitoring and logging all activities. The forensic value of a honeypot depends on the detailed information it can capture about attacks.

Third, a honeypot should be isolated from the real network. Since honeypots are intended to attract attacks, there is a real risk that the honeypot could be compromised and used as a launching pad to attack more hosts in the network.

Honeypots are often classified according to their level of interaction, ranging from low to high. Low-interaction honeypots, such as Honeyd, offer the appearance of simple services. An attacker could try to compromise the honeypot but would not have much to gain. The limited interactions pose a risk that an attacker could discover that the host is a honeypot. At the other end of the range, high-interaction honeypots behave more like real systems. They have more capabilities to interact with an attacker and log activities, but they offer more to gain if they are compromised.

Honeypots are related to the concepts of black holes or network telescopes, which are monitored blocks of unused IP addresses. Since the addresses are unused, any traffic seen at those addresses is naturally suspicious (though not necessarily malicious).

Traditional honeypots suffer a drawback in that they are passive and wait to see malicious activity. The idea of honeypots has been extended to active clients that search for malicious servers and interact with them. The active version of a honeypot has been called a *honey-monkey* or *client honeypot*.

Network Access Control

A vulnerable host might place not only itself but an entire community at risk. For one thing, a vulnerable host might attract attacks. If compromised, the host could be used to launch attacks on other hosts. The compromised host might give information to the attacker, or there might be trust relationships between hosts that could help the attacker. In any case, it is not desirable to have a weakly protected host on your network.

The general idea of *network access control* (NAC) is to restrict a host from accessing a network unless the host can provide evidence of a strong security posture. The NAC process involves the host, the network (usually routers or switches, and servers), and a security policy, as shown in Figure 3.4.

The details of the NAC process vary with various implementations, which unfortunately currently lack standards for interoperability. A host's security posture includes its IP address, operating system, antivirus software, personal firewall, and host intrusion detection system. In some implementations, a software agent runs on the host, collects information about the host's security posture, and reports it to the network as part of a

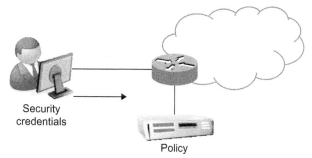

FIGURE 3.4   Network access control.

Security
credentials

Policy

request for admission to the network. The network refers to a policy server to compare the host's security posture to the security policy, to make an admission decision.

The admission decision could be anything from rejection to partial admission or full admission. Rejection might be prompted by out-of-date antivirus software, an operating system needing patches, or firewall misconfiguration. Rejection might lead to quarantine (routing to an isolated network) or forced remediation.

5. INTRUSION MONITORING AND DETECTION

Preventive measures are necessary and help reduce the risk of attacks, but it is practically impossible to prevent all attacks. Intrusion detection is also necessary to detect and diagnose malicious activities, analogous to a burglar alarm. Intrusion detection is essentially a combination of monitoring, analysis, and response.[22] Typically, an IDS supports a console for human interface and display. Monitoring and analysis are usually viewed as passive techniques because they do not interfere with ongoing activities. The typical IDS response is an alert to systems administrators, who may or may not choose to pursue further investigation. In other words, traditional IDSs do not offer much response beyond alerts, under the presumption that security incidents need human expertise and judgment for follow-up.

Detection accuracy is the critical problem for intrusion detection. Intrusion detection should ideally minimize false positives (normal incidents mistaken for suspicious ones) and false negatives (malicious incidents escaping detection). Naturally, false negatives are contrary to the essential purpose of intrusion detection. False positives are also harmful because they are troublesome for systems administrators who must waste time investigating false alarms. Intrusion detection should also seek to more than identify security incidents. In addition to relating the facts of an incident, intrusion detection should ascertain the nature of the incident, the perpetrator, the seriousness (malicious vs. suspicious), scope, and potential consequences (such as stepping from one target to more targets).

22. Richard Bejtlich, *The Tao of Network Security Monitoring: Beyond Intrusion Detection*, Addison-Wesley, 2005.

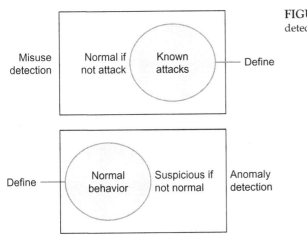

FIGURE 3.5 Misuse detection and anomaly detection.

IDS approaches can be categorized in at least two ways. One way is to differentiate host-based and network-based IDS, depending on where sensing is done. A host-based IDS monitors an individual host, whereas a network-based IDS works on network packets. Another way to view IDS is by their approach to analysis. Traditionally, the two analysis approaches are misuse (signature-based) detection and anomaly (behavior-based) detection. As shown in Figure 3.5, these two views are complementary and are often used in combination.

In practice, intrusion detection faces several difficult challenges: Signature-based detection can recognize only incidents matching a known signature; behavior-based detection relies on an understanding of normal behavior, but "normal" can vary widely. Attackers are intelligent and evasive; attackers might try to confuse IDS with fragmented, encrypted, tunneled, or junk packets; an IDS might not react to an incident in real time or quickly enough to stop an attack; and incidents can occur anywhere at any time, which necessitates continual and extensive monitoring, with correlation of multiple distributed sensors.

Host-Based Monitoring

Host-based IDS runs on a host and monitors system activities for signs of suspicious behavior. Examples could be changes to the system Registry, repeated failed login attempts, or installation of a backdoor. Host-based IDSs usually monitor system objects, processes, and regions of memory. For each system object, the IDS will usually keep track of attributes such as permissions, size, modification dates, and hashed contents, to recognize changes.

A concern for a host-based IDS is possible tampering by an attacker. If an attacker gains control of a system, the IDS cannot be trusted. Hence, special protection of the IDS against tampering should be architected into a host.

A host-based IDS is not a complete solution by itself. Although monitoring the host is logical, it has three significant drawbacks: Visibility is limited to a single host; the IDS process consumes resources, possibly impacting performance on the host; and attacks will not be seen until they have already reached the host. Host-based and network-based IDS are often used together to combine strengths.

Traffic Monitoring

Network-based IDSs typically monitor network packets for signs of reconnaissance, exploits, DoS attacks, and malware. They have strengths to complement host-based IDSs: Network-based IDSs can see traffic for a population of hosts; they can recognize patterns shared by multiple hosts; and they have the potential to see attacks before they reach the hosts.

IDSs are placed in various locations for different views, as shown in Figure 3.6. An IDS outside a firewall is useful for learning about malicious activities on the Internet. An IDS in the DMZ will see attacks originating from the Internet that are able to get through the outer firewall to public servers. Lastly, an IDS in the private network is necessary to detect any attacks that are able to successfully penetrate perimeter security.

Signature-Based Detection

Signature-based intrusion detection depends on patterns that uniquely identify an attack. If an incident matches a known signature, the signature identifies the specific attack. The central issue is how to define signatures or model attacks. If signatures are too specific, a change in an attack tactic could result in a false negative (missed alarm). An attack signature should be broad enough to cover an entire class of attacks. On the other hand, if signatures are too general, it can result in false positives.

Signature-based approaches have three inherent drawbacks: New attacks can be missed if a matching signature is not known; signatures require time to develop for new attacks; and new signatures must be distributed continually.

Snort is a popular example of a signature-based IDS (www.snort.org). Snort signatures are rules that define fields that match packets of information about the represented attack.

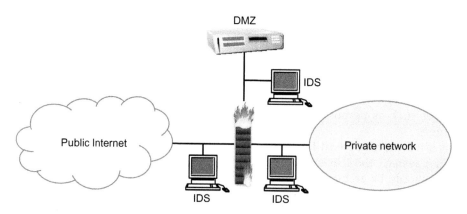

FIGURE 3.6   IDSs monitoring various network zones.

Snort is packaged with more than 1800 rules covering a broad range of attacks, and new rules are constantly being written.

Behavior Anomalies

A behavior-based IDS is appealing for its potential to recognize new attacks without a known signature. It presumes that attacks will be different from normal behavior. Hence the critical issue is how to define normal behavior, and anything outside of normal (anomalous) is classified as suspicious. A common approach is to define normal behavior in statistical terms, which allows for deviations within a range.

Behavior-based approaches have considerable challenges. First, normal behavior is based on past behavior. Thus, data about past behavior must be available for training the IDS. Second, behavior can and does change over time, so any IDS approach must be adaptive. Third, anomalies are just unusual events, not necessarily malicious ones. A behavior-based IDS might point out incidents to investigate further, but it is not good at discerning the exact nature of attacks.

Intrusion Prevention Systems

IDSs are passive techniques. They typically notify the systems administrator to investigate further and take the appropriate action. The response might be slow if the systems administrator is busy or the incident is time consuming to investigate.

A variation called an *intrusion prevention system* (IPS) seeks to combine the traditional monitoring and analysis functions of an IDS with more active automated responses, such as automatically reconfiguring firewalls to block an attack. An IPS aims for a faster response than humans can achieve, but its accuracy depends on the same techniques as the traditional IDS. The response should not harm legitimate traffic, so accuracy is critical.

6. REACTIVE MEASURES

When an attack is detected and analyzed, systems administrators must exercise an appropriate response to the attack. One of the principles in security is that the response should be proportional to the threat. Obviously, the response will depend on the circumstances, but various options are available. Generally, it is possible to block, slow, modify, or redirect any malicious traffic. It is not possible to delineate every possible response. Here we describe only two responses: quarantine and traceback.

Quarantine

Dynamic quarantine in computer security is analogous to quarantine for infectious diseases. It is an appropriate response, particularly in the context of malware, to prevent an infected host from contaminating other hosts. Infectious malware requires connectivity between an infected host and a new target, so it is logical to disrupt the connectivity between hosts or networks as a means to impede the malware from spreading further.

Within the network, traffic can be blocked by firewalls or routers with access control lists (ACLs). ACLs are similar to firewall rules, allowing routers to selectively drop packets.

Traceback

One of the critical aspects of an attack is the identity or location of the perpetrator. Unfortunately, discovery of an attacker in IP networks is almost impossible because:

- The source address in IP packets can be easily spoofed (forged).
- Routers are stateless by design and do not keep records of forwarded packets.
- Attackers can use a series of intermediary hosts (called *stepping stones* or *zombies*) to carry out their attacks.

Intermediaries are usually innocent computers taken over by an exploit or malware and put under control of the attacker. In practice, it might be possible to trace an attack back to the closest intermediary, but it might be too much to expect to trace an attack all the way back to the real attacker.

To trace a packet's route, some tracking information must be either stored at routers when the packet is forwarded or carried in the packet, as shown in Figure 3.7. An example of the first approach is to store a hash of a packet for some amount of time. If an attack occurs, the target host will query routers for a hash of the attack packet. If a router has the hash, it is evidence that the packet had been forwarded by that router. To reduce memory consumption, the hash is stored instead of storing the entire packet. The storage is temporary instead of permanent so that routers will not run out of memory.

An example of the second approach is to stamp packets with a unique router identifier, such as an IP address. Thus the packet carries a record of its route. The main advantage

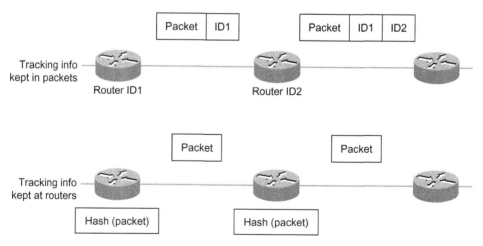

FIGURE 3.7   Tracking information stored at routers or carried in packets to enable packet traceback.

here is that routers can remain stateless. The problem is that there is no space in the IP packet header for this scheme.

Finally, let's briefly look at how a network-based intrusion protection system (IPS) monitors network traffic for particular network segments or devices and analyzes network, transport, and application protocols to identify suspicious activity. The following section describes common intrusion protection components.

7. NETWORK-BASED INTRUSION PROTECTION

Network-based IPS components are similar to other types of IPS technologies, except for the sensors. A network-based IPS sensor monitors and analyzes network activity on one or more network segments. Sensors are available in two formats: appliance-based sensors, which are comprised of specialized hardware and software optimized for IPS sensor use, and software-only sensors, which can be installed onto hosts that meet certain specifications.

Network-based IPSs also provide a wide variety of security capabilities. Some products can collect information on hosts such as which OSs they use and which application versions they use that communicate over networks. Network-based IPSs can also perform extensive logging of data related to detected events (see checklist: An Agenda for Action for Logging Capabilities Activities); most can also perform packet captures.

AN AGENDA FOR ACTION FOR LOGGING CAPABILITIES ACTIVITIES

As previously stated, network-based IPSs typically perform extensive logging of data related to detected events. This data can be used to confirm the validity of alerts, to investigate incidents, and to correlate events between the IPS and other logging sources. Data fields commonly logged by network-based IPSs include the following key activities (check all tasks completed):

_____1. Timestamp (usually date and time).

_____2. Connection or session ID (typically a consecutive or unique number assigned to each TCP connection or to like groups of packets for connectionless protocols).

_____3. Event or alert type. In the console, the event or alert type often links to supporting information for the specific vulnerability or exploit, such as references for additional information and associated Common Vulnerabilities and Exposures (CVE) numbers.

_____4. Rating (priority, severity, impact, confidence).

_____5. Network, transport, and application layer protocols.

_____6. Source and destination IP addresses.

_____7. Source and destination TCP or UDP ports, or ICMP types and codes.

_____ **8.** Number of bytes transmitted over the connection.

_____ **9.** Decoded payload data, such as application requests and responses.

_____ **10.** State-related information (authenticated username).

_____ **11.** Prevention action performed (if any).

8. SUMMARY

This chapter made it perfectly clear that, to guard against network intrusions, we must understand the variety of attacks, from exploits to malware to social engineering. Direct attacks are prevalent, but a class of *pull attacks* has emerged, relying on lures to bring victims to a malicious Web site. Pull attacks are much more difficult to uncover and in a way defend against. Just about anyone can become victimized.

Much can be done to fortify hosts and reduce their risk exposure, but some attacks are unavoidable. Defense in depth is a most practical defense strategy, combining layers of defenses. Although each defensive layer is imperfect, the cost becomes harder to surmount for intruders.

One of the essential defenses is *intrusion detection*. Host-based and network-based intrusion detection systems have their respective strengths and weaknesses. Research continues to be needed to improve intrusion detection, particularly behavior-based techniques. As more attacks are invented, signature-based techniques will have more difficulty keeping up.

Finally, let's move on to the real interactive part of this chapter: review questions/exercises, hands-on projects, case projects and optional team case project. The answers and/or solutions by chapter can be found in the Online Instructor's Solutions Manual.

CHAPTER REVIEW QUESTIONS/EXERCISES

True/False

1. True or False? Traditionally, attack methods do not follow sequential steps analogous to physical attacks.
2. True or False? Malicious software, or malware, is not an enormous problem for Internet users because of its variety and prevalence and the level of danger it presents.
3. True or False? Traditional network attacks can be viewed as an "active" approach in which the attacker takes the initiative of a series of actions directed at a target.
4. True or False? The basic idea behind the *defense-in-depth strategy* is to hinder the attacker as much as possible with multiple layers of defense, even though each layer might be surmountable.
5. True or False? In computer security, *access control* refers to mechanisms to allow users to perform functions up to their unauthorized level and restrict users from performing authorized functions.

Multiple Choice

1. A stealthy type of malicious software (*malware*) designed to hide the existence of certain processes or programs from normal methods of detection is known as a:
   A. wireless sniffer.
   B. rootkit.
   C. port scanner.
   D. port knocker.
   E. keystroke logger.

2. If an intruder has installed malware for covert control, he or she will want to conceal the communications between him- or herself and the compromised target from discovery by:
   A. network-based intrusion detection systems (IDSs).
   B. tunneling.
   C. multiple time zones.
   D. budgets.
   E. networks.

3. What is a commonly used method to place packets of one protocol into the payload of another packet?
   A. Encryption.
   B. Signature-based.
   C. Tunneling.
   D. Hybrid detection.
   E. Host-based.

4. What is another obvious concealment method?
   A. Infection.
   B. Rate.
   C. Host.
   D. Back door.
   E. Encryption.

5. What can be a Trojan horse or other form of malware?
   A. Antivirus.
   B. Unified threat management.
   C. Keylogger.
   D. Firewall.
   E. Antispam.

EXERCISE

Problem

A physical security company has an innovative, patented product and critical secrets to protect. For this company, protecting physical security and safeguarding network security go hand-in-hand. A Web application in the data center tracks the serialized keycodes and allows customers to manage their key sets. The customers include everyone from theft-conscious retail chains to security-sensitive government agencies. In this case project, how would the security company go about establishing solid network security to protect them against intrusions?

Hands-On Projects

Project

A solution services company is also a managed service provider specializing in IT infrastructure, Voice over Internet Protocol (VoIP), wireless broadband, data centers, and procurement. As part of a customer network security upgrade, how would the company go about establishing a solid network to protect a school district's network from external threats; as well as the risk of unauthorized intrusions by users within the network?

Case Projects

Problem

For a international town's 10-person IT staff, upgrading its network security initiative meant expanding its multivendor Gigabit and Fast Ethernet network and ensuring that its growing volume of e-government services, including online tax payments, license application filings, and housing services, function without network intrusions. To accomplish this purpose, how would the town go about guarding against increasing waves of computer viruses, malware, and denial-ofservice (DoS) attacks?

Optional Team Case Project

Problem

Intrusion types of systems are put in place to serve business needs for meeting an objective of network security; IDSs and IPSs provide a foundation of technology needs and for tracking; and, identifying network attacks which detect intrusions through logs of IDS systems and preventing an action through IPS systems. If a company hosts critical systems, confidential data, and strict compliance regulations, then it's great to use IDS or IPS or both in guarding network environments. So, what are the basic benefits of IDS and IPS systems?

Securing Cloud Computing Systems

Cem Gurkok
Verizon Terremark

1. CLOUD COMPUTING ESSENTIALS: EXAMINING THE CLOUD LAYERS

Cloud computing is composed of several layers, such as public, private, hybrid, and community deployment models: SaaS, PaaS, IaaS (service, platform, infrastructure as a service or SPI) service models. The NIST Model of Cloud Computing is shown in Figure 4.1.

Infrastructure as a service (IaaS) provides online processing, data storage capacity, or network capacity on a virtualized environment. It offers the ability to provision processing, storage, networks, and other basic computing resources, allowing the customer to install and run their software, which can involve operating systems (OSs) and applications. IaaS customers buy these resources as a fully outsourced service. IaaS provides a set of application programming interfaces, which allows management and other forms of interaction with the infrastructure by consumers. Amazon, Terremark, and Rackspace are typical IaaS providers.

Platform as a service (PaaS) sits on top of IaaS. It provides an application development and deployment environment in the cloud. PaaS offers the ability to deploy applications by utilizing computer programming languages and tools available from the service provider. The service provider offers developers application building blocks to configure a new business application. This provides all of the facilities required to support the complete life cycle of building and delivering Web applications and services entirely available from the Internet. Google App Engine, Microsoft Azure, Engine Yard and Collabnet are some PaaS providers.

Service as a service (SaaS) is built on IaaS and PaaS. It serves business applications utilized by individuals or enterprises, and it can also be referred to as on-demand software. SaaS offers the most popular cloud applications to almost everyone that is online. Salesforce.com, Google Docs, and Microsoft Online Services are all popular consumer and

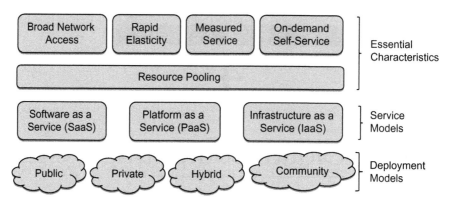

FIGURE 4.1   NIST model of cloud computing [1].

TABLE 4.1   Deployment Model's Responsibilities.

Model/ Infrastructure	Managed by	Owned by	Location	Used by
Public	External CSP	External CSP	Off-Site	Untrusted
Private	Customer or external CSP	Customer or external CSP	On-site or off-site	Trusted
Hybrid	Customer and external CSP	Customer and external CSP	On-site and off-site	Trusted and untrusted

Note: CSP, Cloud Service Provider.

enterprise-directed SaaS applications. The applications are accessible from various client devices through a thin client interface such as a Web browser.

Analyzing Cloud Options in Depth

Table 4.1 shows us that different cloud deployment models have varying management, ownership, locations, and access levels.

Public

Public cloud is an offering from one service provider to many clients who share the cloud-processing resources concurrently. Public cloud clients share applications, processing power, network resources, and data storage space. Differing levels of segregation are provided depending on the resource.

Private

A private cloud hosts one enterprise as a user. Various departments may be present in the cloud, but all are in the same enterprise. Private clouds often employ virtualization within an enterprise's existing computer servers to improve computer utilization. A private cloud also includes provisioning and metering facilities that enable fast deployment and removal where applicable. This model is similar to the conventional IT outsourcing models, but can also exist as an enterprise's internal delivery model. A variety of private cloud implementations have emerged:

- *Dedicated private cloud*: These are hosted within a customer-owned data center or at a collocation facility, and are operated by internal IT departments.
- *Community private cloud*: These are located at the premises of a third party and are owned, managed, and operated by a vendor who is bound by customized service-level agreements (SLAs) and contractual clauses with security and compliance requirements.
- *Managed private cloud*: In this implementation, the infrastructure is owned by the customer and management is performed by a third party.

Virtual Private

A virtual private cloud is a private cloud that exists within a shared or public cloud also called the Intercloud. The Intercloud comprises several interconnected clouds and legacy infrastructure. Amazon Web Services provides Amazon Virtual Private Cloud, which allows the Amazon Elastic Compute Cloud service to be connected to legacy infrastructure over an IPsec virtual private network connection. Google App Engine provides similar functionality via their Secure Data Connector product.

Hybrid

A hybrid cloud is a combination of two or more of the previously mentioned deployment models. Each of the three cloud deployment models has specific advantages and disadvantages relative to the other deployment models. A hybrid cloud leverages the advantage of the other cloud models, providing a more optimal user experience. By utilizing the hybrid cloud architecture, users are able to obtain degrees of fault tolerance combined with locally immediate usability without dependency on Internet connectivity.

Establishing Cloud Security Fundamentals

Security in cloud computing, for the most part, is no different than security in a regular IT environment. However, due to the different deployment models as described above, cloud environments present different risks to an organization.The European Network and Information Security Agency (ENISA) generally groups the risks into policy and organizational, technical, legal, and general risks and describes them as follows [2]:

Policy and Organizational Risks

Let's look at the following policy and organizational risks:

- Lock-in
- Loss of governance
- Compliance challenges

- Loss of business reputation due to co-tenant activities
- Cloud service termination or failure
- Cloud provider acquisition
- Supply chain failure

LOCK-IN

The potential dependency on a particular cloud provider, depending on the provider's commitments, may lead to a catastrophic business failure, should the cloud provider go bankrupt or the content and application migration path to another provider become too costly. There is little or no incentive for cloud providers to make migrating to another provider easy if they are not contractually bound to do so.

LOSS OF GOVERNANCE

By using cloud infrastructures, the client necessarily cedes control to the cloud provider on a number of issues that may affect security. This could have a severe impact on the organization's strategy and therefore on the capacity to meet its mission and goals. The loss of control and governance could lead to the impossibility of complying with the security requirements, a lack of confidentiality, integrity and availability of data, and a deterioration of performance and quality of service, not to mention the introduction of compliance challenges.

COMPLIANCE CHALLENGES

Certain companies migrating to the cloud might need to meet certain industry standards or regulatory requirements, such as Payment Card Industry (PCI) Data Security Standard (DSS). Migrating to the cloud could compromise these business needs if the cloud provider cannot furnish evidence of its own compliance to the relevant requirements or if the provider does not permit audits by the customer.

LOSS OF BUSINESS REPUTATION DUE TO CO-TENANT ACTIVITIES

Resource sharing can give rise to problems when the shared resources' reputation becomes tainted by a bad neighbor's activities. This would also include that certain measures be taken to mitigate, such as IP address blocking and equipment confiscation.

CLOUD SERVICE TERMINATION OR FAILURE

If the cloud provider faces the risk of going out of business due to financial, legal, or other reasons, the customer could suffer from loss or deterioration of service delivery performance and quality of service; as well as loss of investment.

CLOUD PROVIDER ACQUISITION

The acquisition of the cloud provider could increase the possibility of a strategic change and could put previous agreements at risk. This could make it impossible to comply with existing security requirements. The final impact could be damaging for crucial assets, such as the organization's reputation, customer or patient trust, and employee loyalty and experience.

SUPPLY CHAIN FAILURE

A cloud computing provider can outsource certain specialized tasks of its infrastructure to third parties. In such a situation, the cloud provider's level of security may depend on the level of security of each one of the links and the level of dependency of the cloud provider on the third party. In general, lack of transparency in the contract can be a problem for the whole system.

Technical Risks

Let's continue now by taking a look at the following technical risks:

- Resource exhaustion
- Resource segregation failure
- Abuse of high-privilege roles
- Management interface compromise
- Intercepting data in transit, data leakage
- Insecure deletion of data
- Distributed denial of service (DDoS)
- Economic denial of service (EDoS)
- Encryption and key management (loss of encryption keys)
- Undertaking malicious probes or scans
- Compromise of the service engine
- Customer requirements and cloud environment conflicts

RESOURCE EXHAUSTION

Inaccurate modeling of customer demands by the cloud provider can lead to service unavailability, access control compromise, and economic and reputation losses due to resource exhaustion. The customer takes a level of calculated risk in allocating all the resources of a cloud service because resources are allocated according to statistical projections.

RESOURCE SEGREGATION FAILURE

This class of risks includes the failure of mechanisms separating storage, memory, routing, and even reputation between different tenants of the shared infrastructure (guest-hopping attacks, SQL injection attacks exposing multiple customers' data, and side-channel attacks). The likelihood of this incident scenario depends on the cloud model adopted by the customer. It is less likely to occur for private cloud customers compared to public cloud customers.

ABUSE OF HIGH PRIVILEGE ROLES

The malicious activities of an insider could potentially have an impact on the confidentiality, integrity, and availability of all kinds of data, on all kinds of services, and therefore indirectly on the organization's reputation, customer trust, and employee experiences. This can be considered especially important in the case of cloud computing due to the fact that cloud architectures necessitate certain roles, which are extremely high risk. Examples of such roles include the cloud provider's system administrators and auditors and managed security service providers dealing with intrusion detection reports and incident response.

MANAGEMENT INTERFACE COMPROMISE

The customer management interfaces of public cloud providers are Internet accessible and mediate access to larger sets of resources (than traditional hosting providers). They also pose an increased risk, especially when combined with remote access and Web browser vulnerabilities.

INTERCEPTING DATA IN TRANSIT, DATA LEAKAGE

Cloud computing, being a distributed architecture, implies more data is in transit than with traditional infrastructures. Sniffing, spoofing, man-in–the-middle attacks, side channel, and replay attacks should be considered as possible threat sources.

INSECURE DELETION OF DATA

Whenever a provider is changed, resources are scaled down, physical hardware is real-located, and data may be available beyond the lifetime specified in the security policy. Where true data wiping is required, special procedures must be followed, and this may not be supported by the cloud provider.

DISTRIBUTED DENIAL OF DERVICE (DDOS)

A common method of attack involves saturating the target environment with external communications requests, such that it cannot respond to legitimate traffic, or responds so slowly as to be rendered effectively unavailable. This can result in financial and economic losses.

ECONOMIC DENIAL OF SERVICE (EDOS)

EDoS destroys economic resources; the worst-case scenario would be the bankruptcy of the customer or a serious economic impact. The following scenarios are possible: An attacker can use an account and the customer's resources for his own gain or in order to damage the customer economically. The customer has not set effective limits on the use of paid resources and experiences unexpected loads on these resources. An attacker can use a public channel to deplete the customer's metered resources. For example, where the customer pays per HTTP request, a DDoS attack can have this effect.

ENCRYPTION AND KEY MANAGEMENT (LOSS OF ENCRYPTION KEYS)

This risk includes the disclosure of secret keys (Secure Socket Layer [SSL], file encryption, customer private keys) or passwords to malicious parties. It also includes the loss or corruption of those keys, or their unauthorized use for authentication and no-repudiation (digital signature).

UNDERTAKING MALICIOUS PROBES OR SCANS

Malicious probes or scanning, as well as network mapping, are indirect threats to the assets being considered. They can be used to collect information in the context of a hacking attempt. A possible impact could be a loss of confidentiality, integrity, and availability of service and data.

COMPROMISE OF THE SERVICE ENGINE

Each cloud architecture relies on a highly specialized platform and the service engine. The service engine sits above the physical hardware resources and manages customer resources at different levels of abstraction. For example, in IaaS clouds this software component can be the hypervisor. Like any other software layer, the service engine code can have vulnerabilities and is prone to attacks or unexpected failure. Cloud providers must set out a clear segregation of responsibilities that articulate the minimum actions customers must undertake.

CUSTOMER REQUIREMENTS AND CLOUD ENVIRONMENT CONFLICTS

Cloud providers must set out a clear segregation of responsibilities that specify the minimum actions customers must undertake. The failure of the customers to properly secure their environments may pose a vulnerability to the cloud platform if the cloud provider has not taken the necessary steps to provide isolation. Cloud providers should further articulate their isolation mechanisms and provide best practice guidelines to assist customers in securing their resources.

Legal Risks

Now, let's look at the following legal risks:

- Subpoena and e-discovery
- Varying jurisdiction
- Data protection
- Licensing

SUBPOENA AND E-DISCOVERY

In the event of the confiscation of physical hardware as a result of subpoena by law enforcement agencies or civil suits, the centralization of storage as well as shared tenancy of physical hardware means that many more clients are at risk of the disclosure of their data to unwanted parties. At the same time, it may become impossible for the agency of a single nation to confiscate "a cloud," given pending advances around long-distance hypervisor migration.

VARYING JURISDICTION

Customer data may be held in multiple jurisdictions, some of which may be high risk or subject to higher restrictions. Certain countries are regarded as high risk because of their unpredictable legal frameworks and disrespect of international agreements. In these cases customer data can be accessed by various parties without the customer's consent. On the other hand, other countries can have stricter privacy laws and might require that certain data cannot be stored or tracked.

DATA PROTECTION

It has to be clear that the cloud customer will be the main person responsible for processing personal data, even when such processing is carried out by the cloud provider in its role of external processor. While some cloud providers, such as SAS 70-compliant ones, provide information about their data processing and security activities, others are opaque about these activities and can cause legal problems for the customer. There may also be data security breaches that are not notified to the controller by the cloud provider. In some cases, customers might be storing illegal or illegally obtained data, which might put the cloud provider and other customers at risk.

LICENSING

Licensing conditions, such as per-seat agreements, and online licensing checks may become unworkable in a cloud environment. For example, if software is charged on a per-instance basis every time a new machine is instantiated, then the cloud customer's licensing costs may increase exponentially, even though they are using the same number of machine instances for the same duration.

General Risks

Let's continue by looking at the following general risks:

- Network failures
- Privilege escalation
- Social engineering
- Loss or compromise of operational and security logs or audit trails
- Backup loss
- Unauthorized physical access and theft of equipment
- Natural disasters

NETWORK FAILURES

Network failure is one of the highest risks since it directly affects service delivery. It exists due to network misconfiguration, system vulnerabilities, lack of resource isolation, and poor or untested business continuity and disaster recovery plans. Network traffic modification can also be a risk for a customer and cloud provider; if provisioning isn't done properly, there is no traffic encryption or vulnerability assessment.

PRIVILEGE ESCALATION

Although this risk has a low probability of exploitation, it can cause loss of customer data and access control. A malicious entity can therefore take control of large portions of the cloud platform. The risk manifests itself owing to authentication, authorization, and other access control vulnerabilities, hypervisor vulnerabilities (cloud bursting), and misconfiguration.

SOCIAL ENGINEERING

This risk is one of the most disregarded risks since most technical staff focuses on the nonhuman aspects of their platforms. The exploitation of this risk has caused loss of reputation for cloud service providers, such as Amazon and Apple due to the publicity of the events. This risk can be easily minimized by security awareness training, proper user provisioning, resource isolation, data encryption, and proper physical security procedures.

LOSS OR COMPROMISE OF OPERATIONAL AND SECURITY LOGS OR AUDIT TRAILS

Operational logs can be vulnerable due to lack of policy or poor procedures for log collection. This would also include retention, access management vulnerabilities, user deprovisioning vulnerabilities, lack of forensic readiness, and operating system vulnerabilities.

BACKUP LOSS

This high-impact risk affects company reputation, all backed up data, and service delivery. It also occurs owing to inadequate physical security procedures, access management vulnerabilities, and user deprovisioning vulnerabilities.

UNAUTHORIZED PHYSICAL ACCESS AND THEFT OF EQUIPMENT

The probability of malicious actors gaining access to a physical location is very low, but in the event of such an occurrence, the impact to the cloud provider and its customers is very high. It can affect company reputation and data hosted on premises; the risk is due to inadequate physical security procedures.

NATURAL DISASTERS

This risk is another ignored risk that can have a high impact on the businesses involved in the event of its occurrence. If a business has a poor or an untested business continuity and disaster recovery plan or lacks one, its reputation, data, and service delivery can be severely compromised.

Other Cloud Security Concepts

Finally, let's look at the following cloud security concepts:

- Incident response (IR), notification, and remediation
- Virtualization
- External accreditations

INCIDENT RESPONSE (IR), NOTIFICATION AND REMEDIATION

Incident response comprises a set of procedures for an investigator to examine a computer security incident. Although cloud computing brings change on many levels, certain characteristics of cloud computing pose more direct challenges to IR activities than others. The on-demand self-service nature of cloud computing environments makes it hard or even impossible to receive cooperation from the cloud service provider when handling a security incident. Also, the resource pooling practiced by cloud services, in addition to the rapid elasticity offered by cloud infrastructures, may dramatically complicate the IR process, especially the forensic activities carried out as part of the incident analysis. Resource pooling as practiced by cloud services causes privacy concerns for co-tenants regarding the collection and analysis of telemetry and artifacts associated with an incident (e.g., logging, netflow data, memory, machine images) without compromising the privacy of co-tenants. The cross-border nature of cloud computing might cause the IR team to run into legal and regulatory hurdles due to limitations placed on what data can be accessed and used in investigations.

VIRTUALIZATION

Virtualization brings with it all the security concerns of the guest operating system, along with new virtualization-specific threats. A cloud service provider and customers would need to address virtual device hardening, hypervisor security, intervirtual device attacks, performance concerns, encryption, data commingling, data destruction, virtual device image tampering, and in-motion virtual devices.

External Accreditations

Rather than have a cloud service provider respond to numerous contract requests to ensure that all risks are covered, providers can obtain a number of external accreditations that will present evidence that they have both implemented appropriate security controls and follow sound security practices. One of these is the Statement on Auditing Standards (SAS) number 70, commonly known as an SAS 70 audit, which was originally published by the American Institute of Certified Public Accountants (AICPA). The audit is for service organizations and is designed to ensure that the company has sufficient controls and defenses when it is hosting or processing data belonging to one of its customers. A company that has a SAS 70 certificate has been audited by an external auditor, and the control objectives and activities have been found to be acceptable per SAS 70 requirements. When considering cloud providers, customers should look for not only SAS 70, but SAS 70 Type II. Type I certification only states that policies and procedures exist, although there is no audit to ensure that the organization adheres to these procedures. Type II certification comes only after a lengthy and rigorous in-person audit that ensures the service provider adheres to their procedures. Cloud providers, such as Terremark, Rackspace, and Amazon, are SAS 70 Type II certified.

Determining When Security Goals Require a Private Cloud

While the low cost and elastic nature of cloud computing can be beneficial for customers, due to security concerns the deployment method needs to be carefully selected. The security concerns that a potential customer needs to pay attention to are as follows:

- *Data protection (network and storage):* Sensitive and personal data, such as medical, human resources, e-mail, and government communications, will traverse the cloud environment. Securing this data in transit and storage will be important from contractual, legal, and regulatory perspectives.
- *Confidentiality:* Business processes and related information that are crucial to a company's survival may be utilized in a cloud environment. Any leakage of that information caused by voluntary communication by the cloud service provider or the cloud environment's security breach may jeopardize the customer's business and services.

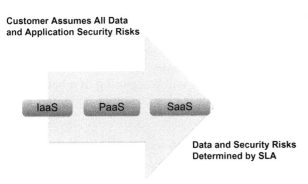

Customer Assumes All Data and Application Security Risks

laaS   PaaS   SaaS

Data and Security Risks Determined by SLA

FIGURE 4.2 Risk assumption in cloud service models.

- *Intellectual property:* It is important to determine who will own the intellectual property rights deployed in a cloud environment prior to engaging in cloud computing activities, and further determine the use that the parties can make of the objects of such rights.
- *Professional negligence:* The customer may be exposed to contractual and tortuous liability to its customers based on negligence due to functions outsourced to the cloud service provider.
- *Outsourcing services and changes in operational control:* A customer may select working with a cloud service provider due to its perceived qualities. If the cloud service provider decides to outsource these services, security concerns could arise owing to the lack of information regarding the processes and their qualities that are adopted by the third parties.

A private cloud deployment model would address all of these concerns by providing an environment owned and managed by the customer or trusted third party, located on-premise or at a trusted location and accessible only by trusted resources. Certain government entities and financial institutions prefer private cloud deployments because of the level of control and physical separation they provide. The progression of risk assumption in cloud service models is shown in Figure 4.2.

2. SOFTWARE AS A SERVICE (SAAS): MANAGING RISKS IN THE CLOUD

In SaaS environments the service levels, privacy, compliance, security controls, and their scope are negotiated into the contracts for service. Therefore, a SaaS customer has the least tactical responsibility compared to the other cloud service models for implementing and managing security solutions.

Centralizing Information with SaaS to Increase Data Security

SaaS storage is always accessed via a Web-based user interface or a client/server application. Data is entered into the system via the Web interface and stored within the SaaS application. SaaS may consume database systems, object and file storage, or dedicated

IaaS storage volumes. Data is tagged and encrypted in the SaaS application and generally managed by the provider if natively supported. Data passes through an encryption proxy before being sent to the SaaS application. This proxy can be implemented by the customer or the cloud service provider. This single point of exit and entry provides the means to easily monitor and control data being processed. Since data will be residing in a heterogeneous environment, the provider will need to encrypt data at a customer level and use separate database instances.

Implementing and Managing User Authentication and Authorization

In a SaaS environment, authentication and authorization is managed with a federated ID management solution (also known as a single sign on (SSO)). Federation is the use of Security Assertion Markup Language (SAML) to offer portability to disparate and independent security domains, with some organizations extending their DS (Directory Service) environment via a gateway product that will handle SAML assertions. Other organizations will consume native SAML assertions from an identity service. The following steps will be taken in a simplified SSO approach:

1. The user attempts to access the SaaS provider and will need to do so with some form of identifying information. For example, in the event the SaaS platform is Web based, the identifying information may be in the form of encrypted data in the URL or a cookie.
2. That information will be authenticated against the customer's user directory via a direct Web service call.
3. The customer's user directory will then reply with an assertion containing authorization and authentication information.
4. The resulting request is either fulfilled or denied based on the authentication and authorization of the assertion.

Permission and Password Protection

In a SaaS environment, the provider will offer a comprehensive password protection and permissions system. Password granting and password management (including read, write, delete options) should be clear and straightforward. Passwords will be required to change periodically to random values and will be stored in an encrypted and replicated manner.

Permissions will be assignable at different levels (workgroup, folder, subfolder), depending on the data the employee needs to access, and requestor's permissions will be validated with every access request as described in the authorization steps. The SaaS platform will capture event logs to track what data was accessed by whom at a given time.

Negotiating Security Requirements with Vendors

Service levels, security, governance, compliance, and liability expectations of the service and provider are contractually stipulated, managed to, and enforced, when the cloud provider offers a service level agreement (SLA) to the consumer. There are two types of SLAs: negotiable and nonnegotiable. When a nonnegotiable SLA is offered, the provider administers those portions stipulated in the agreement. An SLA generally comprises the parties involved, dates, scope of agreement, service hours, security, availability, reliability, support, performance metrics, and penalties.

Identifying Needed Security Measures

The security risks that were previously mentioned need to be identified and addressed by the consumer and stipulated in the SLA. Security departments should be engaged during the establishment of SLAs and contractual obligations to ensure that security requirements are contractually enforceable. SaaS providers that generate extensive customer-specific application logs and provide secure storage as well as analysis facilities will ease the burden on the customer. SLAs should cover data protection, business continuity and recovery, incident response, e-discovery, data retention, and removal [3].

Establishing a Service Level Agreement

Since multiple organizations are involved, SLAs and contracts between the parties become the primary means of communicating and enforcing expectations for responsibilities. It is important to note that the SLAs must be such that the cloud provider informs customers in a timely and reliable manner to allow for agreed actions to be taken. The customer should make sure that SLA clauses are not in conflict with promises made by other clauses or clauses from other providers [3].

SLAs may carry too much business risk for a provider, given the actual risk of technical failures. From the customer's point of view, SLAs may contain clauses that turn out to be detrimental; for example, in the area of intellectual property, an SLA might specify that the cloud provider has the rights to any content stored on the cloud infrastructure.

Ensuring SLAs Meet Organizational Security Requirements

Contracts should provide for third-party review of SLA metrics and compliance (e.g., by a mutually selected mediator). The need to quantify penalties for various risk scenarios in SLAs and the possible impact of security breaches on reputation motivate more rigorous internal audit and risk assessment procedures than would otherwise exist. The frequent audits imposed on cloud providers tend to expose risks that would not otherwise have been discovered, having therefore the same positive effect.

3. PLATFORM AS A SERVICE (PAAS): SECURING THE PLATFORM

A customer's administrator has limited control and accountability in a PaaS environment. With PaaS, securing the platform falls onto the provider, but both securing the applications developed against the platform and developing them securely belong to the customer. Customers need to trust the provider to offer sufficient control, while realizing that they will need to adjust their expectations for the amount of control that is reasonable within PaaS.

PaaS should provide functionality to allow customers to implement intrusion or anomaly detection and should permit the customers to send select events or alerts to the cloud provider's security monitoring platform. PaaS should provide encryption in the application, between client and application, in the database and proxies, as well as any application programming interface (API) that deals with the hosted data. PaaS providers generally permit their customers to perform vulnerability assessments and penetration tests on their systems.

Restricting Network Access Through Security Groups

Segregation through security groups is illustrated in Figure 4.3.

By isolating the network into physically separate parts, the cloud provider can limit traffic between public subnets and infrastructure control subnets. The network can be isolated up to a degree by utilizing network virtualization, but this can suffer from vulnerabilities and misconfiguration. Physical separation is also open to error, but this problem can be minimized by the use of process controls. Network isolation can be achieved by having physically separate networks for administrative and operational traffic, for security and network operations traffic, for storage networks, and for publicly accessible components.

Firewalls are traditionally used for network separation, and when used together with network controls, a firewall can become an extra supporting layer. This is particularly helpful when multiple subnets profit from a shared service, such as a directory.

In a PaaS environment, security groups (SGs) can act as a firewall, allowing the customer to choose which protocols and ports are open to computers over the Internet. In Amazon EC2, a security group is a set of ACCEPT firewall rules for *incoming* transmission control protocol (TCP), user datagram protocol (UDP), or internet control message protocol (ICMP). When an instance is launched with a given SG, firewall rules from this group are activated for this instance in EC2's internal distributed firewall [4].

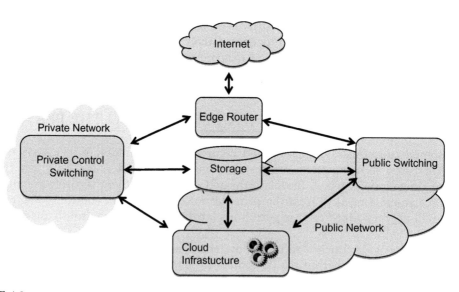

FIGURE 4.3   Segregation through security groups.

Configuring Platform-Specific User Access Control

The cloud service provider is responsible for handling access to the network, servers, and application platforms in the PaaS model. On the other hand, the customer is responsible for access control of the applications they deploy. Application access control includes user access management, such as user provisioning and authentication. Amazon identity and access management let customers define users and their access levels, entity roles, and permissions, and provides access to federated users within the customer's existing enterprise systems. An example of user access control in PaaS is shown in Figure 4.4.

Integrating with Cloud Authentication and Authorization Systems

User access control support is not uniform across cloud providers, and offered features may differ. A PaaS provider may provide a standard API like OAuth (an open standard for authorization) to manage authentication and access control to applications. Google supports a hybrid version of an OpenID (an open, decentralized standard for user authentication and access control) and OAuth protocol that combines the authorization and authentication flow in fewer steps to enhance usability. The customer could also delegate authentication to the customer's identity provider if the cloud provider supports federation standards, such as SAML. Microsoft announced the "Geneva" Claims-Based Access Platform that is compliant with SAML 2.0 standards. The platform's objective is to help developers delegate authentication, authorization, and personalization so that they don't have to implement these futures themselves.

Compartmentalizing Access to Protect Data Confidentiality

When data is stored with a PaaS provider, the provider assumes partial responsibility as the data custodian. Although the responsibilities for data ownership and data custodianship are segregated, the data owner is still accountable for ensuring that data is suitably

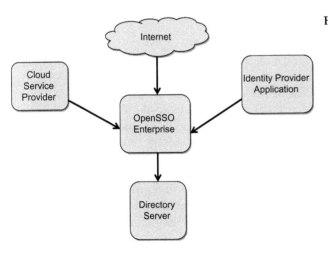

FIGURE 4.4 User access control in PaaS.

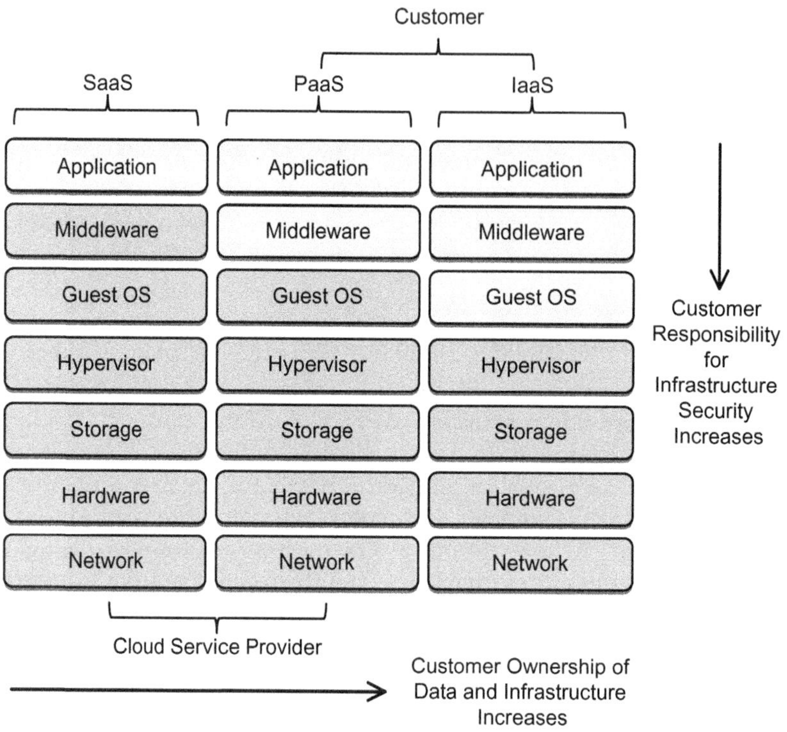

FIGURE 4.5 Ownership in different service models.

safeguarded by the custodian, as seen in Figure 4.5. In a PaaS environment, compartmentalizing access provides data confidentiality since users are prevented from being able to access certain information because they do not need access to it to perform their job functions and they have not been given formal approval to access this data (least privilege design).

Securing Data in Motion and Data at Rest

Data at rest denotes data stored in computer systems, including files on an employee's laptop, company files on a server, or copies of these files on an off-site tape backup. Securing data at rest in a cloud is not drastically different than securing it outside a cloud environment. A customer deploying in a PaaS environment needs to find the risk level acceptable and to make sure that the cloud provider is the primary custodian of the data.

Data in motion indicates data that is transitioning from storage, such as a file or database entry, to another storage format in the same or to a different system. Data in motion can also include data that is not permanently stored. Because data in motion only exists in transition (e.g., computer memory, between end points), its integrity and confidentiality must be ensured. The risk of third party observation of the data in motion exists. Data may be cached on intermediate systems, or temporary files may be created at either endpoint. The best method to protect data in in motion is to apply encryption.

Identifying Your Security Perimeter

With the acceptance of cloud services, an organization's security perimeter has evolved to become more dynamic and has moved beyond the control of the traditional IT department. Cloud computing has extended an organization's network, system, and application realms into the cloud service provider's domain.

The Jericho Forum, an open-group consortium of IT security officers, has addressed deperimeterization. In the view of the Jericho Forum, it is essential to pinpoint the components that are critical to the customer's operation and to ensure that those are sufficiently secured, regardless of the source of the threat. In a completely deperimeterized environment, every component will be sufficiently secured to ensure that confidentiality, integrity, and availability of the data are maintained.

Techniques for Recovering Critical Data

A PaaS customer should review the available options for backup and recovery of their critical data and understand the different options available to secure the data transfer in case of an emergency. The customer should also ensure that backups and other copies of logs, access records, and any other pertinent information that may be required for legal and compliance reasons can be migrated. Data validation should be an automated or user-initiated validation protocol that allows the customer to check its data at any time to ensure the data's integrity. The cloud provider should implement fast SLA-based data recovery. The SLA should be negotiated upfront, and the customer should pay for the SLA required to ensure that there is no conflict of interest. No data, no file, or no system disk, should take more than 30 minutes to recover. PaaS providers can offer one or more of the following options:

- Basic backup and restore
- Pilot light
- Warm standby
- Multisite

BASIC BACKUP AND RESTORE

PaaS providers can offer storage space on their own platform where the transfer of data is performed over the network. The storage service enables snapshots of the data to be transparently copied into the storage systems. Some providers permit the transfer of large data sets by shipping the storage devices directly.

PILOT LIGHT

The notion of the pilot light is an analogy that originates from the gas heater. In a gas heater, a small flame that is always burning can rapidly kindle the entire heater to warm up a house when desired. This situation is comparable to a backup and restore scenario; nevertheless, the customer must make sure that the critical core components of the system are already configured and running in a PaaS environment (the pilot light). When it's time for recovery, the customer would quickly provision a full-scale production environment based on the critical core components. The pilot light method will provide the customer with a shorter recovery time than the backup and restore option, because the core components of the system already exist, are running, and are continuously updated. There remains some installation and configuration tasks that need to be performed by the customer to fully recover the applications. The PaaS environment allows customers to automate the provisioning and configuration of the resources, which can save time and minimize human errors.

WARM STANDBY

The warm standby option extends the pilot light components and preparation. The recovery time decreases further because some services are always operating. After identifying the business-critical components, the customer would duplicate these systems in the PaaS environment and configure them to be always running. This solution is not configured to handle a maximum production load, but it provides all of the available functions. This option may be utilized for testing, quality assurance, and internal use. In case of a catastrophe, additional resources are rapidly added to handle the production load.

MULTISITE

The multisite option exists in the PaaS environment as well as on the customer's on-site infrastructure where both are running. The recovery point selected will determine the data replication method that the customer employs. Various replication methods exist, such as synchronous or asynchronous. A Domain Naming Service (DNS) load balancing service can be used to direct production traffic to the backup and production sites. Part of the traffic will go to the infrastructure in PaaS, and the rest will go to the on-site infrastructure. In case of a catastrophe, the customer can adjust the DNS configuration and send all traffic to the PaaS environment. The capacity of the PaaS service can be rapidly increased to handle the full production load. PaaS resource bursting can be used to automate this process if available from the provider. The customer may need to deploy application logic to detect the failure of the primary site and divert the traffic to the parallel site running in PaaS. The cost of this option is determined by resource consumption.

4. INFRASTRUCTURE AS A SERVICE (IAAS)

Unlike PaaS and SaaS, IaaS customers are primarily responsible for securing the hosts provisioned in the cloud.

Locking Down Cloud Servers

Unlike PaaS and SaaS, IaaS customers are accountable for securing the systems provisioned in the cloud environment. Knowing that most IaaS services available today implement virtualization at the host level, host security in IaaS could be classified as follows.

Virtualization Software Security

Virtualization software is the software that exists on top of hardware and provides customers the capability to create and delete virtual instances. Virtualization at the host level can be achieved by utilizing virtualization models, such as paravirtualization (specialized host-operating system, hardware and hypervisor), operating system-level virtualization (FreeBSD jails, Solaris Containers, Linux-VServer), or hardware-based virtualization (VMware, Xen). In a public IaaS environment, customers cannot access the hypervisor because it is administered solely by the cloud services provider. Cloud services providers should implement the essential security controls, including limiting physical and logical access to the hypervisor and the other virtualization layers. IaaS customers need to comprehend the technology and access controls implemented by the cloud services provider to guard the hypervisor. This will aid the customer to recognize the compliance needs and gaps in relation to the host security standards, policies, and regulations. To show the weakness of the virtualization layer, during Black Hat 2008 and Black Hat DC 2009 Joanna Rutkowska, Alexander Tereshkin, and Rafal Wojtczuk from Invisible Things Lab showed various methods to compromise the Xen hypervisor's virtualization, including the "Blue Pill" attack.

Customer Guest Operating System (OS) or Virtual Instance Security

The virtual incarnation of an operating system is created over the virtualization layer, and it is usually configured to be exposed to the Internet. Customers have complete access to their virtual machines. Public IaaS systems can be exposed to security threats, such as the theft of keys used to access hosts (e.g., SSH private keys), the attack of exposed vulnerable services (e.g., FTP, NetBIOS, SSH), the hijacking of insecure accounts (i.e., weak or no passwords), and the deployment of malware as software or embedded in the operating system.

Ensuring the Cloud is Configured According to Best Practices

Cloud computing is still subject to conventional security best practices, but cloud services providers and their customers may find it difficult to adopt these practices since they are not tailored to the cloud space. The security best practices for cloud computing has been maturing rapidly through the contribution of the players involved in cloud computing, such as hardware manufacturers, software providers, cloud providers, and customers. The key best practices are as follows and can be seen in Figure 4.6:

- Policy
- Risk management
- Configuration management and change control
- Auditing
- Vulnerability scanning
- Segregation of duties
- Security monitoring

Policy

It is a best practice for cloud services providers and their customers to define a solid policy for cloud security. This policy should include all security-related aspects of information security, including staff, information, infrastructure, hardware, and software.

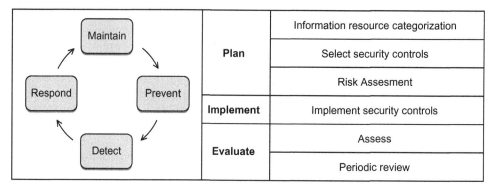

		Information resource categorization
	Plan	Select security controls
		Risk Assesment
	Implement	Implement security controls
	Evaluate	Assess
		Periodic review

FIGURE 4.6   Cloud computing key best practices.

Policies are crucial to provide organizational direction. To succeed, they must be available and visible across the organization, they must have the backing of management, and they must assign responsibilities. Policies should be updated continuously, and they should be accompanied by the use of standards, procedures, and guidelines that enable the implementation of policy.

Risk Management

The goals of risk management best practices are to assess, address, and mitigate security risks in a cloud environment. This should be done in the context of determining the risks from a business standpoint. Choosing security controls and monitoring their efficacy are part of risk management. Basically, a best practice for risk management is to begin with an understanding and assessment of the risks one faces (risk analysis) and orient the selection of security controls along with appropriate security practices and procedures toward managing risks.

Configuration Management and Change Control

It is a best practice to have a configuration and change management process that can govern proposed changes. This would also include identifying possible security consequences, and providing assurance that the current operational system is correct in version and configuration.

Auditing

In auditing, the customer should seek to verify compliance, review the efficacy of controls, and validate security processes. The customer should follow a schedule in auditing, regularly evaluate security controls, use automated and manual processes to validate compliance to a policy, regularly use third-party vulnerability assessment services, and manually examine system logs to validate the effectiveness of the security monitoring systems.

Vulnerability Scanning

It is a best practice to perform periodic cloud infrastructure vulnerability scanning. This should encompass all cloud management systems, servers, and network devices.

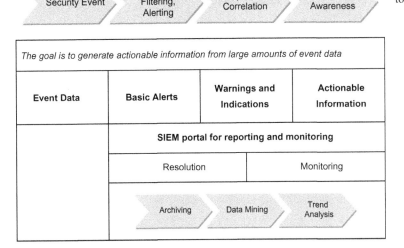

FIGURE 4.7 Security monitoring life cycle.

The purpose of vulnerability scanning is to locate any new or existing vulnerability so that the related risk may be reduced or eliminated.

Segregation of Duties

It is a best practice to limit the user's privileges to the level necessary for them to perform their duties. This comes from the idea of separation of duties, which in turn originates from the principle of least privilege.

Security Monitoring

It is a best practice to automate the collection of security logs from all network devices, servers, and applications. These logs should be kept in their original formats in order to preserve a legal record of all activity and so that they can be queried in an event of an alert. The purposes of security monitoring are to detect threats, expose bugs, keep a legal record of activity, and enable forensics. The most likely sources of security events are operating system logs (event logs and syslogs), application logs, intrusion detection and prevention logs, anti-virus logs, netflow logs, network device logs, and storage equipment logs. These security events are aggregated in streams and redirected via the network to a central collection service, usually a Security Information and Event Management (SIEM) system. Once these events are collected, they should be subject to an ongoing correlation and analysis process, usually performed by a Security Operation Center (SOC). The events get escalated as they are evaluated and assigned alert levels and priorities. The security monitoring life cycle is shown in Figure 4.7.

Confirming Safeguards have been Implemented

Once the IaaS environment has been implemented, it should undergo a continuous evaluation in the form of change management and periodic evaluation in the form of control review. The outcome of these evaluations would be to remedy the issues and to continue the evaluation the process. The following can be used as a generalized checklist to evaluate the IaaS environment:

- Foundations of Security
  - Policies, standards, and guidelines
  - Transparency
  - Employee security
  - External providers
- Business Concerns
  - Business continuity
  - Disaster recovery
  - Legal considerations
  - Resource planning
- Layers of Defense
  - Software assurance
  - Authentication
  - Key management
  - Cryptography
  - Network security
  - Hypervisor and virtual machine security
  - Identity and access management
- Operational Security
  - Operational practices
  - Incident response management
  - Data center: Physical security, power and networking, asset management

Networking

The primary factor in determining whether to use private, public, or hybrid cloud deployments is the risk level an organization can tolerate. Although various IaaS providers implement virtual network zoning, they may not be the same as an internal private cloud that employs stateful inspection and other network security services. If customers have the budget to afford the services of a private cloud, their risks will decline, given they have a private cloud that is internal to their network. In some instances, a private cloud located at a cloud provider's facility can help satisfy security requirements, but will be dependent on the provider's capabilities and maturity. Confidentiality risk can be reduced by using encryption for data in transit. Secure digital signatures can make it more difficult for malicious players to tamper with data and therefore, ensure the integrity of data. The cloud service provider should provide the following information to the customer:

- Data and access control threats
- Access and authentication controls
- Information about security gateways (firewalls, Web application firewalls, service-oriented architecture, and application programming interface)

- Secure services like DNSSEC, NTP, OAuth, SNMP, and management network segmentation
- Traffic and network flow monitoring capabilities
- Hypervisor integration availability
- Security products (IDS/IPS, Server Tier Firewall, File Integrity Monitoring, DLP, Anti-Virus, Anti-Spam)
- Security monitoring and incident response capabilities
- Denial-of-service (DoS) protection and mitigation capabilities

Operating Systems

The ease of self-provisioning new virtual instances on an IaaS platform creates a possibility that insecure virtual servers may be created. Secure-by-default configuration should be implemented by default by mirroring or surpassing industry best practices. Securing a virtual instance in the cloud requires solid operational security procedures supported by automation of procedures. The following steps can be used to evaluate host and virtual machine (VM) security:

- Use a hardened system configuration. A best practice for cloud applications is to build hardened virtual machine images that have only the configuration sufficient to support the application stack. Limiting the abilities of the basic application stack not only limits the server's attack surface, but also greatly decreases the number of updates needed to maintain a secure application stack.
- Keep track of the available virtual machine images and operating system versions that are offered for cloud hosting. The IaaS provider offers some of these VM images through their infrastructure. If a virtual machine image from the IaaS provider is utilized, it should go through the same security verification and hardening process for systems within the enterprise infrastructure. The best substitute for the customer is to build its image that matches the security standards of the internal trusted systems.
- Maintain the integrity of the hardened image.
- Secure the private keys required to access hosts in the cloud.
- Separate the cryptographic keys from the cloud where the data is hosted. The exception to this would be when the keys are necessary for decryption, and this would be limited to the duration of the decryption activity. If the application needs a key to continuously encrypt and decrypt, it may not be feasible to protect the key since it will be hosted with the application.
- Do not place credentials in the virtual machine images except for a key to decrypt the file system.
- Do not permit password-based authentication for remote access.
- Require passwords to execute administrative functions.
- Install a host firewall and open to the public only the minimum ports necessary to support the services.
- Run only the needed services, and turn off the unused services (e.g., turn off FTP, print services, network file services, and database services if they are not required).
- Install a host-based intrusion detection system (IDS).

- Log system and event logs to a dedicated log aggregator. Isolate the log server with strong access controls.
- Ensure a system to provide patching images in the cloud; both online and offline is available.
- Ensure that isolation between different customers (network and data) is provided.

Applications

The integrity and security of a cloud environment is dependent on the integrity of its components. Software is a primary route for vulnerabilities and exploits. IaaS providers, such as Amazon EC2 and Terremark, handle the applications on customer virtual machines as black boxes. This makes the providers completely independent of the operations and management of the customer's applications. Therefore, customers bear the full responsibility for securing their applications deployed in the cloud.

Web applications installed on a public cloud should be designed with an Internet facing threat model and protected with typical security measures against Web application vulnerabilities, such as those listed in the the Open Web Application Security Project (OWASP) Top 10 Web application security risks. Following common security development practices, they should also be periodically audited for vulnerabilities. Security should be embedded into the software development life cycle. It's the customers' responsibility to keep their applications and runtime platform up to date to protect their systems from a compromise. It is in the customer's best interest to designs and implement applications with the least-privileged access model.

Developers creating applications for IaaS clouds should develop their own mechanisms for authentication and authorization. Similar to traditional identity management implementations, cloud applications should also be designed to use delegated authentication services offered by an enterprise identity provider. If in-house implementations of authentication, authorization, and accounting are not properly designed, they can become a weakness. Cloud customers should avoid using in-house authentication, authorization, and accounting solutions when possible.

Scanning for and Patching Vulnerabilities

Penetration testing and vulnerability assessments of cloud infrastructure should be carried out on a periodic basis. Usually, the customer may not have the specialized skills and expertise to perform these tests; therefore, the customer should work with a third party that is professional and has the necessary skills and certifications. Penetration testing should be geared toward the entire cloud infrastructure and not just individual components. Security is only as good as the weakest link.

A penetration test and vulnerability assessment can uncover multiple vulnerabilities, not all of which can or should be fixed. Newly found vulnerabilities need to be classified by their severity. Generally, a vulnerability that is categorized as critical should be addressed to safeguard the entire cloud. Vulnerabilities categorized as having low and medium severity may be accepted as reasonable risks. Vulnerabilities that are not addressed need to have their residual risk evaluated and then accepted by the customer. If it is found that the same vulnerability exists across all servers with the virtual machine image, then this should be fixed in the golden virtual machine image.

Vulnerability scanning has additional benefits. If one collects scan data against the same targets and stores the scan results in a database, configuration errors and attack trends can be detected by analysis of this data over time. Likewise, use of a database to store scanning results, makes these immediately available to auditors and automated tools for compliance and other security checking.

Controlling and Verifying Configuration Management

The relationship between configuration management and security control procedures is an often-neglected one in commercial implementations of Internet-facing systems. The root cause is typically a process failure in configuration management or change control (CC). A recognition of this problem is found in NIST SP 800−64, Security Considerations in the Information System Development Life Cycle, which states: "Changes to the hardware, software, or firmware of a system can have a significant impact on the security of the system ... changes should be documented, and their potential impact on security should be assessed regularly." Configuration management and change management should be well defined and provide a structured method for causing technical and administrative changes. They should also provide assurances that the information technology resources in operation are correct in their version and configuration. Configuration management and change management are essential to controlling and managing an accurate inventory of components and changes.

Vulnerability assessments can be used to confirm the configuration management data. When issues that have not been previously identified are discovered, more thorough investigation becomes necessary.

Most of the time cloud providers are responsible for the vulnerability, patch, and configuration administration of the infrastructure (hosts, storage, networks, and applications). Cloud providers should assure their customers of their technical vulnerability management program using ISO/IEC 27002 type control and assurance frameworks.

IaaS configuration management and change control focuses on infrastructure managed by the cloud provider, as well as the customer infrastructure interfacing with the IaaS environment. Therefore, the provider should be responsible for systems, networks, hypervisors, employee systems, and storage and management applications owned and operated by the provider and third parties. Instead, IaaS customers are responsible for their virtual servers, image standardization, configuration standardization, configuration management of the customer environment, and network access policies.

5. LEVERAGING PROVIDER-SPECIFIC SECURITY OPTIONS

Due to the elastic model of services delivered via the cloud, customers need only pay for the amount of security they require, such as the number of workstations to be protected or the amount of network traffic monitored, and not for the supporting infra-structure and staffing to support the various security services. A security-focused provider offers greater security expertise than is typically available within an organization. Finally, outsourcing administrative tasks, such as log management, can save time and money, allowing an organization to devote more resources to its core competencies. The security options that are provided by various cloud providers are as follows:

- Network security
- Multifactor authentication
- Identity and access management
- Data loss prevention
- Encryption
- Business continuity and disaster recovery
- Web security
- Email security
- Security assessments
- Intrusion management, detection, and prevention
- Security information and event management

Defining Security Groups to Control Access

The conventional model of network zones and tiers has been supplanted in public clouds with security groups, security domains, or virtual data centers that have logical boundaries between tiers but are less exact and offer less protection than the earlier model. A security group acts as a firewall that controls the traffic allowed into a group of instances. When the customer launches a virtual instance, it can assign the instance to one or more security groups. For each security group, the customer adds rules that govern the allowed inbound traffic to instances in the group. All other inbound traffic is discarded. The customer can modify rules for a security group at any time. The new rules are auto-matically enforced for all existing and future instances in the group. The default security group usually allows no inbound traffic and permits all outbound traffic. A virtual instance can have as many security groups as needed.

Filtering Traffic by Port Number

Each security group rule enables a specific source to access the instances in the group using a certain protocol (TCP, UDP, ICMP) and destination port or ports. For example, a rule could allow a source IP address 1.1.1.1 to access the instances in the group on TCP port 80 (the protocol and destination port).

Discovering and Benefiting from the Provider's Built-in Security

Some IaaS providers have the mentioned security options built into their systems. Amazon EC2 provides its customers with identity and access management (IAM) policies and security groups (SGs). Other providers such as Terremark have multifactor authentication built into their Enterprise Cloud solutions besides IAM and SG. These built-in features decrease the time needed to launch a secure environment and reduce the cost further.

Protecting Archived Data

The same three information security principles are associated with data stored in the cloud as with data stored elsewhere: confidentiality, integrity, and availability.

Confidentiality

Confidentiality is usually provided by encrypting customer data. Data can be at the volume storage level or object storage level.

Volume storage encryption prevents snapshot cloning or exposure, exploration by the cloud provider, and exposure due to physical loss of drives. IaaS volumes can be encrypted using instance-managed encryption (instance managed, keys stored in volume and protected by a secret or key pair), externally managed encryption (instance managed, keys are managed externally, provided on request), or proxy encryption (external software or appliance managed).

Object or file storage encryption allows the user to implement virtual private storage (VPS). Like a virtual private network, VPS allows the use of a public shared infrastructure while still protecting data, since only those with encryption keys can read the data. The objects can be encrypted by standard tools, by the application using the data, or by a proxy before being placed in storage.

IaaS providers can also offer IAM policies and access control lists (ACLs) to further protect stored data. The transfer of data is also protected by provider-implemented SSL or VPN connections.

Integrity

Besides the confidentiality of data, the customer also needs to consider the integrity of their data. Confidentiality does not mean integrity. Data can be encrypted for confidentiality reasons, but the customer might not have a method to validate the integrity of that data. IaaS providers should regularly check for integrity by keeping track of data checksums and repair data if corruptions are detected by using redundant data. Data in transfer should also be checksum validated to detect corruption.

Availability

Supposing that customers' data has preserved its confidentiality and integrity, the customers should also be worried about the availability of their data. They should be concerned about three main threats: network-based attacks; the cloud service provider's own availability; and backups or redundancy. Availability is usually stated in the SLA, and customers pay for varying levels of availability based on their risk tolerances. IaaS providers may provide redundant storage (geographic and systemic), versioning, and high-bandwidth connectivity to prevent problems arising from availability issues.

6. ACHIEVING SECURITY IN A PRIVATE CLOUD

In private clouds, computing and storage infrastructure are dedicated to a single organization and are not shared with any other organization. However, just because they are private does not mean that they are more secure.

Taking Full Responsibility for Security

The security management and day-to-day operation of the environment are relegated to internal IT or to a third party with contractual SLAs. The risks faced by internal IT departments still remain. Private cloud security should be considered from different perspectives:

- *Infrastructure security:* This perspective includes physical access and data leakage concerns (loss of hard drives), energy supply security, facility security, network security, hardware security (hardware cryptography modules, trusted protection modules), compute security (process, memory isolation), storage security, operation system security, virtualization security, and update security (hypervisor, virtual machines).
- *Platform security:* This perspective includes user experience security, application framework security, data security, development environment security, and update security.
- *Software security:* This perspective includes application security (multi-tenant partitioning, and user permissions) and update security.
- *Service delivery security:* This perspective includes connection security (SSL, authentication), and service endpoint security (traditional network security).
- *User security:* This perspective includes making sure that the users and the systems they are using to access the private cloud are trusted and secured.
- *Legal concerns:* This perspective includes governance issues, compliance issues (PCI DSS, HIPPA), data protection (personally identifiable information), and legal agreements (SLA, terms of use, user license agreements).

The advantages of a private cloud in the context of security become apparent mostly when compared to a public cloud implementation.

Managing the Risks of Public Clouds

Although a public cloud deployment is suitable for most uses that are nonsensitive, migrating sensitive, mission-critical, or proprietary data into any cloud environment that is not certified and designed for handling such data introduces high risk. A customer should first select a cloud deployment model and then make sure that sufficient security controls are in place. These actions should be followed by a reasonable risk assessment:

- *Data and encryption*: If the data is stored unencrypted in the cloud, data privacy is at risk. There is the risk for unauthorized access either by a malicious employee on the cloud service provider side or an intruder gaining access to the infrastructure from the outside.
- *Data retention*: When the data is migrated or removed by the cloud provider or customer, there may be data residues that might expose sensitive data to unauthorized parties.

- *Compliance requirements*: Various countries have varying regulations for data privacy. Because some public cloud providers don't offer information about the location of the data, it is crucial to consider the legal and regulatory requirements about where data can be stored.
- *Multi-tenancy risks*: The shared nature of public cloud environments increases security risks, such as unauthorized viewing of data by other customers using the same hardware platform. A shared environment also presents resource competition problems whenever one of the customers uses most of the resources due either to need or to being exposed to targeted attacks, such as DDoS (distributed denial of service).
- *Control and visibility*: Customers have restricted control and visibility over the cloud resources because the cloud provider is responsible for administering the infrastructure. This introduces additional security concerns that originate from the lack of transparency. Customers need to rethink the way they operate as they surrender the control of their IT infrastructure to an external party while utilizing public cloud services.
- *Security responsibility*: In a cloud the vendor and the user share responsibility forsecuring the environment. The amount of responsibility shouldered by each party can change depending on the cloud model adopted.

Identifying and Assigning Security Tasks in Each SPI Service Model: SaaS, PaaS, IaaS

Security-related tasks tend to be the highest for the cloud provider in an SaaS environment, whereas an IaaS environment shifts most of the tasks to the customer.

- SaaS
  - *Attack types:* Elevation of privilege, cross-site scripting attack (XSS), cross-site request forgery (CSRF), SQL injection, encryption, open redirect, buffer overflows, connection polling, canonicalization attacks, brute force attacks, dictionary attacks, token stealing.
  - *Provider security responsibilities:* Identity and access management, data protection, security monitoring, security management, authentication, authorization, role-based access control, auditing, intrusion detection, incident response, forensics.
  - *Consumer security responsibilities:* Other than assessing the risk of being in a cloud environment, the customer has little to do in SaaS environment.
- PaaS
  - *Attack types:* Data tampering, buffer overflows, canonicalization attacks, Structured Query Language (SQL) injection, encryption, disclosure of confidential data, elevation of privilege, side-channel attacks (VM-to-VM).
  - *Provider security responsibilities:* Security monitoring, security management, authentication, authorization, role-based access control, auditing, intrusion detection, incident response, forensics.
  - *Customer security responsibilities:* Identity and access management, data protection.
- IaaS
  - *Attack types:* Data tampering, side-channel attacks (VM-to-VM , VM-to-host or host-to-VM), encryption, network traffic sniffing, physical access, brute force attacks, dictionary attacks.

- *Provider security responsibilities:* Role-based access control, auditing, intrusion detection, incident response, forensics.
- *Customer security responsibilities:* Identity and access management, data protection, security monitoring, security management, authentication, authorization.

Selecting the Appropriate Product

While evaluating cloud computing products, customers usually want to know about how secure the implementation is, if the cloud provider is meeting best practices for security, how well the cloud provider is meeting discrete controls and requirements, and how the product compares with other similar services.

Comparing Product-Specific Security Features

To be able to compare cloud providers, we need to define a set of metrics and standards. Based on the previous discussions of risk and cloud security coverage, we can use the following set:

- *Organizational security:* Staff security, third-party management, SLAs
- *Physical security:* Physical access controls; access to secure areas, environmental controls
- *Identity and access management:* Key management, authorization, authentication
- *Encryption:* Connection encryption (SSL, VPN), stored data encryption
- *Asset management and security:* Asset inventory, classification, destruction of used media
- *Business continuity (BC) and disaster recovery (DR) management:* Recovery point objective and recovery time objective information, information security during DR and BC, recovery priority, dependencies
- *Incident management:* Existence of a formal process, detection capabilities, real-time security monitoring, escalation procedures, statistics
- *Legal concerns and privacy:* Audits, certifications, location of data, jurisdiction, subcontracting, outsourcing, data processing, privacy, intellectual property

The vendors that provide the highest transparency into their services will have higher coverage of metrics and a possibly higher score than the vendor with less documentation. Some vendors will lack the specific feature or will not document it properly and therefore, will not have a score for the specific metric.

Considering Organizational Implementation Requirements

Besides comparing the cloud provider's products, the customers also need to be well aware of their organization's security requirements and how they align with the cloud provider's offerings. The customers should check for the following organizational requirements to see if they apply:

- Data
  - Separation of sensitive and nonsensitive data: Segregate sensitive data from nonsensitive data into separate databases in separate security groups when hosting an application that handles highly sensitive data.

- Encryption of non-root file systems: Use only encrypted file systems for block devices and non-root local devices.
- Encryption of file system key: Pass the file system key encrypted at start-up.
- Signing of content in storage.
- Secure handling of decryption keys and forced removal after use: Decryption keys should be in the cloud only for the duration of use.
- Applications
  - No dependence on a specific virtual machine system (operating system or other cloud services).
  - Source address filtering of network traffic: Only allow needed traffic, such as HTTP and HTTPS.
  - Encryption of network traffic.
  - Strong authentication of network-based access: Authentication should preferably be performed using keys by performing mutual authentication.
  - Use of host-based firewall.
  - Installation of a network-based intrusion detection system (NIDS).
  - Installation of a host-based intrusion detection system (HIDS).
  - Usage of hardening tools: Usage of hardening tools, such as Bastille Linux, and SELinux should be possible.
  - System design for patch roll-out: System should be designed to easily patch and relaunch instances.
  - Support of SAML or other identity and access management systems.
- Other
  - Compliance support: Presence of SAS 70 Type II, PCI DSS, and other compliance certifications.
  - Regular full backups stored in remote secure locations.
  - Instance snapshots in case of a security breach.
  - Role segregation: The infrastructure should be segmented based on roles (development, production).
  - Regular verification of cloud resources configuration: This is especially important since cloud resources can be managed via different channels (Web console and APIs). Thus, if, for example, the Web console access has been hacked, this might not be immediately visible to the customer if normally management is only done via APIs. Therefore, some type of intrusion detection for the cloud resource management is needed.
  - No credentials in end-user devices.
  - Secure storage and generation of credentials.
  - Security groups: Security groups (i.e., named set of firewall rules) should be used to configure IP traffic to and from instances completely in order to isolate every tier, even internally to the cloud.

Virtual Private Cloud (VPC)

VPC can offer public cloud users the privacy of a private cloud environment. In a VPC, while the infrastructure remains public, the cloud provider lets the customers define a virtual network by letting them select their own subnets, IP address ranges, route tables, and network gateways. Optionally virtual private networks (VPNs) are provided to further secure the virtual networks. Stored data can also be protected by assigning ACLs.

Simulating a Private Cloud in a Public Environment

VPCs utilize VPNs to secure communication channels by creating protected, virtually dedicated conduits within the cloud provider network. This eradicates the necessity to specify intricate firewall rules between the application in the cloud and the enterprise, because all locations would be linked by a private network isolated from the public Internet. VPNs form the construct of a private network and address space used by all VPN endpoints. Because VPNs can use specific IP addresses, the cloud provider can permit customers to utilize any IP address ranges without conflicting with other cloud customers. A VPC can contain many cloud data centers, but it appears as a single collection of resources to the customer.

Google Secure Data Connector (SDC)

SDC provides data connectivity and allows IT administrators to control the services and data that are available in Google Apps (Web-based office suite). SDC builds a secure link by encrypting connections between Google Apps and customer networks. Google Apps is the only external service that can make requests over the secured connection. SDC can filter the types of requests that can be routed. The filters can limit which gadgets, spreadsheets, and App Engine applications may access which internal systems. Filters can also be used to limit user access to resources. SDC implements OAuth Signed Fetch that adds authentication information to requests that are made through SDC. The customer can use OAuth to validate requests from Google and provide an additional layer of security to the SDC filters.

Amazon VPC

Amazon VPC lets their customers cut out a private section of their public cloud where they can launch services in a virtual network. Using the Amazon VPC, the customer can delineate a virtual network topology that is similar to a traditional network where the customer can specify its own private IP address range, segregate the IP address range into private and public subnets, administer inbound and outbound access using network access control lists, store data in the Amazon S3 storage service and set access permissions, attach multiple virtual network interfaces, and bridge the VPC with on-site IT infrastructure with a VPN to extend existing security and management policies.

Industry-Standard, VPN-Encrypted Connections

A customer might simply want to extend its organization's perimeter into the external cloud computing environment by using a site-to-site VPN and operating the cloud environment making use of its own directory services to control access. Companies such as Terremark and Rackspace offer site-to-site VPN solutions to extend the existing IT infrastructure into their clouds so that customers can securely use solutions deployed in the cloud (e.g., collaboration solutions, testing and development, data replication, DR).

The Hybrid Cloud Alternative

A hybrid cloud can be created by combining any of the three cloud types: public, private, and virtual private. Hybrid clouds are formed when an organization builds a private cloud and wants to leverage its public and virtual private clouds in conjunction with its private cloud for a particular purpose. An example of a hybrid cloud would be a Web site where its core infrastructure is only accessible by the company, but specific components of the Web site are hosted externally, such as high-bandwidth media (video streaming or image caching). Nevertheless, some requirements can thwart hybrid cloud acceptance. For example, financial services companies, such as banks, might not be able to comply with regulations if customer data is hosted at a third-party site or location, regardless of the security controls. Governments also might not be able to take the risk of being compromised in case of a hybrid cloud breach.

Connecting On-Premises Data with Cloud Applications

Data transferred to the cloud should be encrypted both when on the cloud and during transfer (e.g., with SSL, VPN). The employed encryption service should provide well-thought-out encryption key management policies to guarantee data integrity. Also, the customer should retain encryption key ownership to maintain separation of duties between their business and the other cloud service providers. This permits the customers to use their encryption throughout their private and public clouds and therefore, lets them avoid vendor lock-in and to move between cloud providers.

Securely Bridging with VPC

As the name suggests, a VPC does not deliver a fully private infrastructure, but a virtually private infrastructure. Servers created in the customer's VPC are allocated from the same shared resources that are used by all other provider customers. Hence, the customer still has to consider extra security measures in the cloud, both for networking (interserver traffic) and data in shared storage.

To be able to securely bridge existing infrastructure with VPCs, the customer would need to employ tools such as CloudSwitch or Vyatta. These tools provide data isolation for the data circulating between the in-house data center and the VPCs using data encryption and therefore, applying an additional layer of security. For example, CloudSwitch isolates all network and storage access to data at the device level with AES-256 encryption. It also utilizes roles and permissions-based access to enforce corporate policies.

Dynamically Expanding Capacity to Meet Business Surges

Cloudbursting is the dynamic arrangement of an application operating on a private cloud to use public clouds to meet sudden, unforeseen demand, such as a tax services company's need to meet increasing traffic associated with tax-filing deadlines. The benefit of this type of hybrid cloud usage is that the customer only pays for the additional computing resources when they are in demand. To utilize cloudbursting, a customer would need to address workload migration (ability to clone the application environment with tools such as Chef, Puppet, CFEngine, Cloudify), data synchronization (maintaining real-time data copies), and network connectivity.

7. MEETING COMPLIANCE REQUIREMENTS

Cloud providers recognize the difficulty of meeting a wide range of customer requirements. To build a model that can scale, the cloud provider needs to have solid set of controls that can benefit all of its customers. To achieve this goal, the cloud provider can use the model of governance, risk, and compliance (GRC). GRC acknowledges that compliance is an ongoing activity requiring a formal written compliance program. The cloud provider should undergo a continuous cycle of risk assessment, identifying the key controls, monitoring, and testing to identify gaps in controls (Security Content Automation Protocol or SCAP, Cybersecurity Information Exchange Framework or CYBEX, GRC-XML), reporting, and improving on the reported issues. The cycle of compliance evaluation is shown in Figure 4.8.

Managing Cloud Governance

Governance is the set of processes, technologies, customs, policies, laws, and institutions affecting the way an enterprise is directed, administered, or controlled. Governance also comprises the relationship betwen the stakeholders and the goals of the company. Governance includes auditing supply chains, board and management structure and process, corporate responsibility and compliance, financial transparency and information disclosure, and ownership structure and exercise of control rights. A key factor in a customer's decision to engage a corporation is the confidence that expectations will be met. For cloud services, the interdependencies of services should not hinder the customer from clearly identifying the responsible parties. Stakeholders should carefully consider the monitoring mechanisms that are appropriate and necessary for the company's consistent performance and growth.

Customers should review the specific information security governance structure and processes, as well as specific security controls, as part of their due diligence for future cloud providers. The provider's security governance processes and capabilities should be evaluated to see if they are consistent with the customer's information security management processes. The cloud provider's information security controls should be risk-based and clearly support the customer's management processes. The loss of control and governance could cause noncompliance with the security requirements, a lack of confidentiality, integrity and availability of data, and a worsening of performance and quality of service.

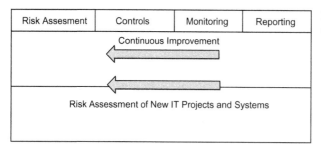

FIGURE 4.8 Cycle of compliance evaluation.

Retaining Responsibility for the Accuracy of the Data

Laws and regulations will usually determine who in an organization should be responsible and held accountable for the accuracy and security of the data. If the customer is storing HIPAA (Health Insurance Portability and Accountability Act) data, then the customer must have a security-related post created to ensure compliance. The Sarbanes–Oxley Act assigns the Chief Financial Officer (CFO) and Chief Executive Officer (CEO) joint responsibility for the financial data. The Gramm-Leach-Bliley Act (GLBA) casts a wider net, making the entire board of directors responsible for security. The Federal Trade Commission (FTC) is less specific by only requiring a certain individual to be responsible for information security in a company.

Verifying Integrity in Stored and Transmitted Data

One of the main difficulties in cloud computing is tracking the location of data during processing. Having control over the data's creation, transfer, storage, use, and destruction becomes crucial. Using data-mining tools and solid IT operational practices will be key to managing data. Although host-level security can be tackled, host-to-host communication and its integrity are harder to secure due to the volume and dynamic nature of data in transition. Although traditional security scanners can be used, real-time reporting provides a better assessment. Thus, an IT GRC solution would display a general view of important metrics to provide a summary of site security and reliability. This solution can keep track of version management and integrity verification of backed-up and in-transit data.

Demonstrating Due Care and Due Diligence

Before signing a contract with a cloud provider, a customer should assess its specific requirements. The range of the services, along with any limitations, regulations, or compliance requirements, should be identified. Any services that will be deployed to the cloud should also be graded as to their importance to the business. A customer should consider if cloud computing is a true core business of the provider, if the provider is financially sound, if the provider is outsourcing, if the physical security of the facilities meet customer needs, if the provider's BC and DR plans are consistent with the customer's needs, if the operations team is technically competent, if they have a verifiable track record, and if the provider offers any indemnifications. Performing due diligence will reduce the negotiation time and make sure that the correct level of security is in place for the customer.

Supporting Electronic Discovery

Electronic discovery (e-discovery) refers to discovery in civil litigation of information in an electronic format. Due to the nature of a cloud environment, a customer might not be able to apply or use e-discovery tools regularly used. The customer also might not have the capability or administrative permissions to search or access all of the data existing in the cloud. Therefore, the customer will need to take into consideration the additional time and expense that will result from performing e-discovery in a cloud environment.

The customers must make clear in the contractual agreement what the cloud provider needs to do if they are contacted to provide data to a third party, such as law enforcement.

The customers might want to contest the request due to the confidentiality of the data or due to an unreasonable request.

Preserving a Chain of Evidence

Chain of evidence or chain of custody refers to the chronological documentation showing seizure, custody, control, transfer, analysis, and disposition of evidence. Several issues touch on the responsibilities and limits that affect customers and providers with regard to collecting legally admissible evidence for prosecution. Identifying the actors is difficult enough with an evidence chain where responsibility for collecting data is shared between the provider and tenant. One party may be the custodian of the data, while the other is the legal owner. Maintaining a chain of evidence can be difficult due to the possibility of compromising the privacy of other cloud customers, unsynchronized log times, and data tampering in open environments, such as public clouds.

Assuring Compliance with Government Certification and Accreditation Regulations

Cloud providers face an increasingly complex variety of compliance requirements from their customers, such as industry standards, regulations, and customer frameworks. Relevant audit frameworks should be used when designing the cloud provider's security control set, and periodic external audits should address the most relevant aspects of these controls.

HIPAA

Cloud providers and customers that handle protected health information (PHI) are required to comply with the security and privacy requirements established in support of HIPAA. The HIPAA security and privacy rules focus on health plans, health care clearinghouses, health care providers, and system vendors. HIPAA requires that PHI is sufficiently protected when entrusted to third parties, such as cloud providers. The level of security should be kept up to standard across all environments. HIPAA addresses administrative safeguards, workforce security, information access management, security awareness and training, security incident procedures, contingency plans, evaluations, physical safeguards (facility and user devices), and technical safeguards (access control, audit control and integrity, authentication, and encryption).

Sarbanes—Oxley

As a reaction to substantial financial reporting fraud in the early 2000s, the Sarbanes—Oxley Act of 2002 (SOX) was passed and signed into law. As a result of SOX, public company CFOs and CEOs are required to certify the efficacy of their internal controls over financial reporting (ICOFR) on a quarterly and annual basis. Management is required to do a yearly assessment of its ICOFR. Third-party auditors are required to provide an opinion about the efficacy of the management's ICOFR at the company's fiscal year end. SOX also influenced the creation of the Public Company Accounting Oversight Board (PCAOB), which was tasked with instituting audit standards. PCAOB Auditing Standard No. 2 pointed to the significance of information technology general controls (ITGCs).

SOX emphasizes the efficacy of an organization's financial reporting process, accounting and finance processes, other vital business, and controls over IT systems that have a material influence on financial reporting. SOX includes internally administered and outsourced systems that can substantially affect financial reporting. A customer using a SaaS environment might make the cloud provider relevant to their SOX scope if financial information is processed in the cloud. Cloud providers need to be clear about their own and the customer's responsibilities about processing information and ensure robust processes for user management/segregation of duties, systems development, program and infrastructure change management, and computer operations. Cloud providers also need to be concerned about physical security; stored and in-transit data; passwords; remote access; provider access to data; data disclosure; other customers accessing the data; data location (data centers, replicas, backups); shared resources; loss of governance; and isolation failures.

Data Protection Act

The Data Protection Act of 1998 is a United Kingdom (UK) Act of Parliament. The Act, defines UK law on the processing of data on identifiable living people (see the checklist: An Agenda for Action for Complying with the Data Protection Act Activities).

AN AGENDA FOR ACTION FOR COMPLYING WITH THE DATA PROTECTION ACT ACTIVITIES

All UK businesses holding personal data about third parties (customers) must comply with the Data Protection Act. The act's principles are as follows (check all tasks completed):

_____1. Personal data shall be processed fairly and lawfully and, in particular, shall not be processed unless:

    _____a. at least one of the conditions in Schedule 2 is met, and

    _____b. in the case of sensitive personal data, at least one of the conditions in Schedule 3 is also met.

_____2. Personal data shall be obtained only for one or more specified and lawful purposes, and shall not be further processed in any manner incompatible with that purpose or those purposes.

_____3. Personal data shall be adequate, relevant, and not excessive in relation to the purpose or purposes for which they are processed.

_____4. Personal data shall be accurate and, where necessary, kept up to date.

_____5. Personal data processed for any purpose or purposes shall not be kept longer than is necessary for that purpose or those purposes.

_____6. Personal data shall be processed in
accordance with the rights of data
subjects under this Act.
_____7. Appropriate technical and
organizational measures shall be
taken against unauthorized or
unlawful processing of personal
data and against accidental loss or
destruction of, or damage to,
personal data.

_____8. Personal data shall not be
transferred to a country or territory
outside the European Economic
Area unless that country or
territory ensures an adequate level
of protection for the rights and
freedoms of data subjects in
relation to the processing of
personal data.

PCI DSS

Organizations that deal with credit-card transactions are required to comply with the Payment Card Industry (PCI) Data Security Standard (DSS). The compliance is ensured by third-party assessments and self-assessments, depending on the volume of credit-card processing transactions. PCI DSS contains 12 high-level requirements:

1. Install and maintain a firewall configuration to protect cardholder data.
2. Do not use vendor-supplied defaults for system passwords and other security parameters.
3. Protect stored cardholder data.
4. Encrypt transmission of cardholder data across open, public networks.
5. Use and regularly update antivirus software.
6. Develop and maintain secure systems and applications.
7. Restrict access to cardholder data based on the business's need to know.
8. Assign a unique ID to each person with computer access.
9. Restrict physical access to cardholder data.
10. Track and monitor all access to network resources and cardholder data.
11. Regularly test security systems and processes.
12. Maintain a policy that addresses information security.

Customers processing or storing cardholder data in a cloud provider need to ensure that the cloud provider and other third parties comply with PCI DSS as well. If the cloud provider has services including processing of credit-card transactions, it is crucial that the cloud provider transparently explains its information flows and how it segregates its credit-card processing and storage activities from others. This approach would limit the extent of the infrastructure that would be subject to PCI DSS. The main objectives of PCI DSS are to ensure the protection of cardholder data, avert breaches, and rapidly contain a breach. These objectives are valid for cloud computing environments as well.

Limiting the Geographic Location of Data

Cloud customers need to ensure that the providers employed outside of their country of residence and jurisdiction have sufficient security controls in place, including their primary and backup sites as well as any intermediate sites that the data crosses. The data protection laws of the European Union (EU) states and other countries are complex and have numerous requirements. The EU stipulates that the data controller and processor must notify entities that the data will be sent and processed in a country other than a member state. They must also have contracts approved by the Data Protection Authority before these activities can be performed. The customer also needs to be aware of the cloud provider subcontracting any data-related functionality since the third parties involved might host or transfer data outside of the customer's jurisdiction.

Following Standards for Auditing Information Systems

Due to multi-tenancy and shared environments, it becomes difficult to conduct an audit without the cloud provider breaching the confidentiality of other customers sharing the infrastructure. In such cases, the cloud provider should adopt a compliance program based on standards such as ISO27001 and provide assurance via SysTrust or ISO certification to its customers. Some audit frameworks are as follows:

- *SAS 70*: This framework involves the audit of controls based on control objectives and control activities (defined by the cloud provider). The auditor provides opinion on the design, operational status, and operating effectiveness of controls. SAS 70 intends to cover services that are relevant for purposes of customers' financial statement audits.
- *SysTrust*: This framework involves the audit of controls based on defined principles and criteria for security, availability, confidentiality, and processing integrity. SysTrust applies to the reliability of any system.
- *WebTrust*: This framework involves the audit of controls based on defined principles and criteria for security, availability, confidentiality, processing integrity, and privacy. WebTrust applies to online or e-commerce systems.
- *ISO 27001*: This framework involves the audit of an organization's Information Security Management System (ISMS).

Negotiating Third-party Provider Audits

When customers engage an audit provider, they should involve proper legal, procurement, and contract teams within their organization. The customer should consider specific compliance requirements and when negotiating must agree on how to collect, store, and share compliance evidence (e.g., audit logs, activity reports, system configurations). If the standard terms of services do not address the customer's compliance needs, they will need to be negotiated. Contracts should include the involvement of a third party for the review of SLA metrics and compliance (e.g., by a mutually selected mediator). Customers should prefer auditors with expertise in cloud computing who are familiar with the assurance challenges of cloud computing environments. Customers should request the cloud provider's SSAE 16 SOC2 (Statements on Standards for Attestation Engagements No. 16 Service Organization Control 2) or ISAE 3402 Type 2 (International Standard on Assurance Engagements 3402 Type 2) reports to provide a starting point of reference for auditors. SSAE 16 SOC2 provides a standard benchmark by which two data center audit reports can be compared and the customer can be assured that the same set of criteria was used to evaluate each. An ISAE 3402 Type 2 Report is known as the report on the description, design, and operating effectiveness of controls at a service organization.

8. PREPARING FOR DISASTER RECOVERY

To make sure the availability of cloud services, business continuity, and disaster recovery address a broad set of activities that are performed. Business continuity is based on standards, policies, guidelines, and procedures that facilitate continuous operation regardless of the incidents. Disaster recovery (DR) is a subsection of business continuity and is concerned with data and IT systems.

Implementing a Plan to Sustain Availability

A cloud service provider (CSP) should have a formal disaster recovery plan in place to assure the provider's viability against natural disasters, human errors, and malicious behavior. This plan should be continuously tested to ensure preparedness and should not compromise the security of the cloud in the event of a disaster.

Customers should review their contracts with the cloud provider and third parties to confirm and verify that the disaster recovery controls and certifications are in place. Customers could also conduct on-site assessments if found necessary. The cloud provider should inform the customer in advance about any disaster recovery tests.

Reliably Connecting to the Cloud across the Public Internet

There may be a substantial amount of latency between the customer's processing and the data stored in the cloud. Contingent on the amount of data being handled, this can result in unacceptable performance. If users access the data in the cloud, the latency may also cause an intolerable user experience. Wide area network optimization between the customer and the cloud provider should be in place so that the cloud enables full data mobility at reduced bandwidth, storage utilization, and cost. These performance issues might be managed with a combination of increased bandwidth or by traffic management. An alternative method is to utilize a cloud storage gateway. An issue to contemplate with a cloud storage gateway is the difference between tiering and caching. The gateways that use the caching method use cloud storage as their primary storage location. On the other hand, the gateways that utilize the tiering method use on-site storage as their primary storage and cloud storage as their secondary storage.

Anticipating a Sudden Provider Change or Loss

Some CSPs will unavoidably cease operating, therefore, making access to the data in the cloud an issue. Access to data might also be jeopardized if the provider or third party dealing with data breaches the contract and does not provide the promised services. When this happens, the customer's efforts should be directed toward finding a replacement cloud provider and confidentially removing and transferring the data from the defunct provider. It is important to clearly state the handling of data in case of bankruptcy or breach of contract in the SLA. Confidential data should be removed properly without leaving any trace.

Archiving SaaS Data Locally

Customers should perform regular extractions and backups to a format that is provider agnostic and make sure metadata can be preserved and migrated. It is also important to understand if any custom tools will have to be developed or if the provider will provide the migration tools. For legal and compliance reasons, the customer should ensure that backups and copies of logs, access records, and any other pertinent information are included in the archive as well.

Addressing Data Portability and Interoperability in Preparation for a Change in Cloud Providers

Depending on the application, it is important to integrate with applications that may be present in other clouds or on traditional infrastructure. Interoperability standards either enable or become a barrier to interoperability, and permit maintenance of the integrity and consistency of an organization's information and processes. SLAs should address the steps to change providers from a portability perspective. The customer should have a good understanding of the cloud provider's APIs, hypervisors, application logic, and other restrictions and build processes to migrate to and handle different cloud architectures. Security should be maintained across migrations. Authentication and IAM mechanisms for user or process access to systems now must operate across all components of a cloud system. Using open standards for identity such as SAML will help to ensure portability. Encryption keys should be stored locally. When moving files and their metadata to new cloud environments, the customer should ensure that copies of file metadata are securely removed to prevent this information from remaining behind and opening a possible opportunity for compromise.

Exploiting the Cloud for Efficient Disaster Recovery Options

Besides providing all the advantages discussed in this chapter, cloud computing has brought advantages in the form of online storage. This feature can be leveraged for backup and disaster recovery and can reduce the cost of infrastructure, applications, and overall business processes. Many cloud storage providers guarantee the reliability and availability of their service. The challenges to cloud storage, cloud backup, and DR in particular involve mobility, information transfer, and availability, assuring business continuity, scalability, and metered payment. Cloud disaster recovery solutions are built on the foundation of three fundamentals: a virtualized storage infrastructure, a scalable file system, and a self-service disaster recovery application that responds to customers' urgent business needs. Some vendors that provide cloud storage services are Amazon, Google, Terremark, and Rackspace.

Achieving Cost-effective Recovery Time Objectives

Recovery Time Objective (RTO) is the maximum amount of time that is acceptable for restoring and regaining access to data after a disruption. To keep RTO low, cloud-based DR requires ongoing server replication, making network bandwidth an important consideration when adopting this approach. To keep bandwidth requirements and related costs low, customers need to identify their critical systems and prioritize them in their DR plan.

Focusing on a narrower set of systems will make DR more efficient and more cost effective by keeping complexity and network bandwidth low.

Employing a Strategy of Redundancy to Better Resist DoS

Denial-of-service (DoS), or distributed-denial-of-service (DDoS) attack, is a type of network-based attack that attempts to make computer or network resources unavailable to their intended users. Customers and cloud providers should ensure that their systems have effective security processes and controls in place so that they can withstand DoS attacks. The controls and processes should have the ability to recognize a DoS attack and utilize the provider's local capacity and geographical redundancies to counter the attack's excessive use of network bandwidth (SYN or UDP floods), CPU, memory, and storage resources (application attacks).

Techniques such as cloudbursting can be used to mitigate the unexpected increase in resource consumption. Third-party cloud-based DDoS mitigation services (e.g., Akamai, Verisign) can be used to offload server functionality, defend the application layer, offload infrastructure functions, obfuscate infrastructure, protect DNS services, and failover gracefully when an attack is overwhelming.

9. SUMMARY

We have seen that cloud computing offers a service or deployment model for almost every type of customer and that each flavor comes with its own security concerns. Advantages offered by cloud solutions need to be weighed with the risks they entail. While public clouds are great for commercial customers, federal customers or other customers dealing with sensitive data need to consider private or hybrid cloud solutions. We have also seen the importance of embodying customer security requirements in SLAs to protect interests for compliance, DR, and other concerns. While delegation of resource management and procurement is a great advantage of cloud computing, customers are still accountable for the security and privacy of the deployed systems and data.

Cloud computing is a new technology that is still emerging. The challenges that appear in the realm of security are being addressed by security experts. If an organization plans to move to a cloud environment, it should do so with caution and weigh the risks to be able to enjoy the low-cost flexibility offered by this empowering technology.

Finally, let's move on to the real interactive part of this chapter: review questions/exercises, hands-on projects, case projects, and optional team case project. The answers and/or solutions by chapter can be found in the Online Instructor's Solutions Manual.

CHAPTER REVIEW QUESTIONS/EXERCISES

True/False

1. True or False? SaaS, PaaS, and IaaS are SPI models.
2. True or False? The risk-based approach is recommended for organizations considering the cloud.

3. True or False? The data and resources asset(s) is supported by the cloud.
4. True or False? A customer hosts its own application and data, while hosting a part of the functionality in the cloud. This service model is referred to as SaaS.
5. True or False? A customer's first step in evaluating its risks while considering a cloud deployment would be to select the data or function that's going to be hosted in the cloud.

Multiple Choice

1. In the criteria to evaluate a potential cloud service model or provider, a customer should consider:
   A. Comfort level for moving to the cloud
   B. Level of control at each SPI cloud model
   C. Importance of assets to move to the cloud
   D. Type of assets to move to the cloud
   E. All of the above
2. Which attack type can affect an IaaS environment?
   A. Cross-site-request-forgery attacks
   B. Side-channel attacks (VM-to-VM)
   C. Token stealing
   D. Canonicalization attacks
   E. All of the above
3. What should a cloud customer prefer for DR?
   A. High RTO, low cost
   B. Low RTO, high cost
   C. Low RTO, low cost, all data
   D. Backup critical data with a low RTO and cost
   E. All of the above
4. Which deployment model is suitable for a customer that needs the flexibility and resources of a public cloud, but needs to secure and define its networks?
   A. Hybrid
   B. Private
   C. Secured
   D. Virtual Private
   E. All of the above
5. What does an SLA cover?
   A. Service levels
   B. Security
   C. Governance
   D. Compliance
   E. All of the above

EXERCISE

Problem

Does the cloud solution offer equal or greater data security capabilities than those provided by your organization's data center?

Hands-On Projects

Project

Have you taken into account the vulnerabilities of the cloud solution?

Case Projects

Problem

As a project to build a small cloud environment, how do you set up a VPC environment on the Amazon EC2 platform ?

Optional Team Case Project

Problem

Have you considered that incident detection and response can be more complicated in a cloud-based environment?

References

[1] Guidelines on Security and Privacy in Public Cloud Computing, NIST Special Publication, pp. 800–144.
[2] Cloud Computing: Benefits, Risks and Recommendations for Information Security, The European Network and Information Security Agency, 2009.
[3] Security Guidance for Critical Areas of Focus in Cloud Computing v3.0, Cloud Security Alliance, 2011.
[4] Amazon Virtual Private Cloud. <http://aws.amazon.com/vpc>.

5

Unix and Linux Security

Gerald Beuchelt

The MITRE Corporation[1], Bedford, MA, U.S.A.

When Unix was first booted on a PDP-8 computer at Bell Labs, it already had a basic notion of user isolation, separation of kernel and user memory space, and process security. It was originally conceived as a multiuser system, and as such, security could not be added on as an afterthought. In this respect, Unix was different from a whole class of computing machinery that had been targeted at single-user environments.

Linux is mostly a GNU software-based operating system with a kernel originally written by Linus Torvalds and many of the popular utilities from the GNU Software Foundation and other open source organizations added. GNU/Linux implements the same interfaces as most current Unix systems, including the Portable Operating System Interface (POSIX) standards. As such, Linux is a Unix-style operating system, despite the fact that it was not derived from the original AT&T/Bell Labs Unix code base.

Debian is a distribution originally developed by Ian Murdock of Purdue University. Debian's express goal is to use only open and free software, as defined by its guidelines. Ubuntu is a derivative Linux distribution that is based on the Debian system. It emphasizes ease of use and allows beginning users easy access to a comprehensive Linux distribution.

All versions of MacOS X are built on top of Unix operating systems, namely, the Mach microkernel and the University of California's FreeBSD code. While the graphical user interface and some other system enhancements are proprietary, MacOS has a XNU kernel and includes most of the command-line utilities commonly found in Unix operating systems.

---

1. The opinions and guidance presented here are those of the author and do not necessarily reflect the positions of The MITRE Corporation, its customers or sponsors, or any part of the U.S. federal government.

DOI: http://dx.doi.org/10.1016/B978-0-12-416689-9.00005-8

The examples in this chapter refer to the Solaris, MacOS, and Ubuntu Linux, a distribution by Canonical Inc., built on the popular Debian distribution.

1. UNIX AND SECURITY

As already indicated, Unix was originally created as a multiuser system. Initially, systems were not necessarily networked, but with the integration of the Berkley Software Distribution (BSD) TCP/IP V4 stack in 1984, Unix-based systems quickly became the backbone of the quickly growing Internet. As such, Unix servers started to provide critical services to network users as well.

The Aims of System Security

In general, secure computing systems must guarantee the confidentiality, integrity, and availability of resources. This is achieved through a combination of different security mechanisms and safeguards, including policy-driven access control and process separation.

Authentication

When a user is granted access to resources on a computing system, it is of vital importance to establish and verify the identity of the requesting entity. This process is commonly referred to as *authentication* (sometimes abbreviated *AuthN*).

Authorization

As a multiuser system, Unix must protect resources from unauthorized access. To protect user data from other users and nonusers, the operating system has to put up safeguards against unauthorized access. Determining the eligibility of an authenticated (or anonymous) user to access or modify a resource is usually called *authorization* (*AuthZ*).

Availability

Guarding a system (including all its subsystems, such as the network) against security breaches is vital to keep the system available for its intended use. *Availability* of a system must be properly defined: Any system is physically available, even if it is turned off; however, a shutdown system would not be too useful. In the same way, a system that has only the core operating system running but not the services that are supposed to run on the system is considered not available.

Integrity

Similar to availability, a system that is compromised cannot be considered available for regular service. Ensuring that the Unix system is running in the intended way is most crucial, especially since the system might otherwise be used by a third party for malicious uses, such as a relay or member in a botnet.

Confidentiality

Protecting resources from unauthorized access and safeguarding the content is referred to as confidentiality. As long as it is not compromised, a Unix system will maintain the confidentiality of system user data by enforcing access control policies and separating processes from each other. There are two fundamentally different types of access control: discretionary and mandatory access control. Users themselves manage the discretionary segment, while the system owner sets the mandatory. We will discuss the differences later in this chapter.

2. BASIC UNIX SECURITY OVERVIEW

Unix security has a long tradition, and though many concepts of the earliest Unix systems still apply, there have been a large number of changes that fundamentally altered the way the operating system implements these security principles.

One of the reasons that it's complicated to talk about Unix security is that there are a lot of variants of Unix and Unix-like operating systems on the market. In fact, if you only look at some of the core Portable Operating System Interface (POSIX) standards that have been set forth to guarantee minimal consistency across different Unix flavors (see Figure 5.1), almost every operating system on the market qualifies as Unix (or, more precisely, as POSIX compliant). Examples include not only the traditional Unix operating systems such as Solaris, HP-UX, or AIX but also Windows NT-based operating systems (such as Windows XP, either through the native POSIX subsystem or the Services for Windows extensions) or even z/OS.

Traditional Unix Systems

Most Unix systems do share some internal features, though: Their authentication and authorization approaches are similar, their delineation between kernel space and user space goes along the same lines, and their security-related kernel structures are roughly comparable. In the last few years, however, major advancements have been made in

---

The term POSIX stands (loosely) for "Portable Operating System Interface for uniX". From the IEEE 1003.1 Standard, 2004 Edition:

"This standard defines a standard operating system interface and environment, including a command interpreter (or "shell"), and common utility programs to support applications portability at the source code level. This standard is the single common revision to IEEE Std 1003.1-1996, IEEE Std 1003.2-1992, and the Base Specifications of The Open Group Single UNIX Specification, Version 2." Partial or full POSIX compliance is often required for government contracts.

FIGURE 5.1   Various Unix and POSIX standards.

extending the original security model by adding role-based access control[2] (RBAC) models to some operating systems.

Kernel Space versus User Land

Unix systems typically execute instructions in one of two general contexts: the kernel or the user space. Code executed in a kernel context has (at least in traditional systems) full access to the entire hardware and software capabilities of the computing environment. Although there are some systems that extend security safeguards into the kernel, in most cases, not only can a rogue kernel execution thread cause massive data corruption, but it can effectively bring down the entire operating system.

Obviously, a normal user of an operating system should not wield so much power. To prevent this, user execution threads in Unix systems are not executed in the context of the kernel but in a less privileged context, the user space—sometimes also facetiously called user land. The Unix kernel defines a structure called *process* (see Figure 5.2) that associates metadata about the user as well as, potentially, other environmental factors with the execution thread and its data. Access to computing resources such as memory and I/O subsystems is safeguarded by the kernel; if a user process wants to allocate a segment of memory or access a device, it has to make a system call, passing some of its metadata as parameters to the kernel. The kernel then performs an authorization decision and either grants the request or returns an error. It is then the process's responsibility to properly react to either the results of the access or the error.

If this model of user space process security is so effective, why not implement it for all operating system functions, including the majority of kernel operations? The answer to this question is that to a large extent the overhead of evaluating authorization metadata is very compute expensive. If most or all operations (that are, in the classical kernel space,

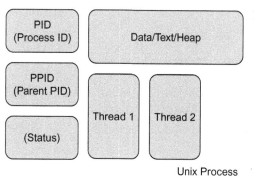

Unix Process

FIGURE 5.2   Kernel structure of a typical Unix process.

2. RBAC was developed in the 1990s as a new approach to access control for computing resources. Authorization to access resources is granted based on role membership, and often allows more fine-grained resource control since specific operations (such as "modify file" or "add printer") can be granted to role members. In 2004, the RBAC model was standardized in American National Standard 359-2004 (see also http://csrc.nist.gov/rbac/ for more information).

often hardware-related device access operations) are run in user space or a comparable way, the performance of the OS would severely suffer. There is a class of operating system with a microkernel that implements this approach; the kernel contains only the most rudimentary functions (processes, scheduling, basic security), and all other operations, including device access and other operations that are typically carried out by the kernel, run in separate user processes. The advantage is a higher level of security and better safeguards against rogue device drivers. Furthermore, new device drivers or other operating system functionality can be added or removed without having to reboot the kernel. The performance penalties are so severe, however, that no major commercial operating system implements a microkernel architecture.

Many modern Unix-based systems operate in a mixed mode: While many device drivers such as hard drives, video, and I/O systems are operating in the kernel space, they also provide a framework for user space drivers. For example, the Filesystems in User Space (FUSE) allows loading additional drivers for file systems. This permits the mounting of devices that are not formatted with the default file system types that the OS supports, without having to execute with elevated privileges. It also allows the use of file systems in situations, where license conflict prevents the integration of a file system driver into the kernel (for example, the CDDL licensed ZFS file system into the GPL licensed Linux kernel).

Semantics of User Space Security

In most Unix systems, security starts with access control to resources. Since users interact with the systems through processes and files, it is important to know that every user space process structure has two important security fields: the user identifier, or UID, and the group identifier, or GID. These identifiers are typically positive integers, which are unique for each user.[3] Every process that is started[4] by or on behalf of a user inherits the UID and GID values for that user account. These values are usually immutable for the live time of the process.

Access to system resources must go through the kernel by calling the appropriate function that is accessible to user processes. For example, a process that wants to reserve some system memory for data access will use the malloc() system call and pass the requested size and an (uninitialized) pointer as parameters. The kernel then evaluates this request, determines whether enough virtual memory (physical memory plus swap space) is available, reserves a section of memory, and sets the pointer to the address where the block starts.

Users who have the UID zero have special privileges: They are considered *superusers*, able to override many of the security guards that the kernel sets up. The default Unix superuser is named *root*.

---

3. If two usernames are associated with the same UID, the operating system will treat them as the same user. Their authentication credentials (username and password) are different, but their authorization with respect to system resources is the same.

4. Processes can be "started" or created in a variety of ways, for example, by calling the fork() system call or by calling the execve() system call to load a new executable file and start it.

Standard File and Device Access Semantics

File access is a very fundamental task, and it is important that only authorized users get read or write access to a given file. If any user was able to access any file, there would be no privacy at all, and security could not be maintained, since the operating system would not be able to protect its own permanent records, such as configuration information or user credentials. Most Unix operating systems use an identity-based access control (IBAC) model, in which access policies are expressed in terms of the user's identity.

The most common IBAC policy describing who may access or modify files and directories is commonly referred to as an *access control list* (ACL). Note that there is more than just one type of ACL; the standard Unix ACLs are very well known, but different Unix variants or POSIX-like operating systems might implement different ACLs and only define a mapping to the simple POSIX 1003 semantics. A good example is the Windows NTFS ACL or the NFS v4 ACLs. ACLs for files and devices represented though device files are stored within the filesystem as meta data for the file information itself. This is different from other access control models where policies may be stored in a central repository.

Read, Write, Execute

From its earliest days, Unix implemented a simple but effective way to set access rights for users. Normal files can be accessed in three fundamental ways: read, write, and execute. The first two ways are obvious; the execution requires a little more explanation. A file on disk may only be executed as either a binary program or a script if the user has the right to execute this file. If the execute permission is not set, the system call exec() or execve() to execute a file image will fail. In addition to a user's permissions, there must be a notion of ownership of files and sometimes other resources. In fact, each file on a traditional Unix file system is associated with a user and a group. The user and group are not identified by their name but by UID and GID instead.

In addition to setting permissions for the user owning the file, two other sets of permissions are set for files: for the group and for all others. Similar to being owned by a user, a file is also associated with one group. All members of this group[5] can access the file with the permissions set for the group. In the same way, the other set of permissions applies to all users of the system.

Special Permissions

In addition to the standard permissions, there are a few special permissions, discussed here.

SET-ID BIT

This permission only applies to executable files, and it can only be set for the user or the group. If this bit is set, the process for this program is not set to the UID or GID of the

---

5. It should be noted that users belong to one primary group, identified by the GID set in the password database. However, group membership is actually determined separately through the /etc/group file. As such, the user can be (and often is) a member of more than one group.

invoking user but instead to the UID or GID of the file. For example, a program owned by the superuser can have the Set-ID bit set and execution allowed for all users. This way a normal user can execute a specific program with elevated privileges.

STICKY BIT

When the sticky bit is set on an executable file, its data (specifically the text segment) is kept in memory, even after the process exits. This is intended to speed execution of commonly used programs. A major drawback of setting the sticky bit is that when the executable file changes (for example, through a patch), the permission must be unset and the program started once more. When this process exits, the executable is unloaded from memory and the file can be changed.

MANDATORY LOCKING

Mandatory file and record locking refers to a file's ability to have its reading or writing permissions locked while a program is accessing that file.

There might be additional implementation-specific permissions. These depend not only on the capabilities of the core operating facilities, including the kernel, but also on the type of file system. For example, most Unix operating systems can mount FAT-based file systems, which do not support any permissions or user and group ownership. Since the internal semantics require some values for ownership and permissions, these are typically set for the entire file system.

Permissions on Directories

The semantics of permissions on directories (see Figure 5.3) are different from those on files.

READ AND WRITE

Mapping these permissions to directories is fairly straightforward: The read permission allows listing files in the directory, and the write permission allows us to create files. For some applications it can be useful to allow writing but not reading.

```
Making a directory readable for everyone:

# chmod o+r /tmp/mydir
# ls -ld /tmp/mydir

drwxr-xr-x   2 root      root          117 Aug  9 12:12 /tmp/mydir


Setting the SetID bit on an executable, thus enabling it to be run with super-user privileges:


# chmod u+s specialprivs
# ls -ld specialprivs

-rwsr-xr-x   2 root      root          117 Aug  9 12:12 specialprivs
```

FIGURE 5.3   Examples of chmod for files and directories.

EXECUTE

With this permission, a process can set its working directory to this directory. Note that with the basic permissions, there is no limitation on traversing directories, so a process might change its working directory to a child of a directory, even if it cannot do so for the directory itself.

SETID

Semantics may differ here. For example, on Solaris this changes the behavior for default ownership of newly created files from the System V to the BSD semantics.

OTHER FILE SYSTEMS

As mentioned, the set of available permissions and authorization policies depends on the underlying operating system capabilities, including the file system. For example, the UFS file system in Solaris since version 2.5 allows additional ACLs on a per-user basis. Furthermore, NFS version 4 or higher defines additional ACLs for file access; it is obvious that the NFS server must have an underlying files system capable of recording this additional metadata.

Discretionary Versus Mandatory Access Control

The access control semantics described so far establish a "discretionary" access control (DAC) model: Any user may determine what type of access he or she wants to give to other specific users, groups, or anybody else. For many applications this is sufficient: For example, for systems that deliver a single network service and do not allow interactive login, the service's ability to determine what data will be shared with network users may be sufficient.

In systems that need to enforce access to data based on centralized, system operator-administered policies, DAC may not be sufficient. For example, for systems that need to operate in Multi-Level Security (MLS) environments, confidentiality of data can only be achieved through a mandatory access control (MAC) model. A number of MAC implementations for Unix-based systems are currently available, including Solaris Trusted Extensions for Solaris 10, SELinux for Linux-based operating systems, and TrustedBSD for BSD-based distributions.

Mandatory access control can be designed and implemented in many different ways. A common approach is to label operating system objects both in user and kernel space with a classification level and enforce appropriate MAC policies, such as the Bell-LaPadua (BLP) model for data confidentiality or the Biba model for data integrity.

Many Unix operating systems today provide a rudimentary set of MAC options by default: The SELinux based Linux Security Module (LSM) interface is now part of the core kernel, and some operating system vendors such as Red Hat ship their OSes with a minimal set of MAC policies enabled. To operate in a true Multi-Level Security environment, further configuration and often additional software modules are necessary to enable a BLP or Biba compliant set of MAC policies.

While MAC-based systems have traditionally been employed in government environments, modern enterprise architectures have a growing need for enforced access control around confidentiality or integrity. For example, data leakage protection (DLP) systems or auditing systems will benefit from certain types of centralized MAC policies.

3. ACHIEVING UNIX SECURITY

Achieving a high level of system security for the Unix system is a complex process that involves technical, operational, and managerial aspects of system operation. Next is a very cursory overview of some of the most important aspects of securing a Unix system.

System Patching

Prior to anything else, it is vitally important to emphasize the need to keep Unix systems up to date. No operating system or other program can be considered safe without being patched up; this point cannot be stressed enough. Having a system with the latest security patches is the first and most often the best line of defense against intruders and other cyber security threats.

All major Unix systems have a patching mechanism; this is a way to get the system up to date. Depending on the vendor and the mechanism used, it is possible to "back out" the patches. For example, on Solaris it is usually possible to remove a patch through the patchrm(1 m) command. On Debian-based systems this is not quite as easy, since in a patch the software package to be updated is replaced by a new version. Undoing this is only possible by installing the earlier package.

Locking Down the System

In general, all system services and facilities that are not needed for regular operation should be disabled or even uninstalled. Since any software package increases the attack surface of the system, removing unnecessary software ensures a better security posture.

Minimizing User Privileges

User accounts that have far-reaching access rights within a system have the ability to affect or damage a large number of resources, potentially including system management or system service resources. As such, user access rights should be minimized by default, in line with the security principle of "least privilege." For example, unless interactive access to the system is absolutely required, users should not be permitted to login.

Detecting Intrusions with Audits and Logs

By default, most Unix systems log kernel messages and important system events from core services. The most common logging tool is the syslog facility, which is controlled from the /etc/syslog.conf file.

4. PROTECTING USER ACCOUNTS AND STRENGTHENING AUTHENTICATION

In general, a clear distinction must be made between users obtaining a command shell for a Unix system ("interactive users") and consumers of Unix network services ("noninteractive users"). The interactive users should in most instances be limited to administrators that need to configure and monitor the system, especially since interactive access is almost always a necessary first step to obtain administrative access.

Establishing Secure Account Use

For any interactive session, Unix systems require the user to log into the system. To do so, the user must present a valid credential that identifies him (he or she must authenticate to the system). The type of credentials a Unix system uses depends on the capabilities of the OS software itself and on the configuration set forth by the systems administrator. The most traditional user credential is a username and a text password, but there are many other ways to authenticate to the operating system, including Kerberos, SSH, or security certificates.

The Unix Login Process

Depending on the desired authentication mechanism (see Figure 5.4), the user will have to use different access protocols or processes. For example, console or directly attached terminal sessions usually support only password credentials or smart card logins, whereas a secure shell connection supports only RSA- or DSA-based cryptographic tokens over the SSH protocol.

Overview of Unix authentication methods

- Simple: a username and a password are used to login to the operating system. The login process must receive both in cleartext. For the password, the Unix crypt hash is calculated and compared to the value in the password or shadow file.

- Kerberos: The user is supposed to have a ticket-granting ticket from the Kerberos Key Distribution Server (KDC). Using the ticket-granting ticket, he obtains a service ticket for an interactive login to the Unix host. This service ticket (encrypted, time limited) is then presented to the login process, and the Unix host validates it with the KDC.

- PKI based Smartcard: the private key on the smart card is used to authenticate with the system.

FIGURE 5.4 Various authentication mechanisms for Unix systems.

The login process is a system daemon that is responsible for coordinating authentication and process setup for interactive users. To do this, the login process does the following:

1. Draw or display the login screen.
2. Collect the credential.
3. Present the user credential to any of the configured user databases (typically, these can be files, NIS, Kerberos servers, or LDAP directories) for authentication.
4. Create a process with the user's default command-line shell, with the home directory as working directory.
5. Execute systemwide, user, and shell-specific start-up scripts.

The commonly available X11 windowing system does not use the text-oriented login process but instead provides its own facility to perform roughly the same kind of login sequence.

Access to interactive sessions using the SSH protocol follows a similar general pattern, but the authentication is significantly different from the traditional login process.

Controlling Account Access

Simple files were the first method available to store user account data. Over the course of years many other user databases have been implemented. We examine these here.

The Local Files

Originally, Unix only supported a simple password file for storing account information. The username and the information required for the login process (UID, GID, shell, home directory, and GECOS information) are stored in this file, which is typically at /etc/passwd. This approach is highly insecure, since this file needs to be readable by all for a number of different services, thus exposing the password hashes to potential hackers. In fact, a simple dictionary or even brute-force attack can reveal simple or even more complex passwords.

To protect against an attack like this, most Unix variants use a separate file for storing the password hashes (/etc/shadow) that is only readable and writable by the system.

Network Information System

The Network Information System (NIS) was introduced to simplify the administration of small groups of computers. Originally, Sun Microsystems called this service Yellow Pages, but the courts decided that this name constituted a trademark infringement on the British Telecom Yellow Pages. However, most commands that are used to administer the NIS still start with the yp prefix (such as ypbind and ypcat).

Systems within the NIS are said to belong to a NIS domain. Although there is absolutely no correlation between the NIS domain and the DNS domain of the system, it is quite common to use DNS-style domain names for naming NIS domains. For example, a system with DNS name system1.sales.example.com might be a member of the NIS domain nis.sales.Example.COM. Note that NIS domains—other than DNS domains—are case sensitive.

The NIS uses a simple master/slave server system: The master NIS server holds all authoritative data and uses an ONC-RPC-based protocol to communicate with the slave servers and clients. Slave servers cannot be easily upgraded to a master server, so careful planning of the infrastructure is highly recommended.

Client systems are bound to one NIS server (master or slave) during runtime. The addresses for the NIS master and the slaves must be provided when joining a system to the NIS domain. Clients (and servers) can always be members of only one NIS domain. To use the NIS user database (and other NIS resources, such as auto-mount maps, netgroups, and host tables) after the system is bound, use the name service configuration file (/etc/nss-witch.conf), as shown in Figure 5.5.

Using PAMs to Modify AuthN

These user databases can easily be configured for use on a given system through the /etc/nsswitch.conf file. However, in more complex situations, the administrator might want to fine-tune the types of acceptable authentication methods, such as Kerberos, or even configure multifactor authentication. Traditionally, the PAM is configured through the /etc/pam.conf file, but more modern implementations use a directory structure, similar to the System V init scripts. For these systems, the administrator needs to modify the configuration files in the /etc/pam.d/ directory.

Using the systemauth PAM, administrators can also enforce users to create and maintain complex passwords, including the setting of specific lengths, minimal number or numeric or nonletter characters, and so on. Figure 5.6 illustrates a typical systemauth PAM configuration.

Noninteractive Access

The security configuration of noninteractive services can vary quite significantly. Especially popular network services, such as LDAP, HTTP, or Windows File Shares

```
# /etc/nsswitch.conf

#
# Example configuration of GNU Name Service Switch functionality.
#
passwd:         files nis

group:          files nis
shadow:         files nis

hosts:          files nis dns
networks:       files

protocols:      db files
services:       db files
ethers:         db files
rpc:            db files
netgroup:       nis
```

FIGURE 5.5   Sample nsswitch.conf for a Debian system.

```
# /etc/pam.d/common-password - password-related modules common to all services
#

# This file is included from other service-specific PAM config files,
# and should contain a list of modules that define the services to be
# used to change user passwords.  The default is pam_unix.

# Explanation of pam_unix options:
#
# The "nullok" option allows users to change an empty password, else
# empty passwords are treated as locked accounts.
#

# The "md5" option enables MD5 passwords.  Without this option, the
# default is Unix crypt.
#

# The "obscure" option replaces the old `OBSCURE_CHECKS_ENAB' option in
# login.defs.
#

# You can also use the "min" option to enforce the length of the new
# password.
#
# See the pam_unix manpage for other options.

password    requisite    pam_unix.so nullok obscure md5

# Alternate strength checking for password. Note that this
# requires the libpam-cracklib package to be installed.
# You will need to comment out the password line above and
# uncomment the next two in order to use this.
# (Replaces the `OBSCURE_CHECKS_ENAB', `CRACKLIB_DICTPATH')
#

password required    pam_cracklib.so retry=3 minlen=6 difok=3

password required    pam_unix.so use_authtok nullok md5
```

FIGURE 5.6   Setting the password strength on a Debian-based system through the PAM system.

(CIFS), can use a wide variety of authentication and authorization mechanisms that do not even need to be provided by the operating system. For example, an Apache Web server or a MySQL database server might use its own user database, without relying on any operating system services such as passwd files or LDAP directory authentication.

Monitoring how noninteractive authentication and authorization are performed is critically important since most users of Unix systems will only utilize them in noninteractive ways. To ensure the most comprehensive control over the system, it is highly recommended that the suggestions presented in this chapter be followed to minimize the attack surface and verify that the system makes only a clearly defined set of services available on the network.

Other Network Authentication Mechanisms

In 1983, BSD introduced the rlogin service. Unix administrators have been using RSH, RCP, and other tools from this package for a long time; they are very easy to use and configure and provide simple access across a small network of computers. The login was facilitated through a very simple trust model: Any user could create a .rhosts file in her home directory and specify foreign hosts and users from which to accept logins without proper credential checking. Over the rlogin protocol (TCP 513), the username of the rlogin client would be transmitted to the host system, and in lieu of an authentication, the rshd daemon would simply verify the preconfigured values. To prevent access from untrusted hosts, the administrator could use the /etc/hosts.equiv file to allow or deny individual hosts or groups of hosts (the latter through the use of NIS netgroups).

Risks of Trusted Hosts and Networks

Since no authentication ever takes place, this trust mechanism should not be used. Not only does this system rely entirely on the correct functioning of the hostname resolution system, but in addition, there is no way to determine whether a host was actually replaced.[6] Also, although rlogin-based trust systems might work for very small deployments, they become extremely hard to set up and operate with large numbers of machines.

Replacing Telnet, Rlogin, and FTP Servers and Clients with SSH

The most sensible alternative to the traditional interactive session protocols such as Telnet is the Secure Shell (SSH) system. It is very popular on Unix systems, and pretty much all versions ship with a version of SSH. Where SSH is not available, the open source package OpenSSH can easily be used instead.[7]

SSH combines the ease-of-use features of the rlogin tools with a strong cryptographic authentication system. On one hand, it is fairly easy for users to enable access from other systems; on the other hand, the secure shell protocol uses strong cryptography to:

- Authenticate the connection, that is, establish the authenticity of the user
- Protect the privacy of the connection through encryption
- Guarantee the integrity of the channel through signatures

6. This could actually be addressed through host authentication, but it is not a feature of the rlogin protocol.

7. "The Open Group Base Specifications Issue 6 IEEE Std 1003.1, 2004 Edition." See [IEEE04]. Copyright © 2001–2004 The IEEE and The Open Group, All Rights Reserved [www.opengroup.org/onlinepubs/ 009695399/], 2004.

```
$ ssh host -luser1 -c aes192-cbc
```

FIGURE 5.7   Create an interactive session on Solaris to host for user1 using the AES cipher with 192 bits.

This is done using either the RSA or DSA security algorithm, which are both available for the SSH v2[8] protocol. The cipher (see Figure 5.7) used for encryption can be explicitly selected.

The user must first create a public/private key pair through the ssh-keygen(1) tool. The output of the key generator is placed in the .ssh subdirectory of the user's home directory. This output consists of a private key file called id_dsa or id_rsa. This file must be owned by the user and can only be readable by the user. In addition, a file containing the public key is created, named in the same way, with the extension .pub appended. The public key file is then placed into the .ssh subdirectory of the user's home directory on the target system.

Once the public and private keys are in place and the SSH daemon is enabled on the host system, all clients that implement the SSH protocol can create connections. There are four common applications using SSH:

- Interactive session is the replacement for Telnet and rlogin. Using the ssh(1) command line, the sshd daemon creates a new shell and transfers control to the user.
- In a remotely executed script/command, ssh(1) allows a single command with arguments to pass. This way, a single remote command (such as a backup script) can be executed on the remote system as long as this command is in the default path for the user.
- An SSH-enabled file transfer program can be used to replace the standard FTP or FTP over SSL protocol.
- Finally, the SSH protocol is able to tunnel arbitrary protocols. This means that any client can use the privacy and integrity protection offered by SSH. In particular, the X-Window system protocol can tunnel through an existing SSH connection by using the -X command-line switch.

5. LIMITING SUPERUSER PRIVILEGES

The superuser[9] has almost unlimited power on a Unix system, which can be a significant problem. On systems that implement mandatory access controls, the superuser account can be configured to not affect user data, but the problem of overly powerful root

8. T. Ylonen and C. Lonvick, Eds., "The Secure Shell (SSH) Authentication Protocol," Network Working Group, Request for Comments: 4252, SSH Communications Security Corp., Category: Standards Track, Cisco Systems, Inc., See [IETF4252]. Copyright © The Internet Society (2006). [http://tools.ietf.org/html/rfc4252], 2006.

9. In all Unix systems "root" is the default name for the superuser. Access to the superuser account may be disabled by default, and administrative access is only granted temporarily to users through the sudo(1) facility.

accounts for standard, DAC-only systems remains. For an organizational and managerial perspective, access to privileged functions on a Unix operating system should be tightly controlled. For example, operators that have access to privileged functions on a Unix system should not only undergo special training, but also have be investigated for their personal background. Finally, it may be advisable to enforce a policy where operators of critical systems can only access privileged functions with at least two operators present (through multifactor authentication technologies).

There are a number of technical ways to limit access for the root user:

Configuring Secure Terminals

Most Unix systems allow us to restrict root logins to special terminals, typically the system console. This approach is quite effective, especially if the console or the allowed terminals are under strict physical access control. The obvious downside of this approach is that remote access to the system can be very limited: using this approach, access through any TCP/IP-based connection cannot be configured, thus requiring a direct connection, such as a directly attached terminal or a modem.

Configuration is quite different for the various Unix systems. Figure 5.8 shows the comparison between Solaris and Debian.

Gaining Root Privileges with su

The su(1) utility allows changing the identity of an interactive session. This is an effective mediation of the issues that come with restricting root access to secure terminals: Although only normal users can get access to the machine through the network (ideally by limiting the access protocols to those that protect the privacy of the communication, such as SSH), they can change their interactive session to a superuser session.

Using Groups Instead of Root

If users should be limited to executing certain commands with superuser privileges, it is possible and common to create special groups of users. For these groups, we can set the execution bit on programs (while disabling execution for all others) and the SetID bit for the owner, in this case the superuser. Therefore, only users of such a special group can execute the given utility with superuser privileges.

Using the sudo(1) Mechanism

By far more flexible and easier to manage than the approach for enabling privileged execution based on groups is the sudo(1) mechanism. Originally an open source program, sudo(1) is available for most Unix distributions. The detailed configuration is quite complex, and the manual page is quite informative.

6. SECURING LOCAL AND NETWORK FILE SYSTEMS

For production systems, there is a very effective way of preventing the modification of system-critical resources by unauthorized users or malicious software. Critical portions of

On Solaris simply edit the file /etc/default/login:

```
# Copyright 2004 Sun Microsystems, Inc.  All rights reserved.
# Use is subject to license terms.

# If CONSOLE is set, root can only login on that device.
# Comment this line out to allow remote login by root.
#

CONSOLE=/dev/console

# PASSREQ determines if login requires a password.
#

PASSREQ=YES

# SUPATH sets the initial shell PATH variable for root
#

SUPATH=/usr/sbin:/usr/bin



# SYSLOG determines whether the syslog(3) LOG_AUTH facility should be used
# to log all root logins at level LOG_NOTICE and multiple failed login
# attempts at LOG_CRIT.
#

SYSLOG=YES

# The SYSLOG_FAILED_LOGINS variable is used to determine how many failed
# login attempts will be allowed by the system before a failed login
# message is logged, using the syslog(3) LOG_NOTICE facility.  For
example,
# if the variable is set to 0, login will log -all- failed login attempts.
#

SYSLOG_FAILED_LOGINS=5


On Debian:

# The PAM configuration file for the Shadow `login' service
#


# Disallows root logins except on tty's listed in /etc/securetty
# (Replaces the `CONSOLE' setting from login.defs)

auth       requisite  pam_securetty.so
# Disallows other than root logins when /etc/nologin exists
# (Replaces the `NOLOGINS_FILE' option from login.defs)

auth       requisite  pam_nologin.so

# Standard Un*x authentication.

@include common-auth

# This allows certain extra groups to be granted to a user
# based on things like time of day, tty, service, and user.
# Please edit /etc/security/group.conf to fit your needs
# (Replaces the `CONSOLE_GROUPS' option in login.defs)
```

FIGURE 5.8   Restricting root access.

```
auth        optional   pam_group.so
```
FIGURE 5.8   Continued.

```
# Uncomment and edit /etc/security/time.conf if you need to set
# time restrainst on logins.
# (Replaces the `PORTTIME_CHECKS_ENAB' option from login.defs
# as well as /etc/porttime)

account     requisite  pam_time.so



# Uncomment and edit /etc/security/access.conf if you need to
# set access limits.
# (Replaces /etc/login.access file)

account  required          pam_access.so

# Sets up user limits according to /etc/security/limits.conf
# (Replaces the use of /etc/limits in old login)

session     required   pam_limits.so

# Prints the last login info upon succesful login
# (Replaces the `LASTLOG_ENAB' option from login.defs)

session     optional   pam_lastlog.so

# Standard Un*x account and session

@include common-account
@include common-session
@include common-password
```

the file systems (such as the locations of binary files, system libraries, and some configuration files) do not necessarily change very often.

Directory Structure and Partitioning for Security

In fact, any systemwide binary code should probably only be modified by the systems administrators. In these cases, it is very effective to properly partition the file system.

Employing Read-Only Partitions

The reason to properly partition the file system (see Figure 5.9) is so that only frequently changing files (such as user data, log files, and the like) are hosted on readable file systems. All other storage can then be mounted on read-only partitions.

The following scheme is a good start for partitioning with read-only partitions:

FIGURE 5.9   Secure partitioning.

- Binaries and Libraries: /bin, /lib, /sbin, /usr - read-only
- Logs and frequently changing system data: /var, /usr/var - writable
- User home directories: /home, /export/home - writable
- Additional software packages: /opt, /usr/local - read-only
- System configuration: /etc, /usr/local/etc - writable
- Everything else: Root (/) - read-only

Obviously, this can only be a start and should be evaluated for each system and application. Updating operating system files, including those on the root file system, should be performed in single-user mode with all partitions mounted writable.

Finding Special Files

To prevent inadvertent or malicious access to critical data, it is vitally important to verify the correct ownership and permission set for all critical files in the file system.

Ownership and Access Permissions

The Unix find(1) command is an effective way to locate files with certain characteristics. In the following, a number of sample command-line options for this utility are given to locate files.

Locate SetID Files

Since executables with the SetID bit set are often used to allow the execution of a program with superuser privileges, it is vitally important to monitor these files on a regular basis.

Another critical permission set is that of world-writable files; there should be no system-critical files in this list, and users should be aware of any files in their home directories that are world-writable (see Figure 5.10). Finally, files and directories that are not owned by current users can be found by the code shown in Figure 5.11. For groups, just use -nogroup instead.

Locate Suspicious Files and Directories

Malicious software is sometimes stored in nonstarted directories such as subdirectories named "..." that will not immediately be noticed. Administrators should pay special attention to such files and verify if the content is part of a legitimate software package.

```
$ find /  \( -perm -04000 -o -perm -02000\) -type f -xdev -print
```

FIGURE 5.10   Finding files with SUID and SGID set.

`$ find / -nouser`   **FIGURE 5.11**   Finding files without users.

---

7. NETWORK CONFIGURATION

Since many Unix systems today are used as network servers, most users will never log in these systems interactively. Consequently, the most significant threat sources for Unix- based systems are initially defective or badly configured network services. However, such initial attacks are often only used to get initial interactive access to the system; once an attacker can access a command-line shell, other layers of security must be in place to prevent an elevation of privileges (superuser access).

Basic Network Setup

Unix user space processes can access networks by calling a variety of functions from the system libraries, namely, the socket() system call and related functions. While other network protocols such as DECNet or IPX may still be supported, the TCP/IP family of protocols plays by far the most important role in today's networks. As such, we will focus on these protocols alone. A number of files are relevant for configuring access to networks, with some of the most important listed here:

1. /etc/hostname (and sometimes also /etc/nodename) set the name under which the system identifies itself. This name is also often used to determine its own IP address, based on hostname resolution.
2. /etc/protocols defines the available list of protocols such as IP, TCP, ICMP, and UDP.
3. /etc/hosts and /etc/networks files define what IP hosts and networks are locally known to the system. They typically include the localhost definition (which is always 127.0.0.1 for IPv4 networks) and the loopback network (defined to be 127.0.0.0/24), respectively.
4. /etc/nsswitch.conf is available on many Unix systems and allows fine-grained setting of name resolution for a number of network and other resources, including the UIDs and GIDs. Typical settings include purely local resolution (i.e., through the files in the /etc directory), resolution through NIS, host resolution through DNS, user and group resolution through LDAP, and so on.
5. /etc/resolv.conf is the main configuration file for the DNS resolver libraries used in most Unix systems. It points to the IP addresses of the default DNS nameservers and may include the local domainname and any other search domains.
6. /etc/services (and/or /etc/protocols) contains a list of well-known services and the port numbers and protocol types they are bound to. Some system commands (such as netstat) use this database to resolve ports and protocols into user-friendly names.

Depending on the Unix flavor and the version, many other network configuration files apply to the base operating system. In addition, many other services that are commonly used on Unix systems such as HTTP servers, application servers, and databases have their own configuration files that will need to be configured and monitored in deployed systems.

Detecting and Disabling Standard UNIX Services

To protect systems against outside attackers and remove the overall attack surface, it is highly recommended to disable any service not needed for providing the intended functionality. The following simple process will likely turn off most system services that are not needed:

1. Examine the start-up scripts for your system. Start-up procedures have been changing for Unix systems quite significantly over time. Early systems used the /etc/inittab to determine runlevels and start-up scripts. Unix System V introduced the /etc/init.d scripts and the symbolic links from the /etc/rc*.d/ directories. Most current Unix systems either still use this technology or implement an interface to start and stop services (like Solaris). Debian-based distributions have a System V backward compatibility facility. Administrators should determine their start-up system and disable any services and feature not required for the function of that system. Ideally, facilities and services not needed should be uninstalled to minimize the potential attack surface for both external attacks, as well as privilege escalation attacks by running potentially harmful binaries.
2. Additionally, administrator can examine the processes that are currently running on a given system (e.g., through running the ps(1) command). Processes that cannot be traced to a particular software package or functionality should be killed and their file images ideally uninstalled or deleted.
3. The netstat(1) command can be used to display currently open network sockets, specifically for TCP and UDP connections. By default, netstat(1) will use the /etc/services and /etc/protocols databases to map numeric values to well-known services. Administrators should verify that there are only those ports open that are expected to be used by the software installed on the system.

Host-Based Firewall

One of the best ways to limit the attack surface for external attackers is to close down all network sockets that are not being actively used by network clients. This is true for systems attached directly to the Internet as well as for systems on private networks. The IP stacks of most Unix systems can be configured to only accept specific protocols (such as TCP) and connections on specific ports (such as port 80). Figure 5.12 shows how to limit ssh(1) access to systems on a specific IP subnet. Depending on the network stack, this can be achieved with a setting in the System Preferences for MacOS, or the iptables(1) command for Linux systems.

Restricting Remote Administrative Access

If possible, interactive access to Unix-based systems should be limited to dedicated administrative terminals. This may be achieved by limiting root access to directly attached

```
iptables -A INPUT -i eth0 -p tcp -s 192.168.1.0/24 --dport 22 -m state --state
NEW,ESTABLISHED -j ACCEPT
iptables -A OUTPUT -o eth0 -p tcp --sport 22 -m state --state ESTABLISHED -j ACCEPT
```

FIGURE 5.12 Configuration for iptables(1) for allowing ssh(1) connections from IP address range 192.168.1.1–192.168.1.254. This can be used to limit interactive access, as described in Chapter 8.

consoles and terminals, or by creating dedicated private networks for the express purpose of allowing remote access through ssh(1), SNMP, or Web administration utilities.

Consoles and Terminals on Restricted Networks

As described earlier, root access to terminals can be limited to specific devices such as terminals or consoles. If the terminals or consoles are provided through TCP/IP-capable terminal concentrators or KVM-switches, interactive network access can be achieved by connecting these console devices through restricted networks to dedicated administrative workstations.

Dedicated Administrative Networks

Similarly, interactive access can be restricted to a small number of workstation and access points through the following technologies:

- Dedicated physical interface or VLAN segmentation—If any interactive or administrative access is limited to separate networks, preferably disconnected from operational networks, the potential attack surface is significantly reduced.
- Logical interface—If no physical or VLAN infrastructure is available, Unix networking stacks typically allow the assignment of additional IP addresses to a single physical networking interface. While more susceptible to lower-level attacks, this approach may still be sufficient for effective separation of networks.
- Routing and firewall table design—As a fairly high-level approach, administrators may limit access to specific services from preconfigured IP addresses or networks through careful design of the host-based firewall and the routing tables of the IP stack.
- Yale University has a somewhat old, but still useful, Unix networking checklist at http://security.yale.edu/network/unix.html that describes a number of general security settings for Unix systems in general, and Solaris specifically. A similar older checklist is also available from the Carnegie Mellon University's Software Engineering Institute CERT at https://www.cert.org/tech_tips/unix_configuration_guidelines.html.
- Special topics in system administration that also address security topics such as auditing, configuration management, and recovery can be found on the Usenix Web site at https://www.usenix.org/lisa/books.
- Apple provides a detailed document on locking down MacOS X 10.6 Server: http://images.apple.com/support/security/guides/docs/SnowLeopard_Server_Security_Config_v10.6.pdf.
- The U.S. federal government operates a Computer Emergency Readiness Team (US-CERT) at https://www.us-cert.gov, targeted at technical and nontechnical users for both the government and the private sector. In addition to general information,

the US-CERT provides information from the National Vulnerability Database (NVD), security bulletins, and current threat information.

Finally, let's briefly look at how to improve the security of Linux and Unix systems. The following part of the chapter, describes how to modify Linus and Unix systems and fix their potential security weaknesses.

8. IMPROVING THE SECURITY OF LINUX AND UNIX SYSTEMS

A security checklist should be structured to follow the life cycle of Linus and Unix systems, from planning and installation to recovery and maintenance. The checklist is best applied to a system before it is connected to the network for the first time. In addition, the checklist can be reapplied on a regular basis, to audit conformance (see checklist: An Agenda for Action for Linux and Unix Security Activities).

AN AGENDA FOR ACTION FOR LINUX AND UNIX SECURITY ACTIVITIES

No two organizations are the same, so in applying the checklist, consideration should be given to the appropriateness of each action to your particular situation. Rather than enforcing a single configuration, the following checklist will identify the specific choices and possible security controls that should be considered at each stage, which includes the following key activities (check all tasks completed):

Determine Appropriate Security

_____1. Computer role.
_____2. Assess security needs of each kind of data handled.
_____3. Trust relationships.
_____4. Uptime requirements and impact if these are not met.
_____5. Determine minimal software packages required for role.
_____6. Determine minimal net access required for role.

Installation

_____7. Install from trusted media.
_____8. Install while not connected to the Internet.
_____9. Use separate partitions.
_____10. Install minimal software.

Apply All Patches and Updates

_____11. Initially apply patches while offline.
_____12. Verify integrity of all patches and updates.
_____13. Subscribe to mailing lists to keep up to date.

Minimize

_____14. Minimize network services.
_____15. Disable all unnecessary start-up scripts.
_____16. Minimize SetUID/SetGID programs.
_____17. Other minimization.

Secure Base OS

_____**18.** Physical, console, and boot security.

_____**19.** User logons.

_____**20.** Authentication.

_____**21.** Access control.

_____**22.** Other.

Secure Major Services

_____**23.** Confinement.

_____**24.** tcp_wrappers.

_____**25.** Other general advice for services.

_____**26.** SSH.

_____**27.** Printing.

_____**28.** RPC/portmapper.

_____**29.** File services NFS/AFS/Samba.

_____**30.** The X Window System.

_____**31.** DNS service.

_____**32.** WWW service.

_____**33.** Squid proxy.

_____**34.** CVS.

_____**35.** Web browsers.

_____**36.** FTP service.

Add Monitoring Capability

_____**37.** syslog configuration.

_____**38.** Monitoring of logs.

_____**39.** Enable trusted audit subsystem if available.

_____**40.** Monitor running processes.

_____**41.** Host-based intrusion detection.

_____**42.** Network intrusion detection.

Connect to the Net

_____**43.** First put in place a host firewall.

_____**44.** Position the computer behind a border firewall.

_____**45.** Network stack hardening/sysctls.

_____**46.** Connect to network for the first time.

Test Backup/Rebuild Strategy

_____**47.** Backup/rebuild strategy.

_____**48.** TEST backup and restore.

_____**49.** Allow separate restore of software and data.

_____**50.** Repatch after restoring.

_____**51.** Process for intrusion response.

Maintain

_____**52.** Mailing lists.

_____**53.** Software inventory.

_____**54.** Rapid patching.

_____**55.** Secure administrative access.

_____**56.** Log book for all sysadmin work.

_____**57.** Configuration change control with.

_____**58.** Regular audit.

9. ADDITIONAL RESOURCES

There is a large number of very useful tools to assist administrators in managing Unix systems. This also includes verifying their security.

Useful Tools

The following discussion of useful tools should not be regarded as exhaustive. Rather, it should be seen as a simple starting point.

Webmin

Webmin is a useful general-purpose graphical system management interface that is available for a large number of Unix systems. It is implemented as a Web application running on port 10,000 by default. Webmin allows management of basic Unix functionality such as user and group management, network and printer configuration, file system management, and many more. It also comes with a module for managing commonly used services such as the OpenLDAP directory server, the BIND DNS server, a number of different mail transfer agents, and databases.

Webmin is particularly useful for casually maintained systems that do not require tight configuration management and may expose a Web application interface. It is not recommended to use Webmin on mission-critical systems or in environments where systems are exposed to unknown external users (such as on the Internet or on large private networks). Even for systems where Webmin is an acceptable risk, it is recommended to ensure that the web interface is protected by transport-level security (HTTP with SSL), and preferably restricted to dedicated administration networks or stations.

nmap

For testing the open ports on a given host or subnet, nmap is an excellent tool. It allows scanning a given IP address or IP address range and testing what TCP and UDP ports are accessible. It is very flexible and can easily be extended, but it comes with a number of modules that allow determining the operating systems of an IP responder based on the fingerprint of the TCP/IP stack responses.

LCFG

Local ConFiGiguration System (LCFG) is an effective configuration management system for complex Unix deployments. It compiles machine-specific and default configurations for all aspects of a given Unix system into an XML file and distributes these files to the client machines. More information on LCFG can be found at http://www.lcfg.org/.

Further Information

Since this chapter can only provide an introduction to fully securing Unix-based systems, the following list of resources is recommended for a more in-depth treatment of this topic. Users are also advised to consult vendor-specific information about secure configuration of their products.

By far the most comprehensive guidance on security configuration for Unix systems is available through the U.S. Defense Information Systems Agency (DISA). DISA and the National Institutes for Standards and Technology (NIST) create, publish, and update Security Technical Implementation Guides (STIGs) for a number of operating systems at http://iase.disa.mil/stigs/os/. Beyond the general STIG for Unix security, there are vendor- specific STIGs for Red Hat Linux, Solaris, HP-UX, and AIX.

10. SUMMARY

This chapter covered communications interfaces between HP-UX, Solaris, Linux, and AIX servers and the communications infrastructure (firewalls, routers, etc.). The use of Oracle in configuring and managing HP-UX, Solaris, Linux and AIX servers to support large databases and applications was also discussed.

Other Unix systems discussed included Solaris, Linux, and AIX, and material was presented on how to perform alternate Information Assurance Officer duties for HP-UX, Solaris, Linux and AIX midtier systems. This chapter also showed entry-level security professionals how to provide support for Unix security error diagnosis, testing strategies, and resolution of problems, which, is normally found in the SMC Ogden server HP-UX, AIX, Solaris, and Linux environments. In addition, the chapter showed security professionals how to provide implementation of DISA security requirements (STIG) and Unix SRR.

This chapter also helped security professionals gain experience in the installation and management of applications in Unix/Sun/Linux/AIX environments. In addition, it showed security professionals how to apply Defense Information Systems Agency (DISA) Security Technical Information Guidelines (STIG) with regard to installing and configuring/setting up Unix/Linux environments under mandatory security requirements.

The chapter showed security professionals how to work with full life-cycle information technology projects; as well as, provides proficiency in the environments of J2EE, EJB, Sun Solaris, IBM WebSphere, Oracle, DB/2, Hibernate, JMS/MQ Series, Web Service, SOAP, and XML. It also helped Unix/Solaris administrators on a large scale, with reference to multiuser enterprise systems.

With regard to certification exams, this chapter is designed to help students gain general experience (which includes operations experience) on large-scale computer systems or multiserver local area networks; broad knowledge and experience with system technologies (including networking concepts, hardware, and software); and the capability to determine system and network and application performance capabilities. It can also help students gain specialized experience in administrating Unix-based systems and Oracle configuration knowledge, with security administration skills.

Finally, let's move on to the real interactive part of this chapter: review questions/exercises, hands-on projects, case projects and optional team case project. The answers and/or solutions by chapter can be found in the Online Instructor's Solutions Manual.

CHAPTER REVIEW QUESTIONS/EXERCISES

True/False

1. True or False? Unix was originally created as a single-user system.
2. True or False? Unix security has a long tradition, and though many concepts of the earliest Unix systems still apply, a large number of changes have taken place that fundamentally altered the way the operating system implements these security principles.

3. True or False? Achieving a high level of system security for the Unix system is a complex process that involves technical, operational, and managerial aspects of system operation.
4. True or False? For any interactive session, Linux systems require the user to log into the system.
5. True or False? The superuser has almost unlimited power on a Unix system, which can be a significant problem.

Multiple Choice

1. When a user is granted access to resources on a computing system, it is of vital importance to establish and verify the identity of the requesting entity. This process is commonly referred to as:
    A. authorization.
    B. availability.
    C. integrity.
    D. authentication.
    E. confidentiality.
2. What allows for the loading of additional drivers for file systems?
    A. File access.
    B. Identity-based access control.
    C. Filesystems in user space.
    D. Access control list.
    E. Meta data.
3. The login process is a system daemon that is responsible for coordinating authentication and process setup for interactive users. To do this, the login process does the following, except which one?
    A. Draw or display the login screen.
    B. Collect the credential.
    C. Present the user credential to only one of the configured user databases (typically, these can be files, NIS, Kerberos servers, or LDAP directories) for authentication.
    D. Create a process with the user's default command-line shell, with the home directory as working directory.
    E. Execute systemwide, user, and shell-specific start-up scripts.
4. What was introduced to simplify the administration of small groups of computers?
    A. Systemauth PAM.
    B. Network Information System.
    C. Noninteractive access.
    D. Trusted hosts.
    E. Trusted networks.
5. The most sensible alternative to the traditional interactive session protocols such as Telnet is the:
    A. open-source package OpenSSH.
    B. SSH daemon.
    C. Secure Shell (SSH) system.

D. SSH protocol.

E. SSH-enabled file transfer program.

EXERCISE

Problem

On a Tuesday morning, a company support team was alerted by a customer who was trying to download a drive update. The customer reported that the FTP server was not responding to connection attempts. Upon failing to log in to the FTP server remotely via the secure shell, the support team member walked to a server room only to discover that the machine crashed and was not able to boot. The reason was simple: No operating system was found. The company gathered the standard set of network servers (all running some version of Unix or Linux): Web, email, DNS servers, and also a dedicated FTP server, used to distribute hardware drivers for the company inventory. In this case project, how would the company go about implementing an incident response plan?

Hands-On Projects

Project

Despite the risks of viruses and malicious attacks, most Linux Web servers are inadequately protected against intrusion. How would a company go about protecting their Linux Web servers against intrusion?

Case Projects

Problem

Rlogin is a software utility for Unix-like computer operating systems that allows users to log in on another host via a network, communicating via TCP port 513. Rlogin is most commonly deployed on corporate or academic networks, where user account information is shared between all the Unix machines on the network (often using NIS). But rlogin does have serious security problems. Please list rlogin's possible security problems.

Optional Team Case Project

Problem

Brute-force attacks against remote services such as SSH, FTP, and telnet are still the most common form of attack to compromise servers facing the Internet. So, how would security administrators go about thwarting these types of attack?

6

Eliminating the Security Weakness of Linux and Unix Operating Systems

Mario Santana

Terremark

1. INTRODUCTION TO LINUX AND UNIX

A simple Google search for define:unix yields many definitions. This definition comes from Microsoft: "A powerful multitasking operating system developed in 1969 for use in a minicomputer environment; still a widely used network operating system."[1]

What is Unix?

Unix is many things. Officially, it is a brand and an operating system specification. In common usage, the word *Unix* is often used to refer to one or more of many operating systems that derive from or are similar to the operating system designed and implemented about 41 years ago at AT & T Bell Laboratories. Throughout this chapter, we'll use the term *Unix* to include official Unix-branded operating systems as well as Unix-like operating systems such as BSD, Linux, and even Macintosh OS X.

History

Years after AT & T's original implementation, there followed decades of aggressive market wars among many operating system vendors, each claiming that its operating system was Unix. The ever-increasing incompatibilities between these different versions of

---

1. Microsoft, n.d., "Glossary of Networking Terms for Visio IT Professionals," retrieved September 22, 2008, from Microsoft TechNet: http://technet.microsoft.com/en-us/library/cc751329.aspx#XSLTsection142121120120.

Network and System Security
DOI: http://dx.doi.org/10.1016/B978-0-12-416689-9.00006-X

Unix were seen as a major deterrent to the marketing and sales of Unix. As personal computers grew more powerful and flexible, running inexpensive operating systems like Microsoft Windows and IBM OS/2, they threatened Unix as the server platform of choice. In response to these and other marketplace pressures, most major Unix vendors eventually backed efforts to standardize the Unix operating system.

Unix Is a Brand

Since the early 1990s, the Unix brand has been owned by The Open Group. This organization manages a set of specifications with which vendors must comply to use the Unix brand in referring to their operating system products. In this way, The Open Group provides a guarantee to the marketplace that any system labeled as Unix conforms to a strict set of standards.

Unix Is a Specification

The Open Group's standard is called the Single Unix Specification. It is created in collaboration with the Institute of Electrical and Electronics Engineers (IEEE), the International Standards Organization (ISO), and others. The specification is developed, refined, and updated in an open, transparent process.

The Single Unix Specification comprises several components, covering core system interfaces such as system calls as well as commands, utilities, and a development environment based on the C programming language. Together, these describe a "functional superset of consensus-based specifications and historical practice."[2]

Lineage

The phrase *historical practice* in the description of the Single Unix Specification refers to the many operating systems historically referring to themselves as Unix. These include everything from AT & T's original releases to the versions released by the University of California at Berkeley and major commercial offerings by the likes of IBM, Sun, Digital Equipment Corporation (DEC), Hewlett-Packard (HP), the Santa Cruz Operation (SCO), Novell, and even Microsoft. But any list of Unix operating systems would be incomplete if it didn't mention Linux (see Figure 6.1).

What is Linux?

Linux is a bit of an oddball in the Unix operating system lineup. That's because, unlike the Unix versions released by the major vendors, Linux did not reuse any existing source code. Instead, Linux was developed from scratch by a Finnish university student named Linus Torvalds.

---

2. The Open Group, n.d., "The Single Unix Specification," retrieved September 22, 2008, from What Is Unix: www.unix.org/what_is_unix/single_unix_specification.html.

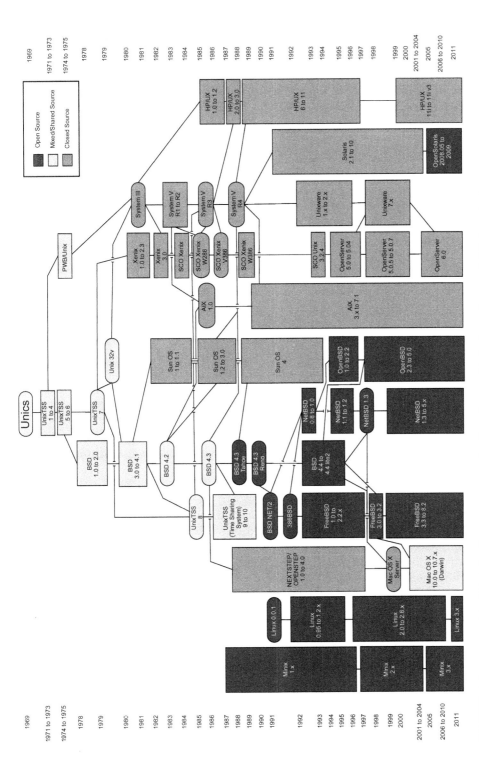

FIGURE 6.1 The simplified Unix family tree presents a timeline of some of today's most successful Unix variants.

Most Popular Unix-like OS

Linux was written from the start to function very similarly to existing Unix products. And because Torvalds worked on Linux as a hobby, with no intention of making money, it was distributed for free. These factors and others contributed to making Linux the most popular Unix operating system today.

Linux Is a Kernel

Strictly speaking, Torvalds's pet project has provided only one part of a fully functional Unix operating system: the kernel. The other parts of the operating system, including the commands, utilities, development environment, desktop environment, and other aspects of a full Unix operating system, are provided by other parties, including GNU, XOrg, and others.

Linux is a Community

Perhaps the most fundamentally different thing about Linux is the process by which it is developed and improved. As the hobby project that it was, Linux was released by Torvalds on the Internet in the hopes that someone out there might find it interesting. A few programmers saw Torvalds's hobby kernel and began working on it for fun, adding features and fleshing out functionality in a sort of unofficial partnership with Torvalds. At this point, everyone was just having fun, tinkering with interesting concepts. As more and more people joined the unofficial club, Torvalds's pet project ballooned into a worldwide phenomenon.

Today, Linux is developed and maintained by hundreds of thousands of contributors all over the world. In 1996, Eric S. Raymond[3] famously described the distributed development methodology used by Linux as a bazaar—a wild, uproarious collection of people, each developing whatever feature they most wanted in an operating system, or improving whatever shortcoming most impacted them. Yet somehow, this quick-moving community resulted in a development process that was stable as a whole and that produced an amazing amount of progress in a very short time.

This is radically different from the way in which Unix systems have typically been developed. If the Linux community is like a bazaar, then other Unix systems can be described as a cathedral—carefully preplanned and painstakingly assembled over a long period of time, according to specifications handed down by master architects from previous generations. Recently, however, some of the traditional Unix vendors have started moving toward a more decentralized, bazaar-like development model similar in many ways to the Linux methodology.

Linux Is Distributions

The open-source movement in general is very important to the success of Linux. Thanks to GNU, XOrg, and other open-source contributors, there was an almost complete Unix already available when the Linux kernel was released. Linux only filled in the final missing component of a no-cost, open-source Unix. Because the majority of the other parts of the operating system came from the GNU project, Linux is also known as GNU/Linux.

3. E. S. Raymond, September 11, 2000, "The Cathedral and the Bazaar," retrieved September 22, 2008, from Eric S. Raymond's homepage: www.catb.org/esr/writings/cathedral-bazaar/cathedral-bazaar/index.html.

To actually install and run Linux, it is necessary to collect all the other operating system components. Because of the interdependency of the operating system components—each component must be compatible with the others—it is important to gather the right versions of all these components. In the early days of Linux, this was quite a challenge!

Soon, however, someone gathered up a self-consistent set of components and made them all available from a central download location. The first such efforts include H. J. Lu's "boot/root" floppies and MCC Interim Linux. These folks did not necessarily develop any of these components; they only redistributed them in a more convenient package. Other people did the same, releasing new bundles called *distributions* whenever a major upgrade was available.

Some distributions touted the latest in hardware support; others specialized in mathematics or graphics or another type of computing; still others built a distribution that would provide the simplest or most attractive user experience. Over time, distributions have become more robust, offering important features such as package management, which allows a user to safely upgrade parts of the system without reinstalling everything else.

Linux Standard Base

Today there are dozens of Linux distributions. Different flavors of distributions have evolved over the years. A primary distinguishing feature is the package management system. Some distributions are primarily volunteer community efforts; others are commercial offerings. See Figure 6.2 for a timeline of Linux development.

The explosion in the number of different Linux distributions created a situation reminiscent of the Unix wars of previous decades. To address this issue, the Linux Standard Base was created to specify certain key standards of behavior for conforming Linux distributions. Most major distributions comply with the Linux Standard Base specifications.

A Word of Warning

Understanding the history and lineage of Unix is important for several reasons. First, it gives us insight into why some things work the way they do—often it's for historical reasons. Second, the wide variety of versions allows us to choose one that best fits our needs for security, functionality, performance, and compatibility. Finally, and most importantly, this understanding shows us that the rich history and many flavors of Unix make it impossible to treat security as a recipe. Similarly, this chapter cannot possibly cover all the details of every variation of the Unix commands that we will introduce.

Instead of memorizing some steps that will harden a Unix system, we must understand the underlying concepts and the overarching architecture, and be willing to adapt our knowledge to the particular details of whatever version we're working with. Keep this in mind as you read this chapter, especially as you apply the lessons in it.

System Architecture

The architecture of Unix operating systems is relatively simple. The kernel interfaces with hardware and provides core functionality for the system. File systems provide

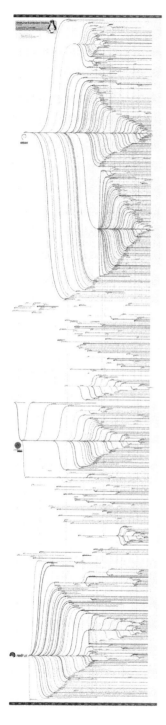

FIGURE 6.2 History of Linux distributions.

permanent storage and access to many other kinds of functionality. Processes embody programs as their instructions are being executed. Permissions describe the actions that users may take on files and other resources.

Kernel

The operating system kernel manages many of the fundamental details that an operating system needs to deal with, including memory, disk storage, and low-level networking. In general, the kernel is the part of the operating system that talks directly to hardware; it presents an abstracted interface to the rest of the operating system components.

Because the kernel understands all the different sorts of hardware that the operating system deals with, the rest of the operating system is freed from needing to understand all those underlying details. The abstracted interface presented by the kernel allows other parts of the operating system to read and write files or communicate on the network without knowing or caring about what kinds of disks or network adapter are installed.

File System

A fundamental aspect of Unix is its file system. Unix pioneered the hierarchical model of directories that contain files and/or other directories to allow the organization of data into a tree structure. Multiple file systems could be accessed by connecting them to empty directories in the root file system. In essence, this is very much like grafting one hierarchy onto an unused branch of another. There is no limit to the number of file systems that can be mounted in this way.

The file system hierarchy is also used to provide more than just access to and organization of local files. Network data shares can also be mounted, just like file systems on local disks. And special files such as device files, first in/first out (FIFO) or pipe files, and others give direct access to hardware or other system features.

Users and Groups

Unix was designed to be a time-sharing system and as such has been a multiuser since its inception. Users are identified in Unix by their usernames, but internally each is represented as a unique identifying integer called a *user ID*, or *UID*. Each user can also belong to one or more groups. Like users, groups are identified by their names, but they are represented internally as a unique integer called a *group ID*, or *GID*. Each file or directory in a Unix file system is associated with a user and a group.

Permissions

Unix has traditionally had a simple permissions architecture, based on the user and group associated with files in the file system. This scheme makes it possible to specify read, write, and/or execute permissions, along with a special permission setting whose effect is context-dependent. Furthermore, it's possible to set these permissions independently for the file's owner; the file's group, in which case the permission applies to all users, other than the owner, who are members of that group, and to all other users. The chmod command is used to set the permissions by adding up the values of all desired permission types, as shown in Table 6.1.

TABLE 6.1   Unix Permissions and Chmod.

Chmod Usage	Read	Write	Execute	Special
User	u + r or 0004	u + w or 0002	u + x or 0001	u + s or 4000
Group	u + r or 0040	u + w or 0020	u + x or 0010	u + s or 2000
Other	u + r or 0400	u + w or 0200	u + x or 0100	u + s or 1000

The Unix permission architecture has historically been the target of criticism for its simplicity and inflexibility. It is not possible, for example, to specify a different permission setting for more than one user or more than one group. These limitations have been addressed in more recent file system implementations using extended file attributes and access control lists.

Processes

When a program is executed, it is represented in a Unix system as a process. The kernel keeps track of many pieces of information about each process. This information is required for basic housekeeping and advanced tasks such as tracing and debugging. This information represents the user, group, and other data used for making security decisions about a process's access rights to files and other resources.

2. HARDENING LINUX AND UNIX

With a basic understanding of the fundamental concepts of the Unix architecture, let's take a look at the practical work of securing a Unix deployment. First, we'll review considerations for securing Unix machines from network-borne attacks. Then we'll look at security from a host-based perspective. Finally, we'll talk about systems management and how different ways of administering a Unix system can impact security.

Network Hardening

Defending from network-borne attacks is arguably the most important aspect of Unix security. Unix machines are used heavily to provide network-based services, running Web sites, domain name server (DNS), firewalls, and many more. To provide these services, Unix systems must be connected to hostile networks, such as the Internet, where legitimate users can easily access and make use of these services.

Unfortunately, providing easy access to legitimate users makes the system readily accessible to bad actors who would subvert access controls and other security measures to steal sensitive information, change reference data, or simply make services unavailable to legitimate users. Attackers can probe systems for security weaknesses, identify and exploit vulnerabilities, and generally wreak digital havoc with relative impunity from anywhere around the globe.

Minimizing Attack Surface

Every way in which an attacker can interact with the system poses a security risk. Any system that makes available a large number of network services, especially complex services such as the custom Web applications of today, suffers a higher likelihood that inadequate permissions or a software bug or some other error will present attackers with an opportunity to compromise security. In contrast, even a very insecure service cannot be compromised if it is not running.

A pillar of any security architecture is the concept of minimizing the attack surface. By reducing the number of enabled network services and the available functionality of those services that are enabled, a system presents a smaller set of functions that can be subverted by an attacker. Other ways to reduce attackable surface areas are to deny network access from unknown hosts when possible and to limit the privileges of running services in order to minimize the damage they might be subverted to cause.

Eliminate Unnecessary Services

The first step in reducing an attack surface is to disable unnecessary services provided by a server. In Unix, services are enabled in one of several ways. The "Internet daemon," or *inetd*, is a historically popular mechanism for managing network services. Like many Unix programs, inetd is configured by editing a text file. In the case of inetd, this text file is /etc/inetd.conf; unnecessary services should be commented out of this file. Today a more modular replacement for inetd, called *xinetd*, is gaining popularity. The configuration for xinetd is not contained in any single file but in many files located in the /etc/xinetd.d/ directory. Each file in this directory configures a single service, and a service may be disabled by removing the file or by making the appropriate changes to the file.

Many Unix services are not managed by inetd or xinetd, however. Network services are often started by the system's initialization scripts during the boot sequence. Derivatives of the BSD Unix family historically used a simple initialization script located in /etc/rc. To control the services that are started during the boot sequence, it is necessary to edit this script.

Recent Unices (the plural of Unix), even BSD derivatives, use something similar to the initialization scheme of the System V or higher family. In this scheme, a "run level" is chosen at boot time. The default run level is defined in /etc/inittab; typically, it is 3 or 5. The initialization scripts for each run level are located in /etc/rc X.d, where X represents the run-level number. The services that are started during the boot process are controlled by adding or removing scripts in the appropriate run-level directory. Some Unices provide tools to help manage these scripts, such as the rcconf command in Debian and derivatives or the chkconfig command in Red Hat Linux and derivatives. Other methods of managing services in Unix include the Service Management Facility of Solaris 10 or higher. No matter how a network service is started or managed, however, it must necessarily listen for network connections to make itself available to users. This fact makes it possible to positively identify all running network services by looking for processes that are listening for network connections. Almost all versions of Unix provide a command that makes this a trivial task. The netstat command can be used to list various kinds of information about the network environment of a Unix host. Running this command with the appropriate

```
travis ~ # netstat -lut
Active Internet connections (only servers)
Proto Recv-Q Send-Q Local Address        Foreign Address      State
tcp        0      0 *:sunrpc             *:*                  LISTEN
tcp        0      0 *:41182              *:*                  LISTEN
tcp6       0      0 [::]:sunrpc          [::]:*               LISTEN
tcp6       0      0 [::]:37434           [::]:*               LISTEN
udp        0      0 *:sunrpc             *:*
udp        0      0 *:725                *:*
udp        0      0 *:743                *:*
udp        0      0 *:45308              *:*
udp6       0      0 [::]:sunrpc          [::]:*
udp6       0      0 [::]:725             [::]:*
udp6       0      0 [::]:58154           [::]:*
```

FIGURE 6.3 Output of netstat -lut.

flags (usually −lut) will produce a listing of all open network ports, including those that are listening for incoming connections (see Figure 6.3).

Finally, let's take a brief look at how services that are necessary can be configured securely. The following checklist (see checklist: An Agenda for Action When Securing Web Server Activities) presents several points to consider when securing a Web server.

Securely Configure Necessary Services

Every such listening port should correspond to a necessary service that is well understood and securely configured. Although we cannot cover every service that might be run on a Unix system, we'll explore a few of the more common services.

One of the most popular services to run on a Unix system is a Web server. The Apache Web server is one of the most popular because it is free, powerful, and flexible, with many third-party add-ons to make it even more powerful and flexible. All this power and flexibility can also make secure Apache configuration a nontrivial exercise.[4]

AN AGENDA FOR ACTION WHEN SECURING WEB SERVER ACTIVITIES

The following items are possible actions that organizations should consider; some of the items may not apply to all organizations. Some important points to consider when securing Apache or any other Web server include[4] (check all tasks completed):

_____1. Keep up to date with server software updates.

_____2. Mitigate denial-of-service attacks by maximizing performance and limiting the resources consumed.

---

4. Apache.org, "Security Tips," retrieved August 22, 2012 from http://httpd.apache.org/docs/2.4/misc/security_tips.html.

_____3. Minimize permissions on Web content directories and files.

_____4. Minimize capabilities for dynamic content.

_____5. When dynamic content (Web applications) is necessary, carefully

check the security of the dynamic content scripts.

_____6. Monitor server logs for malicious or anomalous activity.

Another popular service on Unix servers is the Secure Shell service, or SSH. This service enables secure remote access to the Unix console. To configure it for maximum security, disable the use of passwords and require private key authentication. SSH also allows an administrator to strictly limit which commands can be executed by a given account— a feature that can minimize the risk of SSH accounts used for automated or centralized management functions.

Unix systems are often used to run database software. These databases can contain sensitive information, in which case they must be carefully configured to secure that data; however, even when the data is of little value, the database server itself can be used as a stepping stone in a larger compromise. That's one reason why it's important to secure any Unix system and the services it runs. There are many different kinds of database software, and each one must be hardened according to its own unique capabilities. From the Unix point of view, however, the security of any database can be greatly enhanced by using one of the firewall technologies described below to limit which remote hosts can access the database software.

HOST-BASED

Obviously, it is impossible to disable all the services provided by a server. However, it is possible to limit the hosts that have access to a given service. Often it is possible to identify a well-defined list of hosts or subnets that should be granted access to a network service. There are several ways in which this restriction can be configured.

A classical way of configuring these limitations is through the *tcpwrappers* interface. The tcpwrappers functionality is to limit the network hosts that are allowed to access services provided by the server. These controls are configured in two text files, /etc/hosts. allow and /etc/hosts.deny. This interface was originally designed to be used by inetd and xinetd on behalf of the services they manage. Today most service-providing software directly supports this functionality.

Another, more robust method of controlling network access is through firewall configurations. Most modern Unices include some form of firewall capability: IPFilter, used by many commercial Unices; IPFW, used by most of the BSD variants; and IPTables, used by Linux. In all cases, the best way to arrive at a secure configuration is to create a default rule to deny all traffic and then to create the fewest, most specific exceptions possible.

Modern firewall implementations are able to analyze every aspect of the network traffic they filter as well as aggregate traffic into logical connections and track the state of those connections. The ability to accept or deny connections based on more than just the originating network address and to end a conversation when certain conditions are met makes modern firewalls a much more powerful control for limiting attack surface than tcpwrappers.

CHROOT AND OTHER JAILS

Eventually, some network hosts must be allowed to access a service if it is to be useful at all. In fact, it is often necessary to allow anyone on the Internet to access a service, such as a public Web site. Once a malicious user can access a service, there is a risk that the service will be subverted into executing unauthorized instructions on behalf of the attacker. The potential for damage is limited only by the permissions that the service process has to access resources and to make changes on the system. For this reason, an important security measure is to limit the power of a service to the bare minimum necessary to allow it to perform its duties.

A primary method of achieving this goal is to associate the service process with a user who has limited permissions. In many cases, it's possible to configure a user with very few permissions on the system and to associate that user with a service process. In these cases, the service can only perform a limited amount of damage, even if it is subverted by attackers.

Unfortunately, this is not always very effective or even possible. A service must often access sensitive server resources to perform its work. Configuring a set of permissions to allow access to only the sensitive information required for a service to operate can be complex or impossible.

In answer to this challenge, Unix has long supported the chroot and ulimit interfaces as ways to limit the access that a powerful process has on a system. The chroot interface limits a process's access on the file system. Regardless of actual permissions, a process run under a chroot jail can only access a certain part of the file system. Common practice is to run sensitive or powerful services in a chroot jail and make a copy of only those file system resources that the service needs in order to operate. This allows a service to run with a high level of system access, yet be unable to damage the contents of the file system outside the portion it is allocated.[5]

The ulimit interface is somewhat different in that it can configure limits on the amount of system resources a process or user may consume. A limited amount of disk space, memory, CPU utilization, and other resources can be set for a service process. This can curtail the possibility of a denial-of-service attack because the service cannot exhaust all system resources, even if it has been subverted by an attacker.[6]

Access Control

Reducing the attack surface area of a system limits the ways in which an attacker can interact and therefore subvert a server. Access control can be seen as another way to reduce the attack surface area. By requiring all users to prove their identity before making

5. W. Richard Stevens, *Advanced Programming in the UNIX Environment* Addison-Wesley, Reading, 1992.
6. Ibid.

any use of a service, access control reduces the number of ways in which an anonymous attacker can interact with the system.

In general, access control involves three phases. The first phase is identification, where a user asserts his identity. The second phase is authentication, where the user proves his identity. The third phase is authorization, where the server allows or disallows particular actions based on permissions assigned to the authenticated user.

STRONG AUTHENTICATION

It is critical, therefore, that a secure mechanism is used to prove the user's identity. If this mechanism were to be subverted, an attacker would be able to impersonate a user to access resources or issue commands with whatever authorization level has been granted to that user. For decades, the primary form of authentication has been through the use of passwords. However, passwords suffer from several weaknesses as a form of authentication, presenting attackers with opportunities to impersonate legitimate users for illegitimate ends. Bruce Schneier has argued for years that "passwords have outlived their usefulness as a serious security device."[7] More secure authentication mechanisms include two-factor authentication and PKI certificates.

Two-Factor Authentication

Two-factor authentication involves the presentation of two of the following types of information by users to prove their identity: something they know, something they have, or something they are. The first factor, something they know, is typified by a password or a PIN—some shared secret that only the legitimate user should know. The second factor, something they have, is usually fulfilled by a unique physical token (see Figure 6.4). RSA makes a popular line of such tokens, but cell phones, matrix cards, and other alternatives are becoming more common. The third factor, something they are, usually refers to biometrics.

Unix supports various ways to implement two-factor authentication into the system. Pluggable Authentication Modules, or PAMs, allow a program to use arbitrary authentication mechanisms without needing to manage any of the details. PAMs are used by Solaris, Linux, and other Unices. BSD authentication serves a similar purpose and is used by several major BSD derivatives.

With PAM or BSD authentication, it is possible to configure any combination of authentication mechanisms, including simple passwords, biometrics, RSA tokens, Kerberos, and more. It's also possible to configure a different combination for different services. This kind of flexibility allows a Unix security administrator to implement a very strong authentication requirement as a prerequisite for access to sensitive services.

PKI

Strong authentication can also be implemented using a Private Key Infrastructure (PKI). Secure Socket Layer (SSL), is a simplified PKI designed for secure communications,

7. B. Schneier, December 14, 2006, *Real-World Passwords*, retrieved October 9, 2008, from Schneier on Security: www.schneier.com/blog/archives/2006/12/realworld_passw.html.

FIGURE 6.4 Physical tokens used for two-factor authentication.

familiar from its use in securing traffic on the Web. Through use of a similar foundation of technologies, it's possible to issue and manage certificates to authenticate users rather than Web sites. Additional technologies, such as a trusted platform module or a smart card, simplify the use of these certificates in support of two-factor authentication.

DEDICATED SERVICE ACCOUNTS

After strong authentication, limiting the complexity of the authorization phase is the most important part of access control. User accounts should not be authorized to perform sensitive tasks. Services should be associated with dedicated user accounts, which should then be authorized to perform only those tasks required for providing that service.

Additional Controls

In addition to minimizing the attack surface area and implementing strong access controls, there are several important aspects of securing a Unix network server.

ENCRYPTED COMMUNICATIONS

One of the ways an attacker can steal sensitive information is to eavesdrop on network traffic. Information is vulnerable as it flows across the network, unless it is encrypted.

Sensitive information, including passwords and intellectual property, are routinely transmitted over the network. Even information that is seemingly useless to an attacker can contain important clues to help a bad actor compromise security.

File Transfer Protocol (FTP), World Wide Web (WWW), and many other services that transmit information over the network support the Secure Sockets Layer (SSL) standard for encrypted communications. For server software that doesn't support SSL natively, wrappers like *stunnel* provide transparent SSL functionality.

No discussion of Unix network encryption can be complete without mention of Secure Shell, or SSH. SSH is a replacement for Telnet and RSH, providing remote command-line access to Unix systems as well as other functionality. SSH encrypts all network communications using SSL, mitigating many of the risks of Telnet and RSH.

LOG ANALYSIS

In addition to encrypting network communications, it is important to keep a detailed activity log to provide an audit trail in case of anomalous behavior. At a minimum, the logs should capture system activity such as logon and logoff events as well as service program activity, such as FTP, WWW, or Structured Query Language (SQL) logs.

Since the 1980s, the *syslog* service has been used to manage log entries in Unix. Over the years, the original implementation has been replaced by more feature-rich implementations, such as *syslog-ng* and *rsyslog*. These systems can be configured to send log messages to local files as well as remote destinations, based on independently defined verbosity levels and message sources.

The syslog system can independently route messages based on the facility, or message source, and the level, or message importance. The facility can identify the message as pertaining to the kernel, the email system, user activity, an authentication event, or any of various other services. The level denotes the criticality of the message and can typically be one of *emergency, alert, critical, error, warning, notice, informational*, and *debug*. Under Linux, the *klog* process is responsible for handling log messages generated by the kernel; typically, klog is configured to route these messages through syslog, just like any other process.

Some services, such as the Apache Web server, have limited or no support for syslog. These services typically include the ability to log activity to a file independently. In these cases, simple scripts can redirect the contents of these files to syslog for further distribution and/or processing.

Relevant logs should be copied to a remote, secure server to ensure that they cannot be tampered with. Additionally, file hashes should be used to identify any attempt to tamper with the logs. In this way, the audit trail provided by the log files can be depended on as a source of uncompromised information about the security status of the system.

IDS/IPS

Intrusion detection systems (IDSs) and intrusion prevention systems (IPSs) have become commonplace security items on today's networks. Unix has a rich heritage of such software, including Snort, Prelude, and OSSEC. Correctly deployed, an IDS can provide an early warning of probes and other precursors to attack.

Host Hardening

Unfortunately, not all attacks originate from the network. Malicious users often gain access to a system through legitimate means, bypassing network-based defenses. Various steps can be taken to harden a Unix system from a host-based attack such as this.

Permissions

The most obvious step is to limit the permissions of user accounts on the Unix host. Recall that every file and directory in a Unix file system is associated with a single user and a single group. User accounts should each have permissions that allow full control of their respective home directories. Together with permissions to read and execute system programs, this allows most of the typical functionality required of a Unix user account. Additional permissions that might be required include mail spool files and directories as well as crontab files for scheduling tasks.

ADMINISTRATIVE ACCOUNTS

Setting permissions for administrative users is a more complicated question. These accounts must access very powerful system-level commands and resources in the routine discharge of their administrative functions. For this reason, it's difficult to limit the tasks these users may perform. It's possible, however, to create specialized administrative user accounts, then authorize these accounts to access a well-defined subset of administrative resources. Printer management, Web site administration, email management, database administration, storage management, backup administration, software upgrades, and other specific administrative functions common to Unix systems lend themselves to this approach.

GROUPS

Often it is convenient to apply permissions to a set of users rather than a single user or all users. The Unix group mechanism allows for a single user to belong to one or more groups and for file system permissions and other access controls to be applied to a group.

FILE SYSTEM ATTRIBUTES AND ACLS

It can become unfeasibly complex to implement and manage anything more than a simple permissions scheme using the classical Unix file system permission capabilities. To overcome this issue, modern Unix file systems support access control lists, or ACLs. Most Unix file systems support ACLs using extended attributes that could be used to store arbitrary information about any given file or directory. By recognizing authorization information in these extended attributes, the file system implements a comprehensive mechanism to specify arbitrarily complex permissions for any file system resource.

ACLs contain a list of *access control entries*, or ACEs, which specify the permissions that a user or group has on the file system resource in question. On most Unices, the chacl command is used to view and set the ACEs of a given file or directory. The ACL support in modern Unix file systems provides a fine-grained mechanism for managing complex permissions requirements. ACLs do not make the setting of minimum permissions a trivial matter, but complex scenarios can now be addressed effectively.

Intrusion Detection

Even after hardening a Unix system with restrictive user permissions and ACLs, it's important to maintain logs of system activity. As with activity logs of network services, host-centric activity logs track security-relevant events that could show symptoms of compromise or evidence of attacks in the reconnaissance or planning stages.

AUDIT TRAILS

Again, as with network activity logs, Unix has leaned heavily on syslog to collect, organize, distribute, and store log messages about system activity. Configuring syslog for system messages is the same as for network service messages. The kernel's messages, including those messages generated on behalf of the kernel by klogd under Linux, are especially relevant from a hostcentric point of view.

An additional source of audit trail data about system activity is the history logs kept by a login shell such as *bash*. These logs record every command the user issued at the command line. The bash shell and others can be configured to keep these logs in a secure location and to attach timestamps to each log entry. This information is invaluable in identifying malicious activity, both as it is happening and after the fact.

FILE CHANGES

Besides tracking activity logs, monitoring file changes can be a valuable indicator of suspicious system activity. Attackers often modify system files to elevate privileges, capture passwords or other credentials, establish backdoors to ensure future access to the system, and support other illegitimate uses. Identifying these changes early can often foil an attack in progress before the attacker is able to cause significant damage or loss.

Programs such as Tripwire and Aide have been around for decades; their function is to monitor the file system for unauthorized changes and raise an alert when one is found. Historically, they functioned by scanning the file system and generating a unique *hash*, or fingerprint, of each file. On future runs, the tool would recalculate the hashes and identify changed files by the difference in the hash. Limitations of this approach include the need to regularly scan the entire file system, which can be a slow operation, as well as the need to secure the database of file hashes from tampering.

Today many Unix systems support file change monitoring: Linux has dnotify and inotify; Mac OS X has FSEvents, and other Unices have File Alteration Monitor. All these present an alternative method of identifying file changes and reviewing them for security implications.

Specialized Hardening

Many Unices have specialized hardening features that make it more difficult to exploit software vulnerabilities or to do so without leaving traces on the system and/or to show that the system is so hardened. Linux has been a popular platform for research in this area; even the National Security Agency (NSA) has released code to implement its strict security requirements under Linux. Here we outline two of the most popular Linux hardening packages. Other such packages exist for Linux and other Unices, some of which use innovative techniques such as virtualization to isolate sensitive data, but they are not covered here.

GRSEC/PAX

The grsecurity package provides several major security enhancements for Linux. Perhaps the primary benefit is the flexible policies that define fine-grained permissions it can control. This role-based access control capability is especially powerful when coupled with grsecurity's ability to monitor system activity over a period of time and generate a minimum set of privileges for all users. Additionally, through the PAX subsystem, grsecurity manipulates program memory to make it very difficult to exploit many kinds of security vulnerabilities. Other benefits include a very robust auditing capability and other features that strengthen existing security features, such as chroot jails.

SELINUX

Security Enhanced Linux, or SELinux, is a package developed by the NSA. It adds mandatory access control, or MAC, and related concepts to Linux. MAC involves assigning security attributes as well as system resources such as files and memory to users. When a user attempts to read, write, execute, or perform any other action on a system resource, the security attributes of the user and the resource are both used to determine whether the action is allowed, according to the security policies configured for the system. (See Figure 6.5.[8])

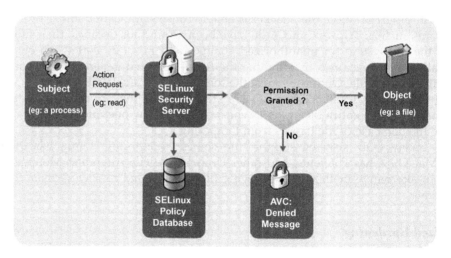

FIGURE 6.5   SELinux decision process.

8. Copyright RedHat, Inc, "Introduction to SELinux," retrieved May 14, 2012 from http://www.centos.org/docs/5/html/Deployment_Guide-en-US/ch-selinux.html.

Systems Management Security

After hardening, a Unix host from network-borne attacks and hardening it from attacks performed by an authorized user of the machine, we will take a look at a few systems management issues. These topics arguably fall outside the purview of security as such; however, by taking certain considerations into account, systems management can both improve and simplify the work of securing a Unix system.

Account Management

User accounts can be thought of as keys to the "castle" of a system. As users require access to the system, they must be issued keys, or accounts, so they can use it. When a user no longer requires access to the system, her key should be taken away or at least disabled.

This sounds simple in theory, but account management in practice is anything but trivial. In all but the smallest environments, it is infeasible to manage user accounts without a centralized account directory where necessary changes can be made and propagated to every server on the network. Through PAM, BSD authentication, and other mechanisms, modern Unices support LDAP, SQL databases, Windows NT and Active Directory, Kerberos, and myriad other centralized account directory technologies.

Patching

Outdated software is perhaps the number-one cause of easily preventable security incidents. Choosing a modern Unix with a robust upgrade mechanism and history of timely updates, at least for security fixes, makes it easier to keep software up to date and secure from well-known exploits. One of the main differentiating factors between the different Unix and Linux families is the software management and upgrade system. There are over 50 different package and upgrade management tools in use on the various Unix flavors.

Backups

When all else fails—especially when attackers have successfully modified or deleted data in ways that are difficult or impossible to positively identify—good backups will save the day. When backups are robust, reliable, and accessible, they put a ceiling on the amount of damage an attacker can do. Unfortunately, good backups don't help if the greatest damage comes from disclosure of sensitive information; in fact, backups could exacerbate the problem if they are not taken and stored in a secure way.

3. PROACTIVE DEFENSE FOR LINUX AND UNIX

As security professionals, we devote ourselves to defending systems from attack. However, it is important to understand the common tools, mind-sets, and motivations that drive attackers. This knowledge can prove invaluable in mounting an effective defense against attack. It's also important to prepare for the possibility of a successful attack and to consider organizational issues so that a secure environment can be developed.

Vulnerability Assessment

A vulnerability assessment looks for security weaknesses in a system. Assessments have become an established best practice, incorporated into many standards and regulations. They can be network-centric or host-based.

Network-based Assessment

Network-centric vulnerability assessment looks for security weaknesses a system presents to the network. Unix has a rich heritage of tools for performing network vulnerability assessments. Most of these tools are available on most Unix flavors.

Nmap is a free, open-source tool for identifying hosts on a network and the services running on those hosts. It's a powerful tool for mapping out the true services being provided on a network. It's also easy to get started with nmap.

Nessus is another free network security tool, though its source code isn't available. It's designed to check for and optionally verify the existence of known security vulnerabilities. It works by looking at various pieces of information about a host on the network, such as detailed version information about the operating system and any software providing services on the network. This information is compared to a database that lists vulnerabilities known to exist in certain software configurations. In many cases, Nessus is also capable of confirming a match in the vulnerability database by attempting an exploit; however, this is likely to crash the service or even the entire system. Many other tools are available for performing network vulnerability assessments. Insecure.Org, the folks behind the nmap tool, also maintain a great list of security tools.[9]

Host-based Assessment

Several tools can examine the security settings of a system from a host-based perspective. These tools are designed to be run on the system that's being checked; no network connections are necessarily initiated. They check things such as file permissions and other insecure configuration settings on Unix systems.

One such tool, *lynis*, is available for various Linux distributions as well as some BSD variants. Another tool is the Linux Security Auditing Tool, or *lsat*. Ironically, lsat supports more versions of Unix than lynis does, including Solaris and AIX.

No discussion of host-based Unix security would be complete without mentioning *Bastille*. Although lynis and lsat are pure auditing tools that report on the status of various security-sensitive host configuration settings, Bastille was designed to help remediate these issues. Recent versions have a reporting-only mode that makes Bastille work like a pure auditing tool.

Incident Response Preparation

Regardless of how hardened a Unix system is, there is always a possibility that an attacker—whether it's a worm, a virus, or a sophisticated custom attack—will successfully

9. Insecure.Org, 2008, "Top 100 Network Security Tools," retrieved October 9, 2008, from http://sectools.org.

compromise the security of the system. For this reason, it is important to think about how to respond to a wide variety of security incidents.

Predefined Roles and Contact List

A fundamental part of incident response preparation is to identify the roles that various personnel will play in the response scenario. The manual, hands-on gestalt of Unix systems administration has historically forced Unix systems administrators to be familiar with all aspects of the Unix systems they manage. These should clearly be on the incident response team. Database, application, backup, and other administrators should be on the team as well, at least as secondary personnel that can be called on as necessary.

Simple Message for End Users

Incident response is a complicated process that must deal with conflicting requirements to bring the systems back online while ensuring that any damage caused by the attack—as well as whatever security flaws were exploited to gain initial access—is corrected. Often, end users without incident response training are the first to handle a system after a security incident has been identified. It is important that these users have clear, simple instructions in this case, to avoid causing additional damage or loss of evidence. In most situations, it is appropriate to simply unplug a Unix system from the network as soon as a compromise of its security is confirmed. It should not be used, logged onto, logged off from, turned off, disconnected from electrical power, or otherwise tampered with in any way. This simple action has the best chance, in most cases, to preserve the status of the incident for further investigation while minimizing the damage that could ensue.

Blue Team/Red Team Exercises

Any incident response plan, no matter how well designed, must be practiced to be effective. Regularly exercising these plans and reviewing the results are important parts of incident response preparation. A common way of organizing such exercises is to assign some personnel (the Red Team) to simulate a successful attack, while other personnel (the Blue Team) are assigned to respond to that attack according to the established incident response plan. These exercises, referred to as Red Team/Blue Team exercises, are invaluable for testing incident response plans. They are also useful in discovering security weaknesses and in fostering a sense of *esprit des corps* among the personnel involved.

Organizational Considerations

Various organizational and personnel management issues can also impact the security of Unix systems. Unix is a complex operating system. Many different duties must be performed in the day-to-day administration of Unix systems. Security suffers when a single individual is responsible for many of these duties; however, that is commonly the skill set of Unix system administration personnel.

Separation of Duties

One way to counter the insecurity of this situation is to force different individuals to perform different duties. Often, simply identifying independent functions, such as backups and log monitoring, and assigning appropriate permissions to independent individuals is enough. Log management, application management, user management, system monitoring, and backup operations are just some of the roles that can be separated.

Forced Vacations

Especially when duties are appropriately separated, unannounced forced vacations are a powerful way to bring fresh perspectives to security tasks. It's also an effective deterrent to internal fraud or mismanagement of security responsibilities. A more robust set of requirements for organizational security comes from the Information Security Management Maturity Model, including its concepts of transparency, partitioning, separation, rotation, and supervision of responsibilities.[10]

4. SUMMARY

This chapter provides the technical security policies, requirements, and implementation details for eliminating the security weaknesses of Linux and Unix operating systems. The chapter also contains general requirements for Linux and Unix operating systems, as well as specific requirements. This chapter may also be used as a guide for enhancing the security configuration of any Linux or Unix-like system. The chapter also contains all requirements, check, and fix procedures that are expected to be applicable to most Linux and Unix-like operating systems.

Finally, let's move on to the real interactive part of this chapter: review questions/exercises, hands-on projects, case projects and optional team case project. The answers and/or solutions by chapter can be found in the Online Instructor's Solutions Manual.

CHAPTER REVIEW QUESTIONS/EXERCISES

True/False

1. True or False? Unix is a brand and an operating system specification.
2. True or False? The architecture of Unix operating systems is relatively difficult.
3. True or False? Defending from network-borne attacks is arguably the least important aspect of Unix security.
4. True or False? The first step in reducing an attack surface is to disable unnecessary services provided by a server.
5. True or False? Every listening port should not correspond to a necessary service that is well understood and securely configured.

10. ISECOM 2008, "Security Operations Maturity Architecture," retrieved October 9, 2008, from ISECOM: www.isecom.org/soma.

Multiple Choice

1. What can be seen as another way to reduce the attack surface area?
   A. Dedicated service accounts.
   B. PKI.
   C. Two-factor authentication.
   D. Strong authentication.
   E. Access control.
2. Information is vulnerable as it flows across the network, unless it is:
   A. log analyzed.
   B. clear texted.
   C. basically authenticated.
   D. encrypted.
   E. All of the above.
3. The Unix group mechanism allows for a single user to belong to one or more:
   A. attributes.
   B. ACLs.
   C. permissions.
   D. groups.
   E. focus groups.
4. Even after hardening a Unix system with restrictive user permissions and ACLs, it's important to maintain logs of:
   A. audit trails.
   B. system messages.
   C. system activity.
   D. bash.
   E. All of the above.
5. An additional source of audit trail data about system activity is the history logs kept by a login shell such as:
   A. log.
   B. file.
   C. password.
   D. bash.
   E. All of the above.

EXERCISE

Problem

Is Linux a secure operating system?

Hands-On Projects

Project

Is it more secure to compile driver support directly into the kernel, instead of making it a module?

Case Projects

Problem

Why does logging in as root from a remote machine always fail?

Optional Team Case Project

Problem

How do you enable shadow passwords on your Red Hat 4.2 or higher, or 5.x or higher Linux box?

7

Internet Security

Jesse Walker

Intel Corporation

The Internet, with all its accompanying complications, is integral to our lives. The security problems besetting the Internet are legendary and have become daily annoyances—and worse—to many users. Given the Net's broad impact on our lives and the widespread security issues associated with it, it is worthwhile understanding what can be done to improve the immunity of our communications from attack.

The Internet can serve as a laboratory for studying network security issues; indeed, we can use it to study nearly every kind of security issue. We will pursue only a modest set of questions related to this theme. The goal of this chapter is to understand how cryptography can be used to address some of the security issues affecting communications protocols. To do so, it will be helpful to first understand the Internet architecture. After that we will survey the types of attacks that are possible against communications. With this background we will be able to understand how cryptography can be used to preserve the confidentiality and integrity of messages.

Our goal is modest: It is only to describe the network architecture and its cryptographic-based security mechanisms sufficiently to understand some of the major issues confronting security systems designers and to appreciate some of the major design decisions they have to make to address these issues.

1. INTERNET PROTOCOL ARCHITECTURE

The Internet was designed to create standardized communication between computers. Computers communicate by exchanging messages. The Internet supports message exchange through a mechanism called *protocols*. Protocols are very detailed and stereotyped rules explaining exactly how to exchange a particular set of messages. Each protocol is defined as a set of automata and a set of message formats. Each protocol specification defines one automaton for sending a message and another for receiving a message. The

Network and System Security
DOI: http://dx.doi.org/10.1016/B978-0-12-416689-9.00007-1

automata specify the timing of symbols that represent the messages; the automata implicitly define a grammar for the messages, indicating whether any particular message is meaningful or is interpreted by the receiver as gibberish. The protocol formats restrict the information that the protocol can express.

Security has little utility as an abstract, disembodied concept. What the word *security* should mean depends very much on the context in which it is applied. The architecture, design, and implementation of a system each determine the kind of vulnerabilities and opportunities that exist and which features are easy or hard to attack or defend.

It is fairly easy to understand why this is true. An attack on a system is an attempt to make the system act outside its specification. An attack is different from "normal" bugs that afflict computers and that occur through random interactions between the system's environment and undetected flaws in the system architecture, design, or implementation. An attack, on the other hand, is an explicit and systematic attempt by a party to search for flaws that make the computer act in a way its designers did not intend.

Computing systems consist of a large number of blocks or modules assembled together, each of which provides an intended set of functions. The system architecture hooks the modules together through *interfaces*, through which the various modules exchange information to activate the functions provided by each module in a coordinated way. These interfaces may be explicit, such as a formal grammar that the automata are supposed to conform, or they may be implicit, as when a parser accepts a larger grammar than is in the specification. An attacker exploits the architecture to compromise the computing system by interjecting inputs into these interfaces that do not conform to the intended specification of inputs into one of the automata. If the targeted module has not been carefully crafted, unexpected inputs can cause it to behave in unintended ways. This implies that the security of a system is determined by its decomposition into modules, which an adversary exploits by injecting messages into the interfaces the architecture exposes. Accordingly, no satisfying discussion of any system is feasible without an understanding of the system architecture. Our first goal, therefore, is to review the architecture of the Internet communication protocols in an effort to gain a deeper understanding of its vulnerabilities.

Communications Architecture Basics

Since communication is an extremely complex activity, it should come as no surprise that the system components providing communication decompose into modules. One standard way to describe each communication module is as a black box with a well-defined service interface. A minimal communications service interface requires four primitives:

- *A send primitive, which an application using the communications module uses to send a message via the module to a peer application executing on another networked device.* The *send* primitive specifies a message payload and a destination, as well as a format forhow messages are encoded from this information. The communication module responding to the *send* transmits the message to the specified destination, reporting its requestor as the message source.
- *A confirm primitive, to report that the module has sent a message to the designated destination in response to a send request or to report when the message transmission failed, along with any*

failure details that might be known. It is possible to combine the *send* and *confirm* primitives, but network architectures rarely take this approach at their lowest layer. The *send* primitive is normally defined to allow the application to pass a message to the communications module for transmission by transferring control of a buffer containing the message. The *confirm* primitive then releases the buffer back to the calling application when the message has indeed been sent. This scheme affects "a conservation of buffers" and enables the communications module and the application using it to operate in parallel, thus enhancing the overall communication performance.

- *A listen primitive, which the receiving application uses to provide the communications module with buffers into which it should put messages arriving from the network.* Each buffer the application posts must be large enough to receive a message of the maximum expected size. The receiving automata must be carefully designed to respond correctly to arriving messages that are too large for the receive buffer.
- *A receive primitive, to deliver a received message from another party to the receiving application.* This releases a posted buffer back to the application and usually generates a signal to notify the application of message arrival. The released buffer contains the received message and the (alleged) message source.

Sometimes the *listen* primitive is replaced with a *release* primitive. In this model, the receive buffer is owned by the receiving communications module instead of the application, and the application must recycle buffers containing received messages back to the communication module upon completion. In this case the buffer size selected by the receiving module determines the maximum message size. In a moment we will explain how network protocols work around this restriction.

It is customary to include a fifth service interface primitive for communications modules:

- A *status* primitive, to report diagnostic and performance information about the underlying communications. This might report statistics, the state of active associations with other network devices, and the like.

Communications is affected by providing a communications module black box on systems, connected by a signaling medium. The medium connecting the two devices constitutes the network communications path. The media can consist of a direct link between the devices or, more commonly, several intermediate relay systems between the two communicating endpoints. Each relay system is itself a communicating device with its own communications module, which receives and then forward messages from the initiating system to the destination system.

Under this architecture, a message is transferred from an application on one networked system to an application on a second networked system as follows:

First, the application sourcing the message invokes the *send* primitive exported by its communications module. This causes the communications module to (attempt) to transmit the message to a destination provided by the application in the *send* primitive.

The communications module encodes the message onto the network's physical medium representing a link to another system. If the communications module implements a *best-effort* message service, it generates the *confirm* primitive as soon as the message has been encoded onto the medium. If the communication module implements a *reliable* message service, the communication delays generation of the *confirm* until it receives an acknowledgment from the message destination. If it has not received an acknowledgment from the receiver after some period of time, it generates a *confirm* indicating that the message delivery failed.

The encoded message traverses the network medium and is placed into a buffer by the receiving communications module of another system attached to the medium. This communications module examines the destination. The module then examines the destination specified by the message. If the module's local system is not the destination, the module reencodes the message onto the medium representing another link; otherwise the module uses the *deliver* primitive to pass the message to the receiving application.

Getting More Specific

This stereotyped description of networked communications is overly simplified. Actually, communications are torturously more difficult in real network modules. To overcome this complexity, communications modules are themselves partitioned further into layers, each providing a different networking function. The Internet decomposes communications into five layers of communications modules:

- The PHY layer
- The MAC layer
- The network layer
- The transport layer
- The sockets layer

These layers are augmented by a handful of cross-layer coordination modules. The Internet depends on the following cross-layer modules:

- ARP
- DHCP
- DNS
- ICMP
- Routing

An application using networking is also part of the overall system design, and the way it uses the network has to be taken into consideration to understand system security.

The PHY Layer

The PHY (pronounced *fie*) layer is technically not part of the Internet architecture per se, but Ethernet jacks and cables, modems, Wi-Fi adapters, and the like represent the most visible aspect of networking, and no security treatment of the Internet can ignore the PHY layer entirely.

The PHY layer module is medium dependent, with a different design for each type of medium: Ethernet, phone lines, Wi-Fi, cellular phone, OC-768, and the like are based on different PHY layer designs. It is the job of the PHY layer to translate between digital bits as represented on a computing device and the analog signals crossing the specific physical medium used by the PHY. This translation is a physics exercise.

To send a message, the PHY layer module encodes each bit of each message from the sending device as a media-specific signal or wave form, representing the bit value 1 or 0. Once encoded, the signal propagates along the medium from the sender to the receiver. The PHY layer module at the receiver decodes the medium-specific signal back into a bit. There are often special symbols representing such things as the frame start and frame end symbols, and training symbols to synchronize the receiver with the transmitter. These special symbols provide control only and are distinct from the symbols representing bits. Wave forms different from the defined symbols are undefined and discarded by the receiver.

It is possible for the encoding step at the transmitting PHY layer module to fail, for a signal to be lost or corrupted while it crosses the medium, and for the decoding step to fail at the receiving PHY layer module. It is the responsibility of higher layers to detect and recover from these potential failures.

The MAC Layer

Like the PHY layer, the MAC (pronounced *mack*) layer is not properly a part of the Internet architecture, but no satisfactory security discussion is possible without considering it. The MAC module is the "application" that uses and controls a particular PHY layer module. A MAC layer is always designed in tandem with a specific PHY (or vice versa), so a PHY–MAC pair together is often referred to as the *data link* layer.

MAC is an acronym for *media access control*. As its name suggests, the MAC layer module determines when to send and receive *frames*, which are messages encoded in a media-specific format. The job of the MAC is to pass frames over a link between the MAC layer modules on different systems.

Although not entirely accurate, it is useful to think of a MAC module as creating *links*, each of which is a communication channel between different MAC modules. It is further useful to distinguish physical links and virtual links. A *physical link* is a direct point-to-point channel between the MAC layers in two endpoint devices. A *virtual link* can be thought of as a shared medium to which more than two devices can connect at the same time. There are no physical endpoints per se; the medium acts as though it is multiplexing links between each pair of attached devices. Some media such as modern Ethernet are implemented as physical point-to-point links but act more like virtual links in that more than a single destination is reachable via the link. This is accomplished by MAC layer switching, which is also called *bridging*. Timing requirements for coordination among communicating MAC layer modules make it difficult to build worldwide networks based on MAC layer switching, however. Mobile devices such as smart phones, laptops, and note-pads also make large-scale bridging difficult, since these devices can shift their attachment points to the network, thus invalidating the data structures used by switches to effect switching. Finally, some media such as Wi-Fi (IEEE 802.11) are *shared* or *broadcast media*. In a shared medium all devices can access the channel, and the MAC design must specify an access control policy that the MAC enforces; this behavior is what gives the MAC layer its name. Ethernet was originally a shared medium, but evolved into its present switched point-to-point structure in order to simplify medium access control. The access control function of a MAC is always a complex security concern.

A MAC frame consists of a header and a data payload. The frame header typically specifies information such as the source and destination for the link endpoints. Devices attached to the medium via their MAC + PHY modules are identified by *MAC addresses*. Each MAC module has its own MAC address assigned by its manufacturer and is supposed to be a globally unique identifier. The *destination address* in a frame allows a particular MAC module to identify frames intended for it, and the *source address* allows the receiver to identify the purported frame source. The frame header also usually includes a preamble, which is a set of special PHY timing signals used to synchronize the interpretation of the PHY layer data signals representing the frame bits.

The payload portion of a frame is the data to be transferred across the network. The maximum payload size is always fixed by the medium type. It is becoming customary for most MACs to support a maximum payload size of 1500 bytes = 12,000 bits, but this is not universal. The maximum fixed size allows the MAC to make efficient use of the underlying physical medium. Since messages can be of an arbitrary length exceeding this fixed size, a higher-layer function is needed to partition messages into segments of the appropriate length.

As we have seen, it is possible for bit errors to creep into communications as signals representing bits traverse the PHY medium. MAC layers differ a great deal in how they respond to errors. Some PHY layers, such as the Ethernet PHY, experience exceedingly low error rates, and for this reason, the MAC layers for these PHYs make no attempt to more than detect errors and discard the mangled frames. Indeed, with these MACs it is cheaper for the Internet to resend message segments at a higher layer than at the MAC layer. These are called *best-effort MACs*. Others, such as the Wi-Fi MAC, experience high error rates due to the shared nature of the channel and natural interference among radio sources; experience has shown that these MACs can deliver better performance by retransmitting damaged or lost frames. It is customary for most MAC layers to append a checksum computed over the entire frame, called *a frame check sequence* (FCS). The FCS allows the receiver to detect bit errors accumulated due to random noise and other physical phenomena during transmission and due to decoding errors. Most MACs discard frames with FCS errors. Some MAC layers also perform error correction on the received bits to remove random bit errors rather than relying on retransmissions.

The Network Layer

The purpose of the network layer module is to represent messages in a media-independent manner and to forward them between various MAC layer modules representing different links. The media-independent message format is called an *Internet Protocol*, or *IP, datagram*. The network layer implements the IP layer and is the lowest layer of the Internet architecture per se.

As well as providing media independence, the network layer provides a vital forwarding function that works even for a worldwide network like the Internet. It is impractical to form a link directly between each communicating system on the planet. Indeed, the cabling costs alone are prohibitive—no one wants billions, or even dozens, of cables connecting their computer to other computers—and too many MAC + PHY interfaces can quickly exhaust the power budget for a single computing system. Hence, each machine is attached by a small number of links to other devices, and some of the machines with multiple links comprise a *switching fabric*. The computing systems constituting the switching fabric are called *routers*.

The forwarding function supported by the network layer module is the key component of a router and works as follows: When a MAC module receives a frame, it passes the frame payload to the network layer module. The payload consists of an *IP datagram*, which is the media-independent representation of the message. The receiving network layer module examines the datagram to see whether to deliver it locally or to pass it on toward the datagram's ultimate destination. To accomplish the latter, the network layer module consults a *forwarding table* to identify some neighbor router closer to the ultimate destination than itself. The forwarding table also identifies the MAC module to use to communicate with the selected neighbor and passes the datagram to that MAC layer module. The MAC module in turn retransmits the datagram as a frame encoded for its medium across its link to the neighbor. This process happens recursively until the datagram is delivered to its ultimate destination.

The network layer forwarding function is based on *IP addresses*, a concept that is critical to understanding the Internet architecture. An IP address is a media-independent name for one of the MAC layer modules within a computing system. Each IP address is structured to represent the "location" of the MAC module within the entire Internet. This notion of location is relative to the graph comprising routers and their interconnecting links, called the *network topology*, not to actual geography. Since this name represents a location, the forwarding table within each IP module can use the IP address of the ultimate destination as a sort of signpost pointing at the MAC module with the greatest likelihood of leading to the ultimate destination of a particular datagram.

An IP address is different from the corresponding MAC address already described. A MAC address is a permanent, globally unique identifier, identifying a particular interface on a particular computing device, whereas an IP address can be dynamic due to device mobility. An IP address cannot be assigned by the equipment manufacturer, since a computing device can change locations frequently. Hence, IP addresses are administered and blocks allocated to different organizations with an Internet presence. It is common, for instance, for an Internet service provider (ISP) to acquire a large block of IP addresses for use by its customers.

An IP datagram has a structure similar to that of a frame: It consists of an IP header, which is "extra" overhead used to control the way a datagram passes through the Internet, and a data payload, which contains the message being transferred. The IP header indicates the ultimate source and destinations, represented as IP addresses.

The IP header format limits the size of an IP datagram payload to 64 K ($2^{16} = 65,536$) bytes. It is common to limit datagram sizes to the underlying media size, although datagrams larger than this do occur. This means that normally each MAC layer frame can carry a single IP datagram as its data payload. IP version 4 or higher, still the dominant version deployed on the Internet today, allows fragmentation of larger datagrams, to split large datagrams into chunks small enough to fit the limited frame size of the underlying MAC layer medium. IPv4 or higher reassembles any fragmented datagrams at the ultimate destination. IP version 6 or higher, which is becoming more widely deployed due to its widespread use in smart phone networks and Asia, does not support fragmentation and reassembly; this removes from IPv6 or higher one of the attack vectors enabled by IPv4 or higher.

Network layer forwarding of IP datagrams is best effort and is not reliable. Network layer modules along the path taken by any message can lose and reorder datagrams. It is common for the network layer in a router to recover from congestion—that is, when the router is overwhelmed by more receive frames than it can process—by discarding late-arriving frames until the router has caught up with its forwarding workload. The network layer can reorder datagrams when the Internet topology changes, because a new path between source and destination might be shorter or longer than an old path, so datagrams in flight before the change can arrive after frames sent following the change. The Internet architecture delegates recovery from these problems to high-layer modules.

Some applications, such as those utilizing voice and video, do not respond well to reordering because it imposes a severe performance penalty on the application. In order to better accommodate the needs of these types of message traffic, the Internet has begun to implement protocols such as MPLS, which mimics the switched circuit mechanisms of phone networks. That is, these protocols create *flows* through the Internet that suppress datagram reordering. Circuit switching uses network resources differently than best-effort forwarding, and network links in the core of the network usually require greater bandwidth for the two technologies to successfully coexist.

The Transport Layer

The transport layer is implemented by TCP and similar protocols. Not all transport protocols provide the same level of service as TCP, but a description of TCP will suffice to help us understand the issues addressed by the transport layer. The transport layer provides a multitude of functions.

First, the transport layer creates and manages instances of two-way channels between communication endpoints. These channels are called *connections*. Each connection represents a virtual endpoint between a pair of communication endpoints. A connection is named by a pair of IP addresses and *port numbers*. Two devices can support simultaneous connections using different port numbers for each connection. It is common to differentiate applications on the same host through the use of port numbers.

A second function of the transport layer is to support delivery of messages of arbitrary length. The 64 K byte limit of the underlying IP module is too small to carry really large messages, and the transport layer module at the message source chops messages into pieces called *segments* that are more easily digestible by lower-layer communications modules. The segment size is negotiated between the two transport endpoints during connection setup. The segment size is chosen by discovering the smallest maximum frame size supported by any MAC + PHY link on the path through the Internet used by the connection setup messages. Once this is known, the transmitter typically partitions a large message into segments no larger than this size, plus room for an IP header. The transport layer module passes each segment to the network layer module, where it becomes the payload for a single IP datagram. The destination network layer module extracts the payload from the IP datagram and passes it to the transport layer module, which interprets the information as a message segment. The destination transport reassembles this into the original message once all the necessary segments arrive.

Of course, as noted, MAC frames and IP datagrams can be lost in transit, so some segments can be lost. It is the responsibility of the transport layer module to detect this loss and retransmit the missing segments. This is accomplished by a sophisticated acknowledgment algorithm defined by the transport layer. The destination sends a special acknowledgment message, often piggybacked with a data segment being sent in the opposite direction, for each segment that arrives. Acknowledgments can be lost as well, and if the message source does not receive the acknowledgment within a time window, the source retransmits the unacknowledged segment. This process is repeated a number of times, and if the failure continues, the network layer tears down the connection because it cannot fulfill its reliability commitment.

One reason for message loss is congestion at routers, something blind retransmission of unacknowledged segments will only exacerbate. The network layer is also responsible for implementing congestion control algorithms as part of its transmit function. TCP, for instance, lowers its transmit rate whenever it fails to receive an acknowledgment message in time, and it slowly increases its rate of transmission until another acknowledgment is lost. This allows TCP to adapt to congestion in the network, helping to minimize frame loss.

It can happen that segments arrive at the destination out of order, since some IP datagrams for the same connection could traverse the Internet through different paths due to dynamic changes in the underlying network topology. The transport layer is responsible for delivering the segments in the order sent, so the receiver caches any segments that arrive out of order prior to delivery. The TCP reordering algorithm is closed tied to the acknowledgment and congestion control scheme so that the receiver never has to buffer too many out-of-order received segments and the sender not too many sent but unacknowledged segments.

Segment data arriving at the receiver can be corrupted due to undetected bit errors on the data link and copy errors within routers and the sending and receiving computing systems. Accordingly, all transport layers use a checksum algorithm called a *cyclic redundancy check* (CRC) to detect such errors. The receiving transport layer module typically discards segments with errors detected by the CRC algorithm, and recovery occurs through retransmission by the sender when it fails to receive an acknowledgment from the receiver for a particular segment.

The Sockets Layer

The top layer of the Internet, the sockets layer, does not *per se* appear in the architecture at all. The sockets layer provides a set of interfaces, each of which represents a logical communications endpoint. An application can use the sockets layer to create, manage, and destroy connection instances using a socket as well as send and receive messages over the connection. The sockets layer has been designed to hide much of the complexity of the transport layer, thereby making TCP easier to use. The sockets layer has been highly optimized over the years to deliver as much performance as possible, but it does impose a performance penalty. Applications with very demanding performance requirements tend to utilize the transport layer directly instead of through the sockets layer module, but this comes with a very high cost in terms of software maintenance.

In most implementations of these communications modules, each message is copied twice, at the sender and the receiver. Most operating systems are organized into user space, which is used to run applications, and kernel space, where the operating system itself runs. The sockets layer occupies the boundary between user space and kernel space. The sockets layer's *send* function copies a message from memory controlled by the sending application into a buffer controlled by the kernel for transmission. This copy prevents the application from changing a message it has posted to send, but it also permits the application and kernel to continue their activities in parallel, thus better utilizing the device's computing resources. The sockets layer invokes the transport layer, which partitions the message buffer into segments and passes the address of each segment to the network layer. The network layer adds its headers to form datagrams from the segments and invokes the right MAC layer module to transmit each datagram to its next hop. A second copy occurs at the boundary between the network layer and the MAC layer, since the data link must be able to asynchronously match transmit requests from the network layer to available transmit slots on the medium provided by its PHY. This process is reversed at the receiver, with a copy of datagrams across the MAC-network layer boundary and of messages between the socket layer and application.

Address Resolution Protocol

The network layer uses Address Resolution Protocol, or ARP, to translate IP addresses into MAC addresses, which it needs to give to the MAC layer in order to deliver frames to the appropriate destination.

The ARP module asks the question, "Who is using IP address X?" The requesting ARP module uses a request/response protocol, with the MAC layer broadcasting the ARP module's requests to all the other devices on the same physical medium segment. A receiving ARP module generates a response only if its network layer has assigned the IP address to one of its MAC modules. Responses are addressed to the requester's MAC address. The requesting ARP module inserts the response received in an address translation table used by the network layer to identify the next hop for all datagrams it forwards.

Dynamic Host Configuration Protocol

Remember that unlike MAC addresses, IP addresses cannot be assigned in the factory, because they are dynamic and must reflect a device's current location within the Internet. A MAC module uses Dynamic Host Configuration Protocol, or DHCP, to acquire an IP address for itself to reflect the device's current location with respect to the Internet topology.

DHCP makes the request: "Please configure my MAC module with an IP address." When one of a device's MAC layer modules connects to a new medium, it invokes DHCP to make this request. The associated DHCP module generates such a request that conveys the MAC address of the MAC module, which the MAC layer module broadcasts to the other devices attached to the same physical medium segment. A DHCP server responds with a unicast DHCP response binding an IP address to the MAC address. When it receives the response, the requesting DHCP module passes the assigned IP address to the network layer to configure in its address translation table.

In addition to binding an IP address to the MAC module used by DHCP, the response also contains a number of network configuration parameters, including the address of one or more routers, to enable reaching arbitrary destinations, the maximum datagram size supported, and the addresses of other servers, such as DNS servers, that translate human-readable names into IP addresses.

Domain Naming Service

IP and MAC addresses are efficient means for identifying different network interfaces, but human beings are incapable of using these as reliably as computing devices can. Instead, human beings rely on names to identify the computing devices with which they want to communication. These names are centrally managed and called *domain names*. The Domain Naming Service, or DNS, is a mechanism for translating human-readable names into IP addresses.

The translation from human-readable names to IP addresses happens within the socket layer module. An application opens a socket with the name of the intended destination. As the first step of opening a connection to that destination, the socket sends a request to a DNS server, asking the server to translate the name into an IP address. When the server responds, the socket can open the connection to the right destination, using the IP address provided.

It is becoming common for devices to register their IP addresses under their names with DNS once DHCP has completed. This permits other devices to locate the registering device so that they can send messages to it.

Internet Control Message Protocol

Internet Control Message Protocol (ICMP) is an important diagnostic tool for trouble-shooting the Internet. Though ICMP provides many specialized message services, three are particularly important:

- *Ping.* Ping is a request/response protocol designed to determine the reachability of another IP address. The requestor sends a ping request message to a designated IP address. If the ping message is delivered, the interface using the destination IP address sends a ping response message to the IP address that sourced the request. The responding ICMP module copies the contents of the ping request into the ping response so that the requestor can match responses to requests. The requestor uses pings to measure the roundtrip time to a destination, among other things.
- *Traceroute.* Traceroute is another request/response protocol. An ICMP module generates a traceroute request to discover the path it is using to traverse the Internet to a destination IP address. The requesting ICMP module transmits a destination. Each router that handles the traceroute request adds a description of its own IP address that received the message and then forwards the updated traceroute request. The destination sends all this information back to the message source in a traceroute response message.
- *Destination unreachable.* When a router receives a datagram for which it has no next hop, it generates a "destination unreachable" message and sends it back to the datagram source. When the message is delivered, the ICMP module marks the forwarding table of the message source so that its network layer will reject further attempts to send messages to the destination IP address. An analogous process happens at the ultimate destination when a message is delivered to a network layer, but the application targeted to receive the message is no longer online. The purpose of "destination unreachable" messages is to suppress messages that will never be successfully delivered in order to reduce network congestion.

Routing

The last cross-layer module we'll discuss is *routing*. Routing is a middleware application to maintain the forwarding tables used by the network layer. Each router advertises itself by periodically broadcasting "hello" messages through each of its MAC interfaces. This allows routers to discover the presence or loss of all neighboring routers, letting them construct the one-hop topology of the part of the Internet directly visible through their directly attached media. The routing application in a router then uses a sophisticated gossiping mechanism to exchange this view of the local topology with their neighbors. Since some of a router's neighbors are not its own direct neighbors, this allows each router to learn the two-hop topology of the Internet. This process repeats recursively until each router knows the entire topology of the Internet. The cost of using each link is part of the information gossiped. A routing module receiving this information uses all of it to compute a lowest-cost route to each destination. Once this is accomplished, the routing module reconfigures the forwarding table maintained by its network layer module. The routine module updates the forwarding table whenever the Internet topology changes, so each network layer can make optimal forwarding decisions in most situations and at the very worst reach any other device that is also connected to the Internet.

There are many different routing protocols, each of which is based on different gossiping mechanisms. The most widely deployed routing protocol between different administrative domains within the Internet is the border gateway protocol (BGP). The most widely deployed routing protocols within wired networks controlled by a single administrative domain are OSPF and RIP. AODV, OLSR, and TBRPF are commonly used in Wi-Fi meshes. Different routing protocols are used in different environments because each one addresses different scaling and administrative issues.

Applications

Applications are the ultimate reason for networking, and the Internet architecture has been shaped by applications' needs. All communicating applications define their own language in which to express what they need to say. Applications generally use the sockets layer to establish communication channels, which they then use for their own purposes.

Since the network modules have been designed to be a generic communications vehicle, that is, designed to meet the needs of all (or at least most) applications, it is rarely meaningful for the network to attempt to make statements on behalf of the applications. There is widespread confusion on this point around authentication and key management, which are the source of many exploitable security flaws.

2. AN INTERNET THREAT MODEL

Now that we have reviewed the architecture of the Internet protocol suite, it is possible to constructively consider the security issues it raises. Before doing so, let's first set the scope of the discussion.

There are two general approaches to attacking a networked computer. The first is to compromise one of the communicating parties so that it responds to queries with lies or otherwise communicates in a manner not foreseen by the system designers of the receiver. For example, it has become common to receive email with virus-infected attachments, whereby opening the attachment infects the receiver with the virus. These messages typically are sent by a machine that has already been compromised, so the sender is no longer acting as intended by the manufacturer of the computing system. Problems of this type are called *Byzantine failures*, named after the Byzantine Generals problem.

The Byzantine Generals problem imagines several armies surrounding Byzantium. The generals commanding these armies can communicate only by exchanging messages transported by couriers between them. Of course the couriers can be captured and the messages replaced by forgeries, but this is not really the issue, since it is possible to devise message schemes that detect lost messages or forgeries. All the armies combined are sufficient to overwhelm the defenses of Byzantium, but if even one army fails to participate in a coordinated attack, the armies of Byzantium have sufficient strength to repulse the attack. Each general must make a decision as to whether to participate in an attack on Byzantium at dawn or withdraw to fight another day. The question is how to determine the veracity of the messages received on which the decision to attack will be made—that is, whether it is possible to detect that one or more generals have become traitors and so will say their armies will join the attack when in fact they plan to hold back so that their allies will be slaughtered by the Byzantines.

Practical solutions addressing Byzantine failures fall largely within the purview of platform rather than network architecture, although the interconnectivity topology is an important consideration. For example, since viruses infect a platform by buffer overrun attacks, platform mechanisms to render buffer overrun attacks futile are needed. Secure logging, to make an accurate record of messages exchanged, is a second deterrent to these sorts of attacks; the way to accomplish secure logging is usually a question of platform design. Most self-propagating viruses and worms utilize the Internet to propagate, but they do not utilize any feature of the Internet architecture per se for their success. The success of these attacks instead depends on the architecture, design, implementation, and policies of the receiving system. Although these sorts of problems are important, we will rarely focus on security issues stemming from Byzantine failures.

What will instead be the focus of the discussion are attacks on the messages exchanged between computers themselves. As we will see, even with this more limited scope, there are plenty of opportunities for things to go wrong.

The Dolev–Yao Adversary Model

Security analyses of systems traditionally begin with a model of the attacker, and we follow this tradition. Daniel Dolev and Andrew Chi-Chih Yao formulated the standard attack model against messages exchanged over a network. The *Dolev-Yao model* makes the following assumptions about an attacker:

- *Eavesdrop.* An adversary can listen to any message exchanged through the network.
- *Forge.* An adversary can create and inject entirely new messages into the datastream or change messages in flight; these messages are called *forgeries*.
- *Replay.* A special type of forgery, called a *replay*, is distinguished. To replay a message, the adversary resends legitimate messages that were sent earlier.

- *Delay and rush.* An adversary can delay the delivery of some messages or accelerate the delivery of others.
- *Reorder.* An adversary can alter the order in which messages are delivered.
- *Delete.* An adversary can destroy in-transit messages, either selectively or all the messages in a datastream.

This model assumes a very powerful adversary, and many people who do not design network security solutions sometimes assert that the model grants adversaries an unrealistic amount of power to disrupt network communications. However, experience demonstrates that it is a reasonably realistic set of assumptions in practice; examples of each threat abound, as we will see. One of the reasons for this is that the environment in which the network operates is exposed and therefore open to attack by a suitably motivated adversary; unlike memory or microprocessors or other devices internal to a computer, there is almost no assurance that the network medium will be deployed in a "safe" way (Indeed, malware has progressed to the point where internal buses and memories can no longer be considered secure against knowledgeable attackers, which is forcing a migration of network security techniques into the platforms themselves). That is, it is comparatively easy for an attacker to anonymously access the physical network fabric, or at least the medium monitored to identify attacks against the medium and the networked traffic it carries. And since a network is intended as a generic communications vehicle, it becomes necessary to adopt a threat model that addresses the needs of all possible applications.

Layer Threats

With the Dolev–Yao model in hand, we can examine each of the architectural components of the Internet protocol suite for vulnerabilities. We next look at threats each component of the Internet architecture exposes through the prism of this model. The first Dolev–Yao assumption about adversaries is that they can eavesdrop on any communications.

Eavesdropping

An attacker can eavesdrop on a communications medium by connecting a receiver to the medium. Ultimately, such a connection has to be implemented at the PHY layer because an adversary has to access some physical media somewhere to be able to listen to anything at all. This connection to the PHY medium might be legitimate, such as when an authorized device is uncompromised, or illegitimate, such as an illegal wiretap; it can be intentional, as when an eavesdropper installs a rogue device, or unintentional, such as a laptop with wireless capabilities that will by default attempt to connect to any Wi-Fi network within range.

With a PHY layer connection, the eavesdropper can receive the analog signals on the medium and decode them into bits. Because of the limited scope of the PHY layer function—there are no messages, only analog signals representing bits and special control symbols—the damage an adversary can do with only PHY layer functionality is rather limited. In particular, to make sense of the bits, an adversary has to impose the higher-layer frame and datagram formats onto the received bits. That is, any eavesdropping attack has to take into account at least the MAC layer to learn anything meaningful about the communications. Real eavesdroppers are more sophisticated than this: They know how to interpret the bits as a medium-specific encoding with regard to the frames that are used by the MAC layer. They also know how to extract the media-independent representation of datagrams conveyed within the MAC frames, as well as how to extract the transport layer segments from the datagrams, which can be reassembled into application messages.

The defenses erected against any threat give some insight into the perceived danger of the threat. People are generally concerned about eavesdropping, and it is easy to illicitly attach listening devices to most PHY media, but detection and removal of wiretaps has not evolved into a comparatively large industry. An apparent explanation of why this is so is that it is easier and more cost effective for an attacker to compromise a legitimate device on the network and configure it to eavesdrop than it is to install an illegitimate device. The evidence for this view is that the antivirus/antibot industry is gigantic by comparison.

There is another reason that an antiwiretapping industry has never developed for the Internet. Almost every MAC module supports a special mode of operation called *promiscuous mode*. A MAC module in promiscuous mode receives every frame appearing on the medium, not just the frames addressed to itself. This allows one MAC module to snoop on frames that are intended for other parties. Promiscuous mode was intended as a troubleshooting mechanism to aid network administrators in diagnosing the source of problems. However, it is also a mechanism that can be easily abused by anyone motivated to enable promiscuous mode on their own networking devices.

Forgeries

A second Dolev–Yao assumption is that the adversary can forge messages. Eavesdropping is usually fairly innocuous compared to forgeries, because eavesdropping merely leaks information, whereas forgeries cause an unsuspecting receiver to take actions based on false information. Hence, the prevention or detection of forgeries is one of the central goals of network security mechanisms. Different kinds of forgeries are possible for each architectural component of the Internet. We will consider only a few for each layer of the Internet protocol suite, to give a taste of their variety and ingenuity.

Unlike the eavesdropping threat, where knowledge of higher layers is essential to any successful compromise, an attacker with only a PHY layer transmitter (and no higher-layer mechanisms) can disrupt communications by *jamming* the medium—that is, outputting noise onto the medium in an effort to disrupt communications. A jammer creates signals that do not necessarily correspond to any wave forms corresponding to bit or other control symbols. The goal of a pure PHY layer jammer is denial of service (DoS)—that is, to fill the medium sufficiently so that no communications can take place.

Sometimes it is feasible to create a jamming device that is sensitive to the MAC layer formats above it, to selectively jam only some frames. Selective jamming requires a means to interpret bits received from the medium as a higher-layer frame or datagram, and the targeted frames to jam are recognized by some criterion, such as being sent from or to a particular address. So that it can enable its own transmitter before the frame has been entirely received by its intended destination, the jammer's receiver must recognize the targeted frames before they are fully transmitted. When this is done correctly, the jammer's transmitter interferes with the legitimate signals, thereby introducing bit errors in the legitimate receiver's decoder. This results in the legitimate receiver's MAC layer detecting the bit errors while trying to verify the frame check sequence, causing it to discard the frame. Selective jamming is harder to implement than continuous jamming, but it is also much harder to detect, because the jammer's signal source transmits only when legitimate devices transmit as well, and only the targeted frames are disrupted. Successful selective jamming usually causes administrators to look for the source of the communications failure on one of the communicating devices instead of in the network for a jammer.

There is also a higher-layer analog to jamming, called *message flooding*. Denial of service (DoS) is also the goal of message flooding. The technique used by message flooding is to create and send messages at a rate high enough to exhaust some resource. It is popular today, for instance, for hackers to compromise thousands of unprotected machines, which they use to generate simultaneous messages to a targeted site. Examples of this kind of attack are to completely fill the physical medium connecting the targeted site to the Internet with network layer datagrams—this is usually hard or impossible—or to generate transport layer connection requests at a rate faster than the targeted site can respond. Other variants—request operations that lead to disk I/O or require expensive cryptographic operations—are also common. Message flooding attacks have the property that they are legitimate messages from authorized parties but simply timed so that collectively their processing exceeds the maximum capacity of the targeted system.

Let's turn away from resource-clogging forgeries and examine forgeries designed to cause a receiver to take an unintended action. It is possible to construct this type of forgery at any higher layer: forged frames, datagrams, network segments, or application messages.

To better understand how forgeries work, we need to examine Internet "identities" more closely—MAC addresses, IP addresses, transport port numbers, and DNS names—as well as the modules that use or support their use. The threats are a bit different at each layer.

Recall that each MAC layer module is manufactured with its own "hardware" address, which is supposed to be a globally unique identifier for the MAC layer module instance. The hardware address is configured in the factory into nonvolatile memory. At boot time, the MAC address is transferred from nonvolatile memory into operational RAM maintained by the MAC module. A transmitting MAC layer module inserts the MAC address from RAM into each frame it sends, thereby advertising an "identity." The transmitter also inserts the MAC address of the intended receiver on each frame, and the receiving MAC layer matches the MAC address in its own RAM against the destination field in each frame sent over the medium. The receiver ignores the frame if the MAC addresses don't match and receives the frame otherwise.

In spite of this system, it is useful—even necessary sometimes—for a MAC module to change its MAC address. For example, sometimes a manufacturer accidentally recycles MAC addresses so that two different modules receive the same MAC address in the factory. If both devices are deployed on the same network, neither works correctly until one of the two changes its address. Because of this problem, all manufacturers provide a way for the MAC module to alter the address in RAM. This can always be specified by software via the MAC module's device driver, by replacing the address retrieved from hardware at boot time.

Since the MAC address can be changed, attacks will find it. A common attack in Wi-Fi networks, for instance, is for the adversary to put the MAC module of the attacking device into promiscuous mode, to receive frames from other nearby systems. It is usually easy to identify another client device from the received frames and extract its MAC address. The attacker then reprograms its own MAC module to transmit frames using the address of its victim. A goal of this attack is usually to "hijack" the session of a customer paying for Wi-Fi service; that is, the attacker wants free Internet access for which someone else has already paid. Another goal of such an attack is often to avoid attribution of the actions being taken by the attacker; any punishment for antisocial or criminal behavior will likely be attributed to the victim instead of the attacker because all the frames that were part of the behavior came from the victim's address.

A similar attack is common at the network layer. The adversary will snoop on the IP addresses appearing in the datagrams encoded in the frames and use these instead of their own IP addresses to source IP datagrams. This is a more powerful attack than that of utilizing only a MAC address, because IP addresses are global; an IP address is an Internet-wide locator, whereas a MAC address is only an identifier on the medium to which the device is physically connected.

Manipulation of MAC and IP addresses leads directly to a veritable menagerie of forgery attacks and enables still others. A very selective list of examples must suffice to illustrate the ingenuity of attackers:

- TCP uses sequence numbers as part of its reliability scheme. TCP is supposed to choose the first sequence number for a connection randomly. If an attacker can predict the first sequence number for a TCP connection, an attacker who spoofs the IP address of one of the parties to the connection can hijack the session by interjecting its own datagrams into the flow that use the correct sequence numbers. This desynchronizes the retry scheme for the device being spoofed, which then drops out from the conversation. This attack seems to have become relatively less common than other attacks over the past few years, since most TCP implementations have begun to utilize better random number generators to seed their sequence numbers.
- An attacker can generate an ARP response to any ARP request, thus claiming to use any requested IP address. This is a common method to hijack another machine's IP address; it is a very effective technique when the attacker has a fast machine and the victim machine has less processing power, and so responds more slowly.
- An attacker can generate DHCP response messages replying to DHCP requests. This technique is often used as part of a larger forgery, such as the evil twin attack, whereby an adversary masquerades as an access point for a Wi-Fi public hot spot. The receipt of DHCP response messages convinces the victim it is connecting to an access point operated by the legitimate hotspot.
- A variant is to generate a DHCP request with the hardware MAC address of another device. This method is useful when the attacker wants to ascribe action it takes over the Internet to another device.
- An attacker can impersonate the DNS server, responding to requests to resolve human-readable names into IP addresses. The IP address in the response messages points the victim to a site controlled by the attacker. This is becoming a common attack used by criminals attempting to commit financial fraud, such as stealing credit card numbers.

Replay

Replay is a special forgery attack. It occurs when an attacker records frames or datagrams and then retransmits them unchanged at a later time.

This might seem like an odd thing to do, but replay attacks are an especially useful way to attack stateful messaging protocols, such as a routing protocol. Since the goal of a routing protocol is to allow every router to know the current topology of the network, a replayed routing message can cause the routers receiving it to utilize out-of-date information.

An attacker might also respond to an ARP request sent to a sabotaged node or to a mobile device that has migrated to another part of the Internet by sending a replayed ARP response. This replay indicates the node is still present, thus masking the true network topology.

Replay is also often a valuable tool for attacking a message encryption scheme. By retransmitting a message, an attacker can sometimes learn valuable information from a message decrypted and then retransmitted without encryption on another link.

A primary use of replay, however, is to attack session start-up protocols. Protocol start-up procedures establish session state, which is used to operate the link or connection and determine when some classes of failures occur. Since this state is not yet established when the session begins, start-up messages replayed from prior instances of the protocol will fool the receiver into allocating a new session. This is a common DoS technique.

Delay and Rushing

Delay is a natural consequence of implementations of the Internet architecture. Datagrams from a single connection typically transit a path across the Internet in bursts. This happens because applications at the sender, when sending large messages, tend to send messages larger than a single datagram. The transport layer partitions these messages into segments to fit the maximum segment size along the path to the destination. The MAC tends to output all the frames together as a single blast after it has accessed the medium. Therefore, routers with many links can receive multiple datagram bursts at the same time. When this happens, a router has to temporarily buffer the burst, since it can output only one frame conveying a datagram per link at a time. Simultaneous arrival of bursts of datagrams is one source of congestion in routers. This condition usually manifests itself at the application by slow communications time over the Internet. Delay can also be intentionally introduced by routers, such as via traffic shaping.

Attackers can induce delays in several ways. We illustrate this idea by describing two different attacks. It is not uncommon for an attacker to take over a router, and when this happens, the attacker can introduce artificial delay, even when the router is uncongested. As a second example, attackers with bot armies can bombard a particular router with "filler" messages, the only purpose of which is to congest the targeted router.

Rushing is the opposite problem: a technique to make it appear that messages can be delivered sooner than can be reasonably expected. Attackers often employ rushing attacks by first hijacking routers that service parts of the Internet that are fairly far apart in terms of network topology. The attackers cause the compromised routers to form a *virtual link* between them. A virtual link emulates a MAC layer protocol but running over a transport layer connection between the two routers instead of a PHY layer. The virtual link, also called a *wormhole*, allows the routers to claim they are connected directly by a link and so are only one hop apart. The two compromised routers can therefore advertise the wormhole as a "low-cost" path between their respective regions of the Internet. The two regions then naturally exchange traffic through the compromised routers and the wormhole.

An adversary usually launches a rushing attack as a prelude to other attacks. By attracting traffic to the wormhole endpoints, the compromised routers can eavesdrop and modify the datagrams flowing through them. Compromised routers at the end of a wormhole are also an ideal vehicle for selective deletion of messages.

Reorder

A second natural event in the Internet is datagram *reordering*. The two most common reordering mechanisms are forwarding table updates and traffic-shaping algorithms. Reordering due to forwarding takes place at the network layer; traffic shaping can be applied at the MAC layer or higher.

The Internet reconfigures itself automatically as routers set up new links with neighboring routers and tear down links between routers. These changes cause the routing application on each affected router to send an update to its neighbors, describing the topology change. These changes are gossiped across the network until every router is aware of what happened. Each router receiving such an update modifies its forwarding table to reflect the new Internet topology.

Since the forwarding table updates take place asynchronously from datagram exchanges, a router can select a different forwarding path for each datagram between even the same two devices. This means that two datagrams sent in order at the message source can arrive in a different order at the destination, since a router can update its forwarding table between the selection of a next hop for different datagrams.

The second reordering mechanism is traffic shaping, which gets imposed on the message flow to make better use of the communication resources. One example is quality of service. Some traffic classes, such as voice or streaming video, might be given higher priority by routers than best-effort traffic, which constitutes file transfers. Higher priority means the router will send datagrams carrying voice or video first while buffering the traffic longer. Endpoint systems also apply traffic-shaping algorithms in an attempt to make real-time applications work better, without gravely affecting the performance of applications that can wait for their data. Any layer of the protocol stack can apply traffic shaping to the messages it generates or receives.

An attacker can emulate reordering any messages it intercepts, but since every device in the Internet must recover from message reordering anyway, reordering attacks are generally useful only in very specific contexts. We will not discuss them further.

Message Deletion

Like reordering, *message deletion* can happen through normal operation of the Internet modules. A MAC layer will drop any frame it receives with an invalid frame check sequence. A network layer module will discard any datagram it receives with an IP header error. A transport layer will drop any data segment received with a data checksum error. A router will drop perfectly good datagrams after receiving too many simultaneous bursts of traffic that lead to congestion and exhaustion of its buffers. For these reasons, TCP was designed to retransmit data segments in an effort to overcome errors.

The last class of attack possible with a Dolev–Yao adversary is message deletion. Two message deletion attacks occur frequently enough to be named: *black-hole attacks* and *gray-hole attacks*.

Black-hole attacks occur when a router deletes all messages it is supposed to forward. From time to time, a router is misconfigured to offer a zero-cost route to every destination in the Internet. This causes all traffic to be sent to this router. Since no device can sustain such a load, the router fails. The neighboring routers cannot detect the failure rapidly enough to configure alternate routes, and they fail as well. This continues until a significant portion of the routers in the Internet fail, resulting in a black hole: Messages flow into the collapsed portion of the Internet and never flow out. A black-hole attack intentionally misconfigures a router. Black-hole attacks also occur frequently in small-scale sensor, mesh, and peer-to-peer file networks.

A gray-hole attack is a selective deletion attack. Targeted jamming is one type of selective message deletion attack. More generally, an adversary can discard any message it intercepts in the Internet, thereby preventing its ultimate delivery. An adversary intercepting and selectively deleting messages can be difficult to detect and diagnose, and so is a powerful attack. It is normally accomplished via compromised routers.

A subtler, indirect form of message deletion is also possible through the introduction of *forwarding loops*. Each IP datagram header has a *time-to-live* (TTL) field, limiting the number of hops that a datagram can make. This field is set to 255 by the initiator and decremented by each router through which the datagram passes. If a router decrements the TTL field to zero, it discards the datagram.

The reason for the TTL field is that the routing protocols that update the forwarding tables can temporarily cause forwarding loops because updates are applied asynchronously as the routing updates are gossiped through the Internet. For instance, if router A gets updated prior to router B, A might believe that the best path to some destination C is via B, whereas B believes the best route to C is via A as the next hop. Messages for C will ping-pong between A and B until one or both are updated with new topology information.

An attacker who compromises a router or forges its routing traffic can intentionally introduce forwarding routes. This causes messages addressed to the destinations affected by the forgery to circulate until the TTL field gets decremented to zero. These attacks are also difficult to detect, because all the routers are behaving according to their specifications, but messages are being mysteriously lost.

Summary

The most striking point to observe about all of the enumerated attacks is that all take advantage of the natural features and structure of the Internet architecture: No one is making any of the protocols misbehave, just "mis-using" the Internet's own features against "legitimate" use. Any I/O channel of any system—and communications over the Internet certainly falls into this bucket—is assumed under the control of an adversary under the Dolev–Yao model. The input parse for any such channel is therefore a programming environment to which we freely grant the adversary access via the language describing protocol messages on the channel. This means our communications architectures necessarily expose our systems to attack, unless we close all possible communications channels. Doing so is impractical because not all people and organizations with which they are affiliated necessarily trust one another for all possible communications, and openness is a necessary condition for our economic models. Vulnerability to attack is therefore a necessary consequence of communications and a judicious mix of security mechanisms with friends and open links with potential business partners is inevitable. Absolutely secure networks and systems have only limited utility.

3. DEFENDING AGAINST ATTACKS ON THE INTERNET

Now that we have a model for thinking about the threats against communication and we understand how the Internet works, we can examine how its communications can sometimes be protected. Here we will explain how cryptography is used to protect messages exchanged between various devices on the Internet and illustrate the techniques with examples.

As might be expected, the techniques vary according to scenario. Methods that are effective for an active session do not work for session establishment. Methods that are required for session establishment are too expensive for an established session. It is interesting that similar methods are used at each layer of the Internet architecture for protecting a session and for session establishment and that each layer defines its own security protocols. Many find the similarity of security solutions at different layers curious and wonder why security is not centralized in a single layer. We will explain why the same mechanisms solve different problems at different layers of the architecture, to give better insight into what each is for.

Layer Session Defenses

A *session* is a series of one or more related messages. The easiest and most straightforward defenses protect the exchange of messages that are organized into sessions, so we will start with session-oriented defenses.

Cryptography, when used properly, can provide reliable defenses against eavesdropping. It can also be used to detect forgery and replay attacks, and the methods used also have some relevance to detecting reordering and message deletion attacks. We will discuss how this is accomplished and illustrate the techniques with TLS, IPsec, and 802.11i.

Defending against Eavesdropping

The primary method used to defend against eavesdropping is encryption. Encryption was invented with the goal of making it infeasible for any computationally limited adversary to be able to learn anything useful about a message that cannot already be deduced by some other means, such as its length. Encryption schemes that appear to meet this goal have been invented and are in widespread use on the Internet. Here we will describe how they are used.

There are two forms of encryption: symmetric encryption, in which the same key is used to both encrypt and decrypt, and asymmetric encryption, in which encryption and decryption use distinct but related keys. The properties of each are different. Asymmetric encryption tends to be used only for applications related to session initiation and assertions about policy (although this is not universally true). The reason for this is that a single asymmetric key operation is generally too expensive across a number of dimensions—computation time, size of encrypted payloads, power consumption—to be applied to a message stream of arbitrary length. We therefore focus on symmetric encryption and how it is used by network security protocols.

A symmetric encryption scheme consists of three operations: *key generate*, *encrypt*, and *decrypt*. The key generate operation creates a *key*, which is a secret. The key generate procedure is usually application specific; we describe some examples of key generate operations in our discussion of session start-up. Once generated, the key is used by the encrypt operation to transform *plaintext* messages—that is, messages that can be read by anyone—into *ciphertext*, which is messages that cannot be read by any computationally limited party who does not possess the key. The key is also used by the decrypt primitive to translate ciphertext messages back into plaintext messages.

There are two kinds of symmetric encryption algorithms. The first type is called a *block cipher*, and the second a *stream cipher*. Block and stream ciphers make different assumptions about the environment in which they operate, making each more effective than the other at different protocol layers.

A block cipher divides a message into chunks of a fixed size called *blocks* and encrypts each block separately. Block ciphers have the random access property, meaning that a block cipher can efficiently encrypt or decrypt any block utilizing an *initialization vector* in conjunction with the key. This property makes block ciphers a good choice for encrypting the content of MAC layer frames and network layer datagrams, for two reasons. First, the chunking behavior of a block cipher corresponds nicely to the packetization process used to form datagrams from segments and frames from datagrams. Second, and perhaps more important, the Internet architecture models the lower layers as "best-effort" services, meaning that it assumes that datagrams and frames are sent and then forgotten. If a transmitted datagram is lost due to congestion or bit error (or attack), it is up to the transport layer or application to recover. The random access property makes it easy to restart a block cipher anywhere it's needed in the datastream. Popular examples of block ciphers include AES, DES, and 3DES, used by Internet security protocols.

Block ciphers are used by the MAC and network layers to encrypt as follows: First, a block cipher mode of operation is selected. A block cipher itself encrypts and decrypts only single blocks. A mode of operation is a set of rules extending the encryption scheme from a single block to messages of arbitrary length. The most popular modes of operation used in the Internet are counter (CTR) mode and cipher-block chaining (CBC) mode. Both require an initialization vector, which is a counter value for counter mode and a randomly generated bit vector for the cipher-block chaining mode. To encrypt a message, the mode of operation first partitions the message into a sequence of blocks whose size equals that of the cipher, padding if needed to bring the message length up to a multiple of the block size. The mode of operation then encrypts each block under the key while combining initialization vectors with the block in a mode-specific fashion.

For example, counter mode uses a counter as its initialization vector, which it increments, encrypts, and then exclusive-ORs the result with the block:

$$\text{counter} \rightarrow \text{counter} + 1; \quad E \leftarrow \text{Encrypt}_{\text{Key}}(\text{counter}); \quad \text{CipherTextBlock} \leftarrow E \oplus \text{PlainTextBlock}$$

where $\oplus$ denotes exclusive OR. The algorithm outputs the new (unencrypted) counter value, which is used to encrypt the next block and CipherTextBlock.

The process of assembling a message from a message encrypted under a mode of operation is very simple: Prepend the original initialization vector to the sequence of ciphertext blocks, which together replace the plaintext payload for the message. The right way to think of this is that the initialization vector becomes a new message header layer. Also prepended is a *key identifier*, which indicates to the receiver which key it should utilize to decrypt the payload. This is important because in many cases it is useful to employ multiple connections between the same pair of endpoints, and so the receiver can have multiple decryption keys to choose from for each message received from a particular source.

A receiver reverses this process: First, it extracts the initialization vector from the data payload, then it uses this and the ciphertext blocks to recover the original plaintext message by reversing the steps in the mode of operation.

This paradigm is widely used in MAC and network layer security protocols, including 802.11i, 802.16e, 802.1ae, and IPsec, each of which utilizes AES in modes related to counter and cipher-block chaining modes.

A stream cipher treats the data as a continuous stream and can be thought of as encrypting and decrypting data one bit at a time. Stream ciphers are usually designed so that each encrypted bit depends on all previously encrypted ones, so decryption becomes possible only if all the bits arrive in order; most true stream ciphers lack the random access property. This means that in principle stream ciphers only work in network protocols when they're used on top of a reliable data delivery service such as TCP. Therefore, they work correctly below the transport layer only when used in conjunction with reliable data links. Stream ciphers are attractive from an implementation perspective because they can often achieve much higher throughputs than block ciphers. RC4 is an example of a popular stream cipher.

Stream ciphers typically do not use a mode of operation or an initialization vector at all, or at least not in the same sense as a block cipher. Instead, they are built as pseudorandom number generators, the output of which is based on a key. The random number generator is used to create a sequence of bits that appear random, called a *key stream*, and the result is exclusive OR'd with the plaintext data to create ciphertext. Since XOR is an idempotent operation, decryption with a stream cipher is just the same operation: Generate the same key stream and exclusive OR it with the ciphertext to recover the plaintext. Since stream ciphers do not utilize initialization vectors, Internet protocols employing stream ciphers do not need the extra overhead of a header to convey the initialization vector needed by the decryptor in the block cipher case. Instead, these protocols rely on the ability of the sender and receiver to keep their respective key stream generators synchronized for each bit transferred. This implies that stream ciphers can only be used over a reliable medium such as TCP—that is, a transport that guarantees delivery of all bits in the proper order and without duplication.

Transport layer security (TLS) is an example of an Internet security protocol that uses the stream cipher RC4. TLS runs on top of TCP, which is a reliable transport and therefore meets one of the preconditions for use of RC4.

Assuming that a symmetric encryption scheme is well designed, its efficacy against eavesdropping depends on four factors. Failing to consider *any* of these factors can cause the encryption scheme to fail catastrophically.

INDEPENDENCE OF KEYS

This is perhaps the most important consideration for the use of encryption. All symmetric encryption schemes assume that the encryption key for each and every session is generated independently of the encryption keys used for every other session. Let's parse this thought:

- *Independent* means selected or generated by a process that is indistinguishable by *any* polynomial time statistical test from the uniform distribution applied to the key space. One common failure is to utilize a key generation algorithm that is not random, such as using the MAC or IP address of a device or time of session creation as the basis for a key, or even basing the key on a password. Schemes that use such public values instead of randomness for keys are easily broken using brute-force search techniques such as dictionary attacks. A second common failure is to pick an initial key randomly but create successive keys by some simple transformation, such as incrementing the initial key, exclusive OR 'ing the MAC address of the device with the key, and so on. Encryption using key generation schemes of this sort are easily broken using differential cryptanalysis and related key attacks.
- *Each and every* mean each and every. For a block cipher, reusing the same key twice with the same initialization vector can allow an adversary to recover information about the plaintext data from the ciphertext *without* using the key. Similarly, each key always causes the pseudorandom number generator at the heart of a stream cipher to generate the same key stream, and reuse of the same key stream again will leak the plaintext data from the ciphertext without using the key.
- Methods effective for the coordinated generation of random keys at the beginning of each session constitute a complicated topic. We address it in our discussion of session start-up later in the chapter.

LIMITED OUTPUT

Perhaps the second most important consideration is to limit the amount of information encrypted under a single key. The modern definition of security for an encryption scheme revolves around the idea of indistinguishability of the scheme's output from random. This goes back to a notion of ideal security proposed by Claude E. Shannon (a research mathematician working for Bell Labs). This has a dramatic effect on how long an encryption key may be safely used before an adversary has sufficient information to begin to learn something about the encrypted data.

Every encryption scheme is ultimately a deterministic algorithm using a finite state space, and no deterministic algorithm using a finite state space can generate an infinite amount of output that is indistinguishable from random. This means that encryption keys must be replaced on a regular basis. The amount of data that can be safely encrypted under a single key depends very much on the encryption scheme. As usual, the limitations for block ciphers and stream ciphers are a bit different.

Let the block size for a block cipher be some integer $n > 0$. Then, for any key K, for every string S_1 there is another string S_2 so that:

$$\text{Encrypt}_K(S_2) = S_1 \text{ and } \text{Decrypt}_K(S_1) = S_2$$

This says that a block cipher's encrypt and decrypt operations are *permutations* of the set of all bit strings whose length equals the block size. In particular, this property says that every pair of distinct n bit strings results in distinct n bit ciphertexts for any block cipher. However, by an elementary theorem from probability called the birthday paradox, random selection of n bit strings should result in a 50 percent probability that some string is chosen at least twice after about $2^{n/2}$ selections. This has a sobering consequence for block ciphers. It says that an algorithm as simple as naïve guessing can distinguish the output of the block cipher from random after about $2^{n/2}$ blocks have been encrypted. This means that an encryption key should never be used to encrypt even close to $2^{n/2}$ blocks before a new, independent key is generated.

To make this specific, DES and 3DES have a block size of 64 bits; AES has a 128-bit block size. Therefore a DES or 3DES key should be used much less than to encrypt $2^{64/2} = 2^{32}$ blocks, whereas an AES key should never be used to encrypt as many as 2^{64} blocks; doing so begins to leak information about the encrypted data without use of the encryption key. As an example, 802.11i has been crafted to limit each key to encrypting 2^{48} before forcing generation of a new key.

This kind of arithmetic does not work for a stream cipher, since its block size is 1 bit. Instead, the length of time a key can be safely used is governed by the periodicity of the pseudorandom number generator at the heart of the stream cipher. RC4, for instance, becomes distinguishable from random after generating about 2^{31} bytes. Note that $31 \approx 32 = \sqrt{256}$, and 256 bytes is the size of the RC4 internal state. This illustrates the rule of thumb that there is a birthday paradox relation between the maximum number of encrypted bits of a stream cipher key and its internal state.

KEY SIZE

The one "fact" about encryption that everyone knows is that larger keys result in stronger encryption. This is indeed true, provided that the generate keys operation is designed according to the independence condition. One common mistake is to properly generate a short key—say, 32 bits long—that is then concatenated to get a key of the length needed by the selected encryption scheme—say, 128 bits. Another similar error is to generate a short key and manufacture the remainder of the key with known public data, such as an IP address. These methods result in a key that is only as strong as the short key that was generated randomly.

MODE OF OPERATION

The final parameter is the mode of operation—that is, the rules for using a block cipher to encrypt messages whose length is different from the block cipher width. The most common problem is failure to respect the documented terms and conditions defined for using the mode of operation.

As an illustration of what can go wrong—even by people who know what they are doing—the cipher-block chaining mode requires that the initialization vector be chosen randomly. The earliest version of the IPsec standard used the cipher-block chaining mode exclusively for encryption. This standard recommended choosing initialization vectors as the final block of any prior message sent. The reasoning behind this recommendation was that, because an encrypted block cannot be distinguished from random if the number of blocks encrypted is limited, a block of a previously encrypted message ought to suffice. However, the advice given by the standard was erroneous because the initialization vector selection algorithm failed to have one property that a real random selection property has: The initialization vector is not unpredictable. A better way to meet the randomness requirement is to increment a counter, prepend it to the message to encrypt, and then encrypt the counter value, which becomes the initialization vector. This preserves the unpredictability property at a cost of encrypting one extra block.

A second common mistake is to design protocols using a mode of operation that was not designed to encrypt multiple blocks. For example, failing to use a mode of operation at all—using the naked encrypt and decrypt operations, with no initialization vector—is itself a mode of operation called *electronic code book* mode. Electronic code book mode was designed to encrypt messages that never span more than a single block—for example, encrypting keys to distribute for other operations. Using electronic code book mode on a message longer than a single block leaks a bit per block, however, because this mode allows an attacker to disguise when two plaintext blocks are the same or different. A classical example of this problem is to encrypt a photograph using electronic code book mode. The main outline of the photograph shows through plainly. This is not a failure of the encryption scheme; it is, rather, using encryption in a way that was never intended.

Now that we understand how encryption works and how it is used in Internet protocols, we should ask why it is needed at different layers. What does encryption at each layer of the Internet architecture accomplish? The best way to answer this question is to watch what it does.

Encryption applied at the MAC layer encrypts a single link. Data is encrypted prior to being put on a link and is decrypted again at the other end of a link. This leaves the IP datagrams conveyed by the MAC layer frames exposed inside each router as they wend their way across the Internet. Encryption at the MAC layer is a good way to transparently prevent data from leaking, since many devices never use encryption. For example, many organizations are distributed geographically and use direct point-to-point links to connect sites; encrypting the links connecting sites prevents an outsider from learning the organization's confidential information merely by eavesdropping. Legal wiretaps also depend on this arrangement because they monitor data inside routers. The case of legal wiretaps also illustrates the problem with link layer encryption only: If an unauthorized party assumes control of a router, he or she is free to read all the datagrams that traverse the router.

IPsec operates essentially at the network layer. Applying encryption via IPsec prevents exposure of the datagrams' payload end to end, so the data is still protected within routers. Since the payload of a datagram includes both the transport layer header and its data segments, applying encryption at the IPsec layer hides the applications being used as well as the data. This provides a big boost in confidentiality but also leads to more inefficient use of the Internet, since traffic-shaping algorithms in routers critically depend on having complete access to the transport headers. Using encryption at the IPsec layer also means the endpoints do not have to know whether each link a datagram traverses through the Internet applies encryption; using encryption at this layer simplifies the security analysis over encryption applied at the MAC layer alone. Finally, like MAC layer encryption, IPsec is a convenient tool for introducing encryption transparently to protect legacy applications, which by and large ignored confidentiality issues. A downside of IPsec is that it still leaves data unprotected within the network protocol implementation, and malware can some-times hook itself between the network and sockets layer to inspect traffic.

The transport layer encryption function can be illustrated by TLS. Like IPsec, TLS oper-ates end to end, but TLS encrypts only the application data carried in the transport data segments, leaving the transport header exposed. Thus, with TLS, routers can still perform their traffic-shaping function, and we still have the simplified security analysis that comes with end-to-end encryption. A second advantage is that TLS protects data essentially from application to application, making malware attacks against the communication channel per se more difficult. There are of course downsides. The first disadvantage of this method is that the exposure of the transport headers gives the attacker greater knowledge about what might be encrypted in the payload. The second disadvantage is that it is somewhat more awkward to introduce encryption transparently at the transport layer; encryption at the transport layer requires cooperation by the application to perform properly. This anal-ysis says that it is reasonable to employ encryption at any one of the network protocol layers because each solves a slightly different problem.

Before leaving the topic of encryption, it is worthwhile to emphasize what encryption does and does not do. Encryption, when properly used, is a *read access control*. If used cor-rectly, no one who lacks access to the encryption key can read the encrypted data. Encryption, however, is *not a write access control*; that is, it does not guarantee the integrity of the encrypted data. Counter mode and stream ciphers are subject to bit-flipping attacks, for instance. An attacker launches a bit-flipping attack by capturing a frame or datagram, changing one or more bits from 0 to 1 (or vice versa) and retransmitting the altered frame. The resulting frame decrypts to some result—the altered message decrypts to something—and if bits are flipped judiciously, the result can be intelligible. As a second example, cipher-block chaining mode is susceptible to cut-and-paste attacks, whereby the attack cuts the final few blocks from one message in a stream and uses them to overwrite the final blocks of a later stream. At most, one block decrypts to gibberish; if the attacker chooses the paste point judiciously, for example, so that it falls where the application ought to have random data anyway, this can be a powerful attack. The upshot is that even encrypted data needs an integrity mechanism to be effective, which leads us to the subject of defenses against forgeries.

Defending against Forgeries and Replays

Forgery and replay detection are usually treated together because replays are a special kind of forgery. We follow this tradition in our own discussion. Forgery detection, not eavesdropping protection, is the central concern for designs to secure network protocol. This is because every accepted forgery of an encrypted frame or datagram is a question whose answer can tell the adversary something about the encryption key or plaintext data. Just as one learns any subject in school, an attacker can learn about the encrypted stream or encryption key faster by asking questions rather than sitting back and passively listening.

Since eavesdropping is a passive attack, whereas creating forgeries is active, turning from the subject of eavesdropping to that of forgeries changes the security goals subtly. Encryption has a security goal of prevention—to prevent the adversary from learning anything useful about the data that cannot be derived in other ways. The comparable security goal for forgeries would be to prevent the adversary from creating forgeries, which is not feasible. This is because any device with a transmitter appropriate for the medium can send forgeries by creating frames and datagrams using addresses employed by other parties. What is feasible is a form of asking forgiveness instead of permission: Prevent the adversary from creating *undetected* forgeries.

The cryptographic tool underlying forgery detection is called a *message authentication code*. Like an encryption scheme, a message authentication code consists of three operations: a *key generation* operation, a *tagging* operation, and a *verification* operation. Also like encryption, the key generation operation, which generates a symmetric key shared between the sender and receiver, is usually application specific. The tagging and verification operations, however, are much different from encrypt and decrypt.

The tagging operation takes the symmetric key, called an *authentication key*, and a message as input parameters and outputs a *tag*, which is a cryptographic checksum depending on the key and message to produce its output.

The verification operation takes three input parameters: the symmetric key, the message, and its tag. The verification algorithm recomputes the tag from the key and message and compares the result against the tag with the received message. If the two fail to match, the verify algorithm outputs a signal that the message is a forgery. If the input and locally computed tag match, the verify algorithm declares that the message is authenticated.

The conclusion drawn by the verify algorithm of a message authentication code is not entirely logically correct. Indeed, if the tag is n bits in length, an attacker could generate a random n bit string as its tag and it would have one chance in 2^n of being valid. A message authentication scheme is considered good if there are no polynomial time algorithms that are significantly better than random guessing at producing correct tags.

Message authentication codes are incorporated into network protocols in a manner similar to encryption. First, a sequence number is prepended to the data that is being forgery protected; the sequence number, we will see, is used to detect replays. Next, a message authentication code tagging operation is applied to the sequence number and message body to produce a tag. The tag is appended to the message, and a key identifier for the authentication key is prepended to the message. The message can then be sent. The receiver determines whether the message was a forgery by first finding the authentication key identified by the key identifier, then by checking the correctness of the tag using the message authentication code's verify operation. If these checks succeed, the receiver finally uses the sequence number to verify that the message is not a replay.

How does replay detection work? When the authentication key is established, the sender initializes to zero the counter that is used in the authenticated message. The receiver meanwhile establishes a replay window, which is a list of all recently received sequence numbers. The replay window is initially empty. To send a replay protected frame, the sender increments his counter by one and prepends this at the front of the data to be authenticated prior to tagging. The receiver extracts the counter value from the received message and compares this to the replay window. If the counter falls before the replay window, which means it is too old to be considered valid, the receiver flags the message as a replay. The receiver does the same thing if the counter is already represented in the replay window data structure. If the counter is greater than the bottom of the replay window and is a counter value that has not yet been received, the frame or datagram is considered "fresh" instead of a replay.

The process is simplest to illustrate for the MAC layer. Over a single MAC link it is ordinarily impossible for frames to be reordered, because only a single device can access the medium at a time; because of the speed of electrons or photons comprising the signals representing bits, at least some of the bits at the start of a frame are received prior to the final bits being transmitted (satellite links are an exception). If frames cannot be reordered by a correctly operating MAC layer, the replay window data structure records the counter for the last received frame, and the replay detection algorithm merely has to decide whether the replay counter value in a received frame is larger than that recorded in its replay window. If the counter is less than or equal to the replay window value, the frame is a forgery; otherwise it is considered genuine. 802.11i, 802.16, and 802.1ae all employ this approach to replay detection. This same approach can be used by a message authentication scheme operating above the transport layer, by protocols such as TLS and SSH (Secure Shell), since the transport eliminates duplicates and delivers bits in the order sent. The replay window is more complicated at the network layer, however, because some reordering is natural, given that the network reorders datagrams. Hence, for the network layer the replay window is usually sized to account for the maximum reordering expected in the "normal" Internet. IPsec uses this more complex replay window.

This works for the following reason: Every message is given a unique, incrementing sequence number in the form of its counter value. The transmitter computes the message authentication code tag over the sequence number and the message data. Since it is not feasible for a computationally bounded adversary to create a valid tag for the data with probability significantly greater than $1/2^n$, a tag validated by the receiver implies that the message, including its sequence number, was created by the transmitter. The worst thing that could have happened, therefore, is that the adversary has delayed the message. However, if the sequence number falls within the replay window, the message could not have been delayed longer than reordering due to the normal operation of forwarding and traffic shaping within the Internet.

A replay detection scheme limits an adversary's opportunities to delete and to reorder messages. If a message does not arrive at its destination, its sequence number is never set in the receive window, so it can be declared a lost message. It is easy to track the percentage of lost messages, and if this exceeds some threshold, then communications become unreliable, but more important, the cause of the unreliability can be investigated. Similarly, messages received outside the replay window can also be tracked, and if the percentage becomes too high, messages are arriving out of order more frequently than might be expected from normal operation of the Internet, pointing to a configuration problem, an equipment failure, or an attack. Again, the cause of the anomaly can be investigated. Mechanisms like these are often how attacks are discovered in the first place. The important lesson is that attacks and even faulty equipment or misconfigurations are often difficult to detect without collecting reliability statistics, and the forgery detection mechanisms can provide some of the best reliability statistics available.

Just like encryption, the correctness of this analysis depends critically on the design enforcing some fundamental assumptions, regardless of the quality of the message authentication code on which it might be based. If any of the following assumptions are violated, the forgery detection scheme can fail catastrophically to accomplish its mission.

INDEPENDENCE OF AUTHENTICATION KEYS

This is absolutely paramount for forgery detection. If the message authentication keys are not independent, an attacker can easily create forged message authentication tags based on authentication keys learned in other ways. This assumption is so important that it is useful to examine in greater detail.

The first point is that a message authentication key utterly fails to accomplish its mission if it is shared among even three parties; only two parties must know any particular authentication key. This is very easy to illustrate. Suppose A, B, and C were to share a message authentication key, and suppose A creates a forgery-protected message it sends to C. What can C conclude when it receives this message? C cannot conclude that the message actually originated from A, even though its addressing indicates it did, because B could have produced the same message and used A's address. C cannot even conclude that B did not change some of the message in transit. Therefore, the algorithm loses all its efficacy for detecting forgeries if message authentication keys are known by more than two parties. They must be known by at least two parties or the receiver cannot verify that the message and its bits originated with the sender.

This is much different than encryption. An encryption/decryption key can be distributed to every member of a group, and as long as the key is not leaked from the group to a third party, the encryption scheme remains an effective read access control against parties that are not members of the group. Message authentication utterly fails if the key is shared beyond two parties. This is due to the active nature of forgery attacks and the fact that forgery handling, being a detection rather than a prevention scheme, already affords the adversary more latitude than encryption toward fooling the good guys.

So for forgery detection schemes to be effective, message authentication keys must be shared between exactly two communicating devices. As with encryption keys, a message authentication key must be generated randomly because brute-force searches and related key attacks can recover the key by observing messages transiting the medium.

NO REUSE OF REPLAY COUNTER VALUES WITH A KEY

Reusing a counter with a message authentication key is analogous to reusing an initialization vector with an encryption key. Instead of leaking data, however, replay counter value reuse leads automatically to trivial forgeries based on replayed messages. The attacker's algorithm is trivial: Using a packet sniffer, record each of the messages protected by the same key and file them in a database. If the attacker ever receives a key identifier and sequence number pair already in the database, the transmitter has begun to reuse replay counter values with a key. The attacker can then replay any message with a higher sequence number and the same key identifier. The receiver will be fooled into accepting the replayed message.

This approach implies that known forgery detection schemes cannot be based on static keys. To the contrary, we could attempt to design such a scheme. One could try to checkpoint in nonvolatile memory the replay counter at the transmitter and the replay window at the receiver. This approach does not work, however, in the presence of a Dolev–Yao adversary. The adversary can capture a forgery-protected frame in flight and then delete all successive messages. At its convenience later, the adversary resends the captured message. The receiver, using its static message authentication key, will verify the tag and, based on its replay window retrieved from nonvolatile storage, verify that the message is indeed in sequence and so accept the message as valid. This experiment demonstrates that forgery detection is not entirely satisfactory because sequence numbers do not take timeliness into account. Secure clock synchronization, however, is a difficult problem with solutions that enjoy only partial success. The construction of better schemes that account for timing remains an open research problem.

KEY SIZE

If message authentication keys must be randomly generated, they must also be of sufficient size to discourage brute-force attack. The key space has to be large enough to make exhaustive search for the message authentication key cost prohibitive. Key sizes for message authentication comparable with those for encryption are sufficient for this task.

MESSAGE AUTHENTICATION CODE TAG SIZE

We have seen many aspects that make message authentication codes somewhat more fragile encryption schemes. Message authentication code size is one in which forgery detection can on the contrary effectively utilize a smaller block size than an encryption scheme. Whereas an encryption scheme based on a 128-bit block size has to replace keys every 2^{48} or so blocks to avoid leaking data, an encryption scheme can maintain the same level of security with about a 48-bit message authentication code tag. The difference is that the block cipher-based encryption scheme leaks information about the encrypted data due to the birthday paradox, whereas an attacker has to create a valid forgery based on an exhaustive search due to the active nature of a forgery attack. In general, to determine the size of a tag needed by a message authentication code, we have only to determine the maximum number of messages sent in the lifetime of the key. As a rule of thumb, if this number of messages is bounded by 2^n, the tag need only be $n + 1$ bits long. This is only a rule of thumb because some MACs cannot be safely truncated to this minimal number of bits.

As with encryption, for many it is confusing that forgery detection schemes are offered at nearly every layer of the Internet architecture. To understand the preceding concept, it is again useful to ask what message forgery detection accomplishes at each layer.

If a MAC module requires forgery detection for every frame received, physical access to the medium being used by the module's PHY layer affords an attacker no opportunity to create forgeries. This is a very strong property. It means that the only MAC layer messages attacking the receiver are either generated by other devices authorized to attach to the medium or else are forwarded by the network layer modules of authorized devices, because all frames received directly off the medium generated by unauthorized devices will be discarded by the forgery detection scheme. A MAC layer forgery detection scheme therefore essentially provides a write access control of the physical medium, closing it to unauthorized parties. Installing a forgery detection scheme at any other layer will not provide this kind of protection. Requiring forgery detection at the MAC layer is therefore desirable whenever feasible.

Forgery detection at the network layer provides a different kind of assurance. IPsec is the protocol designed to accomplish this function. If a network layer module requires IPsec for every datagram received, this essentially cuts off attacks against the device hosting the module to other authorized machines in the entire Internet; datagrams generated by unauthorized devices will be dropped. With this forgery detection scheme it is still possible for an attacker on the same medium to generate frames attacking the device's MAC layer module, but attacks against higher layers become computationally infeasible. Installing a forgery detection scheme at any other layer will not provide this kind of protection. Requiring forgery detection at the network layer is therefore desirable whenever feasible as well.

Applying forgery detection at the transport layer offers different assurances entirely. Forgery detection at this level assures the receiving application that the arriving messages were generated by the peer application, not by some virus or Trojan-horse program that has linked itself between modules between protocol layers on the same or different machine. This kind of assurance cannot be provided by any other layer. Such a scheme at the network or MAC layers only defends against message injection by unauthorized devices on the Internet generally or directly attached to the medium, not against messages generated by unauthorized processes running on an authorized machine. Requiring forgery detection at the transport layer therefore is desirable whenever it is feasible.

The conclusion is that forgery detection schemes accomplish different desirable functions at each protocol layer. The security goals that are achievable are always architecturally dependent, and this comes through clearly with forgery detection schemes.

We began the discussion of forgery detection by noting that encryption by itself is subject to attack. One final issue is how to use encryption and forgery protection together to protect the same message. Three solutions could be formulated to this problem. One approach might be to add forgery detection to a message first—add the authentication key identifier, the replay sequence number, and the message authentication code tag—followed by encryption of the message data and forgery detection headers. TLS is an example Internet protocol that takes this approach. The second approach is to reverse the order of encryption and forgery detection: First encrypt, then compute the tag over the encrypted data and the encryption headers. IPsec is an example Internet protocol defined to use this approach. The last approach is to apply both simultaneously to the plaintext data. SSH is an Internet protocol constructed in this manner.

Session Start-up Defenses

If encryption and forgery detection techniques are such powerful security mechanisms, why aren't they used universally for all network communications? The problem is that not everyone is your friend; everyone has enemies, and in every human endeavor there are those with criminal mind-sets who want to prey on others. Most people do not go out of their way to articulate and maintain relationships with their enemies unless there is some compelling reason to do so, and technology is powerless to change this.

More than anything else, the keys used by encryption and forgery detection are relationship signifiers. Possession of keys is useful not only because they enable encryption and forgery detection but because their use assures the remote party that messages you receive will remain confidential and that messages the peer receives from you actually originated from you. They enable the accountable maintenance of a preexisting relationship. If you receive a message that is protected by a key that only you and I know, and you didn't generate the message yourself, it is reasonable for you to conclude that I sent the message to you and did so intentionally.

If keys are signifiers of preexisting relationships, much of our networked communications cannot be defended by cryptography, because we do not have preexisting relationships with everyone. We send and receive email to and from people we have never met. We buy products online from merchants we have never met. None of these relationships would be possible if we required all messages to be encrypted or authenticated. What is always required is an open, unauthenticated, risky channel to establish new relationships; cryptography can only assure us that communication from parties with whom we already have relationships is indeed occurring with the person with whom we think we are communicating.

A salient and central assumption for both encryption and forgery detection is that the keys these mechanisms use are fresh and independent across sessions. A session is an instance of exercising a relationship to effect communication. This means that secure communications require a state change, transitioning from a state in which two communicating parties are not engaged in an instance of communication to one in which they are. This state change is *session establishment*.

Session establishment is like a greeting between human beings. It is designed to synchronize two entities communicating over the Internet and establish and synchronize their keys, key identifiers, sequence numbers and replay windows, and, indeed, all the states to provide mutual assurance that the communication is genuine and confidential.

The techniques and data structures used to establish a secure session are different from those used to carry on a conversation. Our next goal is to look at some representative mechanisms in this area. The field is vast, and it is impossible to do more than skim the surface briefly to give the reader a glimpse of the beauty and richness of the subject. Secure session establishment techniques typically have three goals, as described in the following sections of this chapter.

Mutual Authentication

First, session establishment techniques seek to mutually authenticate the communicating parties to each other. *Mutually authenticate* means that both parties learn the "identity" of the other. It is not possible to know what is proper to discuss with another party without also knowing the identity of the other party. If only one party learns the identity of the other, it is always possible for an imposter to masquerade as the unknown party.

There are a couple of points to make about this issue. The first is what "learn" means. The kind of learning needed for session establishment is the creation of common knowledge: You know both identities, the peer knows both identities, and the peer knows you know both identities (and vice versa). A lower level of knowledge always enables opportunities for subverting the session establishment protocol.

The second point is what an identity is. Identities in session establishment protocols work differently than they do in real life. In session establishment, an identity is a commitment to a key that identifies you or your computing system. That is, an identity commits its sender to utilizing a particular key during session establishment, and the receiver to reject protocol messages generated using other keys.

KEY SECRECY

Second, session establishment techniques seek to establish a session key that can be maintained as a secret between the two parties and is known to no one else. The session key must be independent from all other keys for all other session instances and indeed from all other keys. This implies that no adversary with limited computational resources can distinguish the key from one selected uniformly at random. Generating such an independent session key is both harder and easier than it sounds; it is always possible to do so if a preexisting relationship already exists between the two communicating parties, and it is impossible to do so reliably if a preexisting relationship does not exist. Relationships begat other relationships, and nonrelationships are sterile with respect to the technology.

SESSION STATE CONSISTENCY

Finally, the parties need to establish a consistent view of the session state. This means that they both agree on the identities of both parties; they agree on the session key instance; they agree on the encryption and forgery detection schemes used, along with any associated state such as sequence counters and replay windows; and they agree on which instance of communication this session represents. If they fail to agree on a single shared parameter, it is always possible for an imposter to convince one of the parties that it is engaged in a conversation that is different from its peer's conversation. As with identities, agree means the two establish common knowledge of all of these parameters, and a session establishment protocol can be considered secure in the Dolev–Yao model only if the protocol proves that both parties share common knowledge of all of the parameters.

Mutual Authentication

There are an enormous number of ways to accomplish the mutual authentication function needed to initiate a new session. Here we examine two approaches that are used in various protocols within the Internet.

A SYMMETRIC KEY MUTUAL AUTHENTICATION METHOD

Our old friend the message authentication code can be used with a static, long-lived key to create a simple and robust mutual authentication scheme. Earlier we stressed that the properties of message authentication are incompatible with the use of a static key to provide forgery detection of session-oriented messages. The incompatibility is due to the use of sequence numbers for replay detection. We will replace sequence numbers with unpredictable quantities in order to resocialize static keys. The cost of this resocialization effort will be a requirement to exchange extra messages.

Suppose parties A and B want to mutually authenticate. We will assume that ID_A is B's name for the key it shares with A, whereas ID_B is A's name for the same key B. We will also assume that A and B share a long-lived message authentication key K and that K is known only to A and B. We will assume that A initiates the authentication. A and B can mutually authenticate using a three-message exchange, as follows: For message 1, A generates a random number R_A and sends a message containing its identity ID_A and random number to B:

$$A \rightarrow B: ID_A, R_A \tag{7.1}$$

The notation $A \rightarrow B: m$ means that A sends message m to B. Here the message being passed is specified as ID_A, R_A, meaning it conveys A's identity ID_A (or, more precisely, the name of the key K) and A's random number R_A. This message asserts B's name for A, to tell B which is the right long-lived key it should use in this instance of the authentication protocol. The random number R_A plays the role of the sequence number in the session-oriented case. It is random in order to provide an unpredictable challenge. If B responds correctly, then this proves that the response is live and was not pre-recorded. R_A also acts as a transaction identifier for the response to A's message 1 (it allows A to recognize which response goes with which message 1). This is important in itself, because without the ability to interleave different instances of the protocol A would have to wait forever for any lost message in order to obtain a correct theory.

If B is willing to have a conversation with A at this time, it fetches the correct message authentication key K, generates its own random number R_B, and computes a message authentication code tag T over the message ID_B, ID_A, R_A, R_B, that is, over the message consisting of both names and both random numbers. B appends the tag to the message, which it then sends to A in response to message 1:

$$B \rightarrow A: ID_B, ID_A, R_A, R_B, T \tag{7.2}$$

B includes A's name in the message to tell A which key to use to authenticate the message. It includes A's random number R_A in the message to signal the protocol instance to which this message responds.

The magic begins when A validates the message authentication code tag T. Since independently generated random numbers are unpredictable, A knows that the second message could not have been produced before A sent the first, because it returns R_A to A. Since the authentication code tag T was computed over the two identities ID_B and ID_A and the two random numbers R_A and R_B using the key K known only to A and B, and since A did not create the second message itself, A knows that B must have created message 2. Hence, message 2 is a response from B to A's message 1 for this instance of the protocol. If the message were to contain some other random number than R_A, A would know the message is not a response to its message 1.

If A verifies message 2, it responds by computing a message authentication code tag T' computed over ID_A and B's random number RB, which it includes in message 3:

$$A \rightarrow B: ID_A, R_B, T' \tag{7.3}$$

Reasoning as before, B knows A produced message 3 in response to its message 2, because message 3 could not have been produced prior to message 2 and only A could have produced the correct tag T'. Thus, after message 3 is delivered, A and B both have been assured of each other's identity, and they also agree on the session instance, which is identified by the pair of random numbers R_A and R_B.

A deeper analysis of the protocol reveals that message 2 must convey both identities and both random numbers protected from forgery by the tag T. This construction binds A's view of the session with B's, and this is providing A with B's view of what they know in common. This binding prevents interleaving or man-in-the-middle attacks. As an example, without this binding, a third party, C, could masquerade as B to A and as A to B. Similarly, message 3 confirms the common knowledge: A knows that B knows that A knows ID_A, ID_B, R_A, and R_B if B verifies the third message; similarly, if B verifies message 3, B knows that A knows that B knows the same parameters.

It is worth noting that message 1 is not protected from either forgery or replay. This lack of any protection is an intrinsic part of the problem statement. During the protocol, A and B must transition from a state where they are unsure about the other's identity and have no communication instance instantiating the long-term relationship signified by the encryption key K to a state where they fully agree on each other's identities and a common instance of communication expressing their long-lived relationship. A makes the transition upon verifying message 2, and there are no known ways to reassure it about B until this point of the protocol. B makes the state transition once it has completed verification of message 3. The point of the protocol is to transition from a mutually suspicious state to a mutually trusted state.

AN ASYMMETRIC KEY MUTUAL AUTHENTICATION METHOD

Authentication based on asymmetric keys is also possible. In addition to asymmetric encryption, there is also an asymmetric key analog of a message authentication code called a *signature scheme*. Just like a message authentication code, a signature scheme consists of three operations: *key generate*, *sign*, and *verify*. The key generate operation outputs two parameters, a signing key S and a related verification key V. S's key holder is never supposed to reveal S to another party, whereas V is meant to be a public value. Under these assumptions, the sign operation takes the signing key S and a message M as input parameters and outputs a signature s of M. The verify operation takes the verification key V, message M, and signature s as inputs, and returns whether it verifies that s was created from S and M. If the signing key S is indeed known by only one party, the signature s must have been produced by that party. This is because it is infeasible for a computationally limited party to compute the signature s without S. Asymmetric signature schemes are often called *public/private key schemes* because S is maintained as a secret, never shared with another party, whereas the verification key is published to everyone.

Signature schemes were invented to facilitate authentication. To accomplish this goal, the verification key must be public, and it is usually published in a certificate, which we will denote as $cert(ID_A, V)$, where ID_A is the identity of the key holder of S and V is the verification key corresponding to A. The certificate is issued by a well-known party called a *certificate authority*. The sole job of the certificate authority is to introduce one party to another. A certificate $cert(ID_A, V)$ issued by a certificate authority is an assertion that entity A has a public verification key V that is used to prove A's identity.

As with symmetric authentication, hundreds of different authentication protocols can be based on signature schemes. The following is one example among legions of examples:

$$A \to B: cert(ID_A, V), R_A \qquad (7.4)$$

Here $cert(ID_A, V)$ is A's certificate, conveying its identity ID_A and verification key V; R_A is a random number generated by A. If B is willing to begin a new session with A, it responds with the message:

$$B \to A: cert(ID_B, V'), R_B, R_A, sig_B(ID_A, R_B, R_A) \qquad (7.5)$$

R_B is a random number generated by B, and sig_B (ID_A, R_B, R_A) is B's signature over the message with fields ID_A, R_B, and R_A. Including IDA under B's signature is essential because it is B's way of asserting that A is the target of message 2. Including RB and RA in the information signed is also necessary to defeat man-in-the-middle attacks. A responds with a third message:

$$A \to B: cert(ID_A, V), R_b, sig_B(ID_B, R_B) \qquad (7.6)$$

A CAVEAT

Mutual authentication is necessary to establish identities. Identities are needed to decide on the access control policies to apply to a particular conversation, that is, to answer the question, Which information that the party knows is suitable for sharing in the context of this communications instance? Authentication—mutual or otherwise—has very limited utility if the communications channel is not protected against eavesdropping and forgeries.

One of the most common mistakes made by Wi-Fi hotspot operators, for instance, is to require authentication but disable eavesdropping and forgery protection for the subsequent Internet access via the hotspot. This is because anyone with a Wi-Fi radio transmitter can access the medium and hijack the session from a paying customer. Another way of saying this is that authentication is useful only when it's used in conjunction with a secure channel. This leads to the topic of session key establishment. The most common use of mutual authentication is to establish ephemeral session keys using the long-lived authentication keys. We will discuss session key establishment next.

Key Establishment

Since it is generally infeasible for authentication to be meaningful without a subsequent secure channel, and since we know how to establish a secure channel across the Internet if we have a key, the next goal is to add key establishment to mutual authentication protocols. In this model, a mutual authentication protocol establishes an ephemeral session key as a side effect of its successful operation; this session key can then be used to construct all the encryption and authentication keys needed to establish a secure channel. All the session states, such as sequence number, replay windows, and key identifiers, can be initialized in conjunction with the completion of the mutual authentication protocol.

It is usually feasible to add key establishment to an authentication protocol. Let's illustrate this with the symmetric key authentication protocol, based on a message authentication code, discussed previously. To extend the protocol to establish a key, we suppose instead that A and B share two long-lived keys K and K'. The first key K is a message authentication key as before. The second key K' is a derivation key, the only function of which is to construct other keys within the context of the authentication protocol. This is accomplished as follows: After verifying message 2 (from line 2 previously), A computes a session key SK as:

$$SK \leftarrow prf(K', R_A, R_B, ID_A, ID_B, length) \tag{7.7}$$

Here prf is another cryptographic primitive called a *pseudorandom function*. A pseudorandom function is characterized by the properties that (a) its output is indistinguishable from random by any computationally limited adversary and (b) it is hard to invert; that is, given a fixed output O, it is infeasible for any computationally limited adversary to find an input I so that $O \leftarrow prf(I)$. The output SK of (7) is *length* bits long and can be split into two pieces to become encryption and message authentication keys. B generates the same SK when it receives message 3. An example of a pseudorandom function is any block cipher, such as AES, in cipher-block chaining MAC mode. Cipher-block chaining MAC mode is just like cipher-block chaining mode, except all but the last block of encrypted data is discarded.

This construction meets the goal of creating an independent, ephemeral set of encryptions of message authentication keys for each session. The construction creates independent keys because any two outputs of a *prf* appear to be independently selected at random to any adversary that is computationally limited. A knows that all the outputs are statistically distinct, because A picks the parameter to the prf R_A randomly for each instance of the protocol; similarly for B. And using the communications instances identifiers RA, RB along with A and B's identities ID_A and ID_B are interpreted as a "contract" to use SK only for this session instance and only between A and B.

Public key versions of key establishment based on signatures and asymmetric encryption also exist, but we will close with one last public key variant based on a completely different asymmetric key principle called the *Diffie–Hellman algorithm*.

The Diffie–Hellman algorithm is based on the discrete logarithm problem in finite groups. A group G is a mathematical object that is closed under an associative multiplication and has inverses for each element in G. The prototypical example of a finite group is the integers under addition modulo a prime number p.

The idea is to begin with an element g of a finite group G that has a long period. This means $g^1 = g$, $g^2 = g \times g$, $g^3 = g^2 \times g$, ... Since G is finite, this sequence must eventually repeat. It turns out that $g = g^{n+1}$ for some integer $n > 1$, and $g^n = e$ is the group's neutral element. The element e has the property that $h \times e = e \times h = h$ *for* every element h in G, and n is called the *period* of g. With such an element it is easy to compute powers of g, but it is hard to compute the logarithm of g^k. If g is chosen carefully, no polynomial time algorithm is known that can compute k from g^k. This property leads to a very elegant key agreement scheme:

$$A \rightarrow B: cert(ID_A, V), g^a B \rightarrow A: g^b, cert(ID_B, V'), sig_B(g^a, g^b, ID_A) A \rightarrow B: sig_A(g^b, g^a, ID_B)$$

The session key is then computed as $SK \leftarrow prf(K, g^a g^b, ID_A, ID_B)$, where $K \leftarrow prf(0, g^{ab})$. In this protocol, a is a random number chosen by A, b is a random number chosen by B, and 0 denotes the all zeros key. Note that A sends g^a unprotected across the channel to B.

The quantity g^{ab} is called the *Diffie–Hellman key*. Since B knows the random secret b, it can compute $g^{ab} = (g^a)^b$ from A's public value g^a, and similarly A can compute g^{ab} from B's public value g^b. This construction poses no risk, because the discrete logarithm problem is intractable, so it is computationally infeasible for an attacker to determine a from g^a. Similarly, B may send g^b across the channel in the clear, because a third party cannot extract b from g^b. B's signature on message 2 prevents forgeries and assures that the response is from B. Since no method is known to compute g^{ab} from g^a and g^b, only A and B will know the Diffie–Hellman key at the end of the protocol. The step $K \leftarrow prf(0, g^{ab})$ extracts all the computational entropy from the Diffie–Hellman key. The construction $SK \leftarrow prf(K, g^a g^b, ID_A, ID_B)$ computes a session key, which can be split into encryption and message authentication keys as before.

The major drawback of Diffie–Hellman is that it is subject to man-in-the-middle attacks. The preceding protocol uses signatures to remove this threat. B's signature authenticates B to a and also binds g^a and g^b together, preventing man-in-the-middle attacks. Similarly, A's signature on message 3 assures B that the session is with A.

These examples illustrate that it is practical to construct session keys that meet the requirements for cryptography, if a long-lived relationship already exists.

State Consistency

We have already observed that the protocol specified in (1) through (3) achieves state consistency when the protocol succeeds. Both parties agree on the identities and on the session instance. When a session key SK is derived, as in (7), both parties also agree on the key. Determining which parties know which pieces of information after each protocol message is the essential tool for a security analysis of this kind of protocol. The analysis of this protocol is typical for authentication and key establishment protocols.

Finally, allowing Internet access in the workplace can create two challenges: ensuring employee efficiency and mitigating security risks. Since you can't simply take away Internet privileges, you must find a way to boost employee productivity while maintaining Internet security. So, with the preceding in mind, because of the frequency of poor security practices or far-too-common security failures on the Internet, let's briefly look at the importance of the process that is used to gather all of these faults into an Internet security checklist and give them a suitable solution.

4. INTERNET SECURITY CHECKLIST

Internet security is a fast-moving challenge and an ever-present threat. There is no one right way to secure a Web site, and all security methods are subject to instant obsolescence, incremental improvement, and constant revision. All public facing Web sites are open to constant attack. So, are you willing and able to invest the time it takes to administer a dynamic, 24×7, world-accessible, database-driven, interactive, user-authenticated Web site? Do you have the time and resources to respond to the constant flow of new Internet security issues? The following high- level checklist helps to answer the preceding questions and addresses a number of far-too-common security failures on the Internet (see checklist: An Agenda for Action in Selecting Internet Security Process Activities).

AN AGENDA FOR ACTION IN SELECTING INTERNET SECURITY PROCESS ACTIVITIES

The following high-level checklist should be addressed in order to find the following Internet security practices helpful (check all tasks completed):

_____**1.** Login pages should be encrypted.

_____**2.** Data validation should be done server-side.

_____**3.** Manage your Web site via encrypted connections.

_____**4.** Use strong, cross-platform compatible encryption.

_____**5.** Connect from a secured network.

_____**6.** Don't share login credentials.

_____**7.** Prefer key-based authentication over password authentication.

_____**8.** Maintain a secure workstation.

_____**9.** Use redundancy to protect the Web site.

_____**10.** Make sure you implement strong security measures that apply to all systems — not just those specific to Web security.

_____**11.** Validate logins trough SSL encryption.

_____**12.** Do not use clear text protocols to manage your server.

_____**13.** Implement security policies that apply to all systems.

5. SUMMARY

This chapter examined how cryptography is used on the Internet to secure protocols. It reviewed the architecture of the Internet protocol suite, for even the meaning of what security means is a function of the underlying system architecture. Next it reviewed the Dolev–Yao model, which describes the threats to which network communications are exposed. In particular, all levels of network protocols are completely exposed to eavesdropping and manipulation by an attacker, so using cryptography properly is a first-class requirement to derive any benefit from its use. We learned that effective security mechanisms to protect session-oriented and session establishment protocols are different, although they can share many cryptographic primitives. Cryptography can be very successful in protecting messages on the Internet, but doing so requires preexisting, long-lived relationships. How to build secure open communities is still an open problem; it is probably an intractable question because a solution would imply the elimination of conflict between human beings who do not know each other.

Finally, let's move on to the real interactive part of this chapter: review questions/exercises, hands-on projects, case projects, and optional team case project. The answers and/or solutions by chapter can be found in the online Instructor's Solutions Manual.

CHAPTER REVIEW QUESTIONS/EXERCISES

True/False

1. True or False? The Internet was designed to create standardized communication between computers.
2. True or False? Since communication is an extremely complex activity, it should come as no surprise that the system components providing communication decompose into modules.
3. True or False? Practical solutions addressing Byzantine failures fall largely within the purview of platform rather than network architecture, although the interconnectivity topology is an important consideration.
4. True or False? Security analyses of systems traditionally begin with a model of the user.
5. True or False? A user can eavesdrop on a communications medium by connecting a receiver to the medium.

Multiple Choice

1. The Internet supports message exchange through a mechanism called:
   A. interfaces.
   B. send primitive.
   C. protocols.
   D. confirm primitive.
   E. listen primitive.
2. A minimal communications service interface requires the following four primitives, except which one?
   A. Send.
   B. Clear.
   C. Confirm.
   D. Listen.
   E. Receive.
3. A report of diagnostic and performance information about underlying communications is known as a:
   A. send primitive.
   B. confirm primitive.
   C. shift cipher.
   D. status primitive.
   E. deliver primitive.
4. What is technically not part of the Internet architecture per se?
   A. PHY Layer.
   B. Chi-square statistic.
   C. Polyalphabetic cipher.

    D. Kerckhoff's principle.

     E. Unicity distance.

5. What is a request/response protocol designed to determine the reachability of another IP address?

    A. Traceroute.

    B. Chisquare test.

    C. Statistical test.

    D. Ping.

     E. Destination unreachable.

EXERCISE

Problem

How would an organization go about deciding an authentication strategy?

Hands-On Projects

Project

How would an organization go about deciding an authorization strategy?

Case Projects

Problem

When should an organization use message security versus transport security?

Optional Team Case Project

Problem

With regard to a Microsoft-based Internet security system, how would an organization go about using its existing Active Directory infrastructure?

Intranet Security

Bill Mansoor

Information Systems Audit and Control Association (ISACA)

Headline dramas like the ones shown in the accompanying sidebar (Intranet Security as News in the Media) (in the mainstream media) are embarrassing nightmares to top brass in any large corporation. These events have a lasting impact on a company's bottom line because the company's reputation and customer trust take a direct hit. Once events like these occur, customers and current and potential investors never look at the company in the same trusting light again, regardless of remediation measures. The smart thing, then, is to avoid the limelight. The onus of preventing such embarrassing security gaffes falls squarely on the shoulders of the IT security chiefs (Chief Information Security Officer and security officers), who are sometimes hobbled by unclear mandates from government regulators and lack of sufficient budgeting to tackle the mandates.

- Intranet Security as News in the Media
- "State Department Contract Employees Fired, Another Disciplined for Looking at Passport File"[1]
- "Laptop stolen with a million customer data records"[2]
- "eBayed VPN kit hands over access to council network"[3]

1. Jake Tapper, and Radia Kirit, "State Department Contract Employees Fired, Another Disciplined for Looking at Passport File," ABCnews.com, March 21, 2008, http://abcnews.go.com/Politics/story?id=4492773&page=1.

2. Laptop security blog, Absolute Software, http://blog.absolute.com/category/real-theft-reports.

3. John Leyden, "eBayed VPN Kit Hands over Access to Council Network," theregister.co.uk, September 29, 2008, www.theregister.co.uk/2008/09/29/second_hand_vpn_security_breach.

- "(Employee) caught selling personal and medical information about ... FBI agent to a confidential source ... for $500"[4]

- "Data thieves gain access to TJX through unsecured wireless access point"[5]

However, federal governments across the world are not taking breaches of personal data lightly (see sidebar, TJX: Data Breach with 45 Million Data Records Stolen). In view of a massive plague of publicized data thefts in the past decade, recent mandates such as the Health Insurance Portability and Accountability Act (HIPAA), Sarbanes-Oxley, and the Payment Card Industry-Data Security Standard (PCI-DSS) Act within the United States now have teeth. These laws even spell out stiff fines and personal jail sentences for CEOs who neglect data breach issues.

TJX: DATA BREACH WITH 45 MILLION DATA RECORDS STOLEN

The largest-scale data breach in history occurred in early 2007 at TJX, the parent company for the TJ Maxx, Marshalls, and HomeGoods retail chains.

In the largest identity-theft case ever investigated by the U.S. Department of Justice, 11 people were convicted of wire fraud. The primary suspect was found to perpetrate the intrusion by wardriving and taking advantage of an unsecured Wi-Fi access point to get in and set up a "sniffer" software instance to capture credit-card information from a database.[12]

Although the intrusion was earlier believed to have taken place from May 2006 to January 2007, TJX later found that it took place as early as July 2005. The data compromised included portions of credit- and debit-card transactions for approximately 45 million customers.[6]

As seen in the TJX case, intranet data breaches can be a serious issue, impacting a company's goodwill in the open marketplace as well as spawning class-action lawsuits.[7] Gone are the days when intranet security was a superficial exercise; security inside the firewall was all but nonexistent. There was a feeling of implicit trust in the internal user. After all, if you hired that person, training him for years, how could you not trust him?

4. Bob Coffield, "Second Criminal Conviction under HIPAA," Health Care Law Blog, March 14, 2006, http://healthcarebloglaw.blogspot.com/2006/03/second-criminal-conviction-under-hipaa.html.

5. "TJX Identity Theft Saga Continues: 11 Charged with Pilfering Millions of Credit Cards," Networkworld.com magazine, August 5, 2008, www.networkworld.com/community/node/30741? nwwpkg=breaches? ap1=rcb.

6. "The TJX Companies, Inc. Updates Information on Computer Systems Intrusion," February 21, 2007, www.tjx.com/Intrusion_Release_email.pdf.

7. "TJX Class Action Lawsuit Settlement Site," The TJX Companies, Inc., and Fifth Third Bancorp, Case No. 07-10162, www.tjxsettlement.com.

In the new millennium, the Internet has come of age, and so have its users. The last largely computer-agnostic generation has exited the user scene; their occupational shoes have been filled with the X and Y generations. Many of these young people have grown up with the Internet, often familiar with it since elementary school. It is not uncommon today to find young college students who started their programming interests in the fifth or sixth grade.

With such a level of computer expertise in users, the game of intranet security has changed (see sidebar: Network Breach Readiness: Many Are Still Complacent). Resourceful as ever, these new users have gotten used to the idea of being hyperconnected to the Internet using mobile technology such as personal digital assistants (PDAs), smartphones, and firewalled barriers. For a corporate intranet that uses older ideas of using access control as the cornerstone of data security, such mobile access to the Internet at work needs careful analysis and control. The idea of building a virtual moat around your well-constructed castle (investing in a firewall and hoping to call it an intranet) is gone. Hyperconnected "knowledge workers" with laptops, PDAs, and USB keys that have whole operating systems built in have made sure of it.

NETWORK BREACH READINESS: MANY ARE STILL COMPLACENT

The level of readiness for breaches among IT shops across the country is still far from optimal. The Ponemon Institute, a security think tank, surveyed some industry personnel and came up with some startling revelations. Hopefully, these statistics will change in the future:

- Eighty-five percent of industry respondents reported that they had experienced a data breach.

- Of those responding, 43 percent had no incident response plan in place, and 82 percent did not consult legal counsel before responding to the incident.
- Following a breach, 46 percent of respondents still had not implemented encryption on portable devices (laptops, PDAs) with company data stored on them.[8]

If we could reuse the familiar vehicle ad tagline of the 1980s, we would say that the new intranet is not "your father's intranet anymore." The intranet as just a simple place to share files and to list a few policies and procedures has ceased to be. The types of changes can be summed up in the following list of features, which shows that the intranet has

8. "Ponemon Institute Announces Result of Survey Assessing the Business Impact of a Data Security Breach," May 15, 2007, www.ponemon.org/press/Ponemon_Survey_Results_Scott_and_Scott_FINAL1.pdf.

become a combined portal as well as a public dashboard. Some of the features can include:

- A searchable corporate personnel directory of phone numbers by department. Often the list is searchable only if the exact name is known.
- Expanded activity guides and a corporate calendar with links for various company divisions.
- Several Really Simple Syndication (RSS) feeds for news according to divisions such as IT, HR, Finance, Accounting, and Purchasing.
- Company blogs (weblogs) by top brass that talk about the current direction for the company in reaction to recent events, a sort of "mission statement of the month."
- A search engine for searching company information, often helped by a search appliance from Google. Microsoft also has its own search software on offer that targets corporate intranets.
- One or several "wiki" repositories for company intellectual property, some of it of a mission-critical nature. Usually granular permissions are applied for access here. One example could be court documents for a legal firm with rigorous security access applied.
- A section describing company financials and other mission-critical indicators. This is often a separate Web page linked to the main intranet page.
- A "live" section with IT alerts regarding specific downtimes, outages, and other critical time-sensitive company notifications. Often embedded within the portal, this is displayed in a "ticker-tape" fashion or like an RSS-type dynamic display.

Of course, this list is not exhaustive; some intranets have other unique features not listed here. In any case, intranets these days do a lot more than simply list corporate phone numbers.

Recently, knowledge management systems have presented another challenge to intranet security postures. Companies that count knowledge as a prime protected asset (virtually all companies these days) have started deploying "mashable" applications that combine social networking (such as Facebook and LinkedIn), texting, and microblogging (such as Twitter) features to encourage employees to "wikify" their knowledge and information within intranets. One of the bigger vendors in this space, Socialtext, has introduced a mashable wiki app that operates like a corporate dashboard for intranets.[9,10]

Socialtext has individual widgets, one of which, "Socialtext signals," is a microblogging engine. In the corporate context, microblogging entails sending short SMS messages to apprise colleagues of recent developments in the daily routine. Examples could be short messages on progress on any major project milestone—for example, joining up major airplane assemblies or getting Food and Drug Administration (FDA) testing approval for a special experimental drug.

9. James Mowery, "Socialtext Melds Media and Collaboration," cmswire.com, October 8, 2008, www.cmswire.com/cms/enterprise-20/socialtext-melds-media-and-collaboration-003270.php.

10. Rob Hof, "Socialtext 3.0: Will Wikis Finally Find Their Place in Business?" Businessweek.com magazine, September 30, 2008, www.business-week.com/the_thread/techbeat/archives/2008/09/socialtext_30_i.html.

These emerging scenarios present special challenges to security personnel guarding the borders of an intranet. The border as it once existed has ceased to be. One cannot block stored knowledge from leaving the intranet when a majority of corporate mobile users are accessing intranet wikis from anywhere using inexpensive mini-notebooks that are given away with cell phone contracts.[11]

If we consider the impact of national and international privacy mandates on these situations, the situation is compounded further for C-level executives in multinational companies who have to come up with responses to privacy mandates in each country in which the company does business. The privacy mandates regarding private customer data have always been more stringent in Europe than in North America, which is a consideration for doing business in Europe.

It is hard enough to block entertainment-related Flash video traffic from time-wasting Internet abuse without blocking a video of last week's corporate meeting at headquarters. Only letting in traffic on an exception basis becomes untenable or impractical because of a high level of personnel involvement needed for every ongoing security change. Simply blocking YouTube.com or Vimeo.com is not sufficient. Video, which has myriad legitimate work uses nowadays, is hosted on all sorts of content-serving (caching and streaming) sites worldwide, which makes it well near impossible to block using Web filters. The evolution of the Internet Content Adaptation Protocol (ICAP), which standardizes Web site categories for content-filtering purposes, is under way. However, ICAP still does not solve the problem of the dissolving networking "periphery."[12]

Guarding movable and dynamic data—which may be moving in and out of the perimeter without notice, flouting every possible mandate—is a key feature of today's intranet. The dynamic nature of data has rendered the traditional confidentiality, integrity, and availability (CIA) architecture somewhat less relevant. The changing nature of data security necessitates some specialized security considerations:

- Intranet security policies and procedures (P&Ps) are the first step toward a legal regulatory framework. The P&Ps needed on any of the security controls listed below should be compliant with federal and state mandates (such as HIPAA, Sarbanes-Oxley, the European Directive 95/46/EC on the protection of personal data, and PCI-DSS, among others). These P&Ps have to be signed off by top management and placed on the intranet for review by employees. There should be sufficient teeth in all procedural sections to enforce the policy, explicitly spelling out sanctions and other consequences of noncompliance, leading up to discharge.
- To be factual, none of these government mandates spell out details on implementing any security controls. That is the vague nature of federal and international mandates. Interpretation of the security controls is better left after the fact to an entity such as the National Institute of Standards and Technology (NIST) in the United States or the Geneva-based International Organization for Standardization (ISO). These organizations

---

11. Matt Hickey, "MSI's 3.5G Wind 120 Coming in November, Offer Subsidized by Taiwanese Telecom," Crave.com, October 20, 2008, http://news.cnet.com/8301-17938_105-10070911-1.html?tag=mncol;title.

12. Network Appliance, Inc., RFC Standards white paper for Internet Content Adaptation Protocol (ICAP), July 30, 2001, www.content-networking.com/references.html.

have extensive research and publication guidance for any specific security initiative. Most of NIST's documents are offered as free downloads from its Web site.[13] ISO security standards such as 27002 ∼ 27005 are also available for a nominal fee from the ISO site.

Policies and procedures, once finalized, need to be automated as much as possible (one example is mandatory password changes every three months). Automating policy compliance takes the error-prone human factor out of the equation (see sidebar: Access Control in the Era of Social Networking). Numerous software tools are available to help accomplish security policy automation.

ACCESS CONTROL IN THE ERA OF SOCIAL NETWORKING

In an age in which younger users have grown up with social networking sites as part of their digital lives, corporate intranet sites are finding it increasingly difficult to block them from using these sites at work. Depending on the company, some are embracing social networking as part of their corporate culture; others, especially government entities, are actively blocking these sites. Detractors mention as concerns wasted bandwidth, lost productivity, and the possibility of infections with spyware and worms.

However, blocking these sites can be difficult because most social networking and video sites such as Vimeo and YouTube can use port 80 to vector Flash videos into an intranet—which is wide open for HTTP access. Flash videos have the potential to provide a convenient Trojan horse for malware to get into the intranet.

To block social networking sites, one needs to block either the Social Networking category or the specific URLs (such as YouTube.com) for these sites in the Web-filtering proxy appliance. Flash videos are rarely downloaded from YouTube itself. More often a redirected caching site is used to send in the video. The caching sites also need to be blocked; this is categorized under Content Servers.

1. SMARTPHONES AND TABLETS IN THE INTRANET

The proliferation of mobile devices for personal and business usage has gained an unprecedented momentum, which only reminds one of the proliferation of personal computers at the start of the 1980s. Back then the rapid proliferation of PCs was rooted in the wide availability of common PC software and productivity packages such as Excel or Borland. Helping with kids' homework and spreadsheets at home was part of the wide appeal.

13. National Institute of Standards and Technology, Computer Security Resource Center, http://csrc.nist.gov/.

A large part of the PC revolution was also rooted in the change in interactivity patterns. Interaction using GUIs and mice had made PCs widely popular compared to the DOS character screen. The consumer PC revolution did not really take off until Windows PCs and Mac Classics brought along mice starting in the early 1990s. It was a quantum leap for ordinary people unfamiliar with DOS commands.

Today, which some now call the post-PC era,[14] the interaction between people and computers has again evolved. The finger (touch) has again replaced keyboards and mice as an input device in smartphones and tablets—which invariably use a mobile-oriented OS like Android or iOS as opposed to MAC OS, Linux, or Windows. Android and iOS were built from the ground up with the "touch interface" in mind.

This marks a sea-change.[15] By the next couple of years, most smartphones will end up with the computing power of a full-size PC that is only five years older. These powerful smartphones and portable tablets (such as iPads and android devices) enabled with multimedia and gaming capabilities are starting to converge toward becoming one and the same device. The increasing speed and functionality for the price ("bang for the buck") will only gather a more rapid pace as user demand becomes more intense. The success of smartphones and tablet devices over traditional full-size laptops stems from two primary reasons:

1. **The functionality and ease of use of using "voice," "gesture," and "touch" interfaces.** As opposed to the use of mice and keyboards, voice-enabled, touch, and gesture-based interfaces used in mobile devices offer a degree of ease unseen in traditional laptops.
2. **The availability of customized apps (applications).** Given the number of specialized apps found in the Apple App Store (and Android's equivalent "market"), they offer increased versatility for these new mobile devices compared to traditional laptops. In Apple's case, the closed ecosystem of apps (securely allowed only after testing for security) decreases the possibility of hacking iPads using uncertified apps.

In the recent iPhone 4s, the use of "Siri" as a speech-aware app only portends the increasing ease of usage for this class of device.[16] Using Siri, the iPhone can be issued voice commands to set appointments, to read back messages, and to notify people if one is going to be late—among a myriad other things—all without touching any keypad. In the recently introduced android version 4.0 or higher, face recognition authentication using the on-board camera is also an ease-of-use feature. There are bugs in these applications of course, but they indisputably point toward a pattern of interactivity change compared to a traditional laptop. There are a few other trends to watch in the integration of mobile devices in the enterprise:

1. Mobile devices let today's employees stretch work far beyond traditional work hours. Because of rich interactivity and ease of use, these devices blur the boundary

14. Ina Fried, "Steve Jobs: Let the Post-PC Era Begin," CNET News, June 1, 2010, http://news.cnet.com/8301-13860_3-20006442-56.html?tag=content;siu-container.

15. Associated Press, "Apple Describes Post-PC Era, Surprise of Success," March 7, 2012, http://news.yahoo.com/apple-describes-post-pc-era-surprise-success-212613625.html.

16. "Siri—Your Wish Is Its Command," http://www.apple.com/iphone/features/siri.html.

between work and play. Companies benefit from this employee availability at non-traditional work hours. The very concept of being at work has changed compared to even 10 years ago.

2. The iteration life cycles of mobile devices are now more rapid. Unlike laptops that had life cycles of almost three years, new version of the iPad comes out almost every year with evolutionary changes. This makes it less and less feasible for IT to set standardization for mobile devices or even pay for them. IT is left in most cases with supporting these devices. IT can, however, put in recommendations on which device it is able or unable to support for feasibility reasons.

3. Because of these cost reasons, it is no longer feasible for most IT departments to dictate the brand or platform of mobile device employees use to access the corporate network. It is often a BYOD (Bring Your Own Device) situation. As long as specialized software can be used to partition the personally owned mobile device for storing company data safely (which cannot be breached), this approach is feasible.

4. The mobile device that seems to be numerically most ready for the enterprise is the same one that has been the most successful commercially, the Apple iPad. Already in its third iteration in 2012 since the first one came out in 2010, the iPad 3 with its security and VPN features seems to be ready to be managed by most Mobile Device Management (MDM) packages. It has been adopted extensively by executives and sales staff at larger corporate entities.[17] It is also starting to be adopted by state and local government to expedite certain e-government initiatives.[18]

5. Compared to the Apple iPhone, however, the Android smartphones generally have had better adoption rates. Blackberry adoption, however, is on the wane.[19] Smartphones will need to have more specially designed Web pages to cope with interactivity on a smaller screen.

6. According to a major vendor in the Mobile Device Management space ("Good Technology") the financial services sector saw the highest level of iPad (iOS) activation, accounting for 46 percent for the third quarter in 2011—which tripled the amount of activation in any other industry (see Figure 8.1). [20]

When it comes to mobile devices (see sidebar: The Commoditization of Mobile Devices and Impact upon Businesses and Society) and smartphones, one can reasonably surmise that the act of balancing security versus business considerations has clearly tilted toward

17. Rachel King, "SAP CIO Bussman on Tablets and Mobile Strategy for Enterprise," September 19, 2011, http://www.zdnet.com/blog/btl/sap-cio-bussman-on-tablets-and-mobile-strategy-for-enterprise/58247.

18. "Better Health Channel—iPhone and iPad Mobile Application," Retrieved March 19, 2012, http://www.egov.vic.gov.au/victorian-government-resources/government-initiatives-victoria/health-and-community-victoria/health-victoria/better-health-channel-iphone-and-ipad-mobile-application.html.

19. Brad Reed, "iOS vs. Android vs. BlackBerry OS vs. Windows Phone," Retrieved November 2, 2011, http://www.networkworld.com/news/2011/102011-tech-arguments-android-ios-blackberry-windows-252223.html.

20. Rachel King, "iPad Driving Massive Growth for iOS in Enterprise (Survey)," October 20, 2011, http://www.zdnet.com/blog/btl/ipad-driving-massive-growth-for-ios-in-enterprise-survey/61229?tag=content; siu-container.

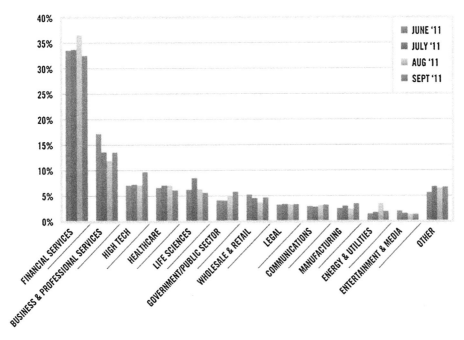

FIGURE 8.1 Net activation by industry. Source: *http://i.zdneMt.com/blogs/zdnet-good-technology-ios-survey-1.jpg? tag = content;siu-container.*

the latter. The age of mobile devices is here, and IT has to adapt security measures to conform to it. The common IT security concept of protecting the host may have to convert to protecting the network from itinerant hosts.

THE COMMODITIZATION OF MOBILE DEVICES AND IMPACT UPON BUSINESSES AND SOCIETY

There are quite a few increasingly visible trends that portend the commoditization of mobile devices and their resulting impact on businesses.

1. The millennial generation is more familiar with mobile technology—Due to widespread usage of smartphones and iPhones as communication devices for computing usage (other than simply voice) in the last few years and now

iPads which have taken their place, their familiarity with mobile hardware is far higher than previous generations. The technological sophistication of these devices has forced the majority of the current generation of young people to be far more tech savvy than previous generations as they have grown up around this mobile-communication-enabled environment.

2. Mobile devices are eating into the sales of PCs and laptops—The millennial generation is no longer simply content with traditional bulky PCs and laptops as computing devices. Lightweight devices with pared-down mobile OSs and battery-efficient mobile devices with 10-hour lives are quickly approaching the computing power of traditional computers and in addition are far more portable. The demand of lowered cost, immediacy, and ease of usage of mobile devices have caused traditional laptop sales to slow down in favor of tablet and iPad sales.

3. Social media usage by mobile devices—Sites like FaceBook, Twitter, and Flickr encourage collaboration and have given rise to usage of these sites using nothing other than mobile devices, whereas this was not possible previously. Most smartphones (even an increasingly common class of GPS-enabled point-and-shoot cameras) enable upload of images and videos to these sites directly from the device itself using Wi-Fi connections and Wi-Fi-enabled storage media (SD cards). This has engendered a mobile lifestyle for this generation that sites such as FaceBook, Twitter, and Flickr are only too happy to cater to. Employees using social media represent new challenges to businesses because protection of business data (enforced by privacy-related federal and state regulations and mandates) has become imperative. Business data has to be separated and protected from personal use of public social media, if they have to exist on the same mobile device. Several vendors already offer products that enable this separation. In industry parlance this area of IT is known as Mobile Device Management.

4. The mobile hardware industry has matured—Margins have been pared to the bone. Mobile devices have become a buyers' market. Because of wider appeal, it is no longer just the tech savvy (opinion leaders and early adopters) who determine the success of a mobile product. It will be the wider swath of nontechie users looking for attractive devices with a standardized set of often-used functions that will determine the success of a product. This will sooner than later force manufacturers to compete on price rather than product innovation. This downward pressure on price will also make it cost-effective for businesses to adopt these mobile devices within their corporate IT infrastructure. Amazon's Kindle and Barnes &Noble's Nook are both nimbly designed and priced at around a $200 price-point compared to the $500 iPad. They have begun to steal some market share from full-featured tablets like the iPad but of course enterprise adoption for the cheaper devices remains to be sorted out.

5. Users expect the "cloud" to be personal—Users in their personal lives have become used to customizing their Internet digital persona by being offered limitless choices in doing so. In their usage of the business cloud," they expect the same level of customization. This customization can be easily built into the backend using the likes of Active Directory and collaboration tools such as Microsoft's SharePoint once a user authenticates through the VPN. Customization can be built upon access permissions in a granular manner per user while tracking their access to company information assets. This accumulated data trend can be used later to refine ease of use for remote users using the company portal.

Mobile device adoption explodes

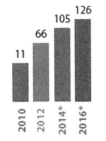

126 million tablets will be in use with US consumers by 2016.[†]

257 million smartphones will be in use with US consumers by 2016.[‡]

Mobile apps are a $6.0 billion market today, growing to $55.7 billion by 2015.[§]

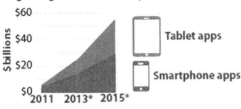

Tablet apps

Smartphone apps

Sources: [†]Forrester Research Consumer PC And Tablet Forecast, 2011 to 2016 (US); [‡]Forrester Research Mobile Adoption Forecast, 2012 to 2017 (US); [§]February 28, 2011, "Mobile App Internet Recasts The Software And Services Landscape" Forrester report
*Forecast

FIGURE 8.2 Mobile device adaptation.
Source: *http://i.zdnet.com/blogs/screen-shot-2012-02-13-at-173416.png.*

In 2011, Apple shipped 172 million portable computing devices including iPads, iPods, and iPhones. Among these were 55 million iPads. The sales of mostly android tablets by other manufacturers are also increasing at a rapid pace. By the end of the first decade of the new millennium, it has become clear that sales of iPads and tablets are making serious dents in the sale of traditional PCs—indicating a shift in consumer preference toward a rapid commoditization of computing. Figure 8.2 from the Forrester Research consumer PC and Tablet forecast helps illustrate this phenomenon.[21]

Several reasons can be attributed to this shift. The millennial generation was already reinventing the idea of how business is conducted and where. Because of increased demands on employee productivity, business had to be conducted in real time at the employee's location (home, hotel, airport) and not just at the traditional workplace. With gas prices hovering in the United States around $5.00 a gallon (essentially a doubling of prices over the first half-decade of the millennium), traditional 9-to-5 work hours with long commutes are no longer practical. iPads and tablets therefore had become *de rigueur* for not only field employees but also workers at headquarters. Instead of imposing rigid 9-to-5 attendance on employees, progressive companies had to let employees be flexible in

21. Zack Whittaker, "One Billion Smartphones by 2016, Says Forrester," February 13, 2012, http://www.zdnet.com/blog/btl/one-billion-smartphones-by-2016-says-forrester/69279.

meeting sales or deliverables on their own deadlines, which improved employee morale and productivity.

Popular devices like the iPad, Samsung Galaxy Android tablet, and many types of smartphones are already capable of accessing company intranets using customized intranet apps. This assures that access to critical company data needed for a sale or demo does not stand in the way of closing an important deal. All this had already been enabled by laptops, but the touchpad-enabled tablet eases this process by using more functional media usage and richer interactivity features.

Ultimately, it will matter less about what device employees use to access the company portal or where they are because their identity will be the deciding factor in what information they will gain access to. Companies will do better in providing customized "private cloud environments" for workers accessible from anywhere. Employees may still use PCs while at the office (see sidebar: Being Secure in the Post-PC Era) and mobile devices while in the field conducting business, but they will increasingly demand the same degree of ease in accessing company data regardless of their location or the means used to access it. The challenge for IT will be in catering to these versatile demands without losing sight of security and protecting privacy.

BEING SECURE IN THE POST-PC ERA

The post-PC era began with the advent of tablets such as iPads as enterprise mobile computing devices. Secure use of tablets in the enterprise presupposes a number of conditionalities:

1. **Backend enterprise network infrastructure support has to be ready** and has to be strong to handle mobile devices interacting with SSL VPNs. Specifically, enterprises need to consider each device platform and their unique issues and idiosyncrasies in trying to connect using an SSL VPN. SSL (or Web) VPNs are preferred because IPSec and L2TP VPNs were not known to be easy to implement on mobile devices (especially Android tablets) as SSL VPNs. PPTP VPNs are dated and not known to have sufficient encryption and security compared to SSL VPNs.

2. **Testing of remote access scenarios such as VPNs is key.** Client Apps for each supported platform (iOS, Android, Windows Phone) against the existing or proposed VPN appliance will need to be thoroughly tested.

3. **This is fundamentally a new paradigm for delivering applications** (email, dashboards, databases) to users. Starting with a practical and functional client App from ground zero will be a better philosophy than sticking to existing GUI ideas or concepts. Instead of pretty but nonfunctional interfaces, spare but well-tested and robust mobile interfaces will afford users time-savings and efficiency to get their job done quicker. Once they are reliably working, additional functions can be slowly added to the app in successive versions.

2. SECURITY CONSIDERATIONS

Quite a few risks need to be resolved when approaching intranet security with regard to mobile devices:

1. **Risk of size and portability**—Mobile devices are prone to loss. An Apple staffer's "loss" of a fourth-generation iPhone to a Gizmodo staffer during a personal outing to a bar is well known. There is no denying that smartphones because of their size are easy theft targets in the wrong place at the wrong time. Loss of a few hundred dollars of hardware, however, is nothing when an invaluable client-list is lost and falls into a competitor's hands. These are nightmare scenarios that keep CIOs up at night.
2. **Risk of access via multiple paradigms**—Mobile devices can access unsafe sites using cellular networks and download malware into storage. The malware in turn can bypass the company firewall to enter the company network to wreak havoc. Old paradigms of security by controlling security using perimeter network access are no longer feasible.
3. **Social media risks**—By definition, mobile devices are designed in such a way that they can easily access social media sites, which are the new target for malware propagating exploits. Being personal devices, mobile media devices are much more at risk of getting exploits sent to them and being "pw" (so to speak).

These issues can be approached and dealt with by using a solid set of technical as well as administrative controls:

1. **Establish a customized corporate usage policy for mobile devices**—This policy/ procedure must be signed by new hires at orientation and by all employees who ask for access to the corporate VPN using mobile devices (even personal ones). This should ideally be in the form of a contract and should be signed by the employee before a portion of the employee's device storage is partitioned for access and storage of corporate data. Normally, there should be yearly training highlighting the do's and dont's of using mobile devices in accessing a corporate VPN. The first thing emphasized in this training should be how to secure company data using passwords and if cost-effective, two-factor authentication using hardware tokens.
2. **Establish a policy for reporting theft or misplacement**—This policy should identify at the very least how quickly one should report thefts of mobile devices containing company data and how quickly remote wipe should be implemented. The policy can optionally detail how the mobile devices feature (app) enabling location of the misplaced stolen device will proceed.
3. **Establish a well-tested SSL VPN for remote access**—Reputed vendors having experience with mobile device VPN clients should be chosen. The quality, functionality, adaptability of usage (and proven reputation) of the VPN clients should be key in determining the choice of the vendor. The advantage of an SSL VPN compared to IPsec or L2TP for mobile usage is well known. The SSL VPNs should be capable of supporting two-factor authentication using hardware tokens. For example, Cisco's "Cisco AnyConnect Secure Mobility Client" and Juniper's "Junos Pulse App" are free app downloads available within the Apple iTunes App store. Other VPN vendors will also have these apps available, and they can be tested to see how smooth and functional the access process is.

4. **Establish inbound and outbound malware scanning**—Inbound scanning should occur for obvious reasons, but outbound scanning should also be scanned in case the company's email servers become SPAM relays and get blacklisted on sites such as Lashback or get blocked to external sites by force.
5. **Establish WPA2 encryption for Wi-Fi traffic access**—WPA2 for now is the best encryption available compared to WEP encryption, which is dated and not recommended.
6. **Establish logging metrics and granular controls**—Keeping regular tabs on information asset access by users and configuring alerting on unusual activity (such as large-scale access or exceeded failed-logon thresholds) is a good way to prevent data leakage.

Mobile devices accessing enterprise intranets using VPNs are subject to the same factors as any other device remotely accessing VPNs, namely (see Figure 8.3):

1. Protection of data while in transmission
2. Protection of data while at rest
3. Protection of the mobile device itself (in case it fell into the wrong hands)
4. App security

At a minimum, the following standards are recommended for managing tablets and smartphones with Mobile Device Management (MDM) appliances:

1. **Protection of data while in transmission:** Transmission security for mobile devices is concerned primarily with VPN security as well as Wi-Fi security. With regard to VPNs, the primary preference for most mobile devices should be for Web-based or SSL VPNs.

Deployment Scenario

The example depicts a typical deployment with a VPN server/concentrator as well as an authentication server controlling access to enterprise network services.

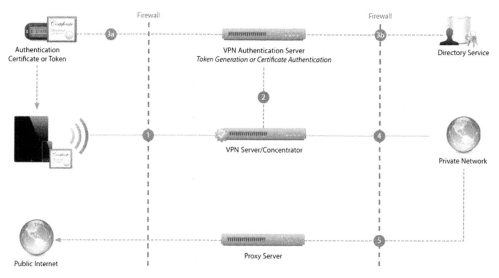

FIGURE 8.3 Mobile device VPN access to company network using token authentication *Courtesy: Apple Inc.*

The reason is that IPsec and L2TP VPN implementations are still buggy as of this writing on all but iOS devices (iPhones and iPads). SSL VPNs can also be implemented as clientless. Regarding Wi-F,i the choice is to simply configure WPA2 Enterprise using 128-bit AES encryption for mobile devices connecting via Wi-Fi. Again, MDM appliances can be used to push out these policies to the mobile devices.

2. **Protection of data while at rest:** The basis of protecting stored data on a mobile device is the password. The stronger the password, the harder to break the encryption. Some devices (including the iPad) support 256-bit AES encryption. Most recent mobile devices also support remote wipe and progressive wipe. The latter feature will progressively increase the time of the lockout duration until finally initiating an automatic remote wipe of all data on the device. These wipe features are designed to protect company data from falling into the wrong hands. All these features can be queried and are configurable for mobile devices via either Exchange ActiveSync policies or configuration policies from MDM appliances.

3. **Protection of the mobile device:** Passwords for mobile devices have to conform to the same corporate "strong password" policy as for other wired network devices. This means the password length, content (minimum of eight characters, alphanumeric, special characters etc.), password rotation and expiry (remember: last three and every two to three months), and password lockout (three to five attempts) have to be enforced. Complete sets of configuration profiles can be pushed to tablets, smartphones, and iPads using MDM appliances specifying app installation privileges, YouTube, and iTunes content ratings permissions, among many others.

4. **App security:** In recent versions of both Android and iOS, significant changes have been made so that app security has become more bolstered. For example, in both OSs, apps run in their own silos and can't access other app or system data. While iPhone apps are theoretically capable of accessing the users' contact information and also their locations in some cases, Apple's signing process for every app that appears in the iTunes app store takes care of this. It is possible on the iOS devices to encrypt data using either software methods such as AES, RC4, 3DES, or hardware accelerated encryption activated when a lockout occurs. In iOS, designating an app as managed can prevent its content from being uploaded to iCloud or iTunes. In this manner, MDM appliances or Exchange ActiveSync can prevent leakage of sensitive company data.

While there are quite a few risks in deploying mobile devices within the Intranet, with careful configuration these risks can be minimized to the point where the myriad benefits outweigh the risks. One thing is certain: These mobile devices and the efficiency they promise are for real, and they are not going away.

Empowering employees is the primary idea in the popularity of these devices. And corporate IT will only serve its own interest by designing enabling security around these devices and letting employees be more productive.

3. PLUGGING THE GAPS: NAC AND ACCESS CONTROL

The first priority of an information security officer in most organizations is to ensure that there is a relevant corporate policy on access controls. Simple on the surface, the subject of access control is often complicated by the variety of ways the intranet is connected to the external world.

Remote users coming in through traditional or SSL (browser-based) virtual private networks (VPNs), control over use of USB keys, printouts, and CD-ROMs all require that a comprehensive endpoint security solution be implemented.

The past couple of years have seen large-scale adoption of network access control (NAC) products in the midlevel and larger IT shops to manage endpoint security. Endpoint security ensures that whoever is plugging into or accessing any hardware anywhere within the intranet has to comply with the minimum baseline corporate security policy standards. This can include add-on access credentials but goes far beyond access. Often these solutions ensure that traveling corporate laptops are compliant with a minimum patching level, scans, and antivirus definition levels before being allowed to connect to the intranet.

The NAC appliances that enforce these policies often require that a NAC fat client is installed on every PC and laptop. This rule can be enforced during logon using a logon script. The client can also be part of the standard OS image for deploying new PCs and laptops.

Microsoft has built an NAC-type framework into some versions of its client OSs (Vista and XP SP3) to ease compliance with its NAC server product called MS Network Policy Server, which closely works with its Windows 2008 Server product (see sidebar: The Cost of a Data Breach). The company has been able to convince quite a few industry networking heavyweights (notably Cisco and Juniper) to adopt its NAP standard.[22]

THE COST OF A DATA BREACH

As of July 2007, the average breach cost per incident was $4.8 million.

- This works out to $182 per exposed record.
- It represents an increase of more than 30 percent from 2005.
- Thirty-five percent of these breaches involved the loss or theft of a laptop or other portable device.

- Seventy percent were due to a mistake or malicious intent by an organization's own staff.
- Since 2005, almost 150 million individuals' identifiable information has been compromised due to a data security breach.
- Nineteen percent of consumers notified of a data breach discontinued their relationship with the business, and a further 40 percent considered doing so.[23]

22. "Juniper and Microsoft Hook Up for NAC work," May 22, 2007, PHYSORG.com, www.physorg.com/news99063542.html.

23. Kevin Bocek, "What Does a Data Breach Cost?" SCmagazine.com, July 2, 2007, www.scmagazineus.com/What-does-a-data-breach-cost/article/35131.

Essentially, the technology has three parts: a policy-enforceable client, a decision point, and an enforcement point. The client could be an XP SP3 or Vista client (either a roaming user or guest user) trying to connect to the company intranet. The decision point in this case would be the Network Policy Server product, checking to see whether the client requesting access meets the minimum baseline to allow it to connect. If it does not, the decision point product would pass this data on to the enforcement point, a network access product such as a router or switch, which would then be able to cut off access.

The scenario would repeat itself at every connection attempt, allowing the network's health to be maintained on an ongoing basis. Microsoft's NAP page has more details and animation to explain this process.[24]

Access control in general terms is a relationship triad among internal users, intranet resources, and the actions internal users can take on those resources. The idea is to give users only the least amount of access they require to perform their job. The tools used to ensure this in Windows shops utilize Active Directory for Windows logon scripting and Windows user profiles. Granular classification is needed for users, actions, and resources to form a logical and comprehensive access control policy that addresses who gets to connect to what, yet keeping the intranet safe from unauthorized access or data-security breaches. Quite a few off-the-shelf solutions geared toward this market often combine inventory control and access control under a "desktop life-cycle" planning umbrella.

Typically, security administrators start with a "Deny-All" policy as a baseline before slowly building in the access permissions. As users migrate from one department to another, are promoted, or leave the company, in large organizations this job can involve one person by herself. This person often has a very close working relationship with Purchasing, Helpdesk, and HR, getting coordination and information from these departments on users who have separated from the organization and computers that have been surplused, deleting and modifying user accounts and assignments of PCs and laptops.

Helpdesk software usually has an inventory control component that is readily available to Helpdesk personnel to update and/or pull up to access details on computer assignments and user status. Optimal use of form automation can ensure that these details occur (such as deleting a user on the day of separation) to avoid any possibility of an unwelcome data breach.

4. MEASURING RISK: AUDITS

Audits are another cornerstone of a comprehensive intranet security policy. To start an audit, an administrator should know and list what he is protecting as well as know the relevant threats and vulnerabilities to those resources.

Assets that need protection can be classified as either tangible or intangible. *Tangible assets* are, of course, removable media (USB keys), PCs, laptops, PDAs, Web servers, networking equipment, DVR security cameras, and employees' physical access cards. *Intangible assets* can include company intellectual property such as corporate email and wikis, user passwords, and, especially for HIPAA and Sarbanes-Oxley mandates, personally identifiable health and financial information, which the company could be legally liable to protect.

24. NAP Program details, Microsoft.com, www.microsoft.com/windowsserver2008/en/us/nap-features.aspx.

Threats can include the theft of USB keys, laptops, PDAs, and PCs from company premises. This results in a data breach (for tangible assets), weak passwords, and unhardened operating systems in servers (for *intangible assets*).

Once a correlated listing of assets and associated threats and vulnerabilities has been made, we have to measure the impact of a breach, which is known as *risk*. The common rule of thumb to measure risk is:

$$\text{Risk} = \text{Value of asset} \times \text{Threat} \times \text{Vulnerability}$$

It is obvious that an Internet-facing Web server faces greater risk and requires priority patching and virus scanning because the vulnerability and threat components are high in that case (these servers routinely get sniffed and scanned over the Internet by hackers looking to find holes in their armor). However, this formula can standardize the priority list so that the actual audit procedure (typically carried out weekly or monthly by a vulnerability-scanning device) is standardized by risk level. Vulnerability-scanning appliances usually scan server farms and networking appliances only because these are high-value targets within the network for hackers who are looking for either unhardened server configurations or network switches with default factory passwords left on by mistake. To illustrate the situation, look at Figure 8.4, which illustrates an SQL injection attack on a corporate database.[25]

The value of an asset is subjective and can be assessed only by the IT personnel in that organization (see sidebar, Questions for a Nontechnical Audit of Intranet Security). If the IT staff has an ITIL (Information Technology Infrastructure Library) process under way, the value of an asset will often already have been classified and can be used. Otherwise, a small spreadsheet can be created with classes of various tangible and intangible assets (as part of a hardware/software cataloguing exercise) and values assigned that way.

QUESTIONS FOR A NONTECHNICAL AUDIT OF INTRANET SECURITY

1. Is all access (especially to high-value assets) logged?
2. In case of laptop theft, is encryption enabled so that the records will be useless to the thief?
3. Are passwords verifiably strong enough to comply with the security policy? Are they changed frequently and held to strong encryption standards?
4. Are all tangible assets (PCs, laptops, PDAs, Web servers, networking equipment) tagged with asset tags?
5. Is the process for surplusing obsolete IT assets secure (that is, are disks wiped for personally identifiable data before surplusing happens)?
6. Are email and Web usage logged?
7. Are peer-to-peer (P2P) and instant messaging (IM) usage controlled?

Based on the answers you get (or don't get), you can start the security audit procedure by finding answers to these questions.

25. "Web Application Security—Check Your Site for Web Application Vulnerabilities," www.acunetix.com/websitesecurity/webapp-security.htm.

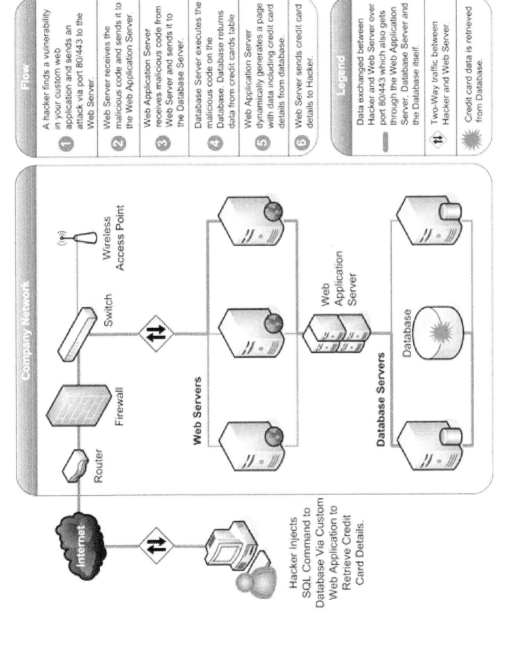

Flow

1. A hacker finds a vulnerability in your custom web application and sends an attack via port 80/443 to the Web Server.

2. Web Server receives the malicious code and sends it to the Web Application Server.

3. Web Application Server receives malicious code from Web Server and sends it to the Database Server.

4. Database Server executes the malicious code on the Database. Database returns data from credit cards table.

5. Web Application Server dynamically generates a page with data including credit card details from database.

6. Web Server sends credit card details to Hacker.

Legend

— Data exchanged between Hacker and Web Server over port 80/443 which also gets through the Web Application Server, Database Server and the Database itself.

⇵ Two-Way traffic between Hacker and Web Server.

✳ Credit card data is retrieved from Database.

Company Network

Router
Firewall
Switch
Wireless Access Point
Web Servers
Web Application Server
Database Servers
Database

Internet

Hacker Injects SQL Command to Database Via Custom Web Application to Retrieve Credit Card Details.

FIGURE 8.4 SQL injection attack. Source: © *acunetix.com.*

5. GUARDIAN AT THE GATE: AUTHENTICATION AND ENCRYPTION

To most lay users, authentication in its most basic form is two-factor authentication—meaning a username and a password. Although adding further factors (such as additional autogenerated personal identification numbers [PINs] and/or biometrics) makes authentication stronger by magnitudes, one can do a lot with just the password within a two-factor situation. Password strength is determined by how hard the password is to crack using a password-cracker application that uses repetitive tries using common words (sometimes from a stored dictionary) to match the password. Some factors will prevent the password from being cracked easily and make it a stronger password:

- Password length (more than eight characters)
- Use of mixed case (both uppercase and lowercase)
- Use of alphanumeric characters (letters as well as numbers)
- Use of special characters (such as !, ?, %, and #)

The ACL in a Windows AD environment can be customized to demand up to all four factors in the setting or renewal of a password, which will render the password strong. Prior to a few years ago, the complexity of a password (the last three items in the preceding list) was favored as a measure of strength in passwords. However, the latest preference as of this writing is to use uncommon passwords—joined-together sentences to form passphrases that are quite long but don't have much in the way of complexity. Password authentication ("what you know") as two-factor authentication is not as secure as adding a third factor to the equation (a dynamic token password). Common types of third-factor authentication include biometrics (fingerprint scan, palm scan, or retina scan—in other words, "what you are") and token-type authentication (software or hardware PIN–generating tokens—that is, "what you have"). Proximity or magnetic swipe cards and tokens have seen common use for physical premises-access authentication in high-security buildings (such as financial and R & D companies), but not for network or hardware access within IT.

When remote or teleworker employees connect to the intranet via VPN tunnels or Web-based SSL VPNs (the outward extension of the intranet once called an *extranet*), the connection needs to be encrypted with strong 3DES or AES type encryption to comply with patient data and financial data privacy mandates. The standard authentication setup is usually a username and a password, with an additional hardware token-generated random PIN entered into a third box. Until lately, RSA as a company was one of the bigger players in the hardware-token field; incidentally, it also invented the RSA algorithm for public-key encryption.

As of this writing, hardware tokens cost under $30 per user in quantities of greater than a couple hundred pieces, compared to about a $100 only a decade ago. Most vendors offer free lifetime replacements for hardware tokens. Instead of a separate hardware token, some inexpensive software token generators can be installed within PC clients, smartphones, and BlackBerry devices. Tokens are probably the most cost-effective enhancement to security today.

6. WIRELESS NETWORK SECURITY

Employees using the convenience of wireless to log into the corporate network (usually via laptop) need to have their laptops configured with strong encryption to prevent data breaches. The first-generation encryption type known as Wireless Equivalent Privacy (WEP) was easily deciphered (cracked) using common hacking tools and is no longer widely used. The latest standard in wireless authentication is WPA or WPA2 (802.11i), which offers stronger encryption compared to WEP. Although wireless cards in laptops can offer all the previously noted choices, they should be configured with WPA or WPA2 if possible.

There are quite a few hobbyists roaming corporate areas looking for open wireless access points (transmitters) equipped with powerful Wi-Fi antennas and wardriving software, a common package being Netstumbler. Wardriving was originally meant to log the presence of open Wi-Fi access points on Web sites (see sidebar: Basic Ways to Prevent Wi-Fi Intrusions in Corporate Intranets), but there is no guarantee that actual access and use (*piggybacking*, in hacker terms) won't occur, curiosity being human nature. If there is a profit motive, as in the TJX example, access to corporate networks will take place, although the risk of getting caught and the resulting risk of criminal prosecution will be high. Furthermore, installing a RADIUS server is a must to check access authentication for roaming laptops.

BASIC WAYS TO PREVENT WI-FI INTRUSIONS IN CORPORATE INTRANETS

1. Reset and customize the default Service Set Identifier (SSID) or Extended Service Set Identifier (ESSID) for the access point device before installation.
2. Change the default admin password.
3. Install a RADIUS server, which checks for laptop user credentials from an Active Directory database (ACL) from the same network before giving access to the wireless laptop. See Figures 8.5 and 8.6 for illustrated explanations of the process.
4. Enable WPA or WPA2 encryption, not WEP, which is easily cracked.
5. Periodically try to wardrive around your campus and try to sniff (and disable) nonsecured network-connected rogue access points set up by naïve users.
6. Document the wireless network by using one of the leading wireless network management software packages made for that purpose.

Note: Contrary to common belief, turning off the SSID broadcast won't help unless you're talking about a home access point situation. Hackers have an extensive suite of tools with which to sniff SSIDs for lucrative corporate targets, which will be broadcast anyway when connecting in clear text (unlike the real traffic, which will be encrypted).

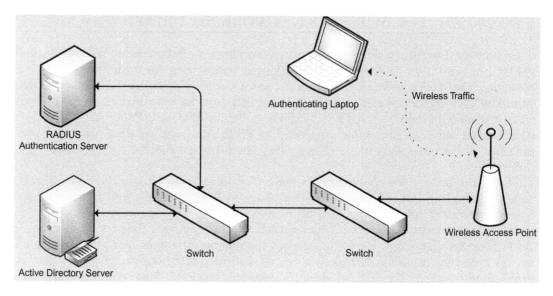

FIGURE 8.5   Wireless EAP authentication using Active Directory and authentication servers.

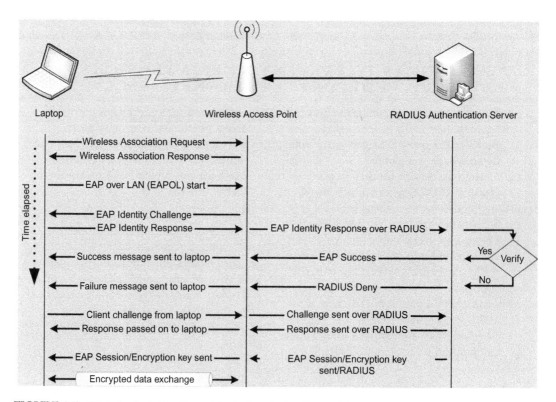

FIGURE 8.6   High-level wireless Extensible Authentication Protocol (EAP) workflow.

7. SHIELDING THE WIRE: NETWORK PROTECTION

Firewalls are, of course, the primary barrier to a network. Typically rule based, firewalls prevent unwarranted traffic from getting into the intranet from the Internet. These days firewalls also do some stateful inspections within packets to peer a little into the header contents of an incoming packet, to check validity—that is, to check whether a streaming video packet is really what it says it is, and not malware masquerading as streaming video.

Intrusion prevention systems (IPSs) are a newer type of inline network appliance that uses heuristic analysis (based on a weekly updated signature engine) to find patterns of malware identity and behavior and to block malware from entering the periphery of the intranet. The IPS and the intrusion detection system (IDS), however, operate differently.

IDSs are typically *not* sitting inline; they sniff traffic occurring anywhere in the network, cache extensively, and can correlate events to find malware. The downside of IDSs is that unless their filters are extensively modified, they generate copious amounts of false positives—so much so that "real" threats become impossible to sift out of all the noise.

IPSs, in contrast, work *inline* and inspect packets rapidly to match packet signatures. The packets pass through many hundreds of parallel filters, each containing matching rules for a different type of malware threat. Most vendors publish new sets of malware signatures for their appliances every week. However, signatures for common worms and injection exploits such as SQL-slammer, Code-red, and NIMDA are sometimes hardcoded into the application-specific integrated chip (ASIC) that controls the processing for the filters. Hardware-enhancing a filter helps avert massive-scale attacks more efficiently because it is performed in hardware, which is more rapid and efficient compared to software signature matching. Incredible numbers of malicious packets can be dropped from the wire using the former method.

The buffers in an enterprise-class IPS are smaller than those in IDSs and are quite fast—akin to a high-speed switch to preclude latency (often as low as 200 microseconds during the highest load). A top-of-the-line midsize IPS box's total processing threshold for all input and output segments can exceed 5 gigabits per second using parallel processing.[26]

However, to avoid overtaxing CPUs and for efficiency's sake, IPSs usually block only a very limited number of important threats out of the thousands of malware signatures listed. Tuning IPSs can be tricky—just enough blocking to silence the false-positive noise but making sure all critical filters are activated to block important threats.

The most important factors in designing a critical data infrastructure are resiliency, robustness, and redundancy regarding the operation of inline appliances. Whether one is talking about firewalls or inline IPSs, redundancy is paramount (see sidebar: Types of Redundancy for Inline Security Appliances). Intranet robustness is a primary concern where data has to available on a 24/7 basis.

26. IPS specification datasheet. "TippingPoint® intrusion prevention system (IPS) technical specifications," www.tippingpoint.com/pdf/resources/datasheets/400918-007_IPStechspecs.pdf.

TYPES OF REDUNDANCY FOR INLINE SECURITY APPLIANCES

1. Security appliances usually have dual power supplies (often hot-swappable) and are designed to be connected to two separate UPS devices, thereby minimizing the chances of a failure within the appliance itself. The hot-swap capability minimizes replacement time for power supplies.

2. We can configure most of these appliances to either shut down the connection or fall back to a level-two switch (in case of hardware failure). If reverting to a fallback state, most IPSs become basically a bump in the wire and, depending on the type of traffic, can be configured to fail open so that traffic remains uninterrupted. Also, inexpensive, small third-party switchboxes are available to enable this failsafe high-availability option for a single IPS box. The idea is to keep traffic flow active regardless of attacks.

3. IPS or firewall devices can be placed in dual-redundant failover mode, either in active-active (load-sharing) or active-passive (primary-secondary) mode. The devices commonly use a protocol called Virtual Router Redundancy Protocol (VRRP) where the secondary pings the primary every second to check live status and assumes leadership to start processing traffic in case pings are not returned from the primary. The switchover is instantaneous and transparent to most network users. Prior to the switchover, all data and connection settings are fully synchronized at identical states between both boxes to ensure failsafe switchover.

4. Inline IPS appliances are relatively immune to attacks because they have highly hardened Linus/Unix operating systems and are designed from the ground up to be robust and low-maintenance appliances (logs usually clear themselves by default).

Most security appliances come with syslog reporting (event and alert logs sent usually via port 514 UDP) and email notification (set to alert beyond a customizable threshold) as standard. The syslog reporting can be forwarded to a security event management (SEM) appliance, which consolidates syslogs into a central threat console for benefit of event correlation and forwards warning emails to administrators based on preset threshold criteria. Moreover, most firewalls and IPSs can be configured to forward their own notification email to administrators in case of an impending threat scenario.

For those special circumstances where a wireless-type LAN connection is the primary one (whether microwave beam, laser beam, or satellite-type connection), redundancy can be ensured by a secondary connection of equal or smaller capacity. For example, in certain northern Alaska towns where digging trenches into the hardened icy permafrost is expensive and rigging wire across the tundra is impractical due to the extreme cold, the primary network connections between towns are always via microwave link, often operating in dual redundant mode.

8. WEAKEST LINK IN SECURITY: USER TRAINING

Intranet security awareness is best communicated to users in two primary ways—during new employee orientation and by ongoing targeted training for users in various departments with specific user audiences in mind. A formal security training policy should be drafted and signed off by management, with well-defined scopes, roles, and responsibilities of various individuals, such as the CIO and the information security officer, and posted on the intranet. New recruits should be given a copy of all security policies to sign off on before they are granted user access. The training policy should also spell out the roles of the HR, Compliance, and PR departments in the training program.

Training can be given using the PowerPoint Seminar method in large gatherings before monthly "all-hands" departmental meetings and also via an emailed Web link to a Flash video format presentation. The latter can also be configured to have an interactive quiz at the end, which should pique audience interest in the subject and help them remember relevant issues.

With regard to topics to be included in the training, any applicable federal or industry mandate such as HIPAA, SOX, PCI-DSS, or ISO 27002 should be discussed extensively first, followed by discussions on tackling social engineering, spyware, viruses, and so on.

The topics of data theft and corporate data breaches are frequently in the news. These topics can be extensively discussed, with emphasis on how to protect personally identifiable information in a corporate setting. Password policy and access control topics are always good things to discuss; users at a minimum need to be reminded to sign off their workstations before going on break.

9. DOCUMENTING THE NETWORK: CHANGE MANAGEMENT

Controlling the IT infrastructure configuration of a large organization is more about change control than other things. Often the change control guidance comes from documents such as the ITIL series of guidebooks.

After a baseline configuration is documented, change control—a deliberate and methodical process that ensures that any changes are made to the baseline IT configuration of the organization (such as changes to network design, AD design, and so on)—is extensively documented and authorized only after prior approval. This is done to ensure that unannounced or unplanned changes are not allowed to hamper the day-to-day efficiency and business functions of the overall intranet infrastructure.

In most government entities, even very small changes are made to go through change management (CM); however, management can give managers leeway to approve a certain minimal level of ad hoc change that has no potential to disrupt operations. In most organizations where mandates are a day-to-day affair, no ad hoc change is allowed unless it goes through supervisory-level change management meetings.

The goal of change management is largely to comply with mandates—but for some organizations, waiting for a weekly meeting can slow things significantly. If justified, an emergency CM meeting can be called to approve a time-sensitive change.

Practically speaking, the change management process works as follows: A formal change management document is filled out (usually a multitab online Excel spreadsheet) and forwarded to the change management ombudsman (maybe a project management person). For some CM form details, see the sidebar: Change Management Spreadsheet Details to Submit to a CM Meeting.

The document must have supervisory approval from the requestor's supervisor before proceeding to the ombudsman. The ombudsman posts this change document on a section of the intranet for all other supervisors and managers within the CM committee to review in advance. Done this way, the change management committee, meeting in its weekly or biweekly change approval meetings, can voice reservations or ask clarification questions of the change-initiating person, who is usually present to explain the change. At the end of the deliberations the decision is then voted on to either approve, deny, modify, or delay the change (sometimes with preconditions).

CHANGE MANAGEMENT SPREADSHEET DETAILS TO SUBMIT TO A CM MEETING

- Name and organizational details of the change-requestor.
- Actual change details, such as the time and duration of the change.
- Any possible impacts (high, low, medium) to significant user groups or critical functions.
- The amount of advance notice needed for impacted users via email (typically two working days).
- Evidence that the change has been tested in advance.

- Signature and approval of the supervisor and her supervisor (manager).
- Whether and how rollback is possible
- Post-change, a "postmortem tab" has to confirm whether the change process was successful and any revealing comments or notes for the conclusion.
- One of the tabs can be an "attachment tab" containing embedded Visio diagrams or word documentation embedded within the Excel sheet to aid discussion.

If approved, the configuration change is then made (usually within the following week). The postmortem section of the change can then be updated to note any issues that occurred during the change (such as a rollback after change reversal and the causes).

In recent years, some organizations have started to operate the change management collaborative process using social networking tools at work. This allows disparate flows of information, such as emails, departmental wikis, and file-share documents, to belong to a unified thread for future reference.

10. REHEARSE THE INEVITABLE: DISASTER RECOVERY

Possible disaster scenarios can range from the mundane to the biblical in proportion. In intranet or general IT terms, successfully recovering from a disaster can mean resuming critical IT support functions for mission-critical business functions. Whether such recovery is smooth and hassle-free depends on how prior disaster-recovery planning occurs and how this plan is tested to address all relevant shortcomings adequately.

The first task when planning for disaster recovery (DR) is to assess the business impact of a certain type of disaster on the functioning of an intranet using business impact analysis (BIA). BIA involves certain metrics; again, off-the shelf software tools are available to assist with this effort. The scenario could be a natural hurricane-induced power outage or a human-induced critical application crash. In any one of these scenarios, one needs to assess the type of impact in time, productivity, and financial terms.

BIAs can take into consideration the breadth of impact. For example, if the power outage is caused by a hurricane or an earthquake, support from generator vendors or the electricity utility could be hard to get, because of the large demands for their services. BIAs also need to take into account historical and local weather priorities. Though there could be possibilities of hurricanes occurring in California or earthquakes occurring along the Gulf Coast of Florida, for most practical purposes the chances of those disasters taking place in those locales are pretty remote. Historical data can be helpful for prioritizing contingencies.

Once the business impacts are assessed to categorize critical systems, a disaster recovery (DR) plan can be organized and tested. The criteria for recovery have two types of metrics: a recovery point objective (RPO) and a recovery time objective (RTO).

In the DR plan, the RPO refers to how far back or "back to what point in time" that backup data has to be recovered. This timeframe generally dictates how often tape backups are taken, which can again depend on the criticality of the data. The most common scenario for medium-sized IT shops is daily incremental backups and a weekly full backup on tape. Tapes are sometimes changed automatically by the tape backup appliances.

One important thing to remember is to rotate tapes (that is, put them on a life-cycle plan by marking them for expiry) to make sure that tapes have complete data integrity during a restore. Most tape manufacturers have marking schemes for this task. Although tapes are still relatively expensive, the extra amount spent on always having fresh tapes ensures that there are no nasty surprises at the time of a crucial data recovery.

RTO refers to how long it takes to restore backed up or recovered data to its original state for resuming normal business processes. The critical factor here is cost. It will cost much more to restore data within an hour using an online backup process or to resume operations using a hotsite rather than a five-hour restore using stored tape backups. If business process resumption is critical, cost becomes a less important factor.

DR also has to take into account resumption of communication channels. If network and telephone links aren't up, having a timely tape restore does little good to resume business functions. Extended campus network links are often dependent on leased lines from major vendors such as Verizon and AT & T, so having a trusted vendor relationship with agreed-on SLA standards is a requirement.

Depending on budgets, one can configure DR to happen almost instantly, if so desired, but that is a far more costly option. Most shops with "normal" data flows are okay with business being resumed within the span of about three to fours hours or even a full working day after a major disaster. Balancing costs with business expectations is the primary factor in the DR game. Spending inordinately for a rare disaster that might never happen is a waste of resources. It is fiscally imprudent (not to mention futile) to try to prepare for every contingency possible.

Once the DR plan is more or less finalized, a DR committee can be set up under an experienced DR professional to orchestrate the routine training of users and managers to simulate disasters on a frequent basis. In most shops this means management meeting every two months to simulate a DR "war room" (command center) situation and employees going through a mandatory interactive six-month disaster recovery training, listing the DR personnel to contact.

Within the command center, roles are preassigned, and each member of the team carries out his or her role as though it were a real emergency or disaster. DR coordination is frequently modeled after the U.S. Federal Emergency Management Agency (FEMA) guidelines, an active entity that has training and certification tracks for DR management professionals.

Simulated "generator shutdowns" in most shops are scheduled on a biweekly or monthly basis to see how the systems actually function. The systems can include uninterrupible power supplies (UPSs), emergency lighting, email and cell phone notification methods, and alarm enunciators and sirens. Since electronics items in a server room are sensitive to moisture damage, gas-based Halon fire-extinguishing systems are used. These Halon systems also have a provision to test them (often twice a year) to determine their readiness. The vendor will be happy to be on retainer for these tests, which can be made part of the purchasing agreement as a service level agreement (SLA). If equipment is tested on a regular basis, shortcomings and major hardware maintenance issues with major DR systems can be easily identified, documented, and redressed.

In a severe disaster situation, priorities need to be exercised on what to salvage first. Clearly, trying to recover employee records, payroll records, and critical business mission data such as customer databases will take precedence. Anything irreplaceable or not easily replaceable needs priority attention.

We can divide the levels of redundancies and backups to a few progressive segments. The level of backup sophistication would of course be dependent on (1) criticality and (2) time-to-recovery criteria of the data involved.

At the very basic level, we can opt not to back up any data or not even have procedures to recover data, which means that data recovery would be a failure. Understandably, this is not a common scenario.

More typical is contracting with an archival company of a local warehouse within a 20-mile periphery. Tapes are backed up onsite and stored offsite, with the archival company picking up the tapes from your facility on a daily basis. The time to recover is dependent on retrieving the tapes from archival storage, getting them onsite, and starting a restore. The advantages here are lower cost. However, the time needed to transport tapes and recover them might not be acceptable, depending on the type of data and the recovery scenario.

Often a "coldsite" or "hotsite" is added to the intranet backup scenario. A coldsite is a smaller and scaled-down copy of the existing intranet data center that has only the most essential pared-down equipment supplied and tested for recovery but not in a perpetually ready state (powered down as in "cold," with no live connection). These coldsites can house the basics, such as a Web server, domain name servers, and SQL databases, to get an informational site started up in very short order.

A hotsite is the same thing as a coldsite except that in this case the servers are always running and the Internet and intranet connections are "live" and ready to be switched over much more quickly than on a coldsite. These are just two examples of how the business resumption and recovery times can be shortened.

Recovery can be made very rapidly if the hotsite is linked to the regular data center using fast leased-line links (such as a DS3 connection). Backups synched in real time with identical RAID disks at the hotsite over redundant high-speed data links afford the shortest recovery time.

In larger intranet shops based in defense-contractor companies, there are sometimes requirements for even faster data recovery with far more rigid standards for data integrity. To-the-second real-time data synchronization in addition to hardware synchronization ensures that duplicate sites thousands of miles away can be up and running within a matter of seconds—even faster than a hotsite. Such extreme redundancy is typically needed for critical national databases (that is, air traffic control or customs databases that are accessed 24/7, for example).

At the highest level of recovery performance, most large database vendors offer "zero data loss" solutions, with a variety of cloned databases synchronized across the country that automatically failover and recover in an instantaneous fashion to preserve a consistent status—often free from human intervention. Oracle's version is called Data Guard; most mainframe vendors offer a similar product, varying in their offerings of tiers and features.

The philosophy here is simple: The more dollars you spend, the more readiness you can buy. However, the expense has to be justified by the level of criticality for the availability of the data.

11. CONTROLLING HAZARDS: PHYSICAL AND ENVIRONMENTAL PROTECTION

Physical access and environmental hazards are very relevant to security within the intranet. People are the primary weak link in security (as previously discussed), and controlling the activity and movement of authorized personnel and preventing access to unauthorized personnel fall within the purview of these security controls. This important area of intranet security must first be formalized within a management-sanctioned and published P&P.

Physical access to data center facilities (as well as IT working facilities) is typically controlled using card readers. These were scanning types in the last two decades but are increasingly being converted to near-field or proximity-type access card systems. Some high-security facilities (such as bank data centers) use smartcards, which use encryption keys stored within the cards for matching keys.

Some important and common-sense topics should be discussed within the subject of physical access. First, disbursal of cards needs to be a deliberate and high-security affair requiring the signatures of at least two supervisory-level people who can be responsible for the authenticity and actual need for access credentials for a person to specific areas.

Access-card permissions need to be highly granular. An administrative person will probably never need to be in the server room, so that person's access to the server room should be blocked. Areas should be categorized and catalogued by sensitivity and access permissions granted accordingly.

Physical data transmission access points to the intranet have to be monitored via digital video recording (DVR) and closed-circuit cameras if possible. Physical electronic eavesdropping can occur to unmonitored network access points in both wireline and wireless ways. There have been known instances of thieves intercepting LAN communication from unshielded Ethernet cable (usually hidden above the plenum or false ceiling for longer runs). All a data thief needs is to place a TAP box and a miniature (Wi-Fi) wireless transmitter at entry or exit points to the intranet to copy and transmit all communications. At the time of this writing, these transmitters are the size of a USB key. The miniaturization of electronics has made data theft possible for part-time thieves. Spy-store sites give determined data thieves plenty of workable options at relatively little cost.

Using a DVR solution to monitor and store access logs to sensitive areas and correlating them to the timestamps on the physical access logs can help forensic investigations in case of a physical data breach, malfeasance, or theft. It is important to remember that DVR records typically rotate and are erased every week. One person has to be in charge of the DVR so records are saved to optical disks weekly before they are erased. DVR tools need some tending to because their sophistication level often does not come up to par with other network tools.

Written or PC-based sign-in logs must be kept at the front reception desk, with timestamps. Visitor cards should have limited access to private and/or secured areas. Visitors must provide official identification, log times coming in and going out, and names of persons to be visited and the reason for their visit. If possible, visitors should be escorted to and from the specific person to be visited, to minimize the chances of subversion or sabotage.

Entries to courthouses and other special facilities have metal detectors, but these may not be needed for every facility. The same goes for bollards and concrete entry barriers to prevent car bombings. In most government facilities where security is paramount, even physical entry points to parking garages have special personnel (usually deputed from the local sheriff's department) to check under cars for hidden explosive devices.

Contractor laptops must be registered and physically checked in by field support personnel. And if these laptops are going to be plugged into the local network, the laptops need to be virus-scanned by data-security personnel and checked for unauthorized utilities or suspicious software (such as hacking utilities, Napster, or other P2P threats).

Supply of emergency power to the data center and the servers has to be robust to protect the intranet from corruption due to power failures. Redundancy has to be exercised all the way from the utility connection to the servers themselves. This means there has to be more than one power connection to the data center (from more than one substation/transformer, if it is a larger data center). There has to be provision of alternate power supply (a ready generator to supply some, if not all, power requirements) in case of power failure.

Power supplied to the servers has to come from more than one single UPS because most servers have two removable power inputs. Data center racks typically have two UPSs on the bottom supplying power to two separate power strips on both sides of the rack for this redundancy purpose (for seamless switchover). In case of a power failure, the UPSs instantly take over the supply of power and start beeping, alerting personnel to gracefully shut down servers. UPSs usually have reserve power for brief periods (less than 10 minutes) until the generator kicks in, relieving the UPS of the large burden of the server power loads. Generators come on trailers or are skid-mounted and are designed to run as long as fuel is available in the tank, which can be about three to five days, depending on the model and capacity to generate (in thousands of kilowatts).

Increasingly, expensive polluting batteries have made UPSs in larger data centers fall out of favor compared to flywheel power supplies, which are a cleaner, battery-less technology to supply interim power. Maintenance of this technology is half as costly as UPS, and it offers the same functionality. Provision has to be made for rechargeable emergency luminaires within the server room, as well as all areas occupied by administrators, so entry and exit are not hampered during a power failure.

Provision for fire detection and firefighting must also be made. As mentioned previously, Halon gas fire-suppression systems are appropriate for server rooms because sprinklers will inevitably damage expensive servers if the servers are still turned on during sprinkler activation.

Sensors have to be placed close to the ground to detect moisture from plumbing disasters and resultant flooding. Master shutoff valve locations for water have to be marked and identified and personnel trained on performing shutoffs periodically. Complete environmental control packages with cameras geared toward detecting any type of temperature, moisture, and sound abnormality are offered by many vendors. These sensors are connected to monitoring workstations using Ethernet LAN cabling. Reporting can occur through emails if customizable thresholds are met or exceeded.

12. KNOW YOUR USERS: PERSONNEL SECURITY

Users working within intranet-related infrastructures have to be known and trusted. Often data contained within the intranet is highly sensitive, such as new product designs and financial or market-intelligence data gathered after much research and at great expense.

Assigning personnel to sensitive areas in IT entails attaching security categories and parameters to the positions, especially within IT. Attaching security parameters to a position is akin to attaching tags to a photograph or blog. Some parameters will be more important than others, but all describe the item to some extent. The categories and parameters listed on the personnel access form should correlate to access permissions to sensitive installations such as server rooms. Access permissions should be compliant to the organizational security policy in force at the time. Personnel, especially those who will be handling sensitive customer data or individually identifiable health records, should be screened before hiring to ensure that they do not have felonies or misdemeanors on their records.

During transfers and terminations, all sensitive access tools should be reassessed and reassigned (or de-assigned, in case termination happens) for logical and physical access. Access tools can include such items as encryption tokens, company cell phones, laptops or PDAs, card keys, metal keys, entry passes, and any other company identification provided for employment. For people who are leaving the organization, an exit interview should be taken. System access should be terminated on the hour after former personnel have ceased to be employees of the company.

13. PROTECTING DATA FLOW: INFORMATION AND SYSTEM INTEGRITY

Information integrity protects information and data flows while they are in movement to and from the users' desktops to the intranet. System integrity measures protect the systems that process the information (usually servers such as email or file servers). The processes to protect information can include antivirus tools, IPS and IDS tools, Web-filtering tools, and email encryption tools.

Antivirus tools are the most common security tools available to protect servers and users' desktops. Typically, enterprise-level antivirus software from larger vendors such as Symantec or McAfee will contain a console listing all machines on the network and will enable the administrators to see graphically (color or icon differentiation) which machines need virus remediation or updates. All machines will have a software client installed that does some scanning and reporting of the individual machines to the console. To save bandwidth, the management server that contains the console will be updated with the latest virus (and spyware) definition from the vendor. Then it is the management console's job to slowly update the software client in each computer with the latest definitions. Sometimes the client itself will need an update, and the console allows this to be done remotely.

IDS detects malware within the network from the traffic and communication malware used. There are certain patterns of behavior attached to each type of malware, and those signatures are what IDSs are used to match. IDSs are mostly defunct nowadays. The major problems with IDSs were that (1) IDSs used to produce too many false positives, which made sifting out actual threats a huge, frustrating exercise, and (2) IDSs had no teeth; that is, their functionality was limited to reporting and raising alarms. IDS devices could not stop malware from spreading because they could not block it.

Compared to IDSs, IPSs have seen much wider adoption across corporate intranets because IPS devices sit inline processing traffic at the periphery and they can block traffic or malware, depending on a much more sophisticated heuristic algorithm than IDS devices. Although IPSs are all mostly signature based, there are already experimental IPS devices that can stop threats, not on signature, but based only on suspicious or anomalous behavior. This is good news because the numbers of "zero-day" threats are on the increase, and their signatures are mostly unknown to the security vendors at the time of infection.

Web-filtering tools have gotten more sophisticated as well. Ten years ago Web filters could only block traffic to specific sites if the URL matched. Today most Web filter vendors have large research arms that try to categorize specific Web sites under certain categories. Some vendors have realized the enormity of this task and have allowed the general public to contribute to this effort. The Web site www.trustedsource.org is an example; a person can go in and submit a single or multiple URLs for categorization. If they're examined and approved, the site category will then be added to the vendor's next signature update for their Web filter solution.

Web filters not only match URLs, but they also do a fair bit of packet-examining these days—just to make sure that a JPEG frame is indeed a JPEG frame and not a worm in disguise. The categories of Web sites blocked by a typical midsized intranet vary, but some surefire blocked categories would be pornography, erotic sites, discrimination/hate, weapons/illegal activities, and dating/relationships.

Web filters are not just there to enforce the moral values of management. These categories—if not blocked at work—openly enable an employee to offend another employee (especially pornography or discriminatory sites) and are fertile grounds for a liability lawsuit against the employer.

Finally, email encryption has been in the news because of the various mandates such as Sarbanes-Oxley and HIPAA. Both mandates specifically mention email or communication encryption to encrypt personally identifiable financial or patient medical data while in transit. Lately, the state of California (among other states) has adopted a resolution to discontinue fund disbursements to any California health organization that does not use email encryption as a matter of practice. This has caught quite a few California companies and local government entities unaware because email encryption software is relatively hard to implement. The toughest challenge yet is to train users to get used to the tool. Email encryption works by entering a set of credentials to access the email rather than just getting email pushed to the user, as within the email client Outlook.

14. SECURITY ASSESSMENTS

A security assessment (usually done on a yearly basis for most midsized shops) not only uncovers various misconfigured items on the network and server-side sections of IT operations; it also serves as a convenient blueprint for IT to activate necessary changes and get credibility for budgetary assistance from the accounting folks.

Typically, most consultants take two to four weeks to conduct a security assessment (depending on the size of the intranet), and they primarily use open-source vulnerability scanners such as Nessus. GFI LANguard, Retina, and Core Impact are other examples of commercial vulnerability-testing tools. Sometimes testers also use other proprietary suites of tools (special open-source tools like the Metasploit Framework or Fragrouter) to conduct "payload-bearing attack exploits," thereby evading the firewall and the IPS to gain entry. In the case of intranet Web servers, cross-site scripting attacks can occur (see sidebar: Types of Scans Conducted on Servers and Network Appliances during a Security Assessment).

TYPES OF SCANS CONDUCTED ON SERVERS AND NETWORK APPLIANCES DURING A SECURITY ASSESSMENT

- Firewalls and IPS devices configuration
- Regular and SSL VPN configuration
- Web server hardening (most critical; available as guides from vendors such as Microsoft)
- DMZ configuration
- Email vulnerabilities

- DNS server anomalies
- Database servers (hardening levels)
- Network design and access control vulnerabilities
- Internal PC health such as patching levels and incidence of spyware, malware, and so on

The results of these penetration tests are usually compiled as two separate items: (1) as a full-fledged technical report for IT and (2) as a high-level executive summary meant for and delivered to top management to discuss strategy with IT after the engagement.

15. RISK ASSESSMENTS

Risk is defined as the probability of loss. In IT terms we're talking about compromising data CIA (confidentiality, integrity, or availability). Risk management is a way to manage the probability of threats causing an impact. Measuring risks using a risk assessment exercise is the first step toward managing or mitigating a risk. Risk assessments can identify network threats, their probabilities, and their impacts. The reduction of risk can be achieved by reducing any of these three factors.

Regarding intranet risks and threats, we're talking about anything from threats such as unpatched PCs getting viruses and spyware (with hidden keylogging software) to network-borne denial-of-service attacks and even large, publicly embarrassing Web vandalism threats, such as someone being able to deface the main page of the company Web site. The last is a very high-impact threat but mostly perceived to be a remote probability—unless, of course, the company has experienced this before. The awareness among vendors as well as users regarding security is at an all-time high due to security being a high-profile news item.

Any security threat assessment needs to explore and list exploitable vulnerabilities and gaps. Many midsized IT shops run specific vulnerability assessment (VA) tools in-house on a monthly basis. eEye's Retina Network Security Scanner and Foundstone's scanning tools appliance are two examples of VA tools that can be found in use at larger IT shops. These tools are consolidated on ready-to-run appliances that are usually managed through remote browser-based consoles. Once the gaps are identified and quantified, steps can be taken to gradually mitigate these vulnerabilities, minimizing the impact of threats.

In intranet risk assessments, we identify primarily Web server and database threats residing within the intranet, but we should also be mindful about the periphery to guard against breaches through the firewall or IPS.

Finally, making intranet infrastructure and applications can be a complex task. This gets even more complex and even confusing when information is obtained from the different sources that are normally found at security conferences around the world. Frequently, these conference sources give a high-level overview, talking about generic compliance; but none gives a full picture and details that are required for quick implementation. So, with the preceding in mind, and because of the frequency of poor security practices or far-too-common security failures on the intranet, let's briefly look at an intranet security implementation process checklist.

16. INTRANET SECURITY IMPLEMENTATION PROCESS CHECKLIST

With this checklist, you get all of your questions in one place. This not only saves time, it's also cost effective. The following high-level checklist lists all of the questions that are typically raised during the implementation process (see checklist: An Agenda for Action for Intranet Security Implementation Process Activities).

AN AGENDA FOR ACTION FOR INTRANET SECURITY IMPLEMENTATION PROCESS ACTIVITIES

The following high-level checklist should be addressed in order to find the following intranet security implemnetation process questions helpful (check all tasks completed):

_____1. How to validate the intranet?

_____2. How to validate web applications?

_____3. How to ensure and verify accuracy of file transfer through the e-mails?

_____4. Does one need third-party certificates for digital signatures?

_____5. How to ensure limited and authorized access to closed and open systems?

_____6. How can one safely access the company intranet while traveling?

_____7. How to best protect the intranet from Internet attacks?

_____8. How to handle security patches?

_____9. Does the stakeholder expect to be able to find a procedure using a simple search interface?

_____10. How many documents will be hosted?

_____11. What design will be used (centralized, hub and spoke, etc.)?

_____12. Who will be involved in evaluating projects?

_____13. What is the budget?

_____14. Who will be responsible for maintaining the site after it goes "live"?

---

17. SUMMARY

It is true that the level of Internet hyperconnectivity among generation X and Y users has mushroomed lately, and the network periphery that we used to take for granted as a security shield has been diminished largely because of the explosive growth of social networking and the resulting connectivity boom. However, with the various new types of incoming application traffic (VoIP, SIP, and XML traffic) to their networks, security administrators need to stay on their toes and deal with these new protocols by implementing newer tools and technology. One recent example of new technology is the application-level firewall for connecting outside vendors to intranets (also known as an XML firewall, placed within a DMZ) that protects the intranet from malformed XML and SOAP message exploits coming from outside sourced applications.[27]

---

27. Latest standard (version 1.1) for SOAP message security standard from OASIS, a consortium for Web Services Security, www.oasisopen.org/committees/download.php/16790/wss-v1.1-spec-os-SOAPMessageSecurity.pdf.

In conclusion, we can say that with the myriad security issues facing intranets today, most IT shops are still well equipped to defend themselves if they assess risks and, most important, train their employees regarding data security practices on an ongoing basis. The problems with threat mitigation remain largely a matter of meeting gaps in procedural controls rather than technical measures. Trained and security-aware employees are the biggest deterrent to data thefts and security breaches.

Finally, let's move on to the real interactive part of this chapter: review questions/exercises, hands-on projects, case projects and optional team case project. The answers and/or solutions by chapter can be found in the Online Instructor's Solutions Manual.

CHAPTER REVIEW QUESTIONS/EXERCISES

True/False

1. True or False? In the corporate context, microblogging entails sending short SMS messages to apprise colleagues of recent developments in the daily routine.
2. True or False? Popular devices like the iPad, Samsung Galaxy Android tablet, and many types of smartphones are already capable of accessing company intranets using customized intranet apps.
3. True or False? Quite a few risks need to be resolved when approaching intranet security concerning mobile devices.
4. True or False? Mobile devices accessing enterprise intranets using VPNs have to be subject to the same factors as any other device remotely accessing VPNs.
5. True or False? While there are few risks in deploying mobile devices within the Intranet, with careful configuration these risks can be increased to the point where the myriad benefits outweigh the risks.

Multiple Choice

1. The intranet, as just a simple place to share files and to list a few policies and procedures, has ceased to be. The types of changes can be summed up in the following list of features, which shows that the intranet has become a combined portal as well as a public dashboard. Some of the features include the following, except which one?
   A. A corporate personnel directory of phone numbers by department.
   B. Several RSS feeds for news according to divisions such as IT, HR, Finance, Accounting, and Purchasing.
   C. A search engine for searching company information, often helped by a search appliance from Google.
   D. A section describing company financials and other mission-critical indicators.
   E. A "live" section with IT alerts regarding specific downtimes, outages, and other critical time-sensitive company notifications.
2. Intranet security policies and procedures (P&Ps) are:
   A. The functionality and ease of use of using voice, gesture, and touch interfaces.
   B. The first step toward a legal regulatory framework.

C. The availability of customized apps (applications).
D. The change in the very concept of "being at work" compared to even 10 years ago.
E. The more rapid iteration life cycles of mobile devices.

3. The millennial generation is more familiar with:
    A. PCs and laptops.
    B. social media.
    C. mobile technology.
    D. mobile hardware industry.
    E. cloud.

4. Backend enterprise network infrastructure support has to be ready and has to be strong to handle mobile devices interacting with:
    A. iPads.
    B. IPSec.
    C. L2TP VPNs.
    D. SSL VPNs.
    E. PPTP VPNs.

5. What policy/procedure must be signed by new hires at orientation and by all employees who ask for access to the corporate VPN using mobile devices (even personal ones)?
    A. WPA2 encryption for Wi-Fi traffic access.
    B. Inbound and outbound malware scanning.
    C. A well-tested SSL VPN for remote access.
    D. A policy for reporting theft or misplacement.
    E. A customized corporate usage policy for mobile devices.

EXERCISE

Problem

How can an organization prevent security breaches to their intranet?

Hands-On Projects

Project

How would an organization handle an intranet attack?

Case Projects

Problem

How would an organization go about handling an unauthorized access of an intranet?

Optional Team Case Project

Problem

How would an organization go about handling the misuse of user privileges on an intranet?

Local Area Network Security

Dr. Pramod Pandya
California State University

Securing available resources on any corporate or academic data network is of paramount importance because most of these networks connect to the Internet for commercial or research activities. Therefore, the network is under attack from hackers on a continual basis, so network security technologies are ever evolving and playing catch-up with hackers. Around 29 years ago the number of potential users was small and the scope of any activity on the network was limited to local networks only. As the Internet expanded in its reach across national boundaries and as the number of users increased, potential risk to the network grew exponentially. Over the past 18 years ecommerce-related activities such as online shopping, banking, stock trading, and social networking have permeated extensively, creating a dilemma for both service providers and their potential clients, as to who is a trusted service provider and a trusted client on the network. Of course, this being a daunting task for security professionals, they have needed to design security policies appropriate for both the servers and their clients. The security policy must be a factor in clients' level of access to the resources. So, in whom do we place trust, and how much trust? Current network designs implement three levels of trust: most trusted, less trusted, and least trusted. Figure 9.1 reflects these levels of trust, as described here:

- The most trusted users belong to the *intranet*. These users have to authenticate to a centralize administrator to access the resources on the network.
- The less trusted users may originate from the intranet as well as the external users who are authenticated to access resources such as email and Web services.
- The least trusted users are the unauthenticated users; most of them are simply browsing the resources on the Internet with no malice intended. Of course, some are scanning the resources with the intent to break in and steal data.

Network and System Security
DOI: http://dx.doi.org/10.1016/B978-0-12-416689-9.00009-5

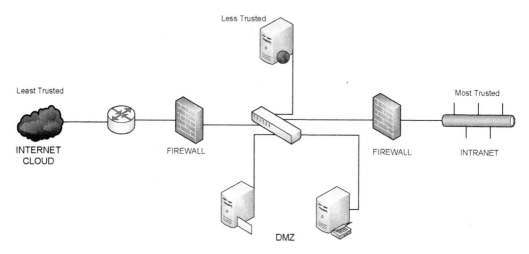

FIGURE 9.1   The DMZ.

These are the objectives of network security:

- *Confidentiality.* Only authorized users have access to the network.
- *Integrity.* Data cannot be modified by unauthorized users.
- *Access.* Security must be designed so that authorized users have uninterrupted access to data.

Finally, the responsibility for the design and implementation of network security, is headed by the chief information officer (CIO) of the enterprise network. The CIO has a pool of network administrators and legal advisers to help with this task. The network administrators define the placing of the network access controls, and the legal advisors underline the consequences and liabilities in the event of network security breaches. We have seen cases of customer records such as credit-card numbers, Social Security numbers, and personal information being stolen. The frequency of these reports have been on the increase in the past years, and consequently this has led to a discussion on the merits of encryption of stored data. One of the most quoted legal requirements on the part of any business, whether small or big, is the protection of consumer data under the Health Insurance Portability and Accountability Act (HIPAA), which restricts disclosure of health-related data and personal information.

1. IDENTIFY NETWORK THREATS

Network security threats can be in one of two categories: (1) disruptive type or (2) unauthorized access type.

Disruptive

Most LANs are designed as collapsed backbone networks using a layer-2 or layer-3 switch. If a switch or a router were to fail due to power failure, a segment or the entire network may cease to function until the power is restored. In some case, the network failure may be due to a virus attack on the secondary storage, thus leading to loss of data.

Unauthorized Access

This access type can be internal (employee) or external (intruder), a person who would attempt to break into resources such as database, file, and email or web servers that they have no permission to access. Banks, financial institutions, major corporations, and major retail businesses employ data networks to process customer transactions and store customer information and any other relevant data. Before the birth of the Internet Age, interin-stitutional transactions were secured because the networks were not accessible to intruders or the general public. In the past 14 years, access to the Internet is almost universal; hence institutional data networks have become the target of frequent intruder attacks to steal customer records. One frequently reads in the news about data network security being compromised by hackers, leading to loss of credit card and debit card numbers, Social Security numbers, drivers' license numbers, and other sensitive information such as purchasing profiles. Over the years, although network security has increased, the frequency of attacks on the networks has also increased because the tools to breach the network security have become freely available on the Internet. In 1988 the U.S. Department of Defense established the Computer Emergency Response Team (CERT), whose mission is to work with the Internet community to prevent and respond to computer and network security breaches. Since the Internet is widely used for commercial activities by all kinds of businesses, the federal government has enacted stiffer penalties for hackers.

2. ESTABLISH NETWORK ACCESS CONTROLS

In this part of the chapter, we outline steps necessary to secure networks through network controls. These network controls are either software or hardware based and are implemented in a hierarchical structure to reflect the network organization. This hierarchy is superimposed on the network from the network's perimeter to the access level per user of the network resources. The functions of the network control are to detect an unauthorized access, to prevent network security from being breached, and finally, to respond to a breach—thus the three categories of detect, prevent, and respond.

The role of prevention control is to stop unauthorized access to any resource available on the network. This could be implemented as simply as a password required to authenticate the user to access the resource on the network. For an authorized user this password can grant login to the network to access the services of a database, file, Web, print, or email server. The network administrator would need a password to access the switch or a router. The prevention control in this case is software based. An analog of hardware-based control would be, for example, if the resources such as server computers, switches, and routers are locked in a network access control room.

The role of the detection control is to monitor the activities on the network and identify an event or a set of events that could breach network security. Such an event may be a virus, spyware, or adware attack. The detection control software must, besides registering the attack, generate or trigger an alarm to notify of an unusual event so that a corrective action can be taken immediately, without compromising security.

The role of the response control is to take corrective action whenever network security is breached so that the same kind of breach is detected and any further damage is prevented.

3. RISK ASSESSMENT

During the initial design phase of a network, the network architects assess the types of risks to the network as well as the costs of recovering from attacks for all the resources that have been compromised. These cost factors can be realized using well-established accounting procedures such as cost/benefit analysis, return on investment (ROI), and total cost of ownership (TCO). These risks could range from natural disaster to an attack by a hacker. Therefore, you need to develop levels of risks to various threats to the network. You need to design some sort of spreadsheet that lists risks versus threats as well as responses to those identified threats. Of course, the spreadsheet would also mark the placing of the network access controls to secure the network.

4. LISTING NETWORK RESOURCES

We need to identify the assets (resources) that are available on the corporate network. Of course, this list could be long, and it would make no sense to protect all the resources, except for those that are mission-critical to the business functions. Table 9.1 identifies mission-critical components of any enterprise network. You will observe that these mission-critical components need to be prioritized, since they do not all provide the same functions. Some resources provide controlled access to a network; other resources carry sensitive corporate data. Hence the threats posed to these resources do not carry the same degree of vulnerabilities to the network. Therefore, the network access control has to be

TABLE 9.1 Mission-Critical Components of any Enterprise Network.

Resources	Threats					
	Fire, Flood, Earthquake	Power Failure	Spam	Virus	Spyware, Adware	Hijacking
Perimeter Router						
DNS Server						
WEB Server						
Email Server						
Core Switches						
Databases						

articulated and applied to each of the components listed, in varying degrees. For example, threats to DNS server pose a different set of problems from threats to the database servers. Next, we itemize the threats to these resources and specific network access controls.

5. THREATS

We need to identify the threats posed to the network from internal users as opposed to those from external users. The reason for such a distinction is that the internal users are easily traceable, compared to the external users. If a threat to the data network is successful, and it could lead to loss or theft of data or denial of access to the services offered by the network, it would lead to monetary loss for the corporation. Once we have identified these threats, we can rank them from most probable to least probable and design network security policy to reflect that ranking.

From Table 9.2, we observe that most frequent threats to the network are from viruses, and we have seen a rapid explosion in antivirus, antispamware, and spyware and adware software. Hijacking of resources such as domain name services, Web services, and perimeter routers would lead to what's most famously known as denial of service (DoS) or distributed denial of service (DDoS). Power failures can always be complemented by standby power supplies that could keep the essential resources from crashing. Natural disasters such as fire, floods, or earthquakes can be most difficult to plan for; therefore we see a tremendous growth in data protection and backup service provider businesses.

6. SECURITY POLICIES

The fundamental goals of security policy are to allow uninterrupted access to the network resources for authenticated users and to deny access to unauthenticated users. Of course, this is always a balancing act between the users' demands on network resources and the evolutionary nature of information technology. The user community would prefer open access, whereas the network administrator insists on restricted and monitored access to the network.

TABLE 9.2 The Most Frequent Threats to the Network Are from Viruses.

Rank	Threat
1	Virus
2	Spam
3	Spyware, Adware
4	Hijacking
5	Power Failure
6	Fire, Flood, Earthquake

The hacker is, in the final analysis, the arbitrator of the network security policy, since it is always the unauthorized user who discovers the potential flaw in the software. Hence, any network is as secure as the last attack that breached its security. It would be totally unrealistic to expect a secured network at all times, once it is built and secured. Therefore, network security design and its implementation represent the ultimate battle of the minds between the chief information security officer (CISO) and the devil, the hacker. We can summarize that the network security policy can be as simple as to allow access to resources, or it can be several hundred pages long, detailing the levels of access and punishment if a breach is discovered. Most corporate network users now have to sign onto the usage policy of the network and are reminded that security breaches are a punishable offence. The critical functions of a good security policy are:

- Appoint a security administrator who is conversant with users' demands and on a continual basis is prepared to accommodate the user community's needs.
- Set up a hierarchical security policy to reflect the corporate structure.
- Define ethical Internet access capabilities.
- Evolve the remote access policy.
- Provide a set of incident-handling procedures.

7. THE INCIDENT-HANDLING PROCESS

The incident-handling process is the most important task of a security policy for the reason that you would not want to shut down the network in case of a network security breach. The purpose of the network is to share the resources; therefore an efficient procedure must be developed to respond to a breach. If news of the network security breach becomes public, the corporation's business practices could become compromised, thus resulting in compromise of its business operations. Therefore set procedures must be developed jointly with the business operations manager and the chief information officer. This calls for a modular design of the enterprise network so that its segments can be shut down in an orderly way, without causing panic.

Toward this end, we need a set of tools to monitor activities on the network—we need an intrusion detection and prevention system. These pieces of software will monitor network activities and log and report an activity that does not conform to usual or acceptable standards as defined by the software. Once an activity is detected and logged, response is activated. It is not merely sufficient to respond to an incident; the network administrator also has to activate tools to trace back to the source of this breach. This is critical so that the network administrator can update the security procedures to make sure that this particular incident does not take place.

8. SECURE DESIGN THROUGH NETWORK ACCESS CONTROLS

A network is as secure as its weakest link in the overall design. To secure it, we need to identify the entry and exit points into the network. Since most data networks have computational nodes to process data and storage nodes to store data, stored data may need to be encrypted so that if network security is breached, stolen data may still remain confidential unless the encryption is broken. As we hear of cases of stolen data from either hacked networks or stolen nodes, encrypting data while it's being stored appears to be necessary to secure data.

The entry point to any network is a perimeter router, which sits between the external firewall and the Internet; this model is applicable to most enterprise networks that engage in some sort of ecommerce activities. Hence our first network access control is to define security policy on the perimeter router by configuring the appropriate parameters on the router. The perimeter router will filter traffic based on the range of IP addresses.

Next in the line of defense is the external firewall that filters traffic based on the state of the network connection. Additionally, the firewall could also check the contents of the traffic packet against the nature of the Transmission Control Protocol (TCP) connection requested. Following the firewall we have the so-called demilitarized zone, or DMZ, where we would place the following servers: Web, DNS, and email. We could harden these servers so that potential threatening traffic can be identified and appropriate incident response generated.

The DMZ is placed between two firewalls, so our last line of defense is the next firewall that would inspect the traffic and possibly filter out the potential threat. The nodes that are placed on the intranet can be protected by commercially available antivirus software. Last but not least, we could install on the network an intrusion detection and prevention system that will generate real-time response to a threat.

Next we address each of the network control access points. The traditional network design includes an access layer, a distribution layer, and the core layer. In the case of a local area network (LAN) we will use the access and distribution layers; the core layer would simply be our perimeter router that we discussed earlier. Thus the LAN will consist of a number of segments reflecting the organizational structure. The segments could sit behind their firewall to protect one another as well, in case of network breach; segments under attack can be isolated, thus preventing a cascade-style attack on the network.

9. IDS DEFINED

An intrusion detection system, or IDS, can be both software and hardware based. IDSs listen to all the activities taking place on both the computer (node on a network) and the network itself. One could think of an IDS as like traffic police, whose function is to monitor the data packet traffic and detect and identify those data packets that match predefined unusual pattern of activities. An IDS can also be programmed to teach itself from its past activities to refine the rules for unusual activities. This should not come as a surprise, since the hackers also get smarter over time.

As we stated, the IDS collects information from a variety of system and network resources, but in actuality it captures packets of data as defined by the TCP/IP protocol stack. In this sense IDS is both a sniffer and analyzer software. IDS in its sniffer role would either capture all the data packets or select ones as specified by the configuration script. This configuration script is a set of rules that tell the analyzer what to look for in a captured data packet, then make an educated guess per rules and generate an alert. Of course, this could lead to four possible outcomes with regard to intrusion detection: false positive, false negative, true positive, or true negative. We address this topic in more detail later in the chapter. IDSs performs a variety of functions:

- Monitor and analyze user and system activities
- Verify the integrity of data files
- Audit system configuration files
- Recognize activity of patterns, reflecting known attacks
- Statistical analysis of any undefined activity pattern

An IDS is capable of distinguishing different types of network traffic, such as an HTTP request over port 80 from some other application such as SMTP being run over port 80. We see here that an IDS understands which TCP/IP applications run over which preassigned port numbers, and therefore falsifying port numbers would be trivially detectable. This is a very easy illustration, but there are more complex attacks that are not that easy to identify, and we shall cover them later in this chapter.

The objective of intrusion detection software packages is to make possible the complex and sometimes virtually impossible task of managing system security. With this in mind, it might be worthwhile to bring to our attention two industrial-grade IDS software packages: Snort (NIDS), which runs on both Linux and Windows, and GFI LANguard S.E.L.M., a host intrusion detection system (HIDS), which runs on Windows only. Commercial-grade IDS software is designed with user-friendly interfaces that make it easy to configure scripts, which lay down the rules for intrusion detection. Next let's examine some critical functions of an IDS:

- Can impose a greater degree of flexibility to the security infrastructure of the network
- Monitors the functionality of routers, including firewalls, key servers, and critical switches
- Can help resolve audit trails, thus often exposing problems before they lead to loss of data
- Can trace user activity from the network point of entry to the point of exit
- Can report on file integrity checks
- Can detect whether a system has been reconfigured by an attack
- Can recognize a potential attack and generate an alert
- Can make possible security management of a network by nonexpert staff

10. NIDS: SCOPE AND LIMITATIONS

Network-based IDS (NIDS) sensors scan network packets at the router or host level, auditing data packets and logging any suspicious packets to a log file. Figure 9.2 is an example of a NIDS. The data packets are captured by a sniffer program, which is a part of the IDS software package. The node on which the IDS software is enabled runs in promiscuous mode. In promiscuous mode, the NIDS node captures all the data packets on the network as defined by the configuration script. NIDSs have become a critical component

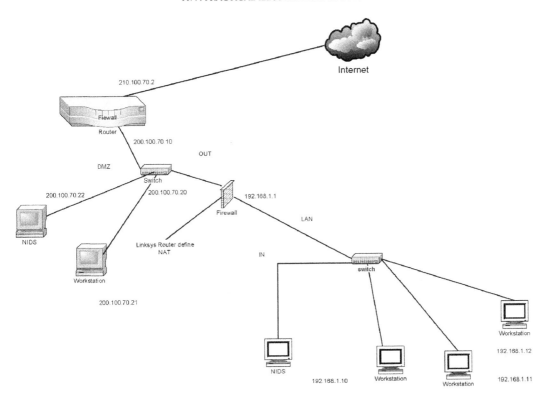

FIGURE 9.2 An example of a network-based intrusion detection system.

of network security management as the number of nodes on the Internet has grown exponentially over last few years. Some of the common malicious attacks on networks are:

- IP address spoofing
- MAC address spoofing
- ARP cache poisoning
- DNS name corruption

11. A PRACTICAL ILLUSTRATION OF NIDS

In this part of the chapter, we illustrate the use of Snort as an example of a NIDS. The signature files are kept in the directory signatures under the directory .doc. Signature files are used to match defined signature against a pattern of bytes in the data packets, to identify a potential attack. Files marked as rules in the rules directory are used to trigger an alarm and write to the file alert.ids. Snort is installed on a node with IP address 192.168.1.22. The security auditing software Nmap is installed on a node with IP address 192.168.1.20. Nmap software is capable of generating ping sweeps, TCP SYN (half-open) scanning, TCP connect() scanning, and much more. Figure 9.2 has a node labeled *NIDS* (behind the Linksys router) on which Snort would be installed. One of the workstations would run Nmap software.

UDP Attacks

A UDP attack is generated from a node with IP address 192.168.1.20 to a node with IP address 192.168.1.22. Snort is used to detect a possible attack. Snort's detect engine uses one of the files in DOS under directory rules to generate the alert file alert.ids. We display a partial listing (see Listing 9.1) of the alert.ids file.

Listing 9.2 shows a partial listing of DOS rules file. The rules stated in the DOS rules file are used to generate the alert.ids file.

```
[**] [1:0:0] DOS Teardrop attack [**]
[Priority: 0]
01/26-11:37:10.667833 192.168.1.20:1631 -> 192.168.1.22:21
UDP TTL:128 TOS:0x0 ID:60940 IpLen:20 DgmLen:69
Len: 41
[**] [1:0:0] DOS Teardrop attack [**]
[Priority: 0]
01/26-11:37:10.668460 192.168.1.20:1631 -> 192.168.1.22:21
UDP TTL:128 TOS:0x0 ID:60940 IpLen:20 DgmLen:69
Len: 41
[**] [1:0:0] DOS Teardrop attack [**]
[Priority: 0]
01/26-11:37:11.667926 192.168.1.20:1631 -> 192.168.1.22:21
UDP TTL:128 TOS:0x0 ID:60941 IpLen:20 DgmLen:69
Len: 41
[**] [1:0:0] DOS Teardrop attack [**]
[Priority: 0]
01/26-11:37:11.669424 192.168.1.20:1631 -> 192.168.1.22:21
UDP TTL:128 TOS:0x0 ID:60941 IpLen:20 DgmLen:69
Len: 41
[**] [1:0:0] DOS Teardrop attack [**]
[Priority: 0]
01/26-11:37:12.669316 192.168.1.20:1631 -> 192.168.1.22:21
UDP TTL:128 TOS:0x0 ID:60942 IpLen:20 DgmLen:69
Len: 41
```

LISTING 9.1   An alert.ids file.

```
# $Id: dos.rules,v 1.30.2.1 2004/01/20 21:31:38 jh8 Exp $
# -----------
# DOS RULES
# -----------
alert ip $EXTERNAL_NET any -> $HOME_NET any (msg:"DOS Jolt attack"; fragbits: M;
dsize:408; reference:cve,CAN-1999-0345; classtype:attempted-dos; sid:268; rev:2;)
alert udp $EXTERNAL_NET any -> $HOME_NET any (msg:"DOS Teardrop attack"; id:242;
fragbits:M; reference:cve,CAN-1999-0015; reference:url,www.cert.org/advisories/CA-1997-
28.html; reference:bugtraq,124; classtype:attempted-dos; sid:270; rev:2;) alert udp any 19 <>
any 7 (msg:"DOS UDP echo+chargen bomb"; reference:cve,CAN-1999-0635;
reference:cve,CVE-1999-0103; classtype:attempted-dos; sid:271; rev:3;)
alert ip $EXTERNAL_NET any -> $HOME_NET any (msg:"DOS IGMP dos attack";
content:"|02 00|"; depth: 2; ip_proto: 2; fragbits: M+; reference:cve,CVE-1999-0918;
classtype:attempted-dos; sid:272; rev:2;)
alert ip $EXTERNAL_NET any -> $HOME_NET any (msg:"DOS IGMP dos attack";
content:"|00 00|"; depth:2; ip_proto:2; fragbits:M+; reference:cve,CVE-1999-0918;
classtype:attempted-dos; sid:273; rev:2;)
alert icmp $EXTERNAL_NET any -> $HOME_NET any (msg:"DOS ath"; content:"+++ath";
nocase; itype: 8; reference:cve,CAN-1999-1228; reference:arachnids,264; classtype:attempted-
dos; sid:274; rev:2;)
```

LISTING 9.2 The DOS rules file.

TCP SYN (Half-Open) Scanning

This technique is often referred to as *half-open* scanning because you don't open a full TCP connection. You send a SYN packet, as though you were going to open a real connection, and wait for a response. A SYN|ACK indicates that the port is listening. An RST is indicative of a nonlistener. If a SYN|ACK is received, you immediately send an RST to tear down the connection (actually, the kernel does this for you). The primary advantage of this scanning technique is that fewer sites will log it! SYN scanning is the -s option of Nmap.

A SYN attack is generated using Nmap software from a node with IP address 192.168.1.20 to a node with IP address 192.168.1.22. Snort is used to detect for a possible attack. Snort's detect engine uses scan and ICMP rules files under directory rules to generate the alert file alert.ids. A partial listing of alert.ids file is shown in Listing 9.3.

A partial listing of the scan rules appears in Listing 9.4. Listing 9.5 contains a partial listing of the ICMP rules. The following points must be noted about NIDS:

- One NIDS is installed per LAN (Ethernet) segment.
- Place NIDS on the auxiliary port on the switch and then link all the ports on the switch to that auxiliary port.
- When the network is saturated with traffic, the NIDS might drop packets and thus create a potential "hole."
- If the data packets are encrypted, the usefulness of an IDS is questionable.

```
[**] [1:469:1] ICMP PING NMAP [**]
[Classification: Attempted Information Leak] [Priority: 2]
01/24-19:28:24.774381 192.168.1.20 -> 192.168.1.22
ICMP TTL:44 TOS:0x0 ID:29746 IpLen:20 DgmLen:28
Type:8 Code:0 ID:35844 Seq:45940 ECHO
[Xref => http://www.whitehats.com/info/IDS162]
[**] [1:469:1] ICMP PING NMAP [**]
[Classification: Attempted Information Leak] [Priority: 2]
01/24-19:28:24.775879 192.168.1.20 -> 192.168.1.22
ICMP TTL:44 TOS:0x0 ID:29746 IpLen:20 DgmLen:28
Type:8 Code:0 ID:35844 Seq:45940 ECHO
[Xref => http://www.whitehats.com/info/IDS162]
[**] [1:620:6] SCAN Proxy Port 8080 attempt [**]
[Classification: Attempted Information Leak] [Priority: 2]
01/24-19:28:42.023770 192.168.1.20:51530 -> 192.168.1.22:8080
TCP TTL:50 TOS:0x0 ID:53819 IpLen:20 DgmLen:40
******S* Seq: 0x94D68C2 Ack: 0x0 Win: 0xC00 TcpLen: 20
[**] [1:620:6] SCAN Proxy Port 8080 attempt [**]
[Classification: Attempted Information Leak] [Priority: 2]
01/24-19:28:42.083817 192.168.1.20:51530 -> 192.168.1.22:8080
TCP TTL:50 TOS:0x0 ID:53819 IpLen:20 DgmLen:40
******S* Seq: 0x94D68C2 Ack: 0x0 Win: 0xC00 TcpLen: 20
[**] [1:615:5] SCAN SOCKS Proxy attempt [**]
[Classification: Attempted Information Leak] [Priority: 2]
01/24-19:28:43.414083 192.168.1.20:51530 -> 192.168.1.22:1080
TCP TTL:59 TOS:0x0 ID:62752 IpLen:20 DgmLen:40
******S* Seq: 0x94D68C2 Ack: 0x0 Win: 0x1000 TcpLen: 20
[Xref => http://help.undernet.org/proxyscan/]
```

LISTING 9.3   Alert.ids file.

Some Not-So-Robust Features of NIDS

Network security is a complex issue with myriad possibilities and difficulties. In networks, security is also a weakest link phenomenon, since it takes vulnerability on one node to allow a hacker to gain access to a network and thus create chaos on the network. Therefore IDS products are vulnerable.

An IDS cannot compensate for weak identification and authentication. Hence you must rely on other means of identification and authentication of users. This is best implemented by token-based or biometric schemes and one-time passwords.

```
# (C) Copyright 2001,2002, Martin Roesch, Brian Caswell, et al.
# All rights reserved.
# $Id: scan.rules,v 1.21.2.1 2004/01/20 21:31:38 jh8 Exp $
# ------------
# SCAN RULES
# -----------
# These signatures are representitive of network scanners. These include
# port scanning, ip mapping, and various application scanners. #
# NOTE: This does NOT include web scanners such as whisker. Those are
# in web* #
alert tcp $EXTERNAL_NET 10101 -> $HOME_NET any (msg:"SCAN myscan"; stateless; ttl:
>220; ack: 0; flags: S;reference:arachnids,439; classtype:attempted-recon; sid:613; rev:2;)
alert tcp $EXTERNAL_NET any -> $HOME_NET 113 (msg:"SCAN ident version request";
flow:to_server,established; content: "VERSION|0A|"; depth: 16;reference:arachnids,303;
classtype:attempted-recon; sid:616; rev:3;)
alert tcp $EXTERNAL_NET any -> $HOME_NET 80 (msg:"SCAN cybercop os probe";
stateless; flags: SF12; dsize: 0; reference:arachnids,146; classtype:attempted-recon; sid:619;
rev:2;)
alert tcp $EXTERNAL_NET any -> $HOME_NET 3128 (msg:"SCAN Squid Proxy attempt";
stateless; flags:S,12; classtype:attempted-recon; sid:618; rev:5;)
alert tcp $EXTERNAL_NET any -> $HOME_NET 1080 (msg:"SCAN SOCKS Proxy attempt";
stateless; flags: S,12; reference:url,help.undernet.org/proxyscan/; classtype:attempted-recon;
sid:615; rev:5;)
alert tcp $EXTERNAL_NET any -> $HOME_NET 8080 (msg:"SCAN Proxy Port 8080
attempt"; stateless; flags:S,12; classtype:attempted-recon; sid:620; rev:6;)
alert tcp $EXTERNAL_NET any -> $HOME_NET any (msg:"SCAN FIN"; stateless; flags:F,12;
reference:arachnids,27; classtype:attempted-recon; sid:621; rev:3;)
alert tcp $EXTERNAL_NET any -> $HOME_NET any (msg:"SCAN ipEye SYN scan"; flags:S;
stateless; seq:1958810375; reference:arachnids,236; classtype:attempted-recon; sid:622; rev:3;)
alert tcp $EXTERNAL_NET any -> $HOME_NET any (msg:"SCAN NULL"; stateless; flags:0;
seq:0; ack:0; reference:arachnids,4; classtype:attempted-recon; sid:623; rev:2;)
```

LISTING 9.4 Scan rules.

An IDS cannot conduct investigations of attacks without human intervention. Therefore when an incident does occur, steps must be defined to handle the incident. The incident must be followed up to determine the responsible party, then the vulnerability that allowed the problem to occur should be diagnosed and corrected. You will observe that an IDS is not capable of identifying the attacker, only the IP address of the node that served as the hacker's point of entry.

An IDS cannot compensate for weaknesses in network protocols. IP and MAC address spoofing is a very common form of attack in which the source IP or MAC address does not correspond to the real source IP or MAC address of the hacker. Spoofed addresses can be mimicked to generate DDoS attacks.

```
# (C) Copyright 2001,2002, Martin Roesch, Brian Caswell, et al.
# All rights reserved.
# $Id: icmp.rules,v 1.19 2003/10/20 15:03:09 chrisgreen Exp $
# -----------
# ICMP RULES
# -----------
#
# Description:
# These rules are potentially bad ICMP traffic. They include most of the
# ICMP scanning tools and other "BAD" ICMP traffic (Such as redirect host)
#
# Other ICMP rules are included in icmp-info.rules
alert icmp $EXTERNAL_NET any -> $HOME_NET any (msg:"ICMP ISS Pinger";
content:"|495353504e4752511|";itype:8;depth:32; reference:arachnids,158; classtype:attempted-
recon; sid:465; rev:1;)
alert icmp $EXTERNAL_NET any -> $HOME_NET any (msg:"ICMP L3retriever Ping";
content: "ABCDEFGHIJKLMNOPQRSTUVWABCDEFGHI"; itype: 8; icode: 0; depth: 32;
reference:arachnids,311; classtype:attempted-recon; sid:466; rev:1;)
alert icmp $EXTERNAL_NET any -> $HOME_NET any (msg:"ICMP Nemesis v1.1 Echo";
dsize: 20; itype: 8; icmp_id: 0; icmp_seq: 0; content:
"|00000000000000000000000000000000000000001|";                reference:arachnids,449;
classtype:attempted-recon; sid:467; rev:1;)
alert icmp $EXTERNAL_NET any -> $HOME_NET any (msg:"ICMP PING NMAP"; dsize: 0;
itype: 8; reference:arachnids,162; classtype:attempted-recon; sid:469; rev:1;)
alert icmp $EXTERNAL_NET any -> $HOME_NET any (msg:"ICMP icmpenum v1.1.1"; id:
666; dsize: 0; itype: 8; icmp_id: 666; icmp_seq: 0; reference:arachnids,450; classtype:attempted-
recon; sid:471; rev:1;) alert icmp $EXTERNAL_NET any -> $HOME_NET any (msg:"ICMP
redirect host";itype:5;icode:1; reference:arachnids,135; reference:cve,CVE-1999-0265;
classtype:bad-unknown; sid:472; rev:1;)
alert icmp $EXTERNAL_NET any -> $HOME_NET any (msg:"ICMP redirect
net";itype:5;icode:0; reference:arachnids,199; reference:cve,CVE-1999-0265; classtype:bad-
unknown; sid:473; rev:1;)
alert icmp $EXTERNAL_NET any -> $HOME_NET any (msg:"ICMP superscan echo";
content:"|00000000000000001|"; itype: 8; dsize:8; classtype:attempted-recon; sid:474; rev:1;)
alert icmp $EXTERNAL_NET any -> $HOME_NET any (msg:"ICMP traceroute ipopts";
ipopts: rr; itype: 0; reference:arachnids,238; classtype
```

LISTING 9.5 ICMP rules.

An IDS cannot compensate for problems in the integrity of information the system provides. Many hacker tools target system logs, selectively erasing records corresponding to the time of the attack and thus covering the hacker's tracks. This calls for redundant information sources.

An IDS cannot analyze all the traffic on a busy network. A network-based IDS in promiscuous mode, can capture all of the data packets; and, as the traffic level raises, NIDS can reach a saturation point and begin to lose data packets.

An IDS cannot always deal with problems involving packet-level attacks. The vulnerabilities lie in the difference between IDS interpretation of the outcome of a network transaction and the destination node for that network session's actual handling of the transaction. Therefore, a hacker can send a series of fragmented network transactions.

Packets that elude detection and can also launch attacks on the destination node. Even worse, the hacker can lead to DoS on the IDS itself.

An IDS has problems dealing with fragmented data packets. Hackers would normally use fragmentation to confuse the IDS and thus launch an attack.

12. FIREWALLS

A firewall is either a single node or a set of nodes that enforce an access policy between two networks. Firewall technology evolved to protect the intranet from unauthorized users on the Internet. This was the case in the earlier years of corporate networks. Since then, the network administrators have realized that networks can also be attacked from trusted users as well as, for example, the employee of a company. The corporate network consists of hundreds of nodes per department and thus aggregates to over a thousand or more, and now there is a need to protect data in each department from other departments. Hence, a need for internal firewalls arose to protect data from unauthorized access, even if they are employees of the corporation. This need has, over the years, led to design of segmented IP networks, such that internal firewalls would form barriers within barriers, to restrict a potential break-in to an IP segment rather than expose the entire corporate network to a hacker. For this reason, network security has grown into a multibillion-dollar business.

Almost every intranet, whether of one node or many nodes, is always connected to the Internet, and thus a potential number of hackers wait to attack it. Thus every intranet is an IP network, with TCP- and UDP-based applications running over it. The design of TCP and UDP protocols require that every client/server application interacts with other client/server applications through TCP and UDP port numbers. As we stated earlier, these TCP and UDP port numbers are well known and hence give rise to a necessary weakness in the network. TCP and UDP port numbers open up "holes" in the networks by their very design. Every Internet and intranet point of entry has to be guarded, and you must monitor the traffic (data packets) that enter and leave the network.

A firewall is a combination of hardware and software technology, namely a sort of sentry, waiting at the points of entry and exit to look out for an unauthorized data packet trying to gain access to the network. The network administrator, with the help of other IT staff, must first identify the resources and the sensitive data that need to be protected from the hackers. Once this task has been accomplished, the next task is to identify who would have access to these identified resources and the data. We should pointed out that most of the networks in any corporation are never designed and built from scratch but are added to an existing network as the demand for networking grows with the growth of the business. So, the design of the network security policy has multilayered facets as well.

Once the network security policy is defined and understood, we can identify the proper placement of the firewalls in relation to the resources on the network. Hence, the next step would be to actually place the firewalls in the network as nodes. The network security policy now defines access to the network, as implemented in the firewall. These access rights to the network resources are based on the characteristics of TCP/IP protocols and the TCP/UDP port numbers.

Firewall Security Policy

The firewall enables the network administrator to centralize access control to the campuswide network. A firewall logs every packet that enters and leaves the network. The network security policy implemented in the firewall provides several types of protection, including the following:

- Block unwanted traffic
- Direct incoming traffic to more trustworthy internal nodes
- Hide vulnerable nodes that cannot easily be secured from external threats
- Log traffic to and from the network

A firewall is transparent to authorized users (both internal and external), whereas it is not transparent to unauthorized users. However, if the authorized user attempts to access a service that is not permitted to that user, a denial of that service will be echoed, and that attempt will be logged.

Firewalls can be configured in a number of architectures, providing various levels of security at different costs of installation and operations. Figure 9.2 is an example of a design termed a *screened Subnet*. In this design, the internal network is a private IP network, so the resources on that network are completely hidden from the users who are external to that network, such as users from the Internet. In an earlier chapter we talked about public versus private IP addresses. It is agreed to by the IP community that nodes with private IP addresses will not be accessible from outside that network. Any number of corporations may use the same private IP network address without creating packets with duplicated IP addresses. This feature of IP networks, namely private IP networks, adds to network security. In Figure 9.2, we used a Linksys router to support a private IP network (192.168.1.0) implementation. For the nodes on the 192.168.1.0 network to access the resources on the Internet, the Linksys router has to translate the private IP address of the data packet to a public IP address. In our scenario, the Linksys router would map the address of the node on the 192.168.1.0 network, to an address on the public network, 200.100.70.0. This feature is known as Network Address Translation (NAT), which is enabled on the Linksys router. You can see in Figure 9.2 that the Linksys router demarks the internal (IN) network from the external (OUT) network.

We illustrate an example of network address translation, as shown in Listing 9.6. The script configures a Cisco router that translates an internal private IP address to a public IP address. Of course, configuring a Linksys router is much simpler using a Web client. An explanation of the commands and their details follow the script.

Configuration Script for sf Router

The access-list command creates an entry in a standard traffic filter list:

- Access-list "access-list-number" permit|deny source [source-mask]

```
ip nat pool net-sf 200.100.70.50 200.100.70.60 netmask 255.255.255.0

ip nat inside source list 1 pool net-sf

!

interface Ethernet0

ip address 192.168.1.1 255.255.255.0

ip nat inside

!

interface Ethernet1

ip address 200.100.70.20 255.255.255.0

ip nat outside

access-list 1 deny 192.168.1.0 0.0.0.255
```

LISTING 9.6   Network Address Translation (NAT).

- Access-list number: identifies the list to which the entry belongs; a number from 1 to 99
- Permit|deny: this entry allows or blocks traffic from the specified address
- Source: identifies source IP address
- Source-mask: identifies the bits in the address field that are matched; it has a 1 in position indicating "don't care" bits, and a 0 in any position that is to be strictly followed

The IP access-group command links an existing access list to an outbound interface. Only one access list per port, per protocol, and per direction is allowed.

- Access-list-number: indicates the number of the access list to be linked to this interface
- In|out: selects whether the access list is applied to the incoming or outgoing interface; out is the default

NAT is a feature that operates on a border router between an inside private addressing scheme and an outside public addressing scheme. The inside private address is 192.168.1.0 and the outside public address is chosen to be 200.100.70.0. Equivalently, we have an intranet on the inside and the Internet on the outside.

13. DYNAMIC NAT CONFIGURATION

First a NAT pool is configured from which outside addresses are allocated to the requesting inside hosts: IP NAT pool "pool name" "start outside IP address" "finish outside IP address." Next the access-list is defined to determine which inside networks are translated by the NAT router: access-list "unique access-list number" permit|deny "inside IP network address." Finally the NAT pool and the access list are correlated:

- IP NAT inside source list "unique access list number" pool "pool name"
- Enable the NAT on each interface of the NAT router
- IP NAT inside + + + + + + + + + + + + + + + + + IP NAT outside

You will note that only one interface may be configured as outside, yet multiple interfaces may be configured as inside, with regard to Static NAT configuration:

- IP NAT inside source static "inside IP address" "outside IP address"
- IP NAT inside source static 192.168.1.100 200.100.70.99

14. THE PERIMETER

In Figure 9.3, you will see yet another IP network labeled *demilitarized zone* (DMZ). You may ask, why yet another network? The rationale behind this design is as follows.

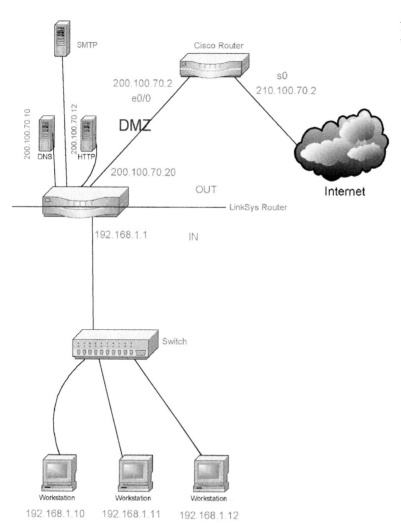

FIGURE 9.3 An illustrative firewall design.

The users that belong to IN might want to access the resources on the Internet, such as read their email and send email to the users on the Internet. The corporation needs to advertise its products on the Internet.

The DMZ is the perimeter network, where resources have public IP addresses, so they are seen and heard on the Internet. The resources such as the Web (HTTP), email (SMTP), and domain name server (DNS) are placed in the DMZ, whereas the rest of the resources that belong to this corporation are completely hidden behind the Linksys router. The resources in the DMZ can be attacked by the hacker because they are open to users on the Internet. The relevant TCP and UDP port numbers on the servers in the DMZ have to be left open to the incoming and outgoing traffic. Does this create a potential "hole" in the corporate network? The answer to this is both yes and no. Someone can compromise the resources in the DMZ without the entire network being exposed to a potential attack.

The first firewall is the Cisco router, and it is the first line of defense, were network security policy implemented. On the Cisco router it is known as the Access Control List (ACL). This firewall will allow external traffic to inbound TCP port 80 on the Web server, TCP port 25 on the email server, and TCP and UDP port 53 on the DNS server. The external traffic to the rest of the ports will be denied and logged.

The second line of defense is the Linksys router that will have well-known ports closed to external traffic. It too will monitor and log the traffic. It is acceptable to place email and the Web server behind the Linksys router on the private IP network address. Then you will have to open up the TCP ports 80 and 25 on the Linksys router so that the external traffic can be mapped to ports 80 and 25, respectively. This would slow down the traffic because the Linksys router (or any commercial-grade router) would have to constantly map the port numbers back and forth. Finally, the DNS server would always need to be placed in the DMZ with a public IP address, since it will be used to resolve domain names by both internal and external users. This decision has to be left to the corporate IT staff.

15. ACCESS LIST DETAILS

The Cisco router in Figure 9.3 can be configured with the following access list to define network security policy. Building an access list in the configuration script of the router does not activate the list unless it is applied to an interface. "ip access-group 101 in" applies the access-list 101 to the serial interface of the router. Some of the access-list commands are explained here. For more information on Cisco access-list commands, visit the Cisco Web site (www.cisco.com):

- ip access-group group no. {in|out}: default is out
- What is the group number?
- The group number is the number that appears in the access-list command line
- What is {in|out}?
- In implies that the packet enters the router's interface from the network
- Out implies that the packet leaves the router's interface to the network

All TCP packets are IP packets, but all IP packets are not TCP packets. Therefore, entries matching on IP packets are more generic than matching on TCP, UDP, or ICMP packets. Each entry in the access list is interpreted (see Listing 9.7) from top to bottom for each packet on the specified interface. Once a match is reached, the remaining access-list entries are ignored. Hence, the order of entries in an access list is very critical, and therefore more specific entries should appear earlier on.

This permits TCP from any host to any host if the ACK or RST bit is set, which indicates that it is part of an established connection. You will note that in a TCP Full Connect, the first packet from the source node does not have the ACK bit set. The keyword *established* is meant to prevent an untrusted user from initiating a connection while allowing packets that are part of already established TCP connections to go through:

- Access-list 101 permit udp any gt 1023 host 200.100.70.10 eq 53
- Permit UDP protocol from any host with port greater than 1023 to the DNS server at port 53
- Access-list 101 permit ip any host 200.100.70.12
- Permit IP from any host to 200.100.70.12

  or

- Access-list 101 permit TCP any 200.100.70.12 eq 80
- Permit any host to engage with our HTTP server on port 80 only
- Access-list 101 permit icmp any echo-reply
- Permit ICMP from any host to any host if the packet is in response to a ping request
- Access-list 101 deny ip any any

The last access-list command is implicit (that is, not explicitly stated). The action of this last access-list is to deny all other packets.

16. TYPES OF FIREWALLS

Conceptually, there are three types of firewalls:

- *Packet filtering*. Permit packets to enter or leave the network through the interface on the router on the basis of protocol, IP address, and port numbers.
- *Application-layer firewall*. A proxy server that acts as an intermediate host between the source and the destination nodes.
- *Stateful-inspection layer*. Validates the packet on the basis of its content.

```
interface serial0
ip address 210.100.70.2
ip access-group 101 in
!
access-list 101 permit tcp any any established
```

LISTING 9.7 Access-list configuration script.

17. PACKET FILTERING: IP FILTERING ROUTERS

An IP packet-filtering router permits or denies the packet to either enter or leave the network through the interface (incoming and outgoing) on the basis of the protocol, IP address, and the port number. The protocol may be TCP, UDP, HTTP, SMTP, or FTP. The IP address under consideration would be both the source and the destination addresses of the nodes. The port numbers would correspond to the well-known port numbers. The packet-filtering firewall has to examine every packet and make a decision on the basis of defined ACL; additionally it will log the following guarded attacks on the network:

- A hacker will attempt to send IP spoofed packets using raw sockets (we will discuss more about usage of raw sockets in the next chapters)
- Log attempted network scanning for open TCP and UDP ports—NIDS will carry out this detective work in more detail
- SYN attacks using TCP connect(), and TCP half open
- Fragment attacks

18. APPLICATION-LAYER FIREWALLS: PROXY SERVERS

These are proxy servers that act as an intermediary host between the source and the destination nodes. Each of the sources would have to set up a session with the proxy server, then the proxy server would set up a session with the destination node. The packets would have to flow through the proxy server. There are examples of Web and FTP proxy servers on the Internet. The proxy servers would also have to be used by the internal users, that is, the traffic from the internal users will have to run through the proxy server to the outside network. Of course, this slows the flow of packets, but you must pay the price for added network security.

19. STATEFUL INSPECTION FIREWALLS

In here the firewall will examine the contents of the packets before permitting them to either enter or leave the network. The contents of the packets must conform with the protocol declared with the packet. For example, if the protocol declared is HTTP, the contents of the packet must be consistent with the HTTP packet definition.

20. NIDS COMPLEMENTS FIREWALLS

A firewall acts as a barrier, if so designed, among various IP network segments. Firewalls may be defined among IP intranet segments to protect resources. In any corporate network, there will always be more than one firewall because an intruder could be one of the authorized network users. Hence the following points should be noted:

- Not all threats originate outside the firewall.
- The most trusted users are also the potential intruders.
- Firewalls themselves may be subject to attack.

Since the firewall sits at the boundary of the IP network segments, it can only monitor the traffic entering and leaving the interface on the firewall that connects to the network. If the intruder is internal to the firewall, the firewall will not be able to detect the security breach. Once an intruder has managed to transit through the interface of the firewall, the intruder would go undetected, which could possibly lead to stealing sensitive information, destroying information, leaving behind viruses, staging attacks on other networks, and most important, leaving spyware software to monitor the activities on the network for future attacks. Hence, a NIDS would play a critical role in monitoring activities on the network and continually looking for possible anomalous patterns of activities.

Firewall technology has been around for the past 25 years, so much has been documented about its weaknesses and strengths. Information about firewalls is freely available on the Internet. Hence a new breed of hackers have utilized *tunneling* as a means of bypassing firewall security policy. NIDS enhances security infrastructure by monitoring system activities for signs of attack and then, based on the system settings, responds to the attack as well as generates an alarm. Response to a potential attack is known as the *incident response* or *incident handling*, which combines investigation and diagnosis phases. Incident response has been an emerging technology in the past 7 years and is now an integral part of intrusion detection and prevention technology.

Finally, but not least, securing network systems is an ongoing process in which new threats arise all the time. Consequently, firewalls, NIDS, and intrusion prevention systems are continuously evolving technologies. In this chapter and subsequent chapters our focus has been and will be wired networks. However, as wireless data networks proliferate and seamlessly connect to the cellular voice networks, the risk of attacks on the wired networks is growing exponentially.

21. MONITOR AND ANALYZE SYSTEM ACTIVITIES

Figure 9.1 shows the placement of a NIDS, one in the DMZ and the other in the private network. This suggests at least two points on the network from which we capture data packets. The next question is the timing of the information collection, although this depends on the degree of threat perceived to the network.

If the level of perceived threat to the network is low, an immediate response to the attack is not very critical. In such a case, interval-oriented data capturing and analysis is most economical in terms of load placed on a NIDS and other resources on the network. Additionally, there might not be full-time network security personnel to respond to an alarm triggered by the NIDS.

If the level of perceived threat is imminent and the time and the data are mission-critical to the organization, real-time data gathering and analysis are of extreme importance. Of course, the real-time data gathering would impact the CPU cycles on the NIDS and would lead to a massive amount of data storage. With real-time data capturing and analysis, real-time response to an attack can be automated with notification. In such a case, network activities can be interrupted, the incident could be isolated, and system and network recovery could be set in motion.

Analysis Levels

Capturing and storing data packets are among the manageable functions of any IDS. How do we analyze the data packets that represent potential or imminent threats to the network?

We need to examine the data packets and look for evidence that could point to a threat. Let's examine the makeup of data packets. Of course, any packet is almost encapsulated by successive protocols from the Internet model, with the data as its kernel. Potential attacks could be generated by IP or MAC spoofing, fragmented IP packets leading to some sort of DoS, saturating the resource with flooding, and much more. We should remind readers that since humans are not going to examine the data packets, this process of examination is relegated to an algorithm. This algorithm must compare the packets with a known format of the packet (signature) that suggests an attack is in progress, or it could be that there is some sort of unusual activity on the network. How does one distinguish abnormal from normal sets of activities? There must be some baseline (statistical) that indicates normal, and deviation from it would be an indicator of abnormal. We explore these concepts in the following paragraphs.

We can identify two levels of analysis: signature and statistical.

22. SIGNATURE ANALYSIS

Signature analysis includes some sort of pattern matching of the contents of the data packets. There are patterns corresponding to known attacks. These known attacks are stored in a database, and a pattern is examined against the known pattern, which defines signature analysis. Most commercial NIDS products perform signature analysis against a database of known attacks, which is part of the NIDS software. Even though the databases of known attacks may be proprietary to the vendor, the client of this software should be able to increase the scope of the NIDS software by adding signatures to the database. Snort is open-source NIDS software, and the database of known attacks is maintained and updated by the user community. This database is an ASCII (human-readable) file.

23. STATISTICAL ANALYSIS

First we have to define what constitutes a normal traffic pattern on the network. Then we must identify deviations away from normal patterns as potential threats. These deviations must be arrived at by statistical analysis of the traffic patterns. A good example would be how many times records are written to a database over a given time interval, and deviations from normally accepted numbers would be an indication of an impending attack. Of course, a clever hacker could mislead the detector into accepting attack activity as normal by gradually varying behavior over time. This would be an example of a false negative.

24. SIGNATURE ALGORITHMS

Signature analysis is based on the following algorithms:

- Pattern matching
- Stateful pattern matching
- Protocol decode-based analysis
- Heuristic-based analysis
- Anomaly-based analysis

Pattern Matching

Pattern matching is based on searching for a fixed sequence of bytes in a single packet. In most cases the pattern is matched against only if the suspect packet is associated with a particular service or, more precisely, destined to and from a particular port. This helps to reduce the number of packets that must get examined and thus speed up the process of detection. However, it tends to make it more difficult for systems to deal with protocols that do not live on well-defined ports.

The structure of a signature based on the simple pattern-matching approach might be as follows: First, the packet is IPv4 or higher and TCP, the destination port is 3333, and the payload contains the fictitious string *psuw*, trigger an alarm. In this example, the pattern *psuw* is what we were searching for, and one of the IDS rules implies to trigger an alarm. One could do a variation on this example to set up more convoluted data packets. The advantage of this simple algorithm is:

- This method allows for direct correlation of an exploit with the pattern; it is highly specific.
- This method is applicable across all protocols.
- This method reliably alerts on the pattern matched.

The disadvantages of this pattern-matching approach are as follows:

- Any modification to the attack can lead to missed events (false negatives).
- This method can lead to high false-positive rates if the pattern is not as unique as the signature writer assumed.
- This method is usually limited to inspection of a single packet and, therefore, does not apply well to the stream-based nature of network traffic such as HTTP traffic. This scenario leads to easily implemented evasion techniques.

Stateful Pattern Matching

This method of signature development adds to the pattern-matching concept because a network stream comprises more than a single atomic packet. Matches should be made in context within the state of the stream. This means that systems that perform this type of signature analysis must consider arrival order of packets in a TCP stream and should handle matching patterns across packet boundaries. This is somewhat similar to a stateful firewall.

Now, instead of looking for the pattern in every packet, the system has to begin to maintain state information on the TCP stream being monitored. To understand the difference, consider the following scenario. Suppose that the attack you are looking for is launched from a client connecting to a server and you have the pattern-match method deployed on the IDS. If the attack is launched so that in any given single TCP packet bound for the target on port 3333 the string is present, this event triggers the alarm. If, however, the attacker causes the offending string to be sent such that the fictitious *gp* is in the first packet sent to the server and *o* is in the second, the alarm does not get triggered. If the stateful pattern-matching algorithm is deployed instead, the sensor has stored the *gp* portion of the string and is able to complete the match when the client forwards the fictitious *p*. The advantages of this technique are as follows:

- This method allows for direct correlation of an exploit with the pattern.
- This method is applicable across all protocols.
- This method makes evasion slightly more difficult.
- This method reliably alerts on the pattern specified.

The disadvantages of the stateful pattern matching-based analysis are as follows:

- Any modification to the attack can lead to missed events (false negatives).
- This method can lead to high false-positive rates if the pattern is not as unique as the signature writer assumed.

Protocol Decode-based Analysis

In many ways, intelligent extensions to stateful pattern matches are protocol decode-based signatures. This class of signature is implemented by decoding the various elements in the same manner as the client or server in the conversation would. When the elements of the protocol are identified, the IDS applies rules defined by the request for comments (RFCs) to look for violations. In some instances, these violations are found with pattern matches within a specific protocol field, and some require more advanced techniques that account for such variables as the length of a field or the number of arguments.

Consider the fictitious example of the *gwb* attack for illustration purposes. Suppose that the base protocol that the attack is being run over is the fictitious OBL protocol, and more specifically, assume that the attack requires that the illegal fictitious argument *gpp* must be passed in the OBL Type field. To further complicate the situation, assume that the Type field is preceded by a field of variable length called OBL Options. The valid list of fictitious options are *gppi, nppi, upsnfs,* and *cvjmep*. Using the simple or the stateful pattern-matching algorithm in this case leads to false positives because the option *gppi* contains the pattern that is being searched for. In addition, because the field lengths are variable, it would be impossible to limit such false positives by specifying search start and stop locations. The only way to be certain that *gpp* is being passed in as the OBL type argument is to fully decode the protocol.

If the protocol allows for behavior that the pattern-matching algorithms have difficulty dealing with, not doing full protocol decodes can also lead to false negatives. For example, if the OBL protocol allows every other byte to be a NULL if a value is set in the OBL header, the pattern matchers would fail to see fx00ox00ox00. The protocol decode-enabled analysis engine would strip the NULLS and fire the alarm as expected, assuming that *gpp* was in the Type field. Thus, with the preceding in mind, the advantages of the protocol decode-based analysis are as follows:

- This method can allow for direct correlation of an exploit.
- This method can be more broad and general to allow catching variations on a theme.
- This method minimizes the chance for false positives if the protocol is well defined and enforced.
- This method reliably alerts on the violation of the protocol rules as defined in the rules script.

The disadvantages of this technique are as follows:

- This method can lead to high false-positive rates if the RFC is ambiguous and allows developers the discretion to interpret and implement as they see fit. These gray area protocol violations are very common.
- This method requires longer development times to properly implement the protocol parser.

Heuristic-based Analysis

A good example of this type of signature is a signature that would be used to detect a port sweep. This signature looks for the presence of a threshold number of unique ports being touched on a particular machine. The signature may further restrict itself through the specification of the types of packets that it is interested in (that is, SYN packets). Additionally, there may be a requirement that all the probes must originate from a single source. Signatures of this type require some threshold manipulations to make them conform to the utilization patterns on the network they are monitoring. This type of signature may be used to look for very complex relationships as well as the simple statistical example given.

The advantages for heuristic-based signature analysis are that some types of suspicious and/or malicious activity cannot be detected through any other means. The disadvantages are that algorithms may require tuning or modification to better conform to network traffic and limit false positives.

Anomaly-based Analysis

From what is seen normally, anomaly-based signatures are typically geared to look for network traffic that deviates. The biggest problem with this methodology is to first define what normal is. Some systems have hardcoded definitions of normal, and in this case they could be considered heuristic-based systems. Some systems are built to learn normal, but the challenge with these systems is in eliminating the possibility of improperly classifying abnormal behavior as normal. Also, if the traffic pattern being learned is assumed to be normal, the system must contend with how to differentiate between allowable deviations and those not allowed or representing attack-based traffic. The work in this area has been mostly limited to academia, although there are a few commercial products that claim to use anomaly-based detection methods. A subcategory of this type of detection is the profile-based detection methods. These systems base their alerts on changes in the way that users or systems interact on the network. They incur many of the same limitations and problems that the overarching category has in inferring the intent of the change in behavior.

Statistical anomalies may also be identified on the network either through learning or teaching of the statistical norms for certain types of traffic, for example, systems that detect traffic floods, such as UDP, TCP, or ICMP floods. These algorithms compare the current rate of arrival of traffic with a historical reference; based on this, the algorithms will alert to statistically significant deviations from the historical mean. Often, a user can provide the statistical threshold for the alerts. The advantages for anomaly-based detection are as follows:

- If this method is implemented properly, it can detect unknown attacks.
- This method offers low overhead because new signatures do not have to be developed.
- In general, these systems are not able to give you intrusion data with any granularity. It looks like something terrible may have happened, but the systems cannot say definitively.
- This method is highly dependent on the environment in which the systems learn what normal is.

The following are Freeware tools to monitor and analyze network activities:

- Network Scanner, Nmap, is available from www.insecure.org. Nmap is a free open-source utility to monitor open ports on a network. The MS-Windows version is a zip file by the name nmap-3.75-win32. zip. You also need to download a packet capture library, WinPcap, under Windows. It is available from http://winpcap.polito.it. In addition to these programs, you need a utility to unzip the zipped file, which you can download from various Internet sites.
- PortPeeker is a freeware utility for capturing network traffic for TCP, UDP, or ICMP protocols. With PortPeeker you can easily and quickly see what traffic is being sent to a given port. This utility is available from www.Linklogger.com.
- Port-scanning tools such as Fport 2.0 or higher and SuperScan 4.0 or higher are easy to use and freely available from www.Foundstone.com.
- Network sniffer Ethereal is available from www.ethereal.com. Ethereal is a packet sniffer and analyzer for a variety of protocols.
- EtherSnoop light is a free network sniffer designed for capturing and analyzing the packets going through the network. It captures the data passing through your network Ethernet card, analyzes the data, and represents it in a readable form. EtherSnoop light is a fully configurable network analyzer program for Win32 environments. It is available from www.arechisoft.com.
- A fairly advanced tool, Snort, an open-source NIDS, is available from www.snort.org.
- UDPFlood is a stress testing tool that could be identified as a DoS agent; it is available from www.Foundstone.com.
- An application that allows you to generate a SYN attack with a spoofed address so that the remote host's CPU cycle's get tied up is Attacker, and is available from www.komodia.com.

Finally, organizations employing legacy LANs should be aware of the limited and weak security controls available to protect communications. Legacy LANs are particularly susceptible to loss of confidentiality, integrity, and availability. Unauthorized users have access to well-documented security flaws and exploits that can easily compromise an organization's systems and information, corrupt the organization's data, consume network bandwidth, degrade network performance, launch attacks that prevent authorized users from accessing the network, or use the organization's resources to launch attacks on other networks. Organizations should mitigate risks to their LANs by applying countermeasures to address specific threats and vulnerabilities. So, with the preceding in mind, let's briefly look at a local area network security countermeasures checklist, which describes management, operational, and technical countermeasures that can be effective in reducing the risks commonly associated with legacy LANs.

25. LOCAL AREA NETWORK SECURITY COUNTERMEASURES IMPLEMENTATION CHECKLIST

With this checklist, these countermeasures do not guarantee a secure LAN environment and cannot prevent all adversary penetrations. Also, security comes at a cost—financial expenses related to security equipment, inconvenience, maintenance, and operation. Each organization needs to evaluate the acceptable level of risk based on numerous factors, which will affect the level of security implemented by that organization. To be effective, LAN security should be incorporated throughout the entire life cycle of LAN solutions. Organizations should create a networking security policy that addresses legacy LAN security. Such a policy and an organization's ability to enforce compliance with it are the foundations for all other countermeasures (see checklist: "An Agenda For Action For Local Area Network Security Countermeasures Implementation Activities"):

AN AGENDA FOR ACTION FOR LOCAL AREA NETWORK SECURITY COUNTERMEASURES IMPLEMENTATION ACTIVITIES

Policy considerations for legacy LANs should include the following (check all tasks completed):

Roles and Responsibilities:

_____1. Which users or groups of users are and are not authorized to use organization LANs?

_____2. Which parties are authorized and responsible for installing and configuring access points (APs) and other LAN equipment?

LAN Infrastructure Security:

_____3. Physical security requirements for LANs and LAN devices, including limitations on the service areas of LANs.

_____4. Types of information that may and may not be sent over LANs,

---

including acceptable use guidelines.

_____ **5.** How LAN transmissions should be protected, including requirements for the use of encryption and for cryptographic key management.

LAN Client Device Security:

_____ **6.** The conditions under which LAN client devices are and are not allowed to be used and operated.

_____ **7.** Standard hardware and software configurations that must be implemented on LAN client devices to ensure the appropriate level of security.

_____ **8.** Limitations on how and when LAN clients device may be used, such as specific locations.

_____ **9.** Guidelines on reporting losses of LAN client devices and reporting LAN security incidents.

_____ **10.** Guidelines for the protection of LAN client devices to reduce theft.

LAN Security Assessments:

_____ **11.** The frequency and scope of LAN security assessments.

_____ **12.** The actions to be taken to address rogue or misconfigured devices that are identified.

Other Recommendations for Management Countermeasures are as Follows:

_____ **13.** Consider designating an individual to track the progress of security standards, features, threats, and vulnerabilities. This helps to ensure the continued secure implementation of LAN technology.

_____ **14.** Maintain an inventory of legacy access points (APs) and connecting devices. This inventory is useful when conducting audits of technologies, particularly in identifying rogue devices.

26. SUMMARY

Local area networks (LANs) are significantly impacting the way organizations do business. As more and more critical work migrates from mainframes to LANs, the need for better controls becomes apparent. This chapter discussed the security and control issues involved with LANs; the types of critical and sensitive data now residing on LANs; the impact of loss, change or disclosure; and, realistic remedies for identified vulnerabilities. Also covered, were how transition technologies, topologies, and architectures create complex security, recovery, and integrity problems. In addition, the security features of popular LAN systems software and add-on packages were also identified. Next, the need for policies, procedures, and administrative controls were covered.

In conclusion, this chapter discussed the basics of how and where to implement effective controls in a local area network (LAN). Security pitfalls existing in both the hardware and software components that make up a LAN were identified. The significant challenges presented by the fast growth of LANs in the workplace was met head on with guidelines for reducing security exposures. Although this chapter di not address the specific implementations of any single network operating system, the topics discussed apply to all of these systems.

Finally, let's move on to the real interactive part of this Chapter: review questions/exercises, hands-on projects, case projects and optional team case project. The answers and/or solutions by chapter can be found in the Online Instructor's Solutions Manual.

CHAPTER REVIEW QUESTIONS/EXERCISES

True/False

1. True or False? Most LANs are designed as collapsed backbone networks using a layer-1 or layer-4 switch.
2. True or False? The LAN consists of a number of segments reflecting the network structure.
3. True or False? The most trusted users belong to the Internet.
4. True or False? During the final design phase of a network, the network architects assess the types of risks to the network; as well as, the costs of recovering from attacks for all the resources that have been compromised.
5. True or False? The fundamental goals of security policy are to allow uninterrupted access to the network resources for authenticated users and to deny access to unauthenticated users.

Multiple Choice

1. The critical functions of a good security policy include the following, except which one?
   A. Appoint a security administrator who is conversant with users' demands and on a continual basis is prepared to accommodate the user community's needs.
   B. Monitor and analyze user and system activities.
   C. Set up a hierarchical security policy to reflect the corporate structure.
   D. Define ethical Internet access capabilities.
   E. Provide a set of incident-handling procedures.
2. IDSs perform the following functions, except which one?
   A. Monitor and analyze user and system activities.
   B. Verify the integrity of data files.
   C. Customize the availability of 'apps' (applications).
   D. Audit system configuration files.
   E. Recognize activity of patterns, reflecting known attacks.
3. IDSs perform the following critical functions, except which one?
   A. Can impose a greater degree of flexibility to the security infrastructure of the network.
   B. Monitors the functionality of routers, including firewalls, key servers, and critical switches.
   C. Can help resolve audit trails, thus often exposing problems before they lead to loss of data.

D. Can trace the mobile hardware industry.

E. Can make possible security management of a network by nonexpert staff.

4. Some of the common malicious attacks on networks include the following, except which one?

A. IP address spoofing.

B. MAC address spoofing.

C. ARP cache poisoning.

D. DNS name corruption.

E. PPTP VPNs address hacking.

5. The following points should be noted about network intrusion detection system (NIDS), except which one?

A. Inbound and outbound NIDS malware scanning.

B. One NIDS is installed per LAN (Ethernet) segment.

C. Place NIDS on the auxiliary port on the switch and then link all the ports on the switch to that auxiliary port.

D. When the network is saturated with traffic, the NIDS might drop packets and thus create a potential "hole."

E. If the data packets are encrypted, the usefulness of an IDS is questionable.

EXERCISE

Problem

What minimum requirements does a computer need to meet to be able to connect to a local area network?

Hands-On Projects

Project

A medium size company needs to know what components they will need to establish a Local Area Network. They plan to have 1,200 users with e-mail, file and print, and Internet services. They also plan to have 20 servers used as LAN, proxy, and database servers. Four departments will need sufficient bandwidth and access applications from a database server. They are also going to expand to eight branch offices located in different states, two with only 10 users needing just a single Internet. What hardware components does the company need to build the LAN for all areas?

Case Projects

Problem

How can an organization correctly route traffic? A small organization has an application server with two network interface cards (NICs): LAN (A) equals a corporate network (in which clients connect to a server for application use); and, LAN (B) equals a digital subscriber line (DSL) Internet and remote connection. The application on this application server is designed to send alerts to the clients (connected via LAN (A)) and it also has email functionality (configured using POP3) that needs to be outbound via LAN (B), due to LAN (A) blocking this traffic. Right now, LAN (A) does not have a default gateway defined, which is allowing the email functionality to work just fine; clients can connect to the servers application via LAN (A) as well; but, the alerts that the application is supposed to send to the client does not work. When LAN (B) is disabled completely, the clients connect to the server application; and, the application successfully sends alerts to the clients as it is designed to do; but, the email functionality no longer works because of the blocked outbound traffic. So, what is the proper way to set this up? Is it something that can be corrected by using static routes? Routing and Remote Access Service (RRAS) perhaps?

Optional Team Case Project

Problem

How would a small company go about connecting a LAN to WAN server? In other words, how would the company connect their default LAN IP (193.279.2. ...) through a Cisco router to a WAN IP (213.81. ...)?

Wireless Network Security

Chunming Rong*, Gansen Zhao†, Liang Yan*, Erdal Cayirci*
and Hongbing Cheng*

*University of Stavanger, Norway, †Sun Yat-sen University, China

With the rapid development of technology in wireless communication and microchips, wireless technology has been widely used in various application areas. The proliferation of wireless devices and wireless networks in the past decade shows the widespread use of wireless technology.

Wireless networks are a general term to refer to various types of networks that communicate without the need of wire lines. Wireless networks can be broadly categorized into two classes based on the structures of the networks: wireless ad hoc networks and cellular networks. The main difference between these two is whether a fixed infrastructure is present.

Three of the well-known cellular networks are the GSM network, the CDMA network, and the 802.11 wireless LAN. The GSM network and the CDMA network are the main network technologies that support modern mobile communication, with most of the mobile phones and mobile networks that are built based on these two wireless networking technologies and their variants. As cellular networks require fixed infrastructures to support the communication between mobile nodes, deployment of the fixed infrastructures is essential. Further, cellular networks require serious and careful topology design of the fixed infrastructures before deployment, because the network topologies of the fixed infrastructures are mostly static and will have a great impact on network performance and network coverage.

Wireless ad hoc networks do not require a fixed infrastructure; thus it is relatively easy to set up and deploy a wireless ad hoc network (see Figure 10.1). Without the fixed infrastructure, the topology of a wireless ad hoc network is dynamic and changes frequently. It is not realistic to assume a static or a specific topology for a wireless ad hoc network. On the other hand, wireless ad hoc networks need to be self-organizing; thus mobile nodes in a wireless ad hoc network can adapt to the change of topology and establish cooperation with other nodes at runtime.

Network and System Security
DOI: http://dx.doi.org/10.1016/B978-0-12-416689-9.00010-1

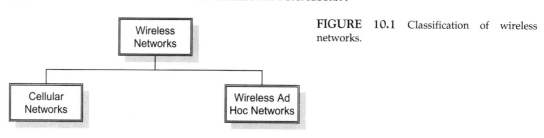

FIGURE 10.1 Classification of wireless networks.

Besides the conventional wireless ad hoc networks, there are two special types that should be mentioned: wireless sensor networks and wireless mesh networks. Wireless sensor networks are wireless ad hoc networks, most of the network nodes of which are sensors that monitor a target scene. The wireless sensors are mostly deprived devices in terms of computation power, power supply, bandwidth, and other computation resources. Wireless mesh networks are wireless networks with either a full mesh topology or a partial mesh topology in which some or all nodes are directly connected to all other nodes. The redundancy in connectivity of wireless networks provides great reliability and excellent flexibility in network packet delivery.

1. CELLULAR NETWORKS

Cellular networks require fixed infrastructures to work (see Figure 10.2). A cellular network comprises a fixed infrastructure and a number of mobile nodes. Mobile nodes connect to the fixed infrastructure through wireless links. They may move around from within the range of one base station to outside the range of the base station, and they can move into the ranges of other base stations. The fixed infrastructure is stationary, or mostly stationary, including base stations, links between base stations, and possibly other conventional network devices such as routers. The links between base stations can be either wired or wireless. The links should be more substantial than those links between base stations and mobile nodes in terms of reliability, transmission range, bandwidth, and so on.

The fixed infrastructure serves as the backbone of a cellular network, providing high speed and stable connection for the whole network, compared to the connectivity between a base station and a mobile node. In most cases, mobile nodes do not communicate with each other directly without going through a base station. A packet from a source mobile node to a destination mobile node is likely to be first transmitted to the base station to which the source mobile node is connected. The packet is then relayed within the fixed infrastructures until reaching the destination base station to which the destination mobile node is connected. The destination base station can then deliver the packet to the destination mobile node to complete the packet delivery.

Cellular Telephone Networks

Cellular telephone networks offer mobile communication for most of us. With a cellular telephone network, base stations are distributed over a region, with each base station

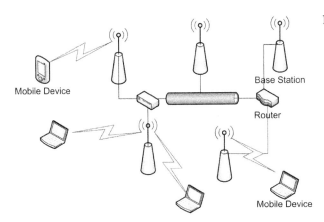

FIGURE 10.2   Cellular networking.

covering a small area. Each part of the small area is called a *cell*. Cell phones within a cell connect to the base station of the cell for communication. When a cell phone moves from one cell to another, its connection will also be migrated from one base station to a new base station. The new base station is the base station of the cell into which the cell phone just moved.

Two of the technologies are the mainstream for cellular telephone networks: the global system for mobile communication (GSM) and code division multiple access (CDMA).

GSM is a wireless cellular network technology for mobile communication that has been widely deployed in most parts of the world. Each GSM mobile phone uses a pair of frequency channels, with one channel for sending data and another for receiving data. Time division multiplexing (TDM) is used to share frequency pairs by multiple mobiles.

CDMA is a technology developed by a company named Qualcomm and has been accepted as an international standard. CDMA assumes that multiple signals add linearly, instead of assuming that colliding frames are completely garbled and of no value. With coding theory and the new assumption, CDMA allows each mobile to transmit over the entire frequency spectrum at all times. The core algorithm of CDMA is how to extract data of interest from the mixed data.

802.11 Wireless LANs

Wireless LANs are specified by the IEEE 802.11 series standard [1], which describes various technologies and protocols for wireless LANs to achieve different targets, allowing the maximum bit rate from 2 Mbits per second to 248 Mbits per second. Wireless LANs can work in either access point (AP) mode or ad hoc mode, as shown in Figure 10.3. When a wireless LAN is working in AP mode, all communication passes through a base station, called an *access point*. The access point then passes the communication data to the destination node, if it is connected to the access point, or forwards the communication data to a router for further routing and relaying. When working in ad hoc mode, wireless LANs work in the absence of base stations. Nodes directly communicate with other nodes within their transmission range, without depending on a base station.

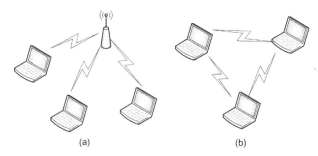

FIGURE 10.3 (a) A wireless network in AP mode; (b) a wireless network in ad hoc mode.

(a)   (b)

One of the complications that 802.11 wireless LANs incur is medium access control in the data link layer. Medium access control in 802.11 wireless LANs can be either distributed or centralized control by a base station. The distributed medium access control relies on the Carrier Sense Multiple Access (CSMA) with Collision Avoidance (CSMA/CA) protocol. CSMA/CA allows network nodes to compete to transmit data when a channel is idle and uses the Ethernet binary exponential backoff algorithm to decide a waiting time before retransmission when a collision occurs. CSMA/CA can also operate based on MACAW (Multiple Access with Collision Avoidance for Wireless) using virtual channel sensing. Request packets and clear-to-send (CTS) packets, are broadcast before data transmission by the sender and the receiver, respectively. All stations within the range of the sender or the receiver will keep silent in the course of data transmission to avoid interference on the transmission.

The centralized medium access control is implemented by having the base station broadcast a beacon frame periodically and poll nodes to check whether they have data to send. The base station serves as a central control over the allocation of the bandwidth. It allocates bandwidth according to the polling results. All nodes connected to the base station must behave in accordance with the allocation decision made by the base station. With the centralized medium access control, it is possible to provide quality-of-service guarantees because the base station can control on the allocation of bandwidth to a specific node to meet the quality requirements.

2. WIRELESS AD HOC NETWORKS

Wireless ad hoc networks are distributed networks that work without fixed infrastructures and in which each network node is willing to forward network packets for other network nodes. The main characteristics of wireless ad hoc networks are as follows:

- Wireless ad hoc networks are distributed networks that do not require fixed infrastructures to work. Network nodes in a wireless ad hoc network can be randomly deployed to form the wireless ad hoc network.
- Network nodes will forward network packets for other network nodes. Network nodes in a wireless ad hoc network directly communicate with other nodes within their ranges. When these networks communicate with network nodes outside of their ranges,

network packets will be forwarded by the nearby network nodes; and, other nodes that are on the path from the source nodes to the destination nodes.

- Wireless ad hoc networks are self-organizing. Without fixed infrastructures and central administration, wireless ad hoc networks must be capable of establishing cooperation between nodes on their own. Network nodes must also be able to adapt to changes in the network, such as the network topology.
- Wireless ad hoc networks have dynamic network topologies. Network nodes of a wireless ad hoc network connect to other network nodes through wireless links. The network nodes are mostly mobile. The topology of a wireless ad hoc network can change from time to time, since network nodes move around from within the range to the outside, and new network nodes may join the network, just as existing network nodes may leave the network.

Wireless Sensor Networks

A wireless sensor network is an ad hoc network mainly comprising sensor nodes, which are normally used to monitor and observe a phenomenon or a scene. The sensor nodes are physically deployed within or close to the phenomenon or the scene. The collected data will be sent back to a base station from time to time through routes dynamically discovered and formed by sensor nodes.

Sensors in wireless sensor networks are normally small network nodes with very limited computation power, limited communication capacity, and limited power supply. Thus a sensor may perform only simple computation and can communicate with sensors and other nodes within a short range. The life spans of sensors are also limited by the power supply.

Wireless sensor networks can be self-organizing, since sensors can be randomly deployed in some inaccessible areas. The randomly deployed sensors can cooperate with other sensors within their range to implement the task of monitoring or observing the target scene or the target phenomenon and to communicate with the base station that collects data from all sensor nodes. The cooperation might involve finding a route to transmit data to a specific destination, relaying data from one neighbor to another neighbor when the two neighbors are not within reach of each other, and so on.

Wireless Multimedia Sensor Networks

Wireless multimedia sensor networks (WMSNs), developed based on wireless sensor networks, are the networks of wireless, interconnected smart devices that enable processing video and audio streams, still images, and scalar sensor data. WMSNs will enable the retrieval of multimedia streams and will store, process in real-time, correlate, and fuse multimedia content captured by heterogeneous sources. The characteristics of a WMSN diverge consistently from traditional network paradigms, such as the Internet and even from scalar sensor networks. Most potential applications of a WMSN require the sensor network paradigm to be rethought to provide mechanisms to deliver multimedia content with a predetermined level of quality of service (QoS). Whereas minimizing energy consumption has been the main objective in sensor network research, mechanisms to efficiently deliver application-level QoS and to map these requirements to network-layer metrics, such as latency and jitter, have not been primary concerns. Delivery of multimedia content in sensor networks presents new, specific system design challenges, which are the object of this article. potential to enable many new applications, includeing Multimedia Surveillance Sensor Networks, Traffic Avoidance, Enforcement, and Control Systems Advanced Health Care Delivery. Environmental and Structural Monitoring and Industrial Process Control.

Internet of Things

The Internet of Things (IoT) is an emerging global Internetbased information architecture facilitating the exchange of goods and services in global supply chain networks, the connection of physical things to the Internet makes it possible to access remote sensor data and to control the physical world from a distance. The applications of Internet of Things are based on real physical objectives. For example, the lack of certain goods would automatically be reported to the provider which in turn immediately causes electronic or physical delivery. From a technical point of view, the IoT architecture is based on data communication tools, primarily RFID-tagged items (Radio-Frequency Identification). The IoT has the purpose of providing an IT-infrastructure facilitating the exchanges of "things" in a secure and reliable manner. The most popular industry proposal for the new IT-infrastructure of the IoT is based on an Electronic Product Code (EPC), introduced by EPCglobal and GS1. The "things" are physical objects carrying RFID tags with a unique EPC; the infrastructure can offer and query EPC Information Services (EPCIS) both locally and remotely to clients. Since some important business processes are concerned, a high degree of reliability about IoT is needed. Generally, the following security and privacy requirements are necessary for IoT:

1. Resilience to attacks: IoT system has to avoid single points of failure and should adjust itself to node failures.
2. Data authentication: Retrieved address and object information must be authenticated is a principle for efficient applications.
3. Access control: Information providers of IoT must be able to implement access control scheme on their confidential data.
4. Client privacy: there should be suitable measures to prevent others retrieving clients' private information and data.

Mesh Networks

One of the emerging technologies of wireless network are wireless mesh networks (WMNs). Nodes in a WMN include mesh routers and mesh clients. Each node in a WMN works as a router as well as a host. When it's a router, each node needs to perform routing and to forward packets for other nodes when necessary, such as when two nodes are not within direct reach of each other and when a route to a specific destination for packet delivery is required to be discovered.

Mesh routers may be equipped with multiple wireless interfaces, built on either the same or different wireless technologies, and are capable of bridging different networks. Mesh routers can also be classified as access mesh routers, backbone mesh routers, or gateway mesh routers. Access mesh routers provide mesh clients with access to mesh networks; backbone mesh routers form the backbone of a mesh network; and a gateway mesh router connects the backbone to an external network.

Each mesh client normally has only one network interface that provides network connectivity with other nodes. Mesh clients are not usually capable of bridging different networks, which is different from mesh routers.

Similar to other ad hoc networks, a wireless mesh network can be self-organizing. Thus nodes can establish and maintain connectivity with other nodes automatically, without human intervention. Wireless mesh networks can divided into backbone mesh networks and access mesh networks.

3. SECURITY PROTOCOLS

Wired Equivalent Privacy (WEP) was defined by the IEEE 802.11 standard [1]. WEP is designed to protect linkage-level data for wireless transmission by providing confidentiality, access control, and data integrity, to provide secure communication between a mobile device and an access point in a 802.11 wireless LAN.

4. WEP

Implemented based on shared key secrets and the RC4 stream cipher [2], WEP's encryption of a frame includes two operations (see Figure 10.4). It first produces a checksum of the data, and then it encrypts the plaintext and the checksum using RC4:

- *Checksumming.* Let c be an integrity checksum function. For a given message M, a checksum $c(M)$ is calculated and then concatenated to the end of M, obtaining a plaintext $P = <M, c(M)>$. Note that the checksum $c(M)$ does not depend on the shared key.
- *Encryption.* The shared key k is concatenated to the end of the initialization vector (IV) v, forming $<v,k>$. $<v,k>$ is then used as the input to the RC4 algorithm to generate a keystream $RC4(v,k)$. The plaintext P is exclusive-or' ed (XOR, denoted by $\oplus$) with the keystream to obtain the ciphertext: $C = P \oplus RC4(v,k)$.

Using the shared key k and the IV v, WEP can greatly simplify the complexity of key distribution because it needs only to distribute k and v but can achieve a relatively very long key sequence. IV changes from time to time, which will force the $RC\ 4$ algorithm to produce a new key sequence, avoiding the situation where the same key sequence is used to encrypt a large amount of data, which potentially leads to several types of attacks [3,4].

WEP combines the shared key k and the IV v as inputs to seed the $RC\ 4$ function. 802.11B [1] specifies that the seed shall be 64 bits long, with 24 bits from the IV v and 40 bits from the shared key k. Bits 0 through 23 of the seed contain bits 0 through 23 of the

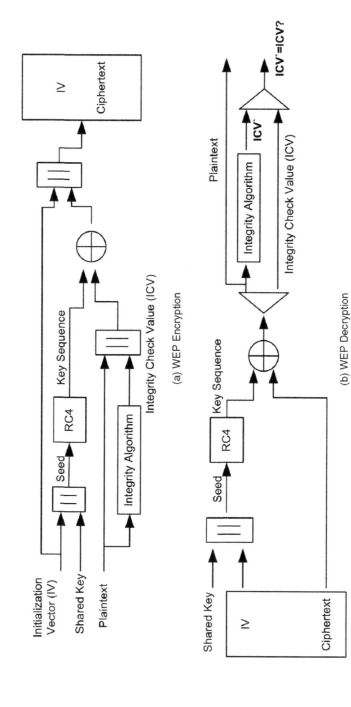

(a) WEP Encryption

(b) WEP Decryption

FIGURE 10.4 WEP encryption and decryption.

IV v, and bits 24 through 63 of the seed contain bits 0 through 39 of the shared key k. When a receiver receives the ciphertext C, it will XOR the ciphertext C with the corresponding keystream to produce the plaintext M' as follows:

$$M' = C \oplus RC4(k, v) = (P \oplus RC4(k, v)) \oplus RC4(k, v) = M$$

WPA and WPA2

Wi-Fi Protected Access (WPA) is specified by the IEEE 802.11i standard. The standard is aimed at providing a stronger security compared to WEP and is expected to tackle most of the weakness found in WEP [5–7].

WPA

WPA has been designed to target both enterprise and consumers. Enterprise deployment of WPA is required to be used with IEEE 802.1x authentication, which is responsible for distributing different keys to each user. Personal deployment of WPA adopts a simpler mechanism, which allows all stations to use the same key. This mechanism is called the *Pre-Shared Key* (PSK) mode.

The WPA protocol works in a similar way to WEP. WPA mandates the use of the *RC 4* stream cipher with a 128 − bit key and a 48 − bit initialization vector (IV), compared with the 40 − bit key and the 24 − bit IV in WEP.

WPA also has a few other improvements over WEP, including the Temporal Key Integrity Protocol (TKIP) and the Message Integrity Code (MIC). With TKIP, WPA will dynamically change keys used by the system periodically. With the much larger IV and the dynamically changing key, the stream cipher *RC4* is able to produce a much longer keystream. The longer keystream improved WPA's protection against the well-known key recovery attacks on WEP, since finding two packets encrypted using the same key sequences is literally impossible due to the extremely long keystream.

With MIC, WPA uses an algorithm named Michael to produce an authentication code for each message, which is termed the *message integrity code*. The message integrity code also contains a frame counter to provide protection over replay attacks.

WPA uses the Extensible Authentication Protocol (EAP) framework [8] to conduct authentication. When a user (supplicant) tries to connect to a network, an authenticator will send a request to the user asking the user to authenticate herself using a specific type of authentication mechanism. The user will respond with corresponding authentication information. The authenticator relies on an authentication server to make the decision regarding the user's authentication.

WPA2

WPA2 is not much different from WPA. Though TKIP is required in WPA, Advanced Encryption Standard (AES) is optional. This is aimed to provide backward compatibility for WPA over hardware designed for WEP, as TKIP can be implemented on the same hardware as those for WEP, but AES cannot be implemented on this hardware. TKIP and AES are both mandatory in WPA2 to provide a higher level of protection over wireless connections. AES is a block cipher, which can only be applied to a fixed length of data block. AES accepts key sizes of 128 bits, 196 bits, and 256 bits.

Besides the mandatory requirement of supporting AES, WPA2 also introduces supports for fast roaming of wireless clients migrating between wireless access points. First, WPA2 allows the caching of a Pair-wise Master Key (PMK), which is the key used for a session between an access point and a wireless client; thus a wireless client can reconnect a recently connected access point without having to reauthenticate. Second, WPA2 enables a wireless client to authenticate itself to a wireless access point that it is moving to while the wireless client maintains its connection to the existing access point. This reduces the time needed for roaming clients to move from one access point to another, and it is especially useful for timing-sensitive applications.

SPINS: Security Protocols for Sensor Networks

Sensor nodes in sensor networks are normally low-end devices with very limited resources, such as memory, computation power, battery, and network bandwidth.

Perrig et al. [9] proposed a family of security protocols named SPINS, which were specially designed for low-end devices with severely limited resources, such as sensor nodes in sensor networks. SPINS consists of two building blocks: Secure Network Encryption Protocol (SNEP) and the "micro" version of the Timed, Efficient, Streaming, Loss-tolerant Authentication Protocol (μTESLA). SNEP uses symmetry encryption to provide data confidentiality, two-party data authentication, and data freshness. μTESLA provides authentication over broadcast streams. SPINS assumes that each sensor node shares a master key with the base station. The master key serves as the base of trust and is used to derive all other keys.

SNEP

As illustrated in Figure 10.5, SNEP uses a block cipher to provide data confidentiality and message authentication code (MAC) to provide authentication. SNEP assumes a shared counter C between the sender and the receiver and two keys, the encryption key K_{encr} and the authentication key K_{mac}. For an outgoing message D, SNEP processes it as follows:

- The message D is first encrypted using a block cipher in counter mode with the key K_{encr} and the counter C, forming the encrypted text $E = \{D\} <Kencr, C>$.
- A message authentication code is produced for the encrypted text E with the key K_{mac} and the counter C, forming the MAC $M = MAC(K_{mac}, C|E)$ where $MAC()$ is a one-way function and $C|E$ stands for the concatenation of C and E.
- SNEP increments the counter C.

To send the message D to the recipient, SNEP actually sends out E and M. In other words, SNEP encrypts D to E using the shared key K_{encr} between the sender and the receiver to prevent unauthorized disclosure of the data, and it uses the shared key K_{mac}, known only to the sender and the receiver, to provide message authentication. Thus data confidentiality and message authentication can both be implemented.

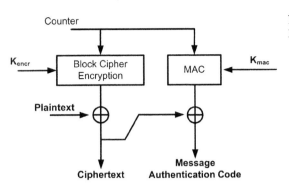

Counter

FIGURE   10.5   Sensor   Network   Encryption
Protocol (SNEP).

The message D is encrypted with the counter C, which will be different in each message. The same message D will be encrypted differently even it is sent multiple times. Thus semantic security is implemented in SNEP. The MAC is also produced using the counter C; thus it enables SNEP to prevent replying to old messages.

μTESLA

TESLA [10−12] was proposed to provide message authentication for multicast. TESLA does not use any asymmetry cryptography, which makes it lightweight in terms of computation and overhead of bandwidth.

μTESLA is a modified version of TESLA, aiming to provide message authentication for multicasting in sensor networks. The general idea of μTESLA is that the sender splits the sending time into intervals. Packets sent out in different intervals are authenticated with different keys. Keys to authenticate packets will be disclosed after a short delay, when the keys are no longer used to send out messages. Thus packets can be authenticated when the authentication keys have been disclosed. Packets will not be tampered with while they are in transit since the keys have not been disclosed yet. The disclosed authentication keys can be verified using previous known keys to prevent malicious nodes from forging authentication keys.

μTESLA has four phases: sender setup, sending authenticated packets, bootstrapping new receivers, and authenticating packets. In the sender setup phase, a sender generates a chain of keys, K_i $(0 \leq i \leq n)$. The keychain is a one-way chain such that K_i can be derived from K_j if $i \leq j$, such as a keychain K_i $(i = 0, \ldots, n)$, $K_i = F(K_{i+1})$, where F is a one-way function. The sender also decides on the starting time T_0, the interval duration T_{int}, and the disclosure delay d (unit is interval), as shown in Figure 10.6.

To send out authenticated packets, the sender attaches a MAC with each packet, where the MAC is produced using a key from the keychain and the data in the network packet. μTESLA has specific requirements on the use of keys for producing MACs. Keys are used in the same order as the key sequence of the keychain. Each of the keys is used in one interval only. For the interval $T_i = T_0 + i \times T_{int}$, the key K_i is used to produce the MACs for the messages sent out in the interval T_i Keys are disclosed with a fixed delay d such that the key K_i used in interval T_i will be disclosed in the interval T_{i+d} The sequence of key usage and the sequence of key disclosure are demonstrated in Figure 10.6.

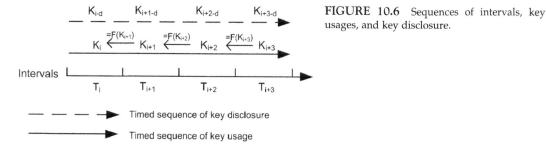

FIGURE 10.6 Sequences of intervals, key usages, and key disclosure.

To bootstrap a new receiver, the sender needs to synchronize the time with the receiver and needs to inform the new receiver of a key K_j that is used in a past interval T_j, the interval duration T_{int}, and the disclosure delay d. With a previous key K_j, the receiver will be able to verify any key K_p where $j \leq p$ using the one-way keychain's property. After this, the new receiver will be able to receive and verify data in the same way as other receivers that join the communication prior to the new receiver.

To receive and authenticate messages, a receiver will check all incoming messages if they have been delayed for more than d. Messages with a delay greater than d will be discarded, since they are suspect as fake messages constructed after the key has been disclosed. The receiver will buffer the remaining messages for at least d intervals until the corresponding keys are disclosed. When a key K_i is disclosed at the moment $T_i + d$, the receiver will verify K_i using K_{i-1} by checking if $K_{i-1} = F(K_i)$. Once the key K_i is verified, K_i will be used to authenticate those messages sent in the interval T_i.

5. SECURE ROUTING

Secure Efficient Ad hoc Distance (SEAD) [13] vector routing is adesign based on Destination-Sequenced Distance Vector (DSDV) routing [14]. SEAD augments DSDV with authentication to provide security in the construction and exchange of routing information.

SEAD

Distance vector routing works as follows. Each router maintains a routing table. Each entry of the table contains a specific destination, a metric (the shortest distance to the destination), and the next hop on the shortest path from the current router to the destination. For a packet that needs to be sent to a certain destination, the router will look up the destination from the routing table to get the matching entry. Then the packet is sent to the next hop specified in the entry.

To allow routers to automatically discover new routes and maintain their routing tables, routers exchange routing information periodically. Each router advises its neighbors of its own routing information by broadcasting its routing table to all its neighbors. Each router will update its routing table according to the information it hears from its neighbors. If a new destination is found from the information advertised by a neighbor, a new entry is added to the routing table with the metric recalculated based on the advertised metric and the linking between the router and the neighbor. If an existing destination is found, the corresponding entry is updated only when a new path that is shorter than the original one has been found. In this case, the metric and the next hop for the specified destination are modified based on the advertised information.

Though distance vector routing is simple and effective, it suffers from possible routing loops, also known as the counting to infinity problem. DSDV [14] is one of the extensions to distance vector routing to tackle this issue. DSDV augments each routing update with a sequence number, which can be used to identify the sequence of routing updates, preventing routing updates being applied in an out-of-order manner. Newer routing updates are advised with sequence numbers greater than those of the previous routing updates. In each routing update, the sequence number will be incremented to the next even number. Only when a broken link has been detected will the router use the next odd sequence number as the sequence number for the new routing update that is to be advertised to all its neighbors. Each router maintains an even sequence number to identify the sequence of every routing update. Neighbors will only accept newer routing updates by discarding routing updates with sequence numbers less than the last sequence number heard from the router.

SEAD provides authentication on metrics' lower bounds and senders' identities by using the one-way hash chain. Let H be a hash function and x be a given value. A list of values is computed as follows:

$$h_0, h_1, h_2, \ldots, h_n$$

where $h_0 = x$ and $h_{i+1} = H(h_i)$ for $0 \le i \le n$. Given any value h_k that has been confirmed to be in the list, to authenticate if a given value d is on the list or not one can compute if d can be derived from h_k by applying H a certain number of times, or if h_k can be derived from d by applying H to d a certain number of times. If either d can be derived from h_k or h_k can be derived from d within a certain number of steps, it is said that d can be authenticated by h_k.

SEAD assumes an upper bound $m - 1$ on the diameter of the ad hoc network, which means that the metric of a routing entry will be less than m. Let $h_0, h_1, h_2, \ldots, h_n$ be a hash chain where $n = m \times k$ and $k \in Z^+$. For an update with the sequence number i and the metric value of j, the value $h_{(k-i)m+j}$ is used to authenticate the routing update entry. By using $h_{(k-i)m+j}$ to authenticate the routing update entry, a node is actually disclosing the value $h_{(k-i)m+j}$ and subsequently all h_p where $p \ge (k-i)m + j$, but not any value h_q where $q \le (k-i)m + j$.

Using a hash value corresponding to the sequence number and metric in a routing update entry allows the authentication of the update and prevents any node from advertising a route to some destination, forging a greater sequence number or a smaller metric. To authenticate the update, a node can use any given earlier authentic hash value h_p from the same hash chain to authenticate the current update with sequence number i and metric j. The current update uses the hash value $h_{(k-i)m+j}$ and $(k-i)m + J \le P$, thus h_p can be computed from $h_{(k-i)m+j}$ by applying H for $(k-i)m + j - p$ times.

The disclosure of $h_{(k-i)m+j}$ does not disclose any value h_q where $q \le (k-i)m + j$. Let a fake update be advised with a sequence number p and metric q, where $p \ge i$ and $q \le j$, or

$q \leq j$. The fake update will need to use the hash value $h_{(k-P)\ m+q}$. If the sequence number p is greater than i or the metric q is less than j, $(k-p)m + q < (k-i)m + j$. This means that a hash value $h_{(k-p)m+q}$ that has not been disclosed is needed to authenticate the update. Since the value $h_{(k-p)m+q}$ has not been disclosed, the malicious node will not be able to have it to fake a routing update.

Ariadne

Ariadne [15] is a secure on-demand routing protocol for ad hoc networks. Ariadne is built on the Dynamic Source Routing protocol (DSR) [16].

Routing in Ariadne is divided into two stages: the route discovery stage and the route maintenance stage. In the route discovery stage, a source node in the ad hoc network tries to find a path to a specific destination node. The discovered path will be used by the source node as the path for all communication from the source node to the destination node until the discovered path becomes invalid. In the route maintenance stage, network nodes identify broken paths that have been found. A node sends a packet along a specified route to some destination. Each node on the route forwards the packet to the next node on the specified route and tries to confirm the delivery of the packet to the next node. If a node fails to receive an acknowledgment from the next node, it will signal the source node using a ROUTE ERROR packet that a broken link has been found. The source node and other nodes on the path can then be advised of the broken link.

The key security features Ariadne adds onto the route discovery and route maintenance are node authentication and data verification for the routing relation packets. Node authentication is the process of verifying the identifiers of nodes that are involved in Ariadne's route discovery and route maintenance, to prevent forging routing packets. In route discovery, a node sends out a ROUTE REQUEST packet to perform a route discovery. When the ROUTE REQUEST packet reaches the destination node, the destination node verifies the originator identity before responding. Similarly, when the source node receives a ROUTE REPLY packet, which is a response to the ROUTE REQUEST packet, the source node will also authenticate the identity of the sender. The authentication of node identities can be of one of the three methods: TELSA, digital signatures, and Message Authentication Code (MAC).

Data verification is the process of verifying the integrity of the node list in route discovery for the prevention of adding and removing nodes from the node list in a ROUTE RQUEST. To build a full list of nodes for a route to a destination, each node will need to add itself into the node list in the ROUTE REQUEST when it forwards the ROUTE REQUEST to its neighbor. Data verification protects the node list by preventing unauthorized adding of nodes and unauthorized removal of nodes.

6. ARAN

Authenticated Routing for Ad hoc Networks (ARAN) [17] is a routing protocol for ad hoc networks with authentication enabled. It allows routing messages to be authenticated at each node between the source nodes and the destination nodes. The authentication that ARAN has implemented is based on cryptographic certificates.

ARAN requires a trusted certificate server, the public key of which is known to all valid nodes. Keys are assumed to have been established between the trusted certificate server and nodes. For each node to enter into a wireless ad hoc network, it needs to have a certificate issued by the trusted server. The certificate contains the IP address of the node, the public key of the node, a time stamp indicating the issue time of the certification, and the expiration time of the certificate. Because all nodes have the public key of the trusted server, a certificate can be verified by all nodes to check whether it is authentic. With an authentic certificate and the corresponding private key, the node that owns the certificate can authenticate itself using its private key.

To discover a route from a source node to the destination node, the source node sends out a route discovery packet (RDP) to all its neighbors. The RDP is signed by the source node's private key and contains a nonce, a time stamp, and the source node's certificate. The time stamp and the nonce work to prevent replay attacks and flooding of the RDP.

The RDP is then rebroadcast in the network until it reaches the destination. The RDP is rebroadcast with the signature and the certificate of the rebroadcaster. On receiving an RDP, each node will first verify the source's signature and the previous node's signature on the RDP.

On receiving an RDP, the destination sends back a reply packet (REP) along the reverse path to the source after validating the RDP. The REP contains the nonce specified in the RDP and the signature from the destination node.

The REP is unicast along the reverse path. Each node on the path will put its own certificate and its own signature on the RDP before forwarding it to the next node. Each node will also verify the signatures on the RDP. An REP is discarded if one or more invalid signatures are found on the REP.

When the source receives the REP, it will first verify the signatures and then the nonce in the REP. A valid REP indicates that a route has been discovered. The node list on a valid REP suggests an operational path from the source node to the destination node that is found.

As an on-demand protocol, nodes keep track of route status. If there has been no traffic for a route's lifetime or a broken link has been detected, the route will be deactivated. Receiving data on an inactive route will force a node to signal an error state by using an error (ERR) message. The ERR message is signed by the node that produces it and will be forwarded to the source without modification. The ERR message contains a nonce and a time stamp to ensure that the ERR message is fresh.

7. SLSP

Secure Link State Routing Protocol (SLSP) [18] is a secure routing protocol for an ad hoc network building based on link state protocols. SLSP assumes that each node has a public/private key pair and has the capability of signing and verifying digital signatures. Keys are bound with the Medium Access Code and the IP address, allowing neighbors within transmission range to uniquely verify nodes if public keys have been known prior to communication.

In SLSP, each node broadcasts its IP address and the MAC to its neighbor with its signature. Neighbors verify the signature and keep a record of the pairing IP address and the MAC. The Neighbor Lookup Protocol (NLP) of SLSP extracts and retains the MAC and IP address of each network frame received by a node. The extracted information is used to maintain the mapping of MACs and IP addresses.

Nodes using SLSP periodically send out link state updates (LSUs) to advise the state of their network links. LSU packets are limited to propagating within a zone of their origin node, which is specified by the maximum number of hops. To restrict the propagation of LSU packets, each LSU packet contains the *zone radius* and the *hops traversed* fields. Let the maximum hop be R; X, a random number; and H be a hash function. *Zone-radius* will be initialized to $H^R(X)$ and *hops−traversed* be initialized to $H(X)$. Each LSU packet also contains a *TTL* field initialized as $R − 1$. If $TTL < 0$ or $H(hops−traversed) = zone\text{-}radius$, a node will not rebroadcast the LSU packet. Otherwise, the node will replace the *hops−traversed* field with $H(hops−traversed)$ and decrease *TTL* by one. In this way, the hop count is authenticated. SLSP also uses signatures to protect LSU packets. Receiving nodes can verify the authenticity and the integrity of the received LSU packets, thus preventing forging or tampering with LSU packets.

8. KEY ESTABLISHMENT

Because wireless communication is open and the signals are accessible by anyone within the vicinity, it is important for wireless networks to establish trust to guard the access to the networks. Key establishment builds relations between nodes using keys; thus security services, such as authentication, confidentiality, and integrity can be achieved for the communication between these nodes with the help of the established keys.

The dynamically changing topology of wireless networks, the lack of fixed infrastructure of wireless ad hoc and sensor networks, and the limited computation and energy resources of sensor networks, have all added complication to the key establishment process in wireless networks.

Bootstrapping

Bootstrapping is the process by which nodes in a wireless network are made aware of the presence of others in the network. On bootstrapping, a node gets its identifying credentials that can be used in the network the node is trying to join. Upon completion of the bootstrapping, the wireless network should be ready to accept the node as a valid node to join the network.

To enter a network, a node needs to present its identifying credential to show its eligibility to access the network. This process is called *preauthentication*. Once the credentials are accepted, network security associations are established with other nodes.

These network security associations will serve as further proof of authorization in the network. Security associations can be of various forms, including symmetric keys, public key pairs, hash key chains, and so on. The security associations can be used to authenticate nodes. Security associations may expire after a certain period of time and can be revoked if necessary. For example, if a node is suspected of being compromised, its security association will be revoked to prevent the node accessing the network. The actual way of revocation depends on the form of the security associations.

Bootstrapping in Wireless Ad Hoc Networks

Wireless ad hoc networks bring new challenges to the bootstrapping process by their lack of a centralized security infrastructure. It is necessary to build a security infrastructure in the bootstrapping phase. The trust infrastructure should be able to accept nodes with valid credentials to enter the network but stop those nodes without valid credentials from joining the network and establish security association between nodes within the network.

To build such a trust infrastructure, we can use any one of the following three supports: prior knowledge, trusted third parties, or self-organizing capability. Prior knowledge is information that has been set on valid nodes in advance, such as predistributed secrets or preset shared keys. This information can be used to distinguish legitimate nodes from malicious ones. Only nodes with prior knowledge will be accepted to enter the network. For example, the predistributed secrets can be used to authenticate legitimate nodes, so the network can simply reject those nodes without the predistributed secrets so that they can't enter the network.

Trusted third parties can also be used to support the establishment of the trust infrastructure. The trusted third party can be a Certificate Authority (CA), a base station of the wireless network, or any nodes that are designated to be trusted. If trusted third parties are used, all nodes must mutually agree to trust them and derive their trust on others from the trusted third parties. One of the issues with this method is that trusted third parties are required to be available for access by all nodes across the whole network, which is a very strong assumption for wireless networks as well as an impractical requirement.

It is desirable to have a self-organizing capability for building the trust infrastructure for wireless networks, taking into account the dynamically changing topology of wireless ad hoc networks. Implementing a self-organizing capability for building the trust infrastructure often requires an out-of-band authenticated communication channel or special hardware support, such as tamper-proof hardware tokens.

Bootstrapping in Wireless Sensor Networks

Bootstrapping nodes in wireless sensor networks is also challenging for the following reasons:

- *Node capture.* Sensor nodes are normally deployed in an area that is geographically close or inside the monitoring environment, which might not be a closed and confined area under guard. Thus sensor nodes are vulnerable to physical capture because it might be difficult to prevent physical access to the area.
- *Node replication.* Once a sensor node is compromised, it is possible for adversaries to replicate sensor nodes by using the secret acquired from the compromised node. In this

case, adversaries can produce fake legitimate node that cannot be distinguished by the network.

- *Scalability.* A single-sensor network may comprise a large number of sensor nodes. The more nodes in a wireless sensor network, the more complicated it is for bootstrapping.
- *Resource limitation.* Sensor nodes normally have extremely limited computation power and memory as well as limited power supply and weak communication capability. This makes some of the deliberate algorithms and methods not applicable to wireless sensor networks. Only those algorithms that require a moderate amount of resources can be implemented in wireless sensor networks.

Bootstrapping a sensor node is achieved using an incremental communication output power level to discover neighbors nearby. The output power level is increased step by step from the minimum level to the maximum level, to send out a HELLO message. This will enable the sensor node to discover neighbors in the order of their distance from the sensor node, from the closest to the farthest away.

Key Management

Key management schemes can be classified according to the way keys are set up (see Figure 10.7). Either keys are managed based on the contribution from all participating nodes in the network or they are managed based on a central node in the network. Thus key management schemes can be divided into contributory key management schemes, in which all nodes work equally together to manage the keys, and distributed key management schemes, in which only one central node is responsible for key management [19].

Classification

The distributed key management scheme can be further divided into symmetric schemes and public key schemes. Symmetric key schemes are based on private key cryptography, whereby shared secrets are used to authenticate legitimate nodes and to provide secure communication between them. The underlying assumption is that the shared secrets are known only to legitimate nodes involved in the interaction. Thus proving the knowledge of the shared secrets is enough to authenticate legitimate nodes. Shared secrets are distributed via secure channels or out-of-band measures. Trust on a node is established if the node has knowledge of a shared secret.

Public key schemes are built on public key cryptography. Keys are constructed in pairs, with a private key and a public key in each pair. Private keys are kept secret by the owners. Public keys are distributed and used to authenticate nodes and to verify credentials.

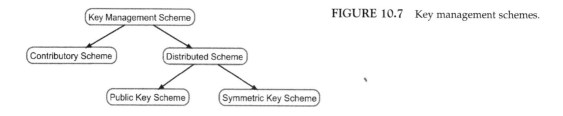

FIGURE 10.7   Key management schemes.

Keys are normally conveyed in certificates for distribution. Certificates are signed by trusted nodes for which the public keys have been known and validated. Trust on the certificates will be derived from the public keys that sign the certificates. Note that given $g^i(mod\ p)$ and $g^j(mod\ p)$, it is hard to compute $gi^*j(mod\ p)$ without the knowledge of i and j.

Contributory Schemes

Diffie-Hellman (D-H) [20] is a well-known algorithm for establishing shared secrets. The D-H algorithm's strength depends on the discrete log problem: It is hard to calculate s if given the value g^s (mod p), where p is a large prime number.

Diffie-hellman Key Exchange

D-H was designed for establishing a shared secret between two parties, namely node A and node B. Each party agrees on a large prime number p and a generator g. A and B each choose a random value i and j, respectively. A and B are then exchanged with the public values g^i (mod p) and g^j (mod p). On the reception of g^j (mod p) from B, A is then able to calculate the value $g^{j \times i}$ (mod p). Similarly, B computes $g^{i \times j}$ (mod p). Thus a shared secret, $g^{i \times j}$ (mod p), has been set up between A and B.

9. ING

Ingemarsson, Tang, and Wong (ING) [21] extends the D-F key exchange to a group of n members, $d_1, \ldots, d_n$. All group members are organized in a ring, where each member has a left neighbor and a right neighbor. Node d_i has a right neighbor d_{i-1} and a left neighbor d_{i+1}. Note that for node d_i, its right neighbor is d_{i+1}; for node d_{i+1}, its left neighbor is d_i.

Same as the D-F algorithm, all members in an ING group assume a large prime number p and a generator g. Initially, node d_i will choose a random number r_i. At the first round of key exchange, node d_i will compute g^{r_i} (mod p) and send it to its left neighbor d_{i+1}. At the same time, node d_i also receives the public value $g^{r_{i-1}}$ (mod p) from its right neighbor d_{i-1}. From the second round on, let q be the value that node d_i received in the previous round, node d_i will compute a new public value q^{d_i} (mod p). After $n-1$ rounds, the node d_i would have received a public value, g^k (mod p) where $k = \Pi_{m=1}^{i-1} r_m \times \Pi_{s=i+1}^{n} r_s$, from its right neighbors. With the public value received at the $n-1$th round, the node d_i can raise it to the power of r_i to compute the value g^l (mod p) where $l = \Pi_{m=1}^{n} r_m$.

Hypercube and Octopus (H & O)

The Hypercube protocol [22] assumes that there are 2^d nodes joining to establish a shared secret and all nodes are organized as a d-dimensional vector space $GF(2)^d$ Let $b_1, \ldots, b_d$ be the basic of $GF(2)^d$. The hypercube protocol takes d rounds to complete:

- In the first round, every participant $v \in GF(2)^d$ chooses a random number r_v and conducts a D-H key exchange with another participant $v + b_1$, with the random values r_v and r_{v+b1}, respectively.

- In the ith round, every participant $v \in GF(2)^d$ performances a D-H key exchange with the participant $v + b_i$, where both v and $v + b_i$ use the value generated in the previous round as the random number for D-H key exchange.

This algorithm can be explained using a complete binary tree to make it more comprehensible. All the nodes are put in a complete binary tree as leaves, with leaves at the $0-$level and the root at the d-level. D-H key exchanges are performed from the leaves up to the root. The key exchange takes d rounds:

- In the first round, each leaf chooses a random number k and performs a D-H key exchange with its sibling leaf, which has a random number j, and the resulting value $g^{k \times j}$ (mod p) is saved as the random value for the parent node of the above two leaves.
- In the ith round, each node at the $i-1$ level performs a D-H key exchange with its sibling node using the random numbers m and n, respectively, that they received in the previous round. The resulting value $g^{m \times n}$ (mod p) is saved as the random value for the parent node of the above two nodes.

After d rounds, the root of the complete binary tree contains the established shared secrets. The hypercube protocol assumes that there are 2^d network nodes. The octopus protocol removes the assumption and extends the hypercube protocol to work with an arbitrary number of nodes. Thus the octopus protocol can be used to establish a shared key for a node set containing an arbitrary number of nodes.

Distributed Schemes

A partially distributed threshold CA scheme [23] works with a normal PKI system where a CA exists. The private key of the CA is split and distributed over a set of n server nodes using a (k,n) secret-sharing scheme [24]. The (k,n) secretsharing scheme allows any k or more server nodes within the n server nodes to work together to reveal the CA's private key. Any set of nodes with fewer than k nodes will not be able to reveal the CA's private key. With the threshold signature scheme [25], any k of the n nodes can cooperate to sign a certificate. Each of the k nodes produces a piece of the signature on the request of signing a given certificate. With all the k pieces of the signature, a valid signature, which is the same as the one produced using the CA's private key, can be produced by combining the k pieces of the signature.

Partially Distributed Threshold CA Scheme

In this way, the partial distributed threshold CA scheme can avoid the bottleneck of the centralized CA of conventional PKI infrastructures. As long as there are at least k of the n nodes available, the network can always issue and sign new certificates. Attacks to any single node will not bring the whole CA down. Only when an attack manages to paralyze $n - k$ or more nodes will the CA's signing service not be available.

To further improve the security of the private key that is distributed over the n nodes, proactive security [26] can be imposed. Proactive security forces the private key shares to be refreshed periodically. Each refreshment will invalidate the previous share held by a node. Attacks on multiple nodes must complete within a refresh period to succeed. To be specific, only when an attack can compromise k or more nodes within a refresh period can the attack succeed.

While conventional PKI systems depend on directories to publish public key certificates, it is suggested that certificates should be disseminated to communication peers when establishing a communication channel with the partial distributed threshold CA scheme. This is due to the fact that the availability of centralized directories cannot be guaranteed in wireless networks. Therefore it is not realistic to assume the availability of a centralized directory.

Self-organized Key Management (PGP-A)

A self-organized key management scheme (PGP-A) [27] has its basis in the Pretty Good Privacy (PGP) [28] scheme. PGP is built based on the "web of trust" model, in which all nodes have equal roles in playing a CA. Each node generates its own public/private key pair and signs other nodes' public keys if it trusts the nodes. The signed certificates are kept by nodes in their own certificate repositories instead of being published by centralized directories in the X.509 PKI systems [29].

PGP-A treats trust as transitive. So, trust can be derived from a trusted node's trust on another node, that is, if node A trusts node B, and node B trusts node C, then A should also trust C if A knows the fact that node B trusts node C.

To verify a key of a node u, a node j will merge its certificate repository with those of j's trusted nodes, and those of the nodes trusted by j's trusted nodes, and so forth. In this way, node j can build up a web of trust in which node j is at the center of the web and j's directly trusted nodes as node j's neighbors. Node l is linked with node k if node k trusts node l. Node j can search the web of trust built as above to find a path from j to u. If such as path exists, let it be a sequence of nodes S: $node_i$ where $i = 1, \ldots, n$, n be the length of the path, and $node_1 = j$ and $node_n = u$. This means that $node_i$ trust $node_{i+1}$ for all $i = 1, \ldots, n-1$. Therefore u can be trusted by j. The path S represents a verifiable chain of certificates. PGP-A does not guarantee that a node u that should be trusted by node j will always be trusted by node j, since there are chances that the node j fails to find a path from node j to node u in the web of trust. This might be due to the reason that node j has not acquired enough certificates from its trusted nodes to cover the path from node j to node u.

Self-Healing Session Key Distribution

The preceding two key management schemes are public key management schemes. The one discussed here, a self-healing session key distribution [30], is a symmetric key management scheme. In such a scheme, keys can be distributed either by an online key distribution server or by key predistribution. A key predistribution scheme normally comprises the key predistribution phase, the shared-key discovery phase, and the path key establishment phase.

In the key predistribution phase, a key pool of a large number of keys is created. Every key can be identified by a unique key identifier. Each network node is given a set of keys from the key pool. The shared-key discovery phase begins when a node tries to communicate with the others. All nodes exchange their key identifiers to find out whether there are any keys shared with others. The shared keys can then be used to establish a secure channel for communication. If no shared key exists, a key path will need to be discovered. The key path is a sequence of nodes with which all adjacent nodes share a key. With the key path, a message can travel from the first node to the last node securely, by which a secure channel can be established between the first node and the last node.

The self-healing session key distribution (S-HEAL) [30] assumes the existence of a group manager and pre-shared secrets. Keys are distributed from the group manager to group members. Let h be a polynomial, where for a node i, node i knows about $h(i)$. Let K be the group key to be distributed, K is covered by h in the distribution: $f(x) = h(x) + K$. The polynomial $f(x)$ is the information that the group manager sends out to all its group members. For node j, node j will calculate $K = f(j) - h(j)$ to reveal the group key. Without the knowledge of $h(j)$, node j will not be able to recover K.

To enable revocation in S-HEAL, the polynomial $h(x)$ is replaced by a bivariate polynomial $s(x,y)$. The group key is covered by the bivariate polynomial $s(x,y)$ when it is distributed to group members, in the way that $f(N,x) = s(N,x) + K$. Node i must calculate $s(N,i)$ to recover K. The revocation enabled S-HEAL tries to stop revoked nodes to calculate $s(N,i)$, thus preventing them to recover K.

Let s of degree t; then $t + 1$ values are needed to compute $s(x,i)$. Assuming that $s(i,i)$ is predistributed to node i, node i will need another t values to recover $s(N,i)$, namely $s(r_1,x)$, ..., $s(r_t,x)$. These values will be disseminating to group members together with the key update. If the group manager wants to revoke node i, the group manager can set one of the values $s(r_1,x)$, ..., $s(r_t,x)$ to $s(i,x)$. In this case, node i obtains only t values instead of $t + 1$ values. Therefore, node i will not be able to compute $s(x,i)$, thus it will not be able to recover K. This scheme can only revoke maximum t nodes at the same time.

Now, let's take a very brief look at wireless network security management countermeasures. Security comes at a cost: either in dollars spent on security equipment, in inconvenience and maintenance, or in operating expenses. Some organizations may be willing to accept risk because applying various management countermeasures may exceed financial or other constraints.

10. MANAGEMENT COUNTERMEASURES

Management countermeasures ensure that all critical personnel are properly trained on the use of wireless technology. Network administrators need to be fully aware of the security risks that wireless networks and devices pose. They must work to ensure security policy compliance and to know what steps to take in the event of an attack (see checklist: "An Agenda For Action When Implementing Wireless Network Security Policies").

Management countermeasures for securing wireless networks begin with a comprehensive security policy. A security policy, and compliance therewith, is the foundation on which other countermeasures (the operational and technical) are rationalized and implemented. Finally, the most important countermeasures are trained and aware users.

AN AGENDA FOR ACTION WHEN IMPLEMENTING WIRELESS NETWORK SECURITY POLICIES

The items below are possible actions that organizations should consider; some of the items may not apply to all organizations. A wireless network security policy should be able to do the following (check all tasks completed):

_____1. Identify who may use WLAN technology in an organization.

_____2. Identify whether Internet access is required.

_____3. Describe who can install access points and other wireless equipment.

_____4. Provide limitations on the location of and physical security for access points.

_____5. Describe the type of information that may be sent over wireless links.

_____6. Describe conditions under which wireless devices are allowed.

_____7. Define standard security settings for access points.

_____8. Describe limitations on how the wireless device may be used, such as location.

_____9. Describe the hardware and software configuration of any access device.

_____10. Provide guidelines on reporting losses of wireless devices and security incidents.

_____11. Provide guidelines on the use of encryption and other security software.

_____12. Define the frequency and scope of security assessments.

---

11. SUMMARY

Organizations should understand that maintaining a secure wireless network is an ongoing process that requires greater effort than for other networks and systems. Moreover, it is important that organizations more frequently assess risks and test and evaluate system security controls when wireless technologies are deployed. Maintaining a secure wireless network (and associated devices) requires significant effort, resources and vigilance and involves the following steps:

• Maintaining a full understanding of the topology of the wireless network.
• Labeling and keeping inventories of the fielded wireless and handheld devices.
• Creating frequent backups of data.
• Performing periodic security testing and assessment of the wireless network.

- Performing ongoing, randomly timed security audits to monitor and track wireless and handheld devices.
- Applying patches and security enhancements.
- Monitoring the wireless industry for changes to standards to enhance to security features and for the release of new products.
- Vigilantly monitoring wireless technology for new threats and vulnerabilities.

Organizations should not undertake wireless deployment for essential operations until they understand and can acceptably manage and mitigate the risks to their information, system operations, and risk to the continuity of essential operations. As described in this chapter, the risks provided by wireless technologies are considerable. Many current communications protocols and commercial products provide inadequate protection and thus present unacceptable risks to organizational operations. Agencies must proactively address such risks to protect their ability to support essential operations, before deployment. Furthermore, many organizations poorly administer their wireless technologies. Some examples include deploying equipment with factory default settings; failing to control or inventory their access points; not implementing the security capabilities provided; and, not developing or employing a security architecture suitable to the wireless environment (firewalls between wired and wireless systems, blocking unneeded services/ports, using strong cryptography, etc.). To a large extent, most of the risks can be mitigated. However, mitigating these risks requires considerable tradeoffs between technical solutions and costs. Today, the vendor and standards community is aggressively working towards more robust, open, and secure solutions for the near future.

Finally, let's move on to the real interactive part of this Chapter: review questions/exercises, hands-on projects, case projects and optional team case project. The answers and/or solutions by chapter can be found in the Online Instructor's Solutions Manual.

CHAPTER REVIEW QUESTIONS/EXERCISES

True/False

1. True or False? Wireless networks are a general term to refer to various types of networks that communicate without the need of wire lines.
2. True or False? Cellular networks require fixed infrastructures to work.
3. True or False? Wireless ad hoc networks are distributed networks that work without fixed infrastructures and in which each network node is willing to forward network packets for other network nodes.
4. True or False? WEP is designed to protect linkage-level data for wireless transmission by providing confidentiality, access control, and data integrity, to provide secure communication between a mobile device and an access point in a 802.11 wireless LAN.
5. True or False? The WPA standard is aimed at providing a stronger security compared to WEP and is expected to tackle most of the weakness found in WEP.

Multiple Choice

1. Personal deployment of WPA adopts a simpler mechanism, which allows all stations to use the same key. This mechanism is called the:
   A. RC 4 stream cipher.
   B. Temporal Key Integrity Protocol (TKIP).
   C. Pre-Shared Key (PSK) mode.
   D. Message Integrity Code (MIC).
   E. Extensible Authentication Protocol (EAP) framework.

2. What are low-end devices with very limited resources, such as memory, computation power, battery, and network bandwidth:
   A. SPINS.
   B. Sequences of intervals.
   C. Key usages.
   D. Sensor nodes.
   E. All of the above.

3. Secure Efficient Ad hoc Distance (SEAD) vector routing is a design based on a:
   A. Secure on-demand routing protocol.
   B. ROUTE RQUEST.
   C. Message Authentication Code (MAC).
   D. Authenticated Routing for Ad hoc Networks (ARAN).
   E. Destination-Sequenced Distance Vector (DSDV) routing.

4. What requires a trusted certificate server, where the public key is known to all valid nodes?
   A. ARAN.
   B. RDP.
   C. REP.
   D. ERR.
   E. All of the above.

5. What is a secure routing protocol for an ad hoc network building based on link state protocols?
   A. Neighbor Lookup Protocol (NLP).
   B. Secure Link State Routing Protocol (SLSP).
   C. Bootstrapping protocol.
   D. Preauthentication protocol.
   E. All of the above.

EXERCISE

Problem

What is WEP?

Hands-On Projects

Project

What is a WEP key?

Case Projects

Problem

Organization A is considering implementing a WLAN so that employees may use their laptop computers anywhere within the boundaries of their office building. Before deciding, however, Organization A has its computer security department perform a risk assessment. The security department first identifies WLAN vulnerabilities and threats. The department, assuming that threat-sources will try to exploit WLAN vulnerabilities, determines the overall risk of operating a WLAN and the impact a successful attack would have on Organization A. The manager reads the risk assessment and decides that the residual risk exceeds the benefit the WLAN provides. The manager directs the computer security department to identify additional countermeasures to mitigate residual risk before the system can be implemented. What are those additional countermeasures?

Optional Team Case Project

Problem

Organization C is considering purchasing mobiles devices for its sales force of 300 employees. Before making a decision to purchase the mobiles devices, the computer security department performs a risk assessment. What did the computer security department find out from the risk assessment?

References

[1] L. M. S. C. of the IEEE Computer Society. Wireless LAN medium access control (MAC) and physical layer (PHY) specifications, technical report, IEEE Standard 802.11, 1999 ed., 1999.

[2] R.L. Rivest, The RC4 encryption algorithm, RSA Data Security, Inc., March 1992 technical report.

[3] E. Dawson, L. Nielsen, Automated cryptanalysis of XOR plaintext strings, Cryptologia 20 (2) (April 1996).

[4] S. Singh, The Code Book: The Evolution of Secrecy from Mary, Queen of Scots, to Quantum Cryptography, Doubleday, 1999.

[5] W.A. Arbaugh, An inductive chosen plaintext attack against WEP/WEP2, IEEE Document 802.11-01/230, May 2001.

[6] J.R. Walker, Unsafe at any key size; an analysis of the WEP encapsulation, IEEE Document 802.11-00/362, October 2000.

[7] N. Borisov, I. Goldberg, D. Wagner, Intercepting Mobile Communications: The Insecurity of 802.11, MobiCom 2001.

[8] B. Aboba, L. Blunk, J. Vollbrecht, J. Carlson, E.H. Levkowetz, Extensible Authentication Protocol (EAP), request for comment, Network Working Group, 2004.

[9] A. Perrig, R. Szewczyk, V. Wen, D. Culler, J.D. Tygar, SPINS: Security protocols for sensor networks, MobiCom '01: Proceedings of the 7th annual international conference on Mobile computing and networking, 2001.

[10] A. Perrig, R. Canetti, D. Xiaodong Song, J.D. Tygar, Efficient and secure source authentication for multicast, NDSS 01: Network and Distributed System Security Symposium, 2001.

[11] A. Perrig, J.D. Tygar, D. Song, R. Canetti, Efficient authentication and signing of multicast streams over lossy channels, SP '00: Proceedings of the 2000 IEEE Symposium on Security and Privacy, 2000.

[12] A. Perrig, R. Canetti, J.D. Tygar, D. Song, RSA CryptoBytes 5 (2002).

[13] Y.-C. Hu, D.B. Johnson, A. Perrig, SEAD: secure efficient distance vector routing for mobile wireless ad hoc networks, WMCSA '02: Proceedings of the Fourth IEEE Workshop on Mobile Computing Systems and Applications, IEEE Computer Society, Washington, DC, 2002. p. 3.

[14] C.E. Perkins, P. Bhagwat, Highly dynamic destination-sequenced distance-vector routing (DSDV) for mobile computers, SIGCOMM Comput. Commun. Rev. 24 (4) (1994) 234−244.

[15] Y.-C. Hu, A. Perrig, D. Johnson, Ariadne: a secure on-demand routing protocol for ad hoc networks, Wire. Netw. J. 11 (1) (2005).

[16] D.B. Johnson, D.A. Maltz, Dynamic source routing in ad hoc wireless networks, Mobile Computing, Kluwer Academic Publishers, 1996, pp. 153−181.

[17] K. Sanzgiri, B. Dahill, B.N. Levine, C. Shields, E.M. Belding-Royer, A secure routing protocol for ad hoc networks, 10th IEEE International Conference on Network Protocols (ICNP'02), 2002.

[18] P. Papadimitratos, Z.J. Haas, Secure link state routing for mobile ad hoc networks, saint-w, 00, 2003.

[19] E. Cayirci, C. Rong, Security in Wireless Ad hoc, Sensor, and Mesh Networks, John Wiley & Sons, 2008.

[20] W. Diffie, M.E. Hellman, New directions in cryptography, IEEE Trans. Inf. Theory IT-22 (6) (1976) 644−654.

[21] I. Ingemarsson, D. Tang, C. Wong, A conference key distribution system, IEEE Trans. Inf. Theory 28 (5) (September 1982) 714−720.

[22] K. Becker, U. Wille, Communication complexity of group key distribution, ACM conference on computer and communications security, 1998.

[23] L. Zhou, Z.J. Haas, Securing ad hoc networks, IEEE Netw. 13 (1999) 24−30.

[24] A. Shamir, How to share a secret, Comm. ACM 22 (11) (1979).

[25] Y. Desmedt, Some recent research aspects of threshold cryptography, ISW (1997) 158−173.

[26] R. Canetti, A. Gennaro, D. Herzberg, Naor, proactive security: long-term protection against break-ins, CryptoBytes 3 (1) (Spring 1997).

[27] S. Capkun, L. Buttyán, J.-P. Hubaux, Self-organized public-key management for mobile ad hoc networks, IEEE Trans. Mob. Comput. 2 (1) (2003) 52−64.

[28] P. Zimmermann, The Official PGP User's Guide, The MIT Press, 1995.

[29] ITU-T. Recommendation X.509, ISO/IEC 9594-8, Information Technology: Open Systems Interconnection − The Directory: Public-key and Attribute Certificate Frameworks, fourth ed., 2000, ITU.

[30] J. Staddon, S.K. Miner, M.K. Franklin, D. Balfanz, M. Malkin, D. Dean, Self-healing key distribution with revocation, IEEE Symposium on Security and Privacy, 2002.

11

Cellular Network Security

Peng Liu, Thomas F. LaPorta and Kameswari Kotapati

Pennsylvania State University

1. INTRODUCTION

Cellular networks are high-speed, high-capacity voice and data communication networks with enhanced multimedia and seamless roaming capabilities for supporting cellular devices. With the increase in popularity of cellular devices, these networks are used for more than just entertainment and phone calls. They have become the primary means of communication for finance-sensitive business transactions, lifesaving emergencies, and life-/mission-critical services such as E-911. Today these networks have become the lifeline of communications.

A breakdown in a cellular network has many adverse effects, ranging from huge economic losses due to financial transaction disruptions; loss of life due to loss of phone calls made to emergency workers; and communication outages during emergencies such as the September 11, 2001, attacks. Therefore, it is a high priority for cellular networks to function accurately.

It must be noted that it is not difficult for unscrupulous elements to break into a cellular network and cause outages. The major reason for this is that cellular networks were not designed with security in mind. They evolved from the old-fashioned telephone networks that were built for performance. To this day, cellular networks have numerous well-known and unsecured vulnerabilities providing access to adversaries. Another feature of cellular networks is network relationships (also called *dependencies*) that cause certain types of errors to propagate to other network locations as a result of regular network activity. Such propagation can be very disruptive to a network, and in turn it can affect subscribers. Finally, Internet connectivity to cellular networks is another major contributor to cellular networks' vulnerability because it gives Internet users direct access to cellular network vulnerabilities from their homes.

To ensure that adversaries do not access cellular networks and cause breakdowns, a high level of security must be maintained in cellular networks. However, though great

Network and System Security
DOI: http://dx.doi.org/10.1016/B978-0-12-416689-9.00011-3

efforts have been made to improve cellular networks in terms of support for new and innovative services, greater number of subscribers, higher speed, and larger bandwidth, very little has been done to update the security of cellular networks. Accordingly, these networks have become highly attractive targets to adversaries, not only because of their lack of security but also due to the ease with which these networks can be exploited to affect millions of subscribers.

In this chapter we analyze the security of cellular networks. Toward understanding the security issues in cellular networks, the rest of the chapter is organized as follows. We present a comprehensive overview of cellular networks with a goal of providing a fundamental understanding of their functioning. Next we present the current state of cellular network security through an in-depth discussion on cellular network vulnerabilities and possible attacks. In addition, we present a cellular network specific attack taxonomy. Finally, we present a review of current cellular network vulnerability assessment techniques and conclude with a discussion.

2. OVERVIEW OF CELLULAR NETWORKS

The current cellular network is an evolution of the early-generation cellular networks that were built for optimal performance. These early-generation cellular networks were proprietary and owned by reputable organizations. They were considered secure due to their proprietary ownership and their *closed nature*, that is, their control infrastructure was unconnected to any public network (such as the Internet) to which end subscribers had direct access. Security was a nonissue in the design of these networks.

Recently, connecting the Internet to cellular networks has not only imported the Internet vulnerabilities to cellular networks, it has also given end subscribers direct access to the control infrastructure of a cellular network, thereby opening the network. Also, with the increasing demand for these networks, a large number of new network operators have come into the picture. Thus, the current cellular environment is no longer a safe, closed network but rather an insecure, open network with many unknown network operators having nonproprietary access to it. Here we present a brief overview of the cellular network architecture.

Overall Cellular Network Architecture

Subscribers gain access to a cellular network via radio signals enabled by a radio access network, as shown in Figure 11.1. The radio access network is connected to the wireline portion of the network, also called the *core network*. Core network functions include servicing subscriber requests and routing traffic. The core network is also connected to the Public Switched Telephone Network (PSTN) and the Internet, as illustrated in Figure 11.1[1].

The PSTN is the circuit-switched public voice telephone network that is used to deliver voice telephone calls on the *fixed landline telephone network*. The PSTN uses Signaling System No. 7 (SS7), a set of telephony signaling protocols defined by the International Telecommunication Union (ITU) for performing telephony functions such as call delivery, call routing, and billing. The SS7 protocols provide a universal structure for telephony

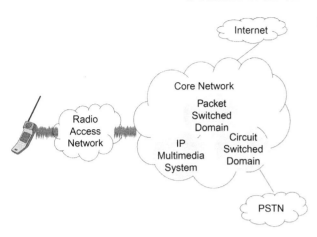

FIGURE 11.1   Cellular network architecture.

network signaling, messaging, interfacing, and network maintenance. PSTN connectivity to the core network enables mobile subscribers to call fixed network subscribers, and vice versa. In the past, PSTN networks were also closed networks because they were unconnected to other public networks.

The core network is also connected to the Internet. Internet connectivity allows the cellular network to provide innovative multimedia services such as weather reports, stock reports, sports information, chat, and electronic mail. Interworking with the Internet is possible using protocol gateways, federated databases, and multiprotocol mobility managers [2]. Interworking with the Internet has created a new generation of services called *cross-network services*. These are multivendor, multidomain services that use a combination of Internet-based data and data from the cellular network to provide a variety of services to the cellular subscriber. A sample cross-network service is the *Email Based Call Forwarding Service* (CFS), which uses Internet-based email data (in a mail server) to decide on the call-forward number (in a call-forward server) and delivers the call via the cellular network.

From a functional viewpoint, the core network may also be further divided into the circuit-switched (CS) domain, the packet-switched (PS) domain, and the IP Multimedia Subsystem (IMS). In the following, we further discuss the core network organization.

Core Network Organization

Cellular networks are organized as collections of interconnected *network areas*, where each network area covers a fixed geographical region (as shown in Figure 11.2). At a particular time, every subscriber is affiliated with two networks: the *home network* and the *visiting network*.

Every subscriber is permanently assigned to the home network (of his device), from which they can roam onto other visiting networks. The home network maintains the subscriber profile and his current location. The visiting network is the network where the subscriber is currently roaming. It provides radio resources, mobility management, routing, and services for roaming subscribers. The visiting network provides service capabilities to the subscribers on behalf of the home environment [3].

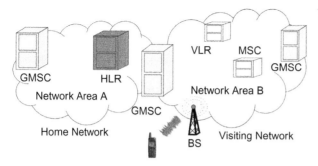

FIGURE 11.2   Core network organization.

The core network is facilitated by network servers (also called *service nodes*). Service nodes are composed of (1) a variety of *data sources* (such as cached read-only, updateable, and shared data sources) to store data such as subscriber profile and (2) *service logic* to perform functions such as computing data items, retrieving data items from data sources, and so on.

Service nodes can be of different types, with each type assigned specific functions. The major service node types in the circuit-switched domain include the Home Location Register (HLR), the Visitor Location Register (VLR), the Mobile Switching Center (MSC), and the Gateway Mobile Switching Center (GMSC) [4].

All subscribers are permanently assigned to a fixed HLR located in the home network. The HLR stores permanent subscriber profile data and relevant temporary data such as current subscriber location (pointer to VLR) of all subscribers assigned to it. Each network area is assigned a VLR. The VLR stores temporary data of subscribers currently roaming in its assigned area; this subscriber data is received from the HLR of the subscriber. Every VLR is always associated with an MSC. The MSC acts as an interface between the radio access network and the core network. It also handles circuit-switched services for subscribers currently roaming in its area. The GMSC is in charge of routing the call to the actual location of the mobile station. Specifically, the GMSC acts as interface between the fixed PSTN network and the cellular network. The radio access network comprises a transmitter, receiver, and speech transcoder called the base station (BS) [5].

Service nodes are geographically distributed and serve the subscriber through collaborative functioning of various network components. Such collaborative functioning is possible due to the inter-component network relationships (called dependencies). A *dependency* means that a network component must rely on other network components to perform a function. For example, there is a *dependency* between service nodes to service subscribers. Such a dependency is made possible through signaling messages containing data items. Service nodes typically request other service nodes to perform specific operations by sending them signaling messages containing data items with predetermined values. On receiving signaling messages, service nodes realize the operations to perform based on values of data items received in signaling messages. Further, dependencies may exist between data items so that received data items may be used to derive other data items. Several application layer protocols are used for signaling messages. Examples of signaling message protocols include Mobile Application Part (MAP), ISDN User Part (ISUP), and Transaction Capabilities Application Part (TCAP) protocols.

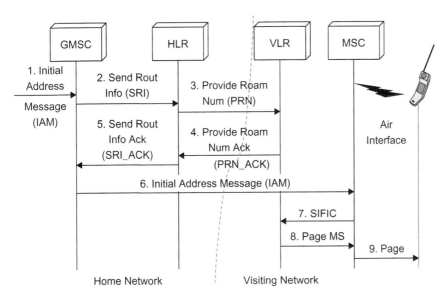

FIGURE 11.3   Signal flow in the call delivery service.

Typically in a cellular network, to provide a specific service a preset group of signaling messages is exchanged between a preset group of service node types. The preset group of signaling messages indicates the operations to be performed at the various service nodes and is called a *signal flow*. In the following, we use the *call delivery service* [6] to illustrate a signal flow and show how the various geographically distributed service nodes function together.

Call Delivery Service

The *call delivery service* is a basic service in the circuit-switched domain. It is used to deliver incoming calls to any subscriber with a mobile device regardless of their location. The signal flow of the call delivery service is illustrated in Figure 11.3. The call delivery service signal flow comprises MAP messages SRI, SRI_ACK, PRN, and PRN_ACK; ISUP message IAM; and TCAP messages SIFIC, Page MS, and Page.

Figure 11.3 illustrates the exchange of signal messages between different network areas. It shows that when a subscriber makes a call using his mobile device, the call is sent in the form of a signaling message IAM to the nearest GMSC, which is in charge of routing calls and passing voice traffic between different networks. This signaling message IAM contains data items such as *called number* that denotes the mobile phone number of the subscriber receiving this call. The *called number* is used by the GMSC to locate the address of the HLR (home network) of the called party. The GMSC uses this address to send the signaling message SRI.

The SRI message is an intimation to the HLR of the arrival of an incoming call to a subscriber with *called number* as mobile phone number. It contains data items such as the *called number* and *alerting pattern*. The *alerting pattern* denotes the pattern (*packet-switched data, short message service*, or *circuit-switched call*) used to alert the subscriber receiving the call. The HLR uses the *called number* to retrieve from its database the current location (pointer to VLR) of the subscriber receiving the call. The HLR uses this subscriber location to send the VLR the message PRN. The PRN message is a request for call routing information (also called *roaming number*) from the VLR where the subscriber is currently roaming. The PRN message contains the *called number, alerting pattern,* and other *subscriber call profile* data items.

The VLR uses the *called number* to store the *alerting pattern* and *subscriber call profile* data items and assign the *roaming number* for routing the call. This *roaming number* data item is passed on to the HLR (in message PRN_ACK), which forwards it to the GMSC (in message SRI_ACK). The GMSC uses this *roaming number* to route the call (message IAM) to the MSC where the subscriber is currently roaming. On receipt of the message IAM, the MSC assigns the *called number* resources for the call and also requests the *subscriber call profile* data items, and *alerting pattern* for the *called number* (using message SIFIC) from the VLR, and receives the same in the Page MS message. The MSC uses the *alerting pattern* in the incoming call profile to *derive* the *page type* data item. The *page type* data item denotes the manner in which to alert the mobile station. It is used to page the mobile subscriber (using message Page). Thus subscribers receive incoming calls irrespective of their locations.

If data item values are inaccurate, a network can misoperate and subscribers will be affected. Hence, accurate functioning of the network is greatly dependent on the integrity of data item values. Thus signal flows allow the various service nodes to function together, ensuring that the network services its subscribers effectively.

3. THE STATE OF THE ART OF CELLULAR NETWORK SECURITY

This part of the chapter presents the current state of the art of cellular network security. Because the security of a cellular network is the security of each aspect of the network, that is, radio access network, core network, Internet connection, and PSTN connection, we detail the security of each in detail.

Security in the Radio Access Network

In a cellular network, the radio access network uses radio signals to connect the subscriber's cellular device with the core network. Hence it would seem that attacks on the radio access network could easily happen because anyone with a transmitter/receiver could capture these signals. This was very true in the case of early-generation cellular networks (first and second generations), where there were no guards against eavesdropping on conversations between the cellular device and BS; cloning of cellular devices to utilize the network resources without paying; and cloning BSs to entice users to camp at the cloned BS in an attack is called a *false base station attack*, so that the target user provides secret information to the adversary.

In the current generation (third-generation) of cellular networks, all these attacks can be prevented because the networks provide adequate security measures. Eavesdropping on signals between the cellular device and BS is not possible, because cipher keys are used to encrypt these signals. Likewise, replay attacks on radio signals are voided by the use of non-repeating random values. Use of integrity keys on radio conversations voids the possibility of deletion and modification of conversations between cellular devices and BSs. By allowing the subscriber to authenticate a network, and vice versa, this generation voids the attacks due to cloned cellular devices and BSs. Finally, as the subscriber's identity is kept confidential by only using a temporary subscriber identifier on the radio network, it is also possible to maintain subscriber location privacy [7].

However, the current generation still cannot prevent a denial-of-service attack from occurring if a large number of registration requests are sent via the radio access network (BS) to the visiting network (MSC). Such a DoS attack is possible because the MSC cannot realize that the registration requests are fake until it attempts to authenticate each request and the request fails. To authenticate each registration request, the MSC must fetch the authentication challenge material from the corresponding HLR. Because the MSC is busy fetching the authentication challenge material, it is kept busy and the genuine registration requests are lost [7]. Overall there is a great improvement in the radio network security in the current third-generation cellular network.

Security in Core Network

Though the current generation of a cellular network has seen many security improvements in the radio access network, the security of the core network is not as improved. Core network security is the security at the service nodes and security on links (or wireline signaling message) between service nodes.

With respect to wireline signaling message security, of the many wireline signaling message protocols, protection is only provided for the Mobile Application Part (MAP) protocol. The MAP protocol is the cleartext application layer protocol that typically runs on the security-free SS7 protocol or the IP protocol. MAP is an essential protocol and it is primarily used for message exchange involving subscriber location management, authentication, and call handling. The reason that protection is provided for only the MAP protocol is that it carries authentication material and other subscriber-specific confidential data; therefore, its security was considered top priority and was standardized [8–10]. Though protection for other signaling message protocols was also considered important, it was left as an improvement for the next-generation networks [11].

Security for the MAP protocol is provided in the form of the newly proposed protocol called Mobile Application Part Security (MAPSec), when MAP runs on the SS7 protocol stack, or Internet Protocol Security (IPSec) when MAP runs on the IP protocol. Both MAPSec and IPSec, protect MAP messages on the link between service nodes by negotiating security associations. Security associations comprise keys, algorithms, protection profiles, and key lifetimes used to protect the MAP message. Both MAPSec and IPSec protect MAP messages by providing source service node authentication and message encryption to prevent eavesdropping, MAP corruption, and fabrication attacks.

It must be noted that though MAPSec and IPSec are deployed to protect individual MAP messages on the link between service nodes, signaling messages typically occur as a group in a signal flow, and hence signaling messages must be protected not only on the link but also in the intermediate service nodes. Also, the deployment of MAPSec and

IPSec is optional; hence if any service provider chooses to omit MAPSec/IPSec's deployment, the efforts of all other providers are wasted. Therefore, to completely protect MAP messages, MAPSec/IPSec must be used by every service provider.

With respect to wireline service nodes, while MAPSec/IPSec protects links between service nodes, there is no standardized method for protecting service nodes [7]. Remote and physical access to service nodes may be subject to operator's security policy and hence could be exploited (insider or outsider) if the network operator is lax with security. Accordingly, the core network suffers from the possibility of node impersonation, corruption of data sources, and service logic attacks. For example, unauthorized access to HLR could deactivate customers or activate customers not seen by the building system. Similarly, unauthorized access to MSC could cause outages for a large number of users in a given network area.

Corrupt data sources or service logic in service nodes have the added disadvantage of propagating this corruption to other service nodes in a cellular network [12–14] via signaling messages. This fact was recently confirmed by a security evaluation of cellular networks [13] that showed the damage potential of a compromised service node to be much greater than the damage potential of compromised signaling messages. Therefore, it is of utmost importance to standardize a scheme for protecting service nodes in the interest of not only preventing node impersonation attacks but also preventing the corruption from propagating to other service nodes.

In brief, the current generation core networks are lacking in security for all types of signaling messages, security for MAP signaling messages in service nodes, and a standardized method for protecting service nodes. To protect all types of signaling message protocols and ensure that messages are secured not only on the links between service nodes but also on the intermediate service nodes (that is, secured end to end), and prevent service logic corruption from propagating to other service nodes, the End-to-End Security (EndSec) protocol was proposed [13].

Because signaling message security essentially depends on security of data item values contained in these messages, EndSec focuses on securing data items. EndSec requires every data item to be signed by its source service nodes using public key encryption. By requiring signatures, if data items are corrupt by compromised intermediate service nodes en route, the compromised status of the service node is revealed to the service nodes receiving the corrupt data items. Revealing the compromised status of service nodes prevents corruption from propagating to other service nodes, because service nodes are unlikely to accept corrupt data items from compromised service nodes.

EndSec also prevents misrouting and node impersonation attacks by requiring every service node in a signal flow to embed the PATH taken by the signal flow in every EndSec message. Finally, EndSec introduces several control messages to handle and correct the detected corruption. Note that EndSec is not a standardized protocol.

Security Implications of Internet Connectivity

Internet connectivity introduces the biggest threat to the security of cellular networks. This is because cheap PC-based equipment with Internet connectivity can now access gateways connecting to the core network (of a cellular network). Therefore, any attack possible in the Internet can now filter into the core network via these gateways. For example, Internet connectivity was the reason for the slammer worm to filter into the E-911 service in Bellevue, Washington, making it completely unresponsive [15]. Other attacks that can filter into the core network from the Internet include spamming and phishing of short messages [16].

We expect low-bandwidth DoS attacks to be the most damaging attacks brought on by Internet connectivity [16,17,18]. These attacks demonstrate that by sending just 240 short messages per second, it is possible to saturate a cellular network and cause the MSC in charge of the region to be flooded and lose legitimate short messages per second. Likewise, it shows that it is possible to cause a specific user to lose short messages by flooding that user with a large number of messages, causing a buffer overflow. Such DoS attacks are possible because the short message delivery time in a cellular network is much greater than the short message submission time using Internet sites [17].

Also, short messages and voices services use the same radio channel, so contention for these limited resources may still occur and cause a loss of voice service. To avoid loss of voice services due to contention, separation of voice and data services on the radio network (of a cellular network) has been suggested [14]. However, such separation requires major standardization and overhaul of the cellular network and is therefore unlikely be implemented very soon. Other minor techniques such as queue management and resource provisioning have been suggested [17].

Though such solutions could reduce the impact of short message flooding, they cannot eliminate other types of low-bandwidth, DoS attacks such as attacks on connection setup and teardown of data services. The root cause for such DoS attacks from the Internet to the core network of a cellular network was identified as the difference in the design principles of these networks. Though the Internet makes no assumptions on the content of traffic and simply passes it on to the next node, the cellular network identifies the traffic content and provides a highly tailored service involving multiple service nodes for each type of traffic [18].

Until this gap is bridged, such attacks will continue, but bridging the gap itself is a major process because either the design of a cellular network must be changed to match the Internet design, or vice versa, which is unlikely to happen soon. Hence a temporary fix would be to secure the gateways connecting the Internet and core network. As a last note, Internet connectivity filters attacks not only into the core network, but also into the PSTN network. Hence PSTN gateways must also be guarded.

Security Implications of PSTN Connectivity

PSTN connectivity to cellular networks allows calls between the fixed and cellular networks. Though the PSTN was a closed network, the security-free SS7 protocol stack on which it is based was of no consequence. However, by connecting the PSTN to the core network that is in turn connected to the Internet, the largest open public network, the SS7-based PSTN network has "no security left" [19].

Because SS7 protocols are plaintext and have no authentication features, it is possible to introduce fake messages, eavesdrop, cause DoS by traffic overload, and incorrectly route signaling messages. Such introduction of SS7 messages into the PSTN network is very easily done using cheap PC-based equipment. Attacks in which calls for 800 and 900 numbers were rerouted to 911 servers so that legitimate calls were lost are documented [20]. Such attacks are more so possible due to the IP interface of the PSTN service nodes and Web-based control of these networks.

Because PSTN networks are to be outdated soon, there is no interest in updating these networks. So, they will remain "security free" until their usage is stopped [19].

So far, we have addressed the security and attacks on each aspect of a cellular network. But an attack that is common to all the aspects of a cellular network is the *cascading attack*. Next we detail the cascading attack and present the corresponding vulnerability assessment techniques.

4. CELLULAR NETWORK ATTACK TAXONOMY

In this part of the chapter, we present a cellular network specific attack taxonomy. This attack taxonomy is called the *three-dimensional taxonomy* because attacks are classified based on the following three dimensions: (1) adversary's physical access to the network when the attack is launched; (2) type of attack launched; and (3) vulnerability exploited to launch the attack.

The three-dimensional attack taxonomy was motivated by a *cellular network specific abstract model*, which is an atomic model of cellular network service nodes. It enables better study of interactions within a cellular network and aids in derivation of several insightful characteristics of attacks on the cellular network.

The abstract model not only led to the development of the three-dimensional attack taxonomy that has been instrumental in uncovering (1) *cascading attacks*, a type of attack in which the adversary targets a specific network location but attacks another location, which in turn propagates the attack to the target location, and (2) *cross-infrastructure cyber-attack*, a new breed of attack in which a cellular network may be attacked from the Internet [21]. In this part of the chapter we further detail the three-dimensional attack taxonomy and cellular network abstract model.

Abstract Model

The abstract model dissects functionality of a cellular network to the basic atomic level, allowing it to systematically isolate and identify vulnerabilities. Such identification of vulnerabilities allows attack classification based on vulnerabilities, and isolation of network functionality aids in extraction of interactions between network components, thereby revealing new vulnerabilities and attack characteristics.

Because service nodes in a cellular network comprise sophisticated *service logic* that performs numerous network functions, the abstract model logically divides the service logic into basic atomic units, called *agents* (represented by the elliptical shape in Figure 11.4). Each agent performs a single function. Service nodes also manage data, so the abstract model also logically divides data sources into data units specific to the agents they support. The abstract model also divides the data sources into *permanent* (represented by the rectangular shape in Figure 11.4) or *cached* (represented by the triangular shape in Figure 11.4) from other service nodes.

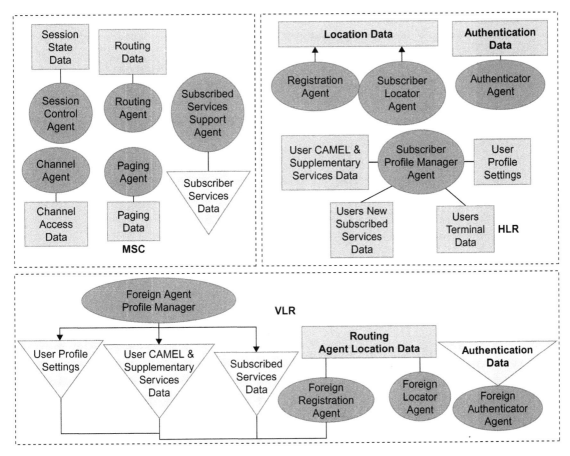

FIGURE 11.4 Abstract model of circuit-switched service nodes.

The abstract model developed for the CS domain is illustrated in Figure 11.4. It shows agents, permanent and cached data sources for the CS service nodes. For example, the *subscriber locator agent* in the HLR is the agent that tracks the subscriber location information. It receives and responds to location requests during an incoming call and stores a subscriber's location every time they move. This location information is stored in the *location data source*. Readers interested in further details may refer to [21,22].

Abstract Model Findings

The abstract model led to many interesting findings. We outline them as follows:

Interactions

To study the network interactions, service nodes in signal flows (call delivery service) were replaced by their corresponding abstract model agents and data sources. Such an abstract-model – based signal flow based on the call delivery service is shown in Figure 11.5.

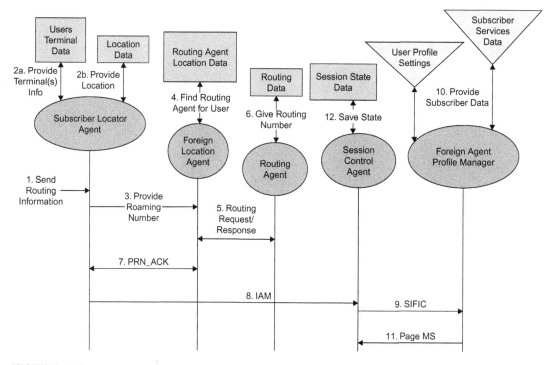

FIGURE 11.5   Abstract model-based signal flow for the call delivery service.

In studying the abstract model signal flow, it was observed that interactions happen (1) between agents typically using procedure calls containing data items; (2) between agents and data sources using queries containing data items; and (3) between agents belonging to different service nodes using signaling messages containing data items.

The common behavior in all these interactions is that they typically involve *data items* whose values are set or modified in agents or data source, or it involves data items passed between agents, data sources, or agents and data sources. Hence, the value of a data item not only can be corrupt in an agent or data source, it can also be easily passed on to other agents, resulting in propagation of corruption. This propagation of corruption is called the *cascading effect*, and attacks that exhibit this effect are called *cascading attacks*. In the following, we present a sample of the cascading attack.

Sample Cascading Attack

In this sample cascading attack, cascading due to corrupt data items and ultimately their service disruption are illustrated in Figure 11.6. Consider the call delivery service explained previously. Here the adversary may corrupt the *roaming number* data item (used to route the call) in the VLR. This corrupt *roaming number* is passed on in message PRN_ACK to the HLR, which in turn passes this information to the GMSC. The GMSC uses the incorrect *roaming number* to route the call to the incorrect MSC_B, instead of the

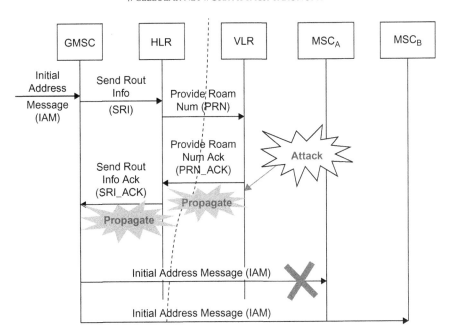

FIGURE 11.6 Sample cascading attacks in the call delivery service.

correct MSC$_A$. This results in the caller losing the call or receiving a wrong-number call. Thus corruption cascades and results in service disruption.

The type of corruption that can cascade is *system-acceptable incorrect value corruption*, a type of corruption in which corrupt values taken on system-acceptable values, albeit incorrect values. Such a corruption can cause the roaming number to be incorrect but a system-acceptable value.

Note that it is easy to cause such system-acceptable incorrect value corruption due to the availability of Web sites that refer to proprietary working manuals of service nodes such as the VLR [23,24]. Such command insertion attacks have become highly commonplace, the most infamous being the telephone tapping of the Greek government and top-ranking civil servants [25].

Cross-Infrastructure Cyber Cascading Attacks

When cascading attacks cross into cellular networks from the Internet through *cross-network services*, they're called *cross-infrastructure cyber cascading attacks*. This attack is illustrated on the CFS in Figure 11.7.

As the CFS forwards calls based on the emails received, corruption is shown to propagate from the mail server to a call-forward (CF) server and finally to the MSC. In the attack, using any standard mail server vulnerabilities, the adversary may compromise the mail server and corrupt the email data source by deleting emails from people the victim is expecting to call. The CF server receives and caches incorrect email from the mail server.

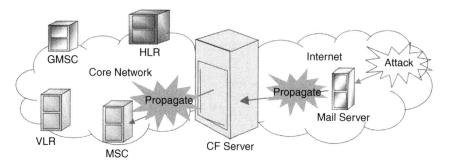

FIGURE 11.7   Cross-infrastructure cyber cascading attacks on call-forward service.

When calls arrive for the subscriber, the call-forwarding service is triggered, and the MSC queries the CF server on how to forward the call. The CF server checks its incorrect email cache, and because there are no emails from the caller, it responds to the MSC to forward the call to the victim's voicemail when in reality the call should have been forwarded to the cellular device. Thus the effect of the attack on the mail server propagates to the CF service nodes. This is a classic example of a cross-infrastructure cyber cascading attack, whereby the adversary gains access to the cross-network server, and attacks by modifying data in the data source of the cross-network server. Note that it has become highly simplified to launch such attacks due to easy accessibility to the Internet and subscriber preference for Internet-based cross-network services.

Isolating Vulnerabilities

From the abstract model, the major vulnerable-to-attacks network components are: (1) data sources; (2) agents (more generally called service logic); and (3) signaling messages. By exploiting each of these vulnerabilities, data items that are crucial to the correct working of a cellular network can be corrupted, leading to ultimate service disruption through cascading effects.

In addition, the effect of corrupt signaling messages is different from the effect of corrupt data sources. By corrupting data items in a data source of a service node, all the subscribers attached to this service node may be affected. However, by corrupting a signaling message, only the subscribers (such as the caller and called party in case of call delivery service) associated with the message are affected. Likewise, corrupting the agent in the service node can affect all subscribers using the agent in the service node. Hence, in the three-dimensional taxonomy, a vulnerability exploited is considered as an attack dimension, since the effect on each vulnerability is different.

Likewise, the adversary's physical access to a cellular network also affects how the vulnerability is exploited and how the attack cascades. For example, consider the case when a subscriber has access to the air interface. The adversary can only affect messages on the air interface. Similarly, if the adversary has access to a service node, the data sources and service logic may be corrupted. Hence, in the three-dimensional taxonomy, the physical access is considered a category as it affects how the vulnerability is exploited and its ultimate effect on the subscriber.

Finally, the way the adversary chooses to launch an attack ultimately affects the service in a different way. Consider a passive attack such as *interception*. Here the service is not affected, but it can have a later effect on the subscriber, such as identity theft or loss of privacy. An active attack such as *interruption* can cause complete service disruption. Hence, in the three-dimensional taxonomy, the attack means are considered a category due the ultimate effect on service. In the next part of the chapter, we detail the cellular network specific three-dimensional taxonomy and the way the previously mentioned dimensions are incorporated (see checklist: "An Agenda For Action When Incorporating The Cellular Network Specific Three-Dimensional Attack Taxonomy").

AN AGENDA FOR ACTION WHEN INCORPORATING THE CELLULAR NETWORK SPECIFIC THREE-DIMENSIONAL ATTACK TAXONOMY

The three dimensions in the taxonomy include Dimension I: Physical Access to the Network, Dimension II: Attack Categories and Dimension III: Vulnerability Exploited. In the following, we outline each dimension (check all tasks completed):

_____**1.** Dimension I—Physical Access to the Network: In this dimension, attacks are classified based on the adversary's level of physical access to a cellular network. Dimension I may be further classified into *single infrastructure attacks* (Level I–III) and *cross-infrastructure cyber-attacks* (Level IV–V):

_____**a.** *Level I: Access to air interface with physical device.* Here the adversary launches attacks via access to the radio access network using standard inexpensive "off-the-shelf" equipment [26]. Attacks include false base station attacks, eavesdropping, and man-in-the-middle attacks and correspond to attacks previously mentioned.

_____**b.** *Level II: Access to links connecting core service nodes.* Here the adversary has access to links connecting to core service nodes. Attacks include disrupting normal transmission of signaling messages and correspond to message corruption attacks previously mentioned.

_____**c.** *Level III: Access core service nodes.* In this case, the adversary could be an insider who managed to gain physical access to core service nodes. Attacks include editing the service logic or modifying data sources, such as subscriber data (profile, security and services) stored in the service node and corresponding to corrupt service logic, data source, and node impersonation attacks previously mentioned.

      d. *Level IV: Access to links connecting the Internet and the core network service nodes.* This is a cross-infrastructure cyber-attack. Here the adversary has access to links connecting the core network and Internet service nodes. Attacks include editing and deleting signaling messages between the two networks. This level of attack is easier to achieve than Level II.

      e. *Level V: Access to Internet servers or cross-network servers*: This is a cross-infrastructure cyber-attack. Here the adversary can cause damage by editing the service logic or modifying subscriber data (profile, security and services) stored in the cross-network servers. Such an attack was previously outlined earlier in the chapter. This level of attack is easier to achieve than Level III.

   2. Dimension II—Attack Type: In this dimension, attacks are classified based on the type of attack. The attack categories are based on Stallings [27] work in this area:

      a. *Interception.* The adversary intercepts signaling messages on a cable (Level II access) but does not modify or delete them. This is a passive attack. This affects the privacy of the subscriber and the network operator. The adversary may use the data obtained from interception to analyze traffic and eliminate the competition provided by the network operator.

      b. *Fabrication or replay.* In this case, the adversary inserts spurious messages, data, or service logic into the system, depending on the level of physical access. For example, via a Level II access, the adversary inserts fake signaling messages; and via a Level III access, the adversary inserts fake service logic or fake subscriber data into this system.

      c. *Modification of resources.* Here the adversary modifies data, messages, or service logic. For example, via a Level II access, the adversary modifies signaling messages on the link; and via a Level III access, the adversary modifies service logic or data.

      d. *Modification of resources.* Here the adversary modifies data, messages, or service logic. For example, via a Level II access, the adversary modifies signaling messages on the link; and via a Level III access, the adversary modifies service logic or data.

_____e. *Denial of service.* In this case, the adversary takes actions to overload a network results in legitimate subscribers not receiving service.

_____f. *Interruption.* Here the adversary causes an interruption by destroying data, messages, or service logic.

_____3. Dimension III—Vulnerability Exploited: In this dimension, attacks are classified based on the vulnerability exploited to cause the attack. Vulnerabilities exploited are explained as follows:

    _____a. *Data.* The adversary attacks the data stored in the system. Damage is inflicted by modifying, inserting, and deleting the data stored in the system.

_____b. *Messages.* The adversary adds, modifies, deletes, or replays signaling messages.

_____c. *Service logic.* Here the adversary inflicts damage by attacking the service logic running in the various cellular core network service nodes.

_____d. *Attack classification.* In classifying attacks, we can group them according to *Case 1: Dimension I versus Dimension II*, and *Case 2: Dimension II versus Dimension III*. Note that the Dimension I versus Dimension III case can be transitively inferred from Case 1 and Case 2.

Table 11.1 shows a sample tabulation of Level I attacks grouped in Case 1. For example, with Level I access an adversary causes interception attacks by observing traffic and eavesdropping. Likewise, fabrication attacks due to Level I access include sending spurious registration messages. Modification of resources due to Level I access includes modifying conversations in the radio access network. DoS due to Level I access occurs when a large number of fake registration messages are sent to keep the network busy so as to not provide service to legitimate subscribers. Finally, interruption attacks due to Level I access occur when adversaries jam the radio access channel so that legitimate subscribers cannot access the network. For further details on attack categories, refer to [22].

5. CELLULAR NETWORK VULNERABILITY ANALYSIS

Regardless of how attacks are launched, if attack actions cause a system-acceptable incorrect value corruption, the corruption propagates, leading to many unexpected cascading effects. To detect remote cascading effects and identify the origin of cascading attacks, cellular network vulnerability assessment tools were developed.

TABLE 11.1 Sample Case 1 Classification.

	Interception	Fabrication/Insertion	Modification of Resources	Denial of Service	Interruption
Level I	• Observe time, rate, length, source, and destination of victim's locations.	• Using modified cellular devices, the adversary can send spurious registration messages to the target network.	• With a modified base station and cellular devices, the adversary modifies conversations between subscribers and their base stations.	• The adversary can cause DoS by sending a large number of fake registration messages.	• Jam victims' traffic channels so that victims cannot access the channels.
	• With modified cellular devices, eavesdrop on victim.	• Likewise, using modified base stations, the adversary can signal victims to camp at their locations.			• Broadcast at a higher intensity than allowed, thereby hogging the bandwidth.

These tools, including the *Cellular Network Vulnerability Assessment Toolkit* (CAT) and the *advanced Cellular Network Vulnerability Assessment Toolkit* (aCAT) [12,28], receive the input from users regarding which data item(s) might be corrupted and output an attack graph. The CAT attack graph not only shows the network location and service where the corruption might originate, it also shows the various messages and service nodes through which the corruption propagates.

An attack graph is a diagrammatic representation of an attack on a real system. It shows various ways an adversary can break into a system or cause corruption and the various ways in which the corruption may propagate within the system. Attack graphs are typically produced manually by red teams and used by systems administrators for protection. CAT and aCAT attack graphs allow users to trace the effect of an attack through a network and determine its side effects, thereby making them the ultimate service disruption.

Cellular networks are at the nascent stage of development with respect to security, so it is necessary to evaluate security protocols before deploying them. Hence, aCAT can be extended with security protocol evaluation capabilities into a tool [13] called *Cellular Network Vulnerability Assessment Toolkit for evaluation* (eCAT). eCAT allows users to quantify the benefits of security solutions by removing attack effects from attack graphs based on the defenses provided. One major advantage of this approach is that solutions may be evaluated before expensive development and deployment.

It must be noted that developing such tools − CAT, aCAT, and eCAT − presented many challenges: (1) cellular networks are extremely complex systems; they comprise several types of service nodes and control protocols, contain hundreds of data elements, and support hundreds of services; hence developing such toolkits requires in-depth working knowledge of these systems; and (2) every cellular network deployment comprises a different physical configuration; toolkits must be immune to the diversity in physical configuration; and finally (3) attacks cascade in a network due to regular network activity as a result of dependencies; toolkits must be able to track the way that corruption cascades due to network dependencies.

The challenge of in-depth cellular network knowledge was overcome by incorporating the toolkits with cellular network specifications defined by the Third Generation Partnership Project (3GPP) and is available at no charge [29]. The 3GPP is a telecommunications standards body formed to produce, maintain, and develop globally applicable "technical specifications and technical reports" for a third-generation mobile system based on evolved GSM core networks and the radio access technologies that they support [24].

Usage of specifications allows handling of the diversity of physical configuration, as specifications detail the functional behavior and not the implementation structure of a cellular network. Specifications are written using simple flow-like diagrams called the Specification and Description Language (SDL) [30], and are referred to as *SDL specifications*. Equipment and service providers use these SDL specifications as the basis for their service implementations.

Corruption propagation is tracked by incorporating the toolkits with novel dependency and propagation models to trace the propagation of corruption. Finally, Boolean properties are superimposed on the propagation model to capture the impact of security solutions.

CAT is the first version of the toolkit developed for cellular network vulnerability assessment. CAT works by taking user input of *seeds* (data items directly corrupted by the adversary and the cascading effect of which leads to a goal) and *goals* (data parameters that are derived incorrectly due to the direct corruption of seeds by the adversary) and uses SDL specification to identify cascading attacks. However, SDL is limited in its expression of relationships and inexplicit in its assumptions and hence cannot capture all the dependencies; therefore CAT misses several cascading attacks.

To detect a complete set of cascading effects, CAT was enhanced with new features, to aCAT. The new features added to aCAT include (1) a network dependency model that explicitly specifies the exact dependencies in a cellular network; (2) infection propagation rules that identify the reasons that cause corruption to cascade; and (3) a small amount of expert knowledge. The network dependency model and infection propagation rules may be applied to SDL specifications and help alleviate their limited expression capability. The expert knowledge helps capture the inexplicit assumptions made by SDL.

In applying these features, aCAT captures all those dependencies that were previously unknown to CAT, and thereby aCAT was able to detect a complete set of cascading effects. Through extensive testing of aCAT, several interesting attacks were found and the areas where SDL is lacking was identified.

To enable evaluation of new security protocols, aCAT was extended to eCAT. eCAT uses Boolean probabilities in attack graphs to detect whether a given security protocol can eliminate a certain cascading effect. Given a security protocol, eCAT can measure effective coverage, identify the types of required security mechanisms to protect the network, and identify the most vulnerable network areas. eCAT was also used to evaluate MAPSec, the new standardized cellular network security protocol. Results from MAPSec's evaluation gave insights into MAPSec's performance and the network's vulnerabilities. In the following, we detail each toolkit.

Cellular Network Vulnerability Assessment Toolkit (CAT)

In this part of the chapter, we present an overview of CAT and its many features. CAT is implemented using the Java programming language. It is made up of a number of subsystems (as shown in Figure 11.8). The *knowledge base* contains the cellular network knowledge obtained from SDL specifications. SDL specifications contain simple flowchart-like diagrams. The flowcharts are converted into data in the *knowledge base*. The *integrated data structure* is similar to that of the knowledge base; it holds intermediate attack graph results.

The GUI subsystem takes user input in the form of seeds and goals. The analysis engine contains algorithms (forward and midpoint) incorporated with cascading effect detection rules. It explores the possibility of the user input *seed* leading to the cascading effect of the user input *goal*, using the knowledge base, and outputs the cascading attack in the form of attack graphs.

Using these attack graphs, realistic attack scenarios may be derived. Attack scenarios explain the effect of the attack on the subscriber in a realistic setting. Each attack graph may have multiple interpretations and give rise to multiple scenarios. Each scenario gives a different perspective on how the attack may affect the subscriber.

Cascading Effect Detection Rules

The Cascading Effect Detection Rules were defined to extract cascading effects from the SDL specifications contained in the knowledge base. They are incorporated into the algorithms in the analysis engine. These rules define what constitutes propagation of corruption from a signaling message to a block, and vice versa, and propagation of corruption within a service node. For example, when a service node receives a signaling message with a corrupt data item and stores the data item, it constitutes propagation of corruption from a signaling message to a block. Note that these rules are high level.

Attack Graph

The CAT attack graph may be defined as a state transition showing the paths through a system, starting with the conditions of the attack, followed by attack action, and ending

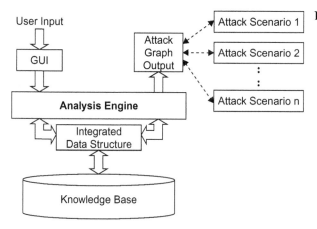

FIGURE 11.8   Architecture of CAT.

with its cascading effects. In Figure 11.9, we present the CAT attack graph output, which was built using user input of *ISDN Bearer Capability* as a seed and *Bearer Service* as goal. The attack graph constitutes nodes and edges. Nodes represent states in the network with respect to the attack, and *edges* represent network state transitions. For description purposes, each node has been given a node label followed by an alphabet, and the attack graph has been divided into layers.

Nodes may be broadly classified as *conditions, actions*, and *goals*, with the conditions of the attack occurring at the lowest layer and the final cascading effect at the highest layer. In the following, we detail each node type.

Condition Nodes

Nodes at the lowest layer typically correspond to the conditions that must exist for the attack to occur. These condition nodes directly follow from the taxonomy. They are an adversary's physical access, target service node, and vulnerability exploited. For example, the adversary has access to links connecting to the GMSC service node, that is, Level II

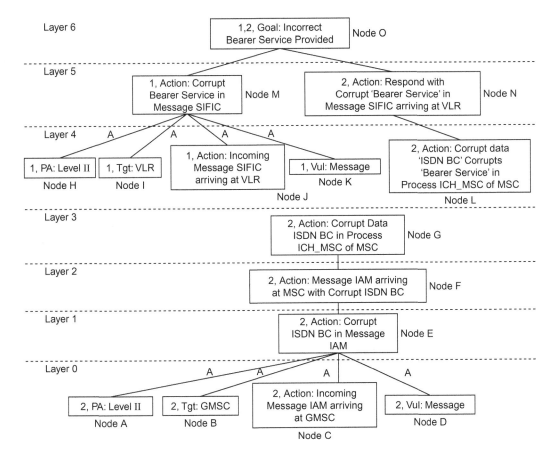

FIGURE 11.9 CAT attack graph output.

physical access; this is represented as Node A in the attack graph. Likewise, the adversary corrupts data item ISDN Bearer Capability in the IAM message arriving at the GMSC. Hence the target of the attack is the GMSC and is represented by Node B. Similarly, the adversary exploits vulnerabilities in a message (IAM); and, this is represented by Node D in the attack graph.

The CAT attack graphs show all the possible conditions for an attack to happen. In other words, we see not only the corruption due to the seed ISDN Bearer Capability in the signaling message, but also IAM arriving at the GMSC. But, there are also other possibilities, such as the corruption of the goal Bearer Service in the signaling message SIFIC, represented by Node M.

Action Nodes

Nodes at higher layers are actions that typically correspond to effects of the attack propagating through the network. Effects typically include propagation of corruption between service nodes, such as from MSC to VLR (Node N), propagation of corruption within service nodes such as ISDN Bearer Capability corrupting Bearer Service (Node L), and so on. Actions may further be classified as adversary actions, normal network operations, or normal subscriber activities. Adversary actions include insertion, corruption, or deletion of data, signaling messages, or service logic represented by Node E. Normal network operations include sending (Node N) and receiving signaling messages (Node E). Subscriber activity may include updating personal data or initiating service.

Goal Nodes

Goal nodes typically occur at the highest layer of the attack graph. They indicate corruption of the goal items due to the direct corruption of seeds by the adversary (Node A).

Edges

In our graph, edges represent network transitions due to both normal network actions and adversary actions. Edges help show the global network view of adversary action. This is the uniqueness of our attack graph. Transitions due to adversary action are indicated by an edge marked by the letter A (edges connecting Layer 0 and Layer 1). By inclusion of normal network transitions in addition to the transitions caused by the adversary, our attack graph shows not only the adversary's activity but also the *global network view of the adversary's action*. This is a unique feature of the attack graph.

Trees

In the graph, trees are distinguished by the tree numbers assigned to its nodes. For example, all the nodes marked with number 2 belong to Tree 2 of the graph. Some nodes in the graph belong to multiple trees. Tree numbers are used to distinguish between AND and OR nodes in the graph. Nodes at a particular layer with the same tree number(s) are AND nodes. For example, at Layer 4, Nodes H, I, J, and K are AND nodes; they all must occur for Node M at Layer 5 to occur. Multiple tree numbers on a node are called OR nodes. The OR node may be arrived at using alternate ways. For example, Node O at Layer 6 is an OR node, the network state indicated by Node O may be arrived at from Node M or Node N.

Each attack tree shows the attack effects due to corruption of a seed at a specific network location (such as signaling message or process in a block). For example, Tree 1 shows the attack due to the corruption of the seed Bearer Service at the VLR. Tree 2 shows the propagation of the seed ISDN Bearer Capability in the signaling message IAM. These trees show that the vulnerability of a cellular network is not limited to one place but can be realized due to the corruption of data in many network locations.

In constructing the attack graph, CAT assumes that an adversary has all the necessary conditions for launching the attack. The CAT attack graph format is well suited to cellular networks because data propagates through the network in various forms during the normal operation of a network; thus an attack that corrupts a data item manifests itself as the corruption of a different data item in a different part of the network after some network operations take place.

Attack Scenario Derivation

The CAT attack graph is in cellular network semantics, and realistic attack scenarios may be derived to understand the implications of the attack graph. Here we detail the principles involved in the derivation of realistic attack scenarios:

END-USER EFFECT

Goal node(s) are used to infer the end effect of the attack on the subscriber. According to the goal node in Figure 11.9, the SIFIC message to the VLR has incorrect goal item Bearer Service. The SIFIC message is used to inform the VLR the calling party's preferences such as voice channel requirements and request the VLR to set up the call based on the calling party and receiving party preferences.

If the calling party's preferences (such as Bearer Service) are incorrect, the call setup by the VLR is incompatible with the calling party, and the communication is ineffective (garbled speech). From the goal node, it can be inferred that Alice, the receiver of the call, is unable to communicate effectively with Bob, the caller, because Alice can only hear garbled speech from Bob's side.

ORIGIN OF ATTACK

Nodes at Layer 0 indicate the origin of the attack, and hence the location of the attack may be inferred. The speech attack may originate at the signaling messages IAM, or the VLR service node.

ATTACK PROPAGATION AND SIDE EFFECTS

Nodes At All Other Layers Show The Propagation Of Corruption Across The Various Service Nodes In The Network. From Other Layers In Figure 11.9, It Can Be Inferred That The Seed Is The ISDN Bearer Capability And The Attack Spreads From The MSC To The VLR.

Example Attack Scenario

Using these guidelines, an attack scenario may be derived as follows. Trudy, the adversary, corrupts the ISDN Bearer Capability of Bob, the victim, at the IAM message arriving at the GMSC. The GMSC propagates this corruption to the MSC, which computes, and hence corrupts, the Bearer Service. The corrupt Bearer Service is passed on to the VLR, which sets up the call between Bob, the caller, and Alice, the receiver. Bob and Alice cannot communicate effectively because Alice is unable to understand Bob.

Though CAT has detected several cascading attacks, its output to a great extent depends on SDL's ability to capture data dependencies. SDL is limited in its expression capability in the sense that it does not always accurately capture the relationship between data items, and in many cases, SDL does even specify the relationship. Without these details CAT may miss some cascading effects due to loss of data relationships. CAT's output to a minor extent also depends on user input in the sense that to accurately capture all the cascading effect of a seed, the user's input must comprise all the seeds that can occur in the cascading effect; otherwise the exact cascading effect is not captured. To alleviate CAT's inadequacies, aCAT was developed.

Advanced Cellular Network Vulnerability Assessment Toolkit (aCAT)

In this section, we present aCAT, an extension of CAT with enhanced features. These enhanced features include (1) incorporating expert knowledge to compensate for the lacking caused by SDL's inexplicit assumptions; expert knowledge added to the knowledge base with the SDL specifications; (2) defining a network dependency model that accurately captures the dependencies in a cellular network; the network dependency model is used to format the data in knowledge base, thereby clarifying the nature of the network dependency; and (3) defining infection propagation rules that define fine-grained rules to detect cascading attacks; these infection propagation rules are incorporated into the analysis engine, which comprises the forward, reverse, and combinatory algorithms. aCAT is also improved in terms of its user input requirements. It requires as input either seeds or goals, whereas CAT required both seeds and goals.

In principle, cascading attacks are the result of propagation of corruption between network components (such as signaling messages, caches, local variables, and service logic) due to dependencies that exist between these network components. Hence, to uncover these attacks, the network dependency model and infection propagation (IP) rules were defined. In the following, we detail the network dependency model and infection propagation model using Figure 11.10.

Network Dependency Model

The network dependency model accurately defines fine-grained dependencies between the various network components. Given that service nodes comprise agents and data sources (from the abstract model), the dependencies are defined as follows. In interagent dependency, agents communicate with each other using agent invocations (as shown by 6 in Figure 11.10) containing data items. Thus, agents are related to each other through data items. Likewise, in agent to data source dependency, agents communicate with data sources using Read and Write operations containing data items. Therefore, agents and data items are related to each other through data items. Within agents, derivative dependencies define relationships between data items. Here data items are used as input to

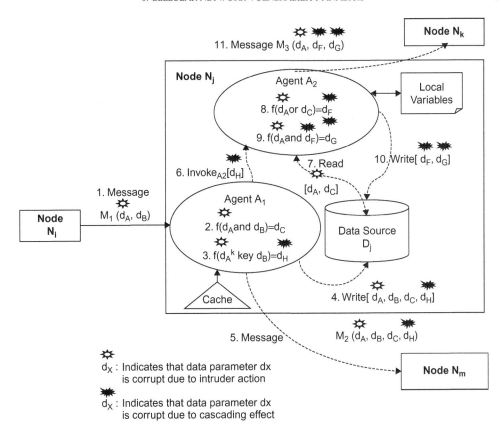

FIGURE 11.10 Network dependency model.

derive data items using derivation operations such as AND, OR operations. Therefore, data items are related to each other through derivation operation. For further detail on the network dependency model, refer to [12].

Infection Propagation (IP) Rules

These are finegrained rules to detect cascading effects. They are incorporated into the algorithms in the analysis engine. An example of the IP rule is that an output data item in the AND dependency is corrupt only if both the input data items are corrupt (as shown by 9 in Figure 11.10). Likewise, an output data item in the OR dependency is corrupt if a single input data item is corrupt (as shown by 8 in Figure 11.10). Similarly, corruption propagates between agents when the data item used to invoke the agent is corrupt, and the same data item is used as an input in the derivative dependency whose output may be corrupt (as shown by 6, 8 in Figure 11.10). Accordingly, corruption propagates from an agent to a data source if the data item written to the data source is corrupt (as shown by 4 in Figure 11.10). Finally, corruption propagates between service nodes if a data item used in the signaling message between the service nodes is corrupt, and the corrupt data item is used to derive corrupt output items or the corrupt data item is stored in the data source (as shown by 1, 3 or 1, 4 in Figure 11.10) [12].

With such a fine-grained dependency model and infection propagation rules, aCAT was very successful in identifying cascading attacks in several key services offered by a cellular network, and it was found that aCAT can indeed identify a better set of cascading effects in comparison to CAT. aCAT has also detected several interesting and unforeseen cascading attacks that are subtle and difficult to identify by other means. These newly identified cascading attacks include the alerting attack, power-off/power-on attack, mixed identity attack, call redirection attack, and missed calls attack.

Alerting Attack

In the following we detail aCAT's output, a cascading attack called the *alerting attack*, shown in Figure 11.11. From goal nodes (Node A at Level 5, and Node C at Level 4) in the alerting attack, it can be inferred that the Page message has incorrect data item *page type*. The Page message is used to inform subscribers of the arrival of incoming calls, and "page type" indicates the type of call. "Page type" must be compatible with the subscriber's mobile station or else the subscriber is not alerted. From the goal node it may be inferred that Alice, a subscriber of the system, is not alerted on the arrival of an incoming call and hence does not receive incoming calls. This attack is subtle to detect because network administrators find that the network processes the incoming call correctly and that the subscriber is alerted correctly. They might not find that this alerting pattern is incompatible with the mobile station itself.

Also, nodes at Level 0 indicate the origin of the attack as signaling messages SRI, PRN, the service nodes VLR, or the HLR. From the other levels it may be inferred that the seed is the *alerting pattern* that the adversary corrupts in the SRI message and the attack spreads from the HLR to the VLR and from the VLR to the MSC. For more details on these attacks, refer to [12].

Cellular Network Vulnerability Assessment Toolkit for Evaluation (eCAT)

In this part of the chapter, we present eCAT an extension to aCAT. eCAT was developed to evaluate new security protocols before their deployment. Though the design goals and threat model of these security protocols are common knowledge, eCAT was designed to find (1) the effective protection coverage of these security protocols in terms of percentage of attacks prevented; (2) the other kinds of security schemes required to tackle the attacks that can evade the security protocol under observation; and (3) the most vulnerable network areas (also called *hotspots*) [13].

eCAT computes security protocol coverage using attack graphs generated by aCAT and Boolean probabilities in a process called *attack graph marking* and quantifies the coverage using *coverage measurement formulas* (CMF). Attack graph marking also identifies network hotspots and exposes if the security protocol being evaluated protects these hotspots. eCAT was also used to evaluate MAPSec, as it is a relatively new protocol, and evaluation results would aid network operators.

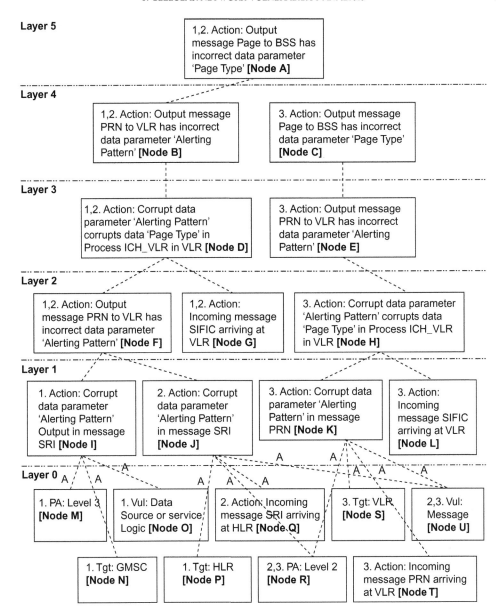

FIGURE 11.11 Attack graph for alerting attack.

Boolean Probabilities

Boolean probabilities are used in attack graphs to distinguish between nodes eliminated (denoted by 0, or shaded node in attack graph) and nodes existing (denoted by 1, or unshaded node in attack graph) due to the security protocol under evaluation. By computing

Boolean probabilities for each node in the attack graph, eCAT can extract the attack effects that may be eliminated by the security protocol under evaluation.

Attack Graph Marking

To mark attack graphs, user input of Boolean probabilities must be provided for Layer 0 nodes. For example, if the security protocol under evaluation is MAPSec, then because MAPSec provides security on links between nodes, it eliminates Level 2 physical access. For example, consider the attack graph generated by eCAT shown in Figure 11.12. Here, Node 5 is set to 0, while all other nodes are set to 1.

eCAT uses the input from Layer 0 nodes to compute the Boolean probabilities for the rest of the nodes starting from Layer 1 and moving upward. For example, the Boolean probability of the AND node (Node 18) is the product of all the nodes in the previous layer with the same tree number. Because Node 5 has the same tree number as Node 18, and Node 5's Boolean probability is 0, Node 18's Boolean probability is also 0. This process of marking attack graphs is continued until Boolean probability of all the nodes is computed till the topmost layer.

Hotspots

Graph marking also marks the network hotspots in the attack graph. With respect to the attack graph, hotspots are the Layer 0 nodes with the highest tree number count. For example in Figure 11.12, Node 3 and Node 4 are the hotspots. A high tree number count indicates an increased attractiveness of the network location to adversaries. This is because by breaking into the network location indicated by the hotspot node, the adversary has a higher likelihood of success and can cause the greatest amount of damage.

Extensive testing of eCAT on several of the network services using MAPSec has revealed hotspots to be "Data Sources and Service Logic." This is because a corrupt data source or service logic may be used by many different services and hence cause many varied cascading effects, spawning a large number of attacks (indicated by multiple trees in attack graphs). Thus attacks that occur due to exploiting service logic and data source vulnerabilities constitute a major portion of the networkwide vulnerabilities and so a major problem. In other words, by exploiting service logic and data sources, the likelihood of attack success is very high. Therefore data source and service logic protection mechanisms must be deployed. It must be noted that MAPSec protects neither service logic nor data sources; rather, it protects MAP messages.

Coverage Measurement Formulas

The CMF comprises the following set of three formulas to capture the coverage of security protocols: (1) *effective coverage*, to capture the average effective number of attacks eliminated by the security protocol; the higher the value of Effective Coverage the greater the protection the security protocol; (2) *deployment coverage*, to capture the coverage of protocol deployments; and (3) *attack coverage*, to capture the attack coverage provided by the security protocol; the higher this value, the greater is the security solution's efficacy in eliminating a large number of attacks on the network.

Extensive use of CMF on several of the network services has revealed that MAPSec has an average networkwide attack coverage of 33%. This may be attributed to the fact that

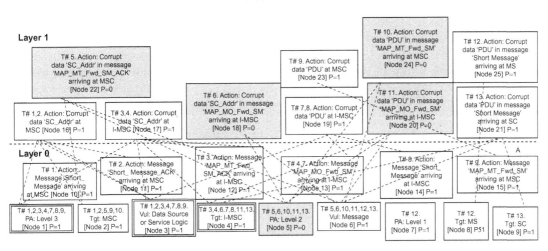

FIGURE 11.12 Fragment of a marked attack graph generated by eCAT.

message corruption has a low spawning effect. Typically a single message corruption causes a single attack, since messages are typically used by a single service. Hence MAPSec is a solution to a small portion of the total network vulnerabilities.

Finally, in evaluating MAPSec using eCAT, it was observed that though MAPSec is 100% effective in preventing MAP message attacks, it cannot prevent a successfully launched attack from cascading. For MAPSec to be truly successful, every leg of the MAP message transport must be secured using MAPSec. However, the overhead for deploying MAPSec can be high, in terms of both processing load and monetary investment. Also, as MAP messages travel through third-party networks en route to their destinations, the risk level of attacks without MAPSec is very high. Hence, MAPSec is vital to protect MAP messages.

In conclusion, because MAPSec can protect against only 33% of attacks, it alone is insufficient to protect the network. A complete protection scheme for the network must include data source and service logic protection.

6. SUMMARY

Next to the Internet, cellular networks are the most highly used communication network. It is also the most vulnerable, with inadequate security measures making it a most attractive target to adversaries that want to cause communication outages during emergencies. As cellular networks are moving in the direction of the Internet, becoming an amalgamation of several types of diverse networks, more attention must be paid to securing these networks. A push from government agencies requiring mandatory security standards for operating cellular networks would be just the momentum needed to securing these networks.

Of all the attacks discussed in this chapter, cascading attacks have the most potential to stealthily cause major network misoperation. At present there is no standardized scheme to protect from such attacks. EndSec is a good solution for protecting from cascading attacks, since it requires every data item to be signed by the source service node. Because service nodes are unlikely to corrupt data items and they are to be accounted for by their signatures, the possibility of cascading attacks is greatly reduced. EndSec has the added advantage of providing end-to-end security for all types of signaling messages. Hence, standardizing EndSec and mandating its deployment would be a good step toward securing the network.

Both Internet and PSTN connectivity are the open gateways that adversaries can use to gain access and attack the network. Because the PSTN's security is not going to be improved, at least its gateway to the core network must be adequately secured. Likewise, since neither the Internet's design nor security will be changed to suit a cellular network, at least its gateways to the core network must be adequately secured.

Finally, because a cellular network is an amalgamation of many diverse networks, it has too many vulnerable points. Hence, the future design of the network must be planned to reduce the number of vulnerable network points and reduce the number of service nodes that participate in servicing the subscriber, thereby reducing the number of points from which an adversary may attack.

Finally, let's move on to the real interactive part of this Chapter: review questions/exercises, hands-on projects, case projects and optional team case project. The answers and/or solutions by chapter can be found in the Online Instructor's Solutions Manual.

CHAPTER REVIEW QUESTIONS/EXERCISES

True/False

1. True or False? Cellular networks are high-speed, high-capacity voice and data communication networks with enhanced multimedia and seamless roaming capabilities for supporting cellular devices.
2. True or False? The current cellular network is an evolution of the early-generation cellular networks that were built for optimal performance.
3. True or False? It would seem that attacks on the radio access network could not easily happen, because anyone with a transmitter/receiver could capture these signals.
4. True or False? Though the current generation of a cellular network has seen many security improvements in the radio access network, the security of the core network is not as improved.
5. True or False? Internet connectivity introduces the biggest threat to the security of cellular networks.

Multiple Choice

1. Cellular networks are organized as collections of interconnected:
   A. Message Integrity Codes (MIC).
   B. Temporal Key Integrity Protocols (TKIP).
   C. Application Program Interfaces.

D. Network Areas.
E. Extensible Authentication Protocol (EAP) framework.
2. The core network is facilitated by network servers, which are also called?
A. Middle Layers.
B. Network Layers.
C. Transport Layers.
D. Service Nodes.
E. All of the above.
3. What is a basic service in the circuit-switched domain?
A. Secure on-demand routing protocol service.
B. Taxonomy service.
C. Caller delivery service.
D. Authenticated Routing for Ad hoc Networks (ARAN) service.
E. Destination-Sequenced Distance Vector (DSDV) routing service.
4. The cloning of cellular devices to utilize the network resources without paying; and cloning BSs to entice users to camp at the cloned BS in an attack, is called a:
A. False base station attack.
B. Privacy attack.
C. Eavesdropping attack.
D. Man-in-the-Middle Attack.
E. Passive attack.
5. What introduces the biggest threat to the security of cellular networks?
A. HELLO Flood connectivity.
B. Denial-of-service attack connectivity.
C. Internet connectivity.
D. Sybil connectivity.
E. All of the above.

EXERCISE

Problem

What are the limitations of cellular network security?

Hands-On Projects

Project

What are the security issues in cellular networks?

Case Projects

Problem

What types of attacks are cellular networks open to?

Optional Team Case Project

Problem

What additional security mechanisms are available to cellular networks?

References

[1] 3GPP, architectural requirements, Technical Standard 3G TS 23.221 V6.3.0, 3G Partnership Project, May 2004.
[2] K. Murakami, O. Haase, J. Shin, T.F. LaPorta, Mobility management alternatives for migration to mobile internet session-based services, IEEE J. Sel. Areas Commun. (J-SAC) 22 (June 2004) 834–848special issue on Mobile Internet.
[3] 3GPP, 3G security, Security threats and requirements, Technical Standard 3G TS 21.133 V3.1.0, 3G Partnership Project, December 1999.
[4] 3GPP, network architecture, Technical Standard 3G TS 23.002 V3.3.0, 3G Partnership Project, May 2000.
[5] V. Eberspacher, GSM Switching, Services and Protocols, John Wiley & Sons, 1999.
[6] 3GPP, Basic call handling - technical realization, Technical Standard 3GPP TS 23.018 V3.4.0, 3G Partnership Project, April 1999.
[7] 3GPP, A guide to 3rd generation security, Technical Standard 3GPP TR 33.900 V1.2.0, 3G Partnership Project, January 2001.
[8] B. Chatras, C. Vernhes, Mobile application part design principles, in: Proceedings of XIII International Switching Symposium, vol. 1, June 1990, pp. 35–42.
[9] J.A. Audestad, The mobile application part (map) of GSM, technical report, Telektronikk 3.2004, Telektronikk, March 2004.
[10] 3GPP, Mobile Application part (MAP) specification, Technical Standard 3GPP TS 29.002 V3.4.0, 3G Partnership Project, April 1999.
[11] K. Boman, G. Horn, P. Howard, V. Niemi, Umts security, Electron. Commun. Eng. J. 14 (5) (October 2002) 191–204Special issue security for mobility.
[12] K. Kotapati, P. Liu, T.F. LaPorta, Dependency relation-based vulnerability analysis of 3G networks: can it identify unforeseen cascading attacks? Special Issue of Springer Telecommunications Systems on Security, Privacy and Trust for Beyond 3G Networks, March 2007.
[13] K. Kotapati, P. Liu, T.F. LaPorta, Evaluating MAPSec by marking attack graphs, ACM/Kluwer J. Wire. Netw. J. (WINET) 12 (March 2008).
[14] K. Kotapati, P. Liu, T.F. LaPorta, EndSec: an end-to-end message security protocol for cellular networks, IEEE workshop on security, privacy and authentication in wireless networks (SPAWN 2008) in IEEE International Symposium on a World of Wireless Mobile and Multimedia Networks (WOWMOM), June 2008.
[15] D. Moore, V. Paxson, S. Savage, C. Shannon, S. Staniford, N. Weaver, Inside the slammer worm, IEEE Secur. Privacy 1 (4) (2003) 33–39.
[16] W. Enck, P. Traynor, P. McDaniel, T.F. LaPorta, Exploiting open functionality in sms-capable cellular networks, CCS '05: Proceedings of the 12th ACM Conference on Computer and Communications Security, ACM Press, 2005.
[17] P. Traynor, W. Enck, P. McDaniel, T.F. LaPorta, Mitigating attacks on open functionality in SMS-capable cellular networks, MobiCom '06: Proceedings of the 12th Annual International Conference on Mobile Computing and Networking, ACM Press, 2006, pp. 182–193.
[18] P. Traynor, P. McDaniel, T.F. LaPorta, On attack causality in internet-connected cellular networks, USENIX Security Symposium (SECURITY), August 2007.
[19] T. Moore, T. Kosloff, J. Keller, G. Manes, S. Shenoi. Signaling system 7 (SS7) network security, in: Proceedings of the IEEE 45th Midwest Symposium on Circuits and Systems, August 2002.
[20] G. Lorenz, T. Moore, G. Manes, J. Hale, S. Shenoi, Securing SS7 telecommunications networks, in: Proceedings of the 2001 IEEE Workshop on Information Assurance and Security, June 2001.
[21] K. Kotapati, P. Liu, Y. Sun, T.F. LaPorta, A taxonomy of cyber attacks on 3G networksISI, Lecture Notes in Computer Science Proceedings IEEE International Conference on Intelligence and Security Informatics, Springer-Verlag, May 2005, pp. 631–633.

[22] K. Kotapati, Assessing Security of Mobile Telecommunication Networks, Ph. D dissertation, Penn State University, August 2008.

[23] Switch, 5ESS Switch, www.alleged.com/telephone/5ESS/.

[24] Telcoman, Central Offices, www.thecentraloffice.com/.

[25] V. Prevelakis, D. Spinellis, The Athens affair, IEEE Spectrum (July 2007).

[26] H. Hannu, Signaling Compression (SigComp) Requirements & Assumptions, RFC 3322 (Informational), January 2003.

[27] W. Stallings, Cryptography and Network Security: Principles and Practice, Prentice Hall, 2000.

[28] K. Kotapati, P. Liu, T. F. LaPorta, CAT - a practical graph & SDL based toolkit for vulnerability assessment of 3G networks, in: Proceedings of the 21st IFIP TC-11 International Information Security Conference, Security and Privacy in Dynamic Environments, SEC 2006, May 2006.

[29] 3GPP2 3GPP, Third Generation Partnership Project, www.3gpp.org/, 2006.

[30] J. Ellsberger, D. Hogrefe, A. Sarma, SDL, *Formal Object-oriented Language for Communicating Systems*, Prentice Hall, 1997.

12

RFID Security

Chunming Rong*, Gansen Zhao[†], Liang Yan*, Erdal Cayirci*
and Hongbing Cheng*

*University of Stavanger, Norway, [†]Sun Yat-sen University, China

1. RFID INTRODUCTION

Generally, an RFID system consists of three basic components: RFID tags, RFID readers, and a back-end database:

- *RFID tags or RFID transponders.* These are the data carriers attached to objects. A typical RFID tag contains information about the attached object, such as an identifier (ID) of the object and other related properties of the object that may help to identify and describe it.
- *The RFID reader or the RFID transceiver.* These devices can read information from tags and may write information into tags if the tags are rewritable.
- *Back-end database.* This is the data repository responsible for the management of data related to the tags and business transactions, such as ID, object properties, reading locations, reading time, and so on.

RFID System Architecture

RFID systems' architecture is illustrated in Figure 12.1. Tags are attached to or embedded in objects to identify or annotate them. An RFID reader send out signals to a tag for requesting information stored on the tag. The tag responses to the request by sending back the appropriate information. With the data from the back-end database, applications can then use the information from the tag to proceed with the business transaction related to the object.

DOI: http://dx.doi.org/10.1016/B978-0-12-416689-9.00012-5

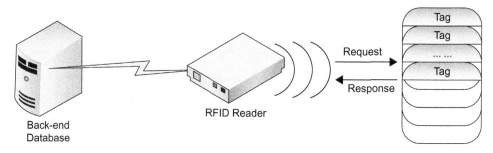

FIGURE 12.1   RFID system architecture.

Tags

In RFID systems, objects are identified or described by information on RFID tags attached to the objects. An RFID tag basically consists of a microchip that is used for data storage and computation and a coupling element for communicating with the RFID reader via radio frequency communication, such as an antenna. Some tags may also have an on-board battery to supply a limited amount of power.

RFID tags can respond to radio frequencies sent out by RFID readers. On receiving the radio signals from a RFID reader, an RFID tag either send back the requested data stored on the tag or write the data into the tag, if the tag is rewritable. Because radio signals are used, RFID tags do not require line of sight to connect with the reader and precise positioning, as barcodes do. Tags may also generate a certain amount of electronic power from the radio signals they receive, to power the computation and transmission of data.

RFID tags can be classified based on four main criteria: power source, type of memory, computational power, and functionality.

A basic and important classification criterion of RFID tags is to classify tags based on power source. Tags can be categorized into three classes: active, semi-active, and passive RFID tags.

Active RFID tags have on-board power sources, such as batteries. Active RFID tags can proactively send radio signals to an RFID reader and possibly to other tags [1] as well. Compared with tags without on-board power, active tags have longer transmission range and are more reliable. Active tags can work in the absence of an RFID reader. On the other hand, the on-board power supply also increases the costs of active tags.

Semi-active RFID tags also have on-board power sources for powering their microchips, but they use RFID readers' energy field for actually transmitting their data [2] when responding to the incoming transmissions. Semi-active tags have the middle transmission range and cost.

Passive RFID tags do not have internal power sources and cannot initiate any communications. Passive RFID tags generate power from radio signals sent out by an RFID reader in the course of communication. Thus passive RFID tags can only work in the presence of an RFID reader. Passive tags have the shortest transmission range and the cheapest cost. The differences of active, semi-active and passive tags are shown in Table 12.1.

RFID tags can be classified into three categories according to the type of memory that a tag uses: read-only tags, write-once/read-many tags, and fully rewritable tags. The

TABLE 12.1 Tags Classified by Power Source.

Power Source	Active Tags	Semiactive Tags	Passive Tags
On-board power supply	Yes	Yes	No
Transmission range	Long	Medium	Short
Communication pattern	Proactive	Passive	Passive
Cost	Expensive	Medium	Cheap

information on read-only tags cannot be changed in the life-cycle of the tags. Write-once/ read-many tags can be initialized with application-specific information. The information on fully rewritable tags can be rewritten many times by an RFID reader.

According to the computational power, RFID tags can be classified into three categories: basic tags, symmetric-key tags, and public-key tags. Basic tags do not have the ability to perform cryptography computation. Symmetric-key tags and public-key tags have the ability to perform symmetric-key and public–key cryptography computation, respectively.

RFID tags can also be classified according to their functionality. The MIT Auto-ID Center defined five classes of tags according to their functionality in 2003 [3]: Class 0, Class 1, Class 2, Class 3, and Class 4 tags. Every class has different functions and different requirements for tag memory and power resource. Class 0 tags are passive and do not contain any memory. They only announce their presence and offer electronic article surveillance (EAS) functionality. Class 1 tags are typically passive. They have read-only or write-once/read-many memory and can only offer identification functionality. Class 2 tags are mostly semi-active and active. They have fully rewritable memory and can offer data-logging functionality. Class 3 tags are semi-active and active tags. They contain on-board environmental sensors that can record temperature, acceleration, motion, or radiation and require fully rewritable memory. Class 4 tags are active tags and have fully rewritable memory. They can establish ad hoc wireless networks with other tags because they are equipped with wireless networking components.

RFID Readers

An RFID reader (transceiver) is a device used to read information from and possibly also write information into RFID tags. An RFID reader is normally connected to a back-end database for sending information to that database for further processing.

An RFID reader consists of two key functional modules: a high-frequency (HF) interface and a control unit. The HF interface can perform three functions: generating the transmission power to activate the tags, modulating the signals for sending requests to RFID tags, and receiving and demodulating signals received from tags. The control unit of an RFID reader has also three basic functions: controlling the communication between the RFID reader and RFID tags, encoding and decoding signals, and communicating with the back-end server for sending information to the back-end database or executing the commands from the back-end server. The control unit can perform more functions in the case of complex RFID systems, such as executing anticollision algorithms in the cause of communicating with multitags, encrypting requests sent by the RFID reader and decrypting responses received from tags, and performing the authentication between RFID readers and RFID tags [4].

RFID readers can provide high-speed tag scanning. Hundreds of objects can be dealt with by a single reader within a second; thus it is scalable enough for applications such as supply chain management, where a large number of objects need to be dealt with frequently. RFID readers need only to be placed at every entrance and exit. When products enter or leave the designated area by passing through an entrance or exit, the RFID readers can instantly identify the products and send the necessary information to the back-end database for further processing.

Back-End Database

The back-end database is in the back-end server that manages the information related to the tags in an RFID system. Every object's information can be stored as a record in the database, and the information on the tag attached to the object can serve as a pointer to the record.

The connection between an RFID reader and a backend database can be assumed as secure, no matter via wireless link or not, because constraints for readers are not very tight and security solutions such as SSL/TLS can be implemented for them [5].

RFID Standards

Currently, as different frequencies are used for RFID systems in various countries and many standards are adopted for different kinds of application, there is no agreement on a universal standard that's accepted by all parties. Several kinds of RFID standards [6] are being used today. These standards include contactless smart cards, item management tags, RFID systems for animal identification, and electronic product code (EPC) tags. These standards specify the physical layer and the link layer characteristics of RFID systems but do not cover the upper layers.

Contactless smart cards can be classified into three types according to the communication ranges. The ISO standards for them are ISO 10536, ISO 14443, and ISO 15693. ISO 10536 sets the standard for close-coupling smart cards, for which the communication range is about 0−1 cm. ISO 14443 sets the standard for proximity-coupling smart cards, which have a communication range of about 0−10 cm. ISO 15693 specifies vicinity-coupling smart cards, which have a communication range of about 0−1 m. The proximity-coupling and vicinity-coupling smart cards have already been implemented with some cryptography algorithms such as 128-bit AES, triple DES, and SHA-1 and challenge-response authentication mechanisms to improve system security [7].

Item management tag standards include ISO 15961, ISO 15962, ISO 15963, and ISO 18000 series [8]. ISO 15961 defines the host interrogator, tag functional commands, and other syntax features of item management. ISO 15962 defines the data syntax of item management, and ISO 15963 is "Unique Identification of RF tag and Registration Authority to manage the uniqueness." For the ISO 18000 standards series, part 1 describes the reference architecture and parameters definition; parts 2, 3, 4, 5, 6, and 7 define the parameters for

TABLE 12.2 EPC Basic Format.

Header	EPC	Object Class	Serial
	Manager		Number
	Number		

air interface communications below 135 kHz, at 13.56 MHz, at 2.45 GHz, at 860 MHz, at 960 MHz, and at 433 MHz, respectively.

Standards for RFID systems for animal identification include ISO 11784, ISO 11785, and ISO 14223 [5]. ISO 11784 and ISO 11784 define the code structure and technical concepts for radiofrequency identification of animals. ISO 14223 includes three parts: air interface, code and command structure, and applications. These kinds of tags use low frequency for communication and have limited protection for animal tracking [7].

The EPC standard was created by the MIT Auto-ID, which is an association of more than 100 companies and university labs. The EPC system is currently operated by EPC global [8]. A typical EPC network has four parts [5]: the electronic product code, the identification system that includes RFID tags and RFID readers, the Savant middleware, and the object naming service (ONS). The first- and second-generation EPC tags cannot support strong cryptography to protect the security of the RFID systems due to the limitation of computational resources, but both of them can provide a kill command to protect the privacy of the consumer [7].

EPC tag encoding includes a Header field followed by one or more Value fields. The Header field defines the overall length and format of the Value fields. There are two kinds of EPC format: EPC 64-bit format and EPC 96-bit format. In the most recent version [9], the 64-bit format was removed from the standard. As shown in Table 12.2, both the formats include four fields: a header (8 bits), an EPC manager number (28 bits), an object class (24 bits), and a serial number (36 bits). The header and the EPC manager number are assigned by EPC global [8], and the object class and the serial number are assigned by EPC manager owner. The EPC header identifies the length, type, structure version, and generation of the EPC. The EPC manager number is the entity responsible for maintaining the subsequent partitions of the EPC. The object class identifies a class of objects. Serial number identifies the instance.

RFID Applications

Recently more and more companies and organizations have begun to use RFID tags rather than traditional barcode because RFID systems have many advantages over traditional barcode systems. First, the information stored in the RFID tags can be read by RFID readers without a line of sight; whereas, barcodes can only be scanned within the line of sight. Second, the distance between a tag and a reader is longer compared with the barcode system. For example, an RFID reader can read information from a tag at a distance as long as 300 feet, whereas the read range for a barcode is typically no more than 15 feet. Third, RFID readers can scan hundreds of tags in seconds. Fourth, since today most RFID tags are produced using silicon technology, more functions can be added to them, such as large memory for more information storage and calculation ability to support various

TABLE 12.3 RFID Application Purpose.

Application Type	Identification Purpose
Asset management	Determine item presence
Tracking	Determine item location
Authenticity verification	Determine item source
Matching	Ensure affiliated items are not separated
Process control	Correlate item information for decision making
Access control	Person authentication
Automated payment	Conduct financial transaction

kinds of encryption and decryption algorithms, so privacy can be better protected and the tags cannot be easily cloned by attackers. In addition, the information stored in the barcode cannot be changed after being imprinted on the barcode, whereas for the RFID tags with rewritable memory the information can be updated when needed.

With these characteristics and advantages, RFID has been widely adopted and deployed in various areas. Currently, RFID can be used in passports, transportation payments, product tracking, lap scoring, animal identification, inventory systems, RFID mandates, promotion tracking, human implants, libraries, schools and universities, museums, and social retailing. These myriad applications of RFID can be classified into seven classes according to the purpose of identifying items [10]. These classes are asset management, tracking, authenticity verification, matching, process control, access control, and automated payment. Table 12.3 lists the identification purposes of various application types.

Asset management involves determining the presence of tagged items and helping manage item inventory. One possible application of asset management is electronic article surveillance (EAS). For example, every good in a supermarket is attached to an EAS tag, which will be deactivated if it is properly checked out. Then RFID readers at the supermarket exits can detect unpaid goods automatically when they pass through.

Tracking is used to identify the location of tagged items. If the readers are fixed, a single reader can cover only one area. To effectively track the items, a group of readers is needed, together with a central system to deal with the information from different readers.

Authenticity verification methods are used to verify the source of tagged items. For example, by adding a cryptography-based digital signature in the tag, the system can prevent tag replication to make sure that a good is labeled with the source information.

Matching is used to ensure that affiliated items are not separated. Samples for matching applications include mothers and their newborn babies to match each other in the hospital and for airline passengers to match their checked luggage and so prevent theft.

Access control is used for person authentication. Buildings may use contactless RFID card systems to identify authorized people. Only those authorized people with the correct RFID card can authenticate themselves to the reader to open a door and enter a building. Using a car key with RFID tags, a car owner can open his own car automatically, another example of RFID's application to access control.

Process control involves decision making by correlating tagged item information. For example, RFID readers in different parts of an assembly line can read the information on the products, which can be used to help production managers make suitable decisions.

Automated payment is used to conduct financial transactions. The applications include payment for toll expressways and at gas stations. These applications can improve the speed of payment to hasten the processing of these transactions.

2. RFID CHALLENGES

RFID systems have been widely deployed in some areas. Perhaps this happened beyond the expectations of RFID researchers and RFID service providers. There are many limitations of the RFID technology that restrain the deployment of RFID applications, such as the lack of universal standardization of RFID in the industry and the concerns about security and privacy problems that may affect the privacy and security of individuals and organizations. The security and privacy issues pose a huge challenge for RFID applications. Here we briefly summarize some of the challenges facing RFID systems.

Counterfeiting

As described earlier in the chapter, RFID tags can be classified into three categories based on the equipped computation power: basic tags, symmetric-key tags, and public-key tags. Symmetric-key and public-key tags can implement cryptography protocols for authentication with private key, and public keys, respectively. Basic tags are not capable of performing cryptography computation. Although they lack the capability to perform cryptography computation, they are most widely used for applications such as supply chain management and travel systems. With the widespread application of fully writable or even reprogrammable basic tags, counterfeiters can easily forge basic tags in real-world applications, and these counterfeit tags can be used in multiple places at the same time, which can cause confusion.

The counterfeiting of tags can be categorized into two areas based on the technique used for tampering with tag data: modifying tag data and adding data to a blank tag. In real-world applications, we face counterfeit threats such as the following [7]:

- The attacker can modify valid tags to make them invalid or modify invalid tags to make them valid.
- The attacker can modify a high-priced object's tag as a low-priced object or modify a low-priced object's tag as a high-priced object.
- The attacker can modify an object's tag to be the same as the tags attached to other objects.
- The attacker can create an additional tag for personal reasons by reading the data from an authorized tag and adding this data to a blank tag in real-world applications, such as in a passport or a shipment of goods.

Sniffing

Another main issue of concern in deploying RFID systems is the sniffing problem. It occurs when third parties use a malicious and unauthorized RFID reader to read the information on RFID tags within their transmission range. Unfortunately, most RFID tags are indiscriminate in their responses to reading requests transmitted by RFID readers and do not have access control functions to provide any protection against an unauthorized reader. Once an RFID tag enters a sufficiently powered reader's field, it receives the reader's requests via radio frequency. As long as the request is well formed, the tag will reply to the request with the corresponding information on the tag. Then the holder of the unauthenticated reader may use this information for other purposes.

Tracking

With multiple RFID readers integrated into one system, the movements of objects can be tracked by fixed RFID readers [11]. For example, once a specific tag can be associated with a particular person or object, when the tag enters a reader's field the reader can obtain the specific identifier of the tag, and the presence of the tag within the range of a specific reader implies specific location information related to the attached person or object. With location information coming from multiple RFID readers, an attacker can follow movements of people or objects. Tracking can also be performed without decrypting the encrypted messages coming from RFID readers [5]. Generally, the more messages the attacker describes, the more location or privacy information can be obtained from the messages.

One way to track is to generate maps of RFID tags with mobile robots [12]. A sensor model is introduced to compute the likelihood of tag detections, given the relative pose of the tag with respect to the robot. In this model a highly accurate FastSLAM algorithm is used to learn the geometrical structure of the environment around the robots, which are equipped with a laser range scanner; then it uses the recursive Bayesian filtering scheme to estimate the posterior locations of the RFID tags, which can be used to localize robots and people in the environment with the geometrical structure of the environment learned by the FastSLAM algorithm.

There is another method to detect the motion of passive RFID tags that are within a detecting antenna's field. Response rate at the reader is used to study the impact of four cases of tag movements that can provide prompt and accurate detection and the influence of the environment. The idea of multiple tags/readers is introduced to improve performance. The movement-detection algorithms can be improved and integrated into the RFID monitoring system to localize the position of the tags. The method does not require any modification of communication protocols nor the addition of hardware. In real-world applications, there exists the following tracking threat: The attacker can track the potential victim by monitoring the movement of the person and performing some illegal actions against the potential victim [13].

Now, let's take a very brief look at denial of service threats. Availability enables a Web services application to detect a Denial of Service (DoS) attack, to continue operation as long as possible, and then to gracefully recover and resume operations after a DoS attack.

There is a need for techniques to replicate data and services to ensure continuity of operations in the event of a fault or threat (see checklist: "An Agenda For Action When Thwarting DoS Threats"). There is also a need for management and monitoring solutions to provide service performance and availability monitoring to meet certain service level objectives.

AN AGENDA FOR ACTION WHEN THWARTING DOS THREATS

Denial of service (DoS) takes place when RFID readers or back-end servers cannot provide excepted services. DoS attacks are easy to accomplish and difficult to guard against [13]. The following are nine DoS threats (check all tasks completed):

_____1. *Killing tags to make them disabled to disrupt readers' normal operations.* EPCglobal had proposed that a tag have a "kill" command to destroy it and protect consumer privacy. If an attacker knows the password of a tag, it can "kill" the tag easily in real-world applications. Now Class-0, Class-1 Generation-1, and Class-1 Generation-2 tags are all equipped with the kill command.

_____2. Carry a blocker tag that can disrupt the communication between an RFID reader and RFID tags. *A blocker tag is a cheap, passive RFID device that can simulate many basic RFID tags at one time and render specific zones private or public. An RFID reader can only communicate with a single RFID tag at any specific time. If more than one tag responds to a request coming from the reader at the same time, "collision" happens. In this case, the reader cannot receive the information sent by the tags, which makes the system unavailable to authorized uses.*

_____3. Carry a special absorbent tag that can be tuned to the same radio frequencies used by legitimate tags. *The absorbent tag can absorb the energy or power generated by radiofrequency signals sent by the reader, and the resulting reduction in the reader's energy may make the reader unavailable to communicate with other tags.*

_____4. *Remove, physically destroy, or erase the information on tags attached to or embedded in objects.* The reader will not communicate with the dilapidated tags in a normal way.

_____5. *Shield the RFID tags from scrutiny using a Faraday cage.* A Faraday cage is a container made of a metal enclosure that can prevent reading radio signals from the readers [14].

_____6. *Carry a device that can actively broadcast more powerful return radio signals or noises than the signals responded to by the tags so as to block or disrupt the communication of any nearby RFID readers and make the system unavailable to authorized users.* The power of the broadcast is so high that it could cause severe blockage or disruption of all nearby RFID systems, even those in legitimate applications where privacy is not a concern [14].

_____7. *Perform a traditional Internet DoS attack and prevent the back-end servers from gathering EPC numbers from the readers.* The servers do not receive enough information from the readers and cannot provide the additional services from the server.

_____8. *Perform a traditional Internet DoS attack against the object-naming service (ONS).* This can deny the service.

_____9. *Send URL queries to a database and make the database busy with these queries.* The database may then deny access to authorized users.

Other Issues

Besides the four basic types of attack (counterfeiting, sniffing, tracking, and denial of service) in real-world applications, there also exists some other threats to RFID systems.

Spoofing

Spoofing attacks take place when an attacker successfully poses as an authorized user of a system [13]. Spoofing attacks are different from counterfeiting and sniffing attacks, though they are all falsification types of attack. Counterfeiting takes place when an attacker forges the RFID tags that can be scanned by authorized readers. Sniffing takes place when an attacker forges authorized readers that can scan the authorized tags to obtain useful information. But the forging object of spoofing is an authorized user of a system. There exist the following spoofing threats in real-world applications [13]:

- *The attacker can pose as an authorized EPC global Information Service Object Naming Service (ONS) user.* If the attacker successfully poses as an authorized ONS user, he can send queries to the ONS to gather EPC numbers. Then, from the EPC numbers, the attacker may easily obtain the location, identification, or other privacy information.
- *The attacker can pose as an authorized database user in an RFID system.* The database stores the complete information from the objects, such as manufacturer, product name, read time, read location, and other privacy information. If the attacker successfully poses as an authorized database user and an authorized user of ONS, he can send queries to the ONS for obtaining the EPC number of one object, then get the complete information on the object by mapping the EPC number to the information stored in the database.
- *The attacker can also pose as an ONS server.* If the attacker's pose is successful, he can easily use the ONS server to gather EPC numbers, respond to invalid requests, deny normal service, and even change the data or write malicious data to the system.

Repudiation

Repudiation takes place when a user denies doing an action or no proof exists to prove that the action has been implemented [13]. There are two kinds of repudiation threats:

- The sender or the receiver denies performing the send and receive actions. A non-repudiation protocol can be used to resolve this problem.
- The owner of the EPC number or the back-end server denies that it has the information from the objects to which the tags are attached.

Insert Attacks

Insert attacks take place when an attacker inserts some system commands to the RFID system where data is normally expected [15]. In real-world applications, there exists the following attack: A system command rather than valid data is carried by a tag in its data storage memory.

Replay Attacks

Replay attacks take place when an attacker intercepts the communication signals between an RFID reader and an RFID tag and records the tag's response. Then the RFID tag's response can be reused if the attacker detects that the reader sends requests to the other tags for querying [16]. There exist the following two threats:

- The attacker can record the communications between proximity cards and a building access reader and play it back to access the building.
- The attacker can record the response that an RFID card in a car gives to an automated highway toll collection system, and the response can be used when the car of the attacker wants to pass the automated toll station.

Physical Attacks

Physical attacks are very strong attacks that physically obtain tags and have unauthorized physical operations on the tags. But it is fortunate that physical attacks cannot be implemented in public or on a widespread scale, except for Transient Electromagnetic Pulse Emanation Standard (TEMPEST) attacks. There exist the following physical attacks [1,17]:

- *Probe attacks.* The attacker can use a probe directly attached to the circuit to obtain or change the information on tags.
- *Material removal.* The attacker can use a knife or other tools to remove the tags attached to objects.
- *Energy attacks.* The attacks can be either of the contact or contactless variety. It is required that contactless energy attacks be close enough to the system.
- *Radiation imprinting.* The attacker can use an X-ray band or other radial bands to destroy the data unit of a tag.
- *Circuit disruption.* The attacker can use strong electromagnetic interference to disrupt tag circuits.
- *Clock glitch.* The attacker can lengthen or shorten the clock pulses to a clocked circuit and destroy normal operations.

Viruses

Viruses are old attacks that threaten the security of all information systems, including RFID systems. RFID viruses always target the back-end database in the server, perhaps destroying and revealing the data or information stored in the database. There exist the following virus threats:

- An RFID virus destroys and reveals the data or information stored in the database.
- An RFID virus disturbs or even stops the normal services provided by the server.
- An RFID virus threatens the security of the communications between RFID readers and RFID tags or between back-end database and RFID readers.

Social Issues

Due to the security challenges in RFID, many people do not trust RFID technologies and fear that they could allow attackers to purloin their privacy information.

Weis [16] presents two main arguments. These arguments make some people choose not to rely on RFID technology and regard RFID tags as the "mark of the beast." However, security issues cannot prevent the success of RFID technology.

The first argument is that RFID tags are regarded as the best replacement for current credit cards and all other ways of paying for goods and services. But RFID tags can also serve as identification. The replacement of current ways of paying by RFID tag requires that people accept RFID tags instead of credit cards, and they cannot sell or buy anything without RFID tags.

There is a second argument [16]: "Since RFID tags are also used as identification, they should be implanted to avoid losing the ID or switching it with someone. Current research has shown that the ideal location for the implant is indeed the forehead or the hand, since they are easy to access and unlike most other body parts they do not contain much fluid, which interferes with the reading of the chip."

Comparison of All Challenges

Previously in this chapter we introduced some of the challenges that RFID systems are facing. Every challenge or attack can have a different method or attack goal, and the consequences of the RFID system after an attack may also be different. In this part of the chapter, we briefly analyze the challenges according to attack methods, attack goals, and the consequences of RFID systems after attacks (see Table 12.4).

The first four challenges are the four basic challenges in RFID systems that correspond to the four basic use cases. *Counterfeiting* happens when counterfeiters forge RFID tags by copying the information from a valid tag or adding some well-formed format information to a new tag in the RFID system. *Sniffing* happens when an unauthorized reader reads the information from a tag, and the information may be utilized by attackers. *Tracking* happens when an attacker who holds some readers unlawfully monitors the movements of objects attached by an RFID tag that can be read by those readers. *Denial of service* happens when the components of RFID systems deny the RFID service.

The last seven challenges or attacks can always happen in RFID systems (see Table 12.4). *Spoofing* happens when an attacker poses as an authorized user of an RFID system on which the attacker can perform invalid operations. *Repudiation* happens when a

TABLE 12.4 Comparison of all Challenges or Attacks in RFID Systems.

Challenge or Attack	Attack Method	Attack Goal	Direct Consequence
Counterfeiting	Forge tags	Tag	Invalid tags
Sniffing	Forge readers	Reader	Reveals information
Tracking	Monitor the movement of objects	Objects of an RFID system	Tracks the movement of object
Denial of service	RF jamming, kill normal command, physical destroy, and so on	Reader, back-end database or server	Denies normal services
Spoofing	Pose as an authorized user	User	Invalid operations by invalid user
Repudiation	Deny action or no proof that the action was implemented	Tag, reader, back-end database or server	Deniable actions
Insert attacks	Insert invalid command	Tag	Invalid operations by invalid commands
Replay attacks	Reuse the response of tags	Communication between RFID tags and readers	Invalid identification
Physical attacks	Physical operations on tag	Tag	Disrupts or destroys communication between RFID tags and readers
Virus	Insert invalid data	Back-end database or server	Destroys the data or service of system
Social issues	Social attitude	Psychology of potential user	Restricts the widespread application

user or component of an RFID system denies the action it performed and there is no proof that the user did perform the action. *Insert attacks* happen when an attacker inserts some invalid system commands into the tags and some operations may be implemented by the invalid command. *Replay attacks* happen when an attacker intercepts the response of the tag and reuses the response for another communication. *Physical attacks* happen when an attacker does some physical operations on RFID tags and these attacks disrupt communications between the RFID readers and tags. A *virus* is the security challenge of all information systems; it can disrupt the operations of RFID systems or reveal the information in those systems. *Social issues* involve users' psychological attitudes that can influence the users' adoption of RFID technologies for real-world applications.

3. RFID PROTECTIONS

According to their computational power, RFID tags can be classified into three categories: basic tags, symmetric-key tags, and public-key tags. In the next part of the chapter, we introduce some protection approaches for these three kinds of RFID tags.

Basic RFID System

Prices have been one of the biggest factors to be considered when we're making decisions on RFID deployments. Basic tags are available for the cheapest price, compared with symmetric-key tags and public-key tags. Due to the limited computation resources built into a basic tag, basic tags are not capable of performing cryptography computations. This imposes a huge challenge to implement protections on basic tags; cryptography has been one of the most important and effective methods to implement protection mechanisms. Recently several approaches have been proposed to tackle this issue.

Most of the approaches to security protection for basic tags focus on protecting consumer privacy. A usual method is by tag killing, proposed by EPCglobal. In this approach, when the reader wants to kill a tag, it sends a kill message to the tag to permanently deactivate it. Together with the kill message, a 32-bit tag-specific PIN code is also sent to the object tag, to avoid killing other tags. On receiving this kill message, a tag will deactivate itself, after which the tag will become inoperative. Generally, tags are killed when the tagged items are checked out in shops or supermarkets. This is very similar to removing the tags from the tagged items when they are purchased. It is an efficient method of protecting the privacy of consumers, since a killed tag can no longer send out information.

The disadvantage of this approach is that it will reduce the post-purchase benefits of RFID tags. In some cases, RFID tags need to be operative only temporarily. For example, RFID tags used in libraries and museums for tagging books and other items need to work at all times and should not be killed or be removed from the tagged items. In these cases, instead of being killed or removed, tags can be made temporarily inactive. When a tag needs to be reawoken, an RFID reader can send a wake message to the tag with a 32-bit tag-specific PIN code, which is sent to avoid waking up other tags. This also results in the management of PIN codes for tags, which brings some inconvenience.

Another approach to protecting privacy is tag relabeling, which was first proposed by Sarma et al [18]. In this scheme, to protect consumers' privacy, identifiers of RFID tags are effaced when tagged items are checked out, but the information on the tags will be kept for later use. Inoue and Yasuuran [19] proposed that consumers can store the identifiers of the tags and give each tag a new identifier. When needed, people can reactivate the tags with the new identifiers. This approach allows users to manage tagged items throughout the items' life cycle. A third approach is to allocate each tag a new random number at each checkout; thus attackers cannot rely on the identifiers to collect information about customers [20]. This method does not solve the problem of tracking [20]. To prevent tracking, random numbers need to be refreshed frequently, which will increase the burden on consumers. Juels proposed a system called the *minimalist system* [21], in which every tag has a list of pseudonyms, and for every reader query, the tag will respond with a different pseudonym from the list and return to the beginning of the list when this list is exhausted. It is assumed that only authorized readers know all these tag pseudonyms. Unauthorized readers that do not know these pseudonyms cannot identify the tags correctly. To prevent unauthorized readers getting the pseudonyms list by frequent query, the tags will response to an RFID reader's request with a relatively low rate, which is called *pseudonym throttling*. Pseudonym throttling is useful, but it cannot provide a high level of privacy for consumers, because with the tag's small memory, the number of pseudonyms in the list is limited. To tackle this problem, the protocol allows an authorized RFID reader to refresh a tag's pseudonyms list.

Juels and Pappu [22] proposed to protect consumers' privacy by using tagged banknotes. The proposed scheme used public-key cryptography to protect the serial numbers of tagged banknotes. The serial number of a tagged banknote is encrypted using a public key to generate a ciphertext, which is saved in the memory of the tag. On receiving a request of the serial number, the tag will respond with this ciphertext. Only law enforcement agencies know the related private key and can decrypt this ciphertext to recover the banknote's serial number. To prevent tracking of banknotes, the ciphertext will be reencrypted periodically. To avoid the ciphertext of a banknote being reencrypted by an attacker, the tagged banknote can use an optical write − access key. A reader that wants to reencrypt this ciphertext needs to scan the write − access key first. In this system only one key pair, a public key and a private key, is used. But this is not enough for the general RFID system. Using multiple key pairs will impair the privacy of RFID systems, since if the reader wants to reencrypt the ciphertext, it needs to know the corresponding public key of this tag.

So, a universal reencryption algorithm has been introduced [23]. In this approach, an RFID reader can reencrypt the ciphertext without knowing the corresponding public key of a tag. The disadvantage of this approach is that attackers can substitute the ciphertext with a new ciphertext, so the integrity of the ciphertext cannot be protected. By signing the ciphertext with a digital signature, this problem can be solved [24], since only the authenticated reader can access the ciphertext.

Floerkemeier (et al.) [25] introduced another approach to protect consumer privacy by using a specially designed protocol. In their approach, they first designed the communication protocol between RFID tags and RFID readers. This protocol requires an RFID reader to provide information about the purpose and the collection type for the query. In addition, a privacy-enforcing device called a *watchdog tag* is used in the system. This watchdog tag is a kind of sophisticated RFID tag that is equipped with a battery, a small screen, and a long-range communication channel. A watchdog tag can be integrated into a PDA or a cell phone and can decode the messages from an RFID reader and display them on the screen for the user to read. With a watchdog tag, a user can know not only the information from the RFID readers in the vicinity of the tag but also the ID, the query purpose, and the collection type of the requests sent by the RFID readers. With this information, the user is able to identify the unwanted communications between tags and an RFID reader, making this method useful for users to avoid the reader ID spoofing attack.

Rieback, Crispo, and Tanebaum [26] proposed another privacy-enforcing device called RFID Guardian, which is also a battery-powered RFID tag that can be integrated into a PDA or a cell phone to protect user privacy. RFID Guardian is actually a user privacy protection platform in RFID systems. It can also work as an RFID reader to request information from RFID tags, or it can work like a tag to communicate with a reader. RFID Guardian has four different security properties: auditing, key management, access control, and authentication. It can audit RFID readers in its vicinity and record information about the RFID readers, such as commands, related parameters, and data, and provide these kinds of information to the user. Using this information, the user can sufficiently identify illegal scanning. In some cases, a user might not know or could forget the tags in his vicinity. With the help of RFID Guardian, the user can detect all the tags within radio range. Then the user can deactivate the tags according to his choice.

For RFID tags that use cryptography methods to provide security, one important issue is key management. RFID Guardian can perform two-way RFID communications and can generate random values. These features are very useful for key exchange and key refresh. Using the features of coordination of security primitives, context awareness, and tag-reader mediation, RFID Guardian can provide access control for RFID systems [26]. Also, using two-way RFID communication and standard challenge-response algorithms, RFID Guardian can provide off-tag authentication for RFID readers.

Another approach for privacy protecting is proposed by Juels, Rivest, and Szydlo [14]. In this approach, a cheap, passive RFID tag is used as the blocker tag. Since this blocker tag can simulate many RFID tags at the same time, it is very difficult for an RFID reader to identify the real tag carried by the user. The blocker tag can both simulate all the possible RFID tags and simulate only a select set of the tags, making it convenient for the user to manage the RFID tags. For example, the user can tell the blocker tag to block only the tags that belong to a certain company. Another advantage of this approach is that if the user wants to reuse these RFID tags, unlike the "killed" tags that need to be activated by the user, the user need only remove the blocker tag. Since the blocker tag can shield the serial numbers of the tags from being read by RFID readers, it can also be used by attackers to disrupt proper operation of an RFID system. A thief can also use the blocker tag to shield the tags attached to the commodities in shops and take them out without being detected.

RFID System Using Symmetric-Key Cryptography

Symmetric-key cryptography, also called *secret-key cryptography* or *single-key cryptography*, uses a single key to perform both encryption and decryption. Due to the limited amount of resources available on an RFID chip, most available symmetric-key cryptographs are too costly to be implemented on an RFID chip. For example, a typical implementation of Advanced Encryption Standard (AES) needs about 2000–3000 gates. This is not appropriate for low-cost RFID tags. It is only possible to implement AES in high-end RFID tags. A successful case of implementing a 128-bit AES on high-end RFID tags has been reported [27].

Using the Symmetric Key to Provide Authentication and Privacy

Symmetric-key cryptography can be applied to prevent tag cloning in RFID systems using a challenge and response protocol. For example, if a tag shares a secret key K with a reader and the tag wants to authenticate itself to the reader, it will first send its identity to the reader. The reader will then generate a nonce N and send it to the tag. The tag will use this nonce and the secret K to generate a hash code $H = h(K,N)$ and send this hash code to the reader. The reader can also generate a hash code $H' = h(K,N)$ and compare these two codes to verify this tag. Using this scheme, it is difficult for an attacker to clone the tags without knowing the secret keys.

Different kinds of symmetric-key cryptography protocol-based RFID tags have been used recently in daily life. For example, an RFID device that uses this symmetric-key challenge-response protocol, called a digital signature transponder, has been introduced by Texas Instruments. This transponder can be built into cars to prevent car theft and can be implemented into wireless payment devices used in filling stations.

One issue of RFID systems that use symmetric-key cryptography is key management. To authenticate itself to an RFID reader, each tag in the system should share a different secret key with the reader, and the reader needs to keep all the keys of these tags. When a tag wants to authenticate itself to an RFID reader, the reader needs to know the secret key shared between them. If the reader does not know the identification of the tag in advance, it cannot determine which key can be used to authenticate this tag. If the tag sends its identification to the reader before the authentication for the reader to search the secret key, the privacy of the tag cannot be protected, since other readers can also obtain the identification of this tag.

To tackle this problem, one simple method is *key searching*. The reader will search all the secret keys in its memory to find the right key for the tag before authentication. There are some protocols proposed for the key search for RFID tags. One general kind of key search scheme [11] has been proposed. In this approach, the tag first generates a random nonce N and hashes this N using its secret key K to generate the hash code. Then it sends both this hash code and N to the reader. Using this nonce N, the reader will generate the hash code with all the secret keys and compare them with the received hash code from the tag. If there is a match, it means it found the right key. In this scheme, since the nonce N is generated randomly every time, the privacy of the tag can be protected.

The problem with this approach is that if there are a large number of tags, the key searching will be very costly. To reduce the cost of the key searching, a modification of this scheme was proposed [28]; in [12], in this approach, a scheme called *tree of secret* is used. Every tag is assigned to a leaf in the tree, and every node in the tree has its secret key. This way the key search cost for each tag can be reduced, but it will add some overlap to the sets of keys for each tag.

Another approach to reduce the cost of key searching is for the RFID tags and RFID reader to keep synchronization with each other. In this kind of approach, every tag will maintain a counter for the reader query times. For each reader's query, the tag should respond with a different value. The reader will also maintain counters for all the tags' responses and maintain a table of all the possible response values. Then, if the reader and tags can keep synchronization, the reader can know the approximate current counter number of the tags. When the reader receives a response from a tag, it can search the table and quickly identify this tag.

Other Symmetric-Key Cryptography-based Approaches

In addition to the basic symmetric-key challenge-response protocol, some symmetric-key cryptography-based approaches have been proposed recently to protect the security and privacy of RFID systems.

One approach is called YA-TRAP: Yet Another Trivial RFID Authentication Protocol, proposed by Tsudik [29]. In this approach, a technique for the inexpensive untraceable identification of RFID tags is introduced. Here *untraceable* means it is computationally difficult to gather the information about the identity of RFID tags from the interaction with them. In YA-TRAP, for the purpose of authentication, only minimal communication between the reader and tags is needed, and the computational burden on the back-end server is very small.

The back-end server in the system is assumed to be secure and maintains all tag information. Each tag should be initialized with three values: K_i, T_0, and T_{max}. K_i is both the identifier and the cryptographic key for this tag. The size of K_i depends on the number of tags and the secure authentication requirement; in practice, 160 bits is enough. T_0 is the initial timestamp of this tag. The value of T_0 of each tag does not need to vary. This means that a group of tags can have the same T_0. T_{max} is the maximum value of T_0, and a group of tags can also have the same T_{max} value. In addition, each tag has a seeded pseudorandom number generator.

YA-TRAP works as follows: First, each tag should store a timestamp T_t in its memory. When an RFID reader wants to interrogate a RFID tag, it will send the current timestamp T_r to this tag. Receiving T_r, the tag will compare T_r with the timestamp value it stores and with T_{max}. If $T_r < T_t$ or $T_r > T_{max}$, this tag will respond to the reader with a random value generated by the seeded pseudo random number generator. Otherwise, the tag will replace T_t with T_r and calculate $H_r = HMACK_i(T_t)$, and then send H_r to the reader. Then the reader will send T_r and H_r to the back-end server. The server will look up its database to find whether this tag is a valid tag. If it's not, the server will send a tag-error message to the reader. If this is a valid tag, the server will send the meta-ID of this tag or the valid message to the reader, according to different application requirements. Since the purpose of this protocol is to minimize the interaction between the reader and tags and minimize the computation burden of the back-end server, it has some vulnerability. One of them is that the adversary can launch a DoS attack to the tag. For example, the attack can send a timestamp $t < T_{max}$, but this t is wildly inaccurate with the current time. In this case, the tag will update its timestamp with the wrong time and the legal reader cannot get access to this tag.

In Ref. [16], another approach called *deterministic hash locks* [11] was proposed. In this scheme, the security of RFID systems is based on the one-way hash function. During initialization, every tag in the system will be given a meta-ID, which is the hash code of a random key. This meta-ID will be stored in the tag's memory. Both the meta-ID and the random key are also stored in the back-end server. After initialization, all the tags will enter the locked state. When they stay in the locked state, tags will respond only with the meta-ID when interrogated by an RFID reader. When a legitimate reader wants to unlock a tag, as shown in Figure 12.2, it will first send a request to the tag. After receiving the meta-ID from the tag, the reader will send this meta-ID to the back-end server. The back-end server will search in its database using this meta-ID to get the random key. Then it will send this key to the reader, and the reader will send it to the tag. Using this random key, the tag will hash this key and compare the hash code with its meta-ID. The tag will unlock itself and send its actual identification to the reader if these two values match. Then the tag will return to the locked state to prevent hijacking of illegal readers. Since the illegal reader cannot contact the back-end server to get the random key, it cannot get the actual identification of the tag.

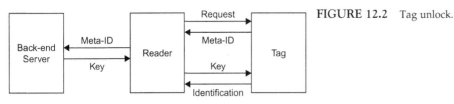

FIGURE 12.2   Tag unlock.

One problem with deterministic hash locks is that when the tag is queried, it will respond with its meta-ID. Since the meta-ID of the tag is a static one and cannot change, the tag can be tracked easily. To solve this problem, Weis, Sarma, Rivest, and Engels proposed the Randomized Hash Locks protocol to prevent tracking of the tag. In this protocol, each tag is equipped with not only the one-way hash function but also a random number generator. When the tag is requested by a reader, it will use the random number generator to generate a random number and will hash this random number together with its identification. The tag will respond with this hash code and the random number to the reader. After receiving this response from the tag, the reader will get all identifications of the tags from the back-end server. Using these identifications, the reader will perform brute-force search by hashing the identification of each tag together with the random number and compare the hash code. If there is a match, the reader can know the identification of the tag. In this approach, the tag response to the reader is not dependent on the request of the reader, which means that the tag is vulnerable to replay attack. To avoid this, Juels and Weis proposed a protocol called Improved Randomized Hash-Locks [30].

RFID System using Public-Key Cryptography

Symmetric-key cryptography can provide security for RFID systems, but it is more suitable to be implemented in a closed environment. If the shared secret keys between them are leaked, it will impose a big problem for the security of RFID systems. Public-key cryptography is more suitable for open systems, since both RFID readers and tags can use their public keys to protect the security of RFID systems. In addition, using public-key cryptography can not only prevent leakage of any information to the eavesdropper attack during communication between reader and tags, it also can provide digital signatures for both the readers and tags for authentication. In the public-key cryptography system, an RFID reader does not need to keep all the secret keys for each tag and does not need to search the appropriate key for each tag as it does in a symmetric-key cryptography system. This will reduce the system burden for key management. Although public-key cryptography has some advantages over symmetric-key cryptography, it is commonly accepted that public-key cryptography is computationally more expensive than symmetric-key cryptography. Because of the limitations of memory and computational power of the ordinary RFID tags, it is difficult for the public-key cryptography to be implemented in RFID systems. In recent years, some research shows that some kinds of public key-based cryptographies such as elliptic curve cryptography and hyperelliptic curve cryptography are feasible to be implemented in high-end RFID tags [31].

Authentication with Public-Key Cryptography

Basically, there are two different kinds of RFID tag authentication methods that use public-key cryptography: one is online authentication and the other is offline authentication [32].

For the authentication of RFID tags in an online situation, the reader is connected with a database server. The database server stores a large number of challenge-response pairs for each tag, making it difficult for the attacker to test all the challenge-response pairs during a limited time period. During the challenge-response pairs enrollment phase, the physical uncloneable function part of RFID systems will be challenged by a Certification Authority with a variety of challenges, and accordingly it will generate responses for these challenges. The physical uncloneable function is embodied in a physical object and can give responses to the given challenges [31]. Then these generated challenge-response pairs will be stored in the database server.

In the authentication phase, when a reader wants to authenticate a tag, first the reader will send a request to the tag for its identification. After getting the ID of the tag, the reader will search the database server to get a challenge-response pair for this ID and send the challenge to the tag. After receiving the challenge from the reader, the tag will challenge its physical uncloneable function to get a response for this challenge and then send this response to the reader. The reader will compare this received response with the response stored in the database server. If the difference between these two responses is less than a certain predetermined threshold, the tag can pass the authentication. Then the database server will remove this challenge-response pair for this ID.

One paper [31] details how the authentication of RFID tags works in an offline situation using public key cryptography. To provide offline authentication for the tags, a PUF-Certificate-Identify-based identification scheme is proposed. In this method, a standard identification scheme and a standard signature scheme are used. Then the security of RFID systems depends on the security of the PUF, the standard identification scheme, and the standard signature scheme. For the standard identification scheme, an elliptic curve discrete log based on Okamoto's Identification protocol [33] is used. This elliptic curve discrete log protocol is feasible to be implemented in the RFID tags.

Identity-Based Cryptography Used in the RFID Networks

An identity-based cryptographic scheme is a kind of public-key-based approach that was first proposed by Shamir [34] in 1984. To use identity-based cryptography in RFID systems, since both the RFID tags and the reader have their identities, it is convenient for them to use their own identities to generate their public keys.

An RFID system based on identity-based cryptography should be set up with the help of a PKG. When the reader and tags enter the system, each of them is allocated a unique identity stored in their memory. The process of key generation and distribution in the RFID system that uses identity-based cryptography is shown in Figure 12.3 and is outlined here:

1. PKG generates a "master" public key PU_{pkg} and a related "master" private key PR_{pkg} and saves them in its memory.
2. The RFID reader authenticates itself to the PKG with its identity ID_{re}.

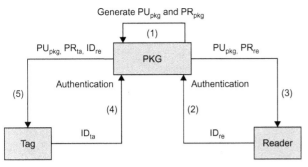

FIGURE 12.3 Key generation and distribution.

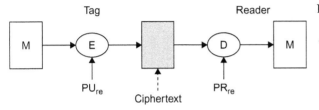

FIGURE 12.4 Message encryption.

3. If the reader can pass the authentication, PKG generates a unique private key PR_{re} for the reader and sends this private key together with PU_{pkg} to reader.

4. When an RFID tag enters the system, it authenticates itself to the PKG with its identity ID_{ta}.

5. If the tag can pass the authentication, PKG generates a unique private key PR_{ta} for the tag and sends PR_{ta} together with PU_{pkg} and the identity of the reader ID_{re} to the tag.

After this process, the reader can know its private key PR_{re} and can use PU_{pkg} and its identity to generate its public key. Every tag entered into the system can know its own private key and can generate a public key of its own and a public key of the reader.

If an RFID tag is required to transmit messages to the reader in security, since the tag can generate the reader's public key PU_{re}, it can use this key PU_{re} to encrypt the message and transmit this encrypted message to the reader. As shown in Figure 12.4, after receiving the message from the tag, the reader can use its private key PR_{re} to decrypt the message. Since only the reader can know its private key PR_{re}, the security of the message can be protected.

Figure 12.5 illustrates the scheme for the reader to create its digital signature and verify it. First, the reader will use the message and the hash function to generate a hash code, and then it uses its private key PR_{re} to encrypt this hash code to generate the digital signature and attach it to the original message and send both the digital signature and message to the tag. After receiving them, the RFID tag can use the public key of the reader PU_{re} to decrypt the digital signature to recover the hash code. By comparing this hash code with the hash code generated from the message, the RFID tag can verify the digital signature.

Figure 12.6 illustrates the scheme for the RFID tag to create its digital signature and verify it. In RFID systems, the reader cannot know the identity of the tag before reading it from the tag. The reader cannot generate the public key of the tag, so the general protocol

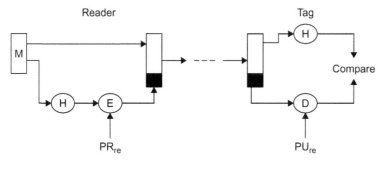

FIGURE 12.5 A digital signature from a reader.

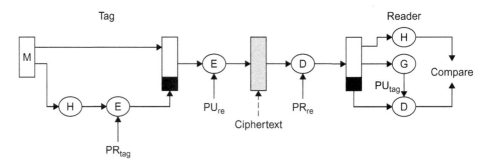

FIGURE 12.6 A digital signature from a tag.

used in identity-based networks cannot be used here. In our approach, first, the tag will use its identity and its private key $PR_{ta}$to generate a digital signature. When the tag needs to authenticate itself to the reader, it will add this digital signature to its identity, encrypt it with the public key of the reader PU_{re}, and send to the reader; only the reader can decrypt this ciphertext and get the identity of the tag and the digital signature. Using the tag identity, the reader can generate the tag's public key PU_{ta}. Then the reader can use this public key to verify the digital signature.

As mentioned, the most important problem for the symmetric-key approach in RFID systems is the key management. The RFID tags need a great deal of memory to store all the secret keys related with each tag in the system for message decryption. Also, if the RFID reader receives a message from a tag, it cannot know which tag this message is from and therefore cannot know which key it can use to decrypt the message. The reader needs to search all the keys until it finds the right one. In RFID systems using identity-based cryptography, every tag can use the public key of the reader to generate the ciphertext that can be decrypted using the reader's private key, so the reader does not need to know the key of the tags; all it needs to keep is its own private key.

In some RFID applications such as epassports and visas, tag authentication is required. However, the symmetric-key approach cannot provide digital signatures for RFID tags to authenticate them to RFID readers. By using an identity-based scheme, the tags can generate digital signatures using their private keys and store them in the tags. When they need to authenticate themselves to RFID readers, they can transmit these digital signatures to the reader, and the reader can verify them using the tags' public keys.

In identity-based cryptography RFID systems, since the identity of the tags and reader can be used to generate public keys, the PKG does not need to keep the key directory, so it can reduce the resource requirements. Another advantage of using identity-based cryptography in RFID systems is that the reader does not need to know the public keys of the tags in advance. If the reader wants to verify the digital signature of an RFID tag, it can read the identity of the tag and use the public key generated from the identity to verify the digital signature.

An inherent weakness of identity-based cryptography is the key escrow problem. But in RFID systems that use identity-based cryptography, because all the devices can be within one company or organization, the PKG can be highly trusted and protected, and the chance of key escrow can be reduced.

Another problem of identity-based cryptography is revocation. For example, people always use their public information such as their names or home addresses to generate their public key. If a person's private keys are compromised by an attacker, since public information cannot be changed easily, this will make it difficult to regenerate new public keys. In contrast, in RFID systems the identity of the tag is used to generate the public key. If the private key of one tag has been compromised, the system can allocate a new identity to the tag and use this new identity to effortlessly create a new private key to the tag.

4. SUMMARY

Like any information technology (IT), radio frequency identification (RFID) presents security and privacy risks that must be carefully mitigated through management, operational, and technical controls in order to realize the numerous benefits the technology has to offer. When practitioners adhere to sound security engineering principles, RFID technology can help a wide range of organizations and individuals realize substantial productivity gains and efficiencies. These organizations and individuals include hospitals and patients, retailers and customers, and manufacturers and distributors throughout the supply chain. This chapter provided detailed coverage of RFID technology, the associated security and privacy risks, and recommended practices that will enable organizations to realize productivity improvements while safeguarding sensitive information and protecting the privacy of individuals. While RFID security is a rapidly evolving field with a number of promising innovations expected in the coming years, these guidelines focus on controls that are commercially available today.

Finally, let's move on to the real interactive part of this Chapter: review questions/exercises, hands-on projects, case projects and optional team case project. The answers and/or solutions by chapter can be found in the Online Instructor's Solutions Manual.

CHAPTER REVIEW QUESTIONS/EXERCISES

True/False

1. True or False? Data carriers attached to objects are called RFID tags.
2. True or False? Currently, as different frequencies are used for RFID systems in various countries and many standards are adopted for different kinds of application, there is an agreement on a universal standard that's accepted by all parties.
3. True or False? Recently more and more companies and organizations have begun to use RFID tags rather than traditional barcode because RFID systems have many advantages over traditional barcode systems.
4. True or False? RFID tags can be classified into three categories based on the equipped computation power: basic tags, symmetric-key tags, and public-key tags.
5. True or False? Another main issue of concern in deploying RFID systems is the sniffing problem.

Multiple Choice

1. Besides the four basic types of attack (counterfeiting, sniffing, tracking, and denial of service) in real-world applications, there also exists some other threats to RFID systems, like:
   A. Spoofing.
   B. Temporal Key Integrity Protocols (TKIP).
   C. Application Program Interfaces.
   D. Network Areas.
   E. Extensible Authentication Protocol (EAP) framework.
2. What happens when counterfeiters forge RFID tags by copying the information from a valid tag or adding some well-formed format information to a new tag in the RFID system?
   A. Middle Layers.
   B. DOS.
   C. Tracking.
   D. Sniffing.
   E. Counterfeiting.
3. What tags are available for the cheapest price, compared with symmetric-key tags and public-key tags?
   A. Symmetric-key tags.
   B. Public-key tags.
   C. Basic tags.
   D. Authenticated Routing tags.
   E. All of the Above.
4. What uses a single key to perform both encryption and decryption?
   A. False base cryptography.
   B. Symmetric-key cryptography.
   C. Eavesdropping cryptography.

D. Man-in-the-Middle cryptography.

E. Passive cryptography.

5. What can provide security for RFID systems, but it is more suitable to be implemented in a closed environment?

A. HELLO Flood connectivity.

B. Denial-of-service attack connectivity.

C. Internet connectivity.

D. Symmetric-key cryptography.

E. All of the above.

EXERCISE

Problem

What provisions are made for code security?

Hands-On Projects

Project

How can you ensure the security of electronic product code (EPC) data?

Case Projects

Problem

Personnel and asset tracking in a health care environment, is a hypothetical case study to illustrate how RFID security might be implemented in practice. Although the case study is fictional, it is intended to resemble real-world activities, including how decision makers address common and expected RFID security problems and their solutions. The case study does not cover *all* of the aspects of RFID system engineering or operations that an organization may encounter in its RFID implementation, but rather a representative sample of salient issues. The case study follows.

The Fringe Science Research Center (FSRC) is a health care facility dedicated to the study of highly contagious diseases—those transmitted through casual human contact. The Center has 80 beds for patient care, a radiology unit with four rooms of sophisticated imaging equipment, and eight laboratories with various diagnostic and research capabilities. The Center confronts the same management issues as many hospitals, including locating portable diagnostic equipment when needed and accounting for missing assets. Another important concern is the ability to quickly locate patients and staff as they move about the facility. Poor asset management results in higher costs, reduced efficiency, and lower quality of care.

The mission of the FSRC also leads to specialized requirements. To prevent unnecessary outbreaks of disease and to understand how transmission occurs, FSRC needs to track the interactions among its staff, patients, and visitors. These tracked interactions provide useful information to researchers about who came into contact with whom and at what time. Additionally, the FSRC must alert caregivers of disease-specific protocols when they are in close proximity to particular patients, including prohibiting staff contact in some cases. It must track blood, urine, and stool samples from patient to laboratory. Finally, the FSRC would like to track the history of in-house diagnostic equipment and trace how the equipment is used to support patients throughout each day. Currently, paper processes are used to achieve these objectives, but they are very labor-intensive and error-prone, sometimes with fatal consequences.

FSRC executives tasked the FSRC's Chief Information Officer (CIO) to use RFID technology to improve the FSRC's traditional asset management function; as well as, meet its specialized requirements. Working with the FSRC executives, how did the CIO go about commissioning a project to reengineer FSRC business practices by using RFID technology as a primary tool to improve organizational performance?

Optional Team Case Project

Problem

Supply chain management of hazardous materials, is also a hypothetical case study to illustrate how RFID security might be implemented in practice. Although the case study is fictional, it is intended to resemble real-world activities, including how decision makers address common and expected RFID security problems and their solutions. The case study does not cover *all* of the aspects of RFID system engineering or operations that an organization may encounter in its RFID implementation, but rather a representative sample of salient issues. The case study follows.

The RAD corporation oversees the movement of radioactive research materials between production facilities, national laboratories, military installations, and other relevant locations. The RAD oversight of the supply chain for these materials involves many of the same issues as in most any other supply chain. RAD wants to know who is in possession of what quantity of materials at any given time. It also wants to locate materials at a site quickly, without having to search through numerous containers to find them. Bar code technology does not provide that capability.

Some of RAD's requirements are more unique. For instance, much of the transported radionuclide material must be closely monitored because extreme temperatures or excessive vibration can make it useless for its intended applications. Consequently, RAD wants temperature and vibration sensors to continuously measure environmental conditions and record readings on the tag. Additionally, the handling of RAD-regulated materials is a homeland and national security issue. If the materials were to fall into unauthorized hands, they could endanger the public welfare. So, with the preceding in mind, how would RAD's project team go about conducting a risk assessment?

References

[1] S.A. Weis, Security and Privacy in Radio-Frequency Identification Devices.
[2] M. Langheinrich, RFID and Privacy.
[3] Auto-ID Center, Draft Protocol Specification for a Class 0 Radio Frequency Identification Tag, February 2003.

[4] K. Finkenzeller, RFID Handbook: Fundamentals and Applications in Contactless Smart Cards and Identification.

[5] P. Peris-Lopez, J.C. Hernandez-Castro, J. Estevez-Tapiador, A. Ribagorda, RFID systems: a survey on security threats and proposed solutions, 11th IFIP International Conference on Personal Wireless Communications – PWC06, Volume 4217 of Lecture Notes in Computer Science, Springer-Verlag, September 2006, pp. 159–170.

[6] RFID Handbook, second ed., J. Wiley & Sons.

[7] T. Phillips, T. Karygiannis, R. Huhn, Security standards for the RFID market, IEEE Secur. & Privacy (November/December 2005) 85–89.

[8] EPCglobal, www.epcglobalinc.org/, June 2005.

[9] EPCglobal Tag Data Standards, Version 1.3.

[10] Guidelines for Securing Radio Frequency Identification (RFID) Systems, Recommendations of the National Institute of Standards and Technology, NIST Special Publication 800–98.

[11] S. Weis, S. Sarma, R. Rivest, D. Engels, Security and privacy aspects of low-cost radio frequency identification systems, in: W. Stephan, D. Hutter, G. Muller, M. Ullmann (Eds.), International Conference on Security in Pervasive computing-SPC 2003, vol. 2802, Springer-Verlag, 2003, pp. 454–469.

[12] D. Haehnel, W. Burgard, D. Fox, K. Fishkin, M. Philipose, Mapping and localization with WID technology, International Conference on Robotics & Automation, 2004.

[13] D.R. Thompson, N. Chaudhry, C.W. Thompson, RFID Security Threat Model.

[14] A. Juels, R.L. Rivest, M. Syzdlo, The blocker tag: selective blocking of RFID tags for consumer privacy, in: V. Atluri (Ed.), 8th ACM Conference on Computer and Communications Security, 2003, pp. 103–111.

[15] F. Thornton, B. Haines, A.M. Das, H. Bhargava, A. Campbell, J. Kleinschmidt, RFID Security.

[16] C. Jechlitschek, A Survey Paper on Radio Frequency Identification (RFID) Trends.

[17] S.H. Weingart, Physical Security Devices for Computer Subsystems: A Survey of Attacks and Defenses.

[18] S.E. Sarma, S.A. Weis, D.W. Engels, RFID systems security and privacy implications, Technical Report, MITAUTOID-WH-014, AutoID Center, MIT, 2002.

[19] S. Inoue, H. Yasuura, RFID privacy using user-controllable uniqueness, in: RFID Privacy Workshop, MIT, November 2003.

[20] N. Good, J. Han, E. Miles, D. Molnar, D. Mulligan, L. Quilter, J. Urban, D. Wagner, Radio frequency ID and privacy with information goods, in: Workshop on Privacy in the Electronic Society (WPES), 2004.

[21] A. Juels, Minimalist cryptography for low-cost RFID tags, in: C. Blundo, S. Cimato (Eds.), The Fourth International Conference on Security in Communication Networks – SCN 2004, Vol. 3352 of Lecture Notes in Computer Science, Springer-Verlag, 2004, pp. 149–164.

[22] A. Juels, R. Pappu, Squealing euros: privacy protection in RFID-enabled banknotes, in: R. Wright (Ed.), Financial Cryptography '03, vol. 2742, Springer-Verlag, 2003, pp. 103–121.

[23] P. Golle, M. Jakobsson, A. Juels, P. Syverson, Universal re-encryption for mixnets, in: T. Okamoto (Ed.), RSA Conference-Cryptographers' Track (CT-RSA), vol. 2964, 2004, pp. 163–178.

[24] G. Ateniese, J. Camenisch, B. de Madeiros, Untraceable RFID tags via insubvertible encryption, in: 12th ACM Conference on Computer and Communication Security, 2005.

[25] C. Floerkemeier, R. Schneider, M. Langheinrich, Scanning with a Purpose Supporting the Fair Information Principles in RFID Protocols, 2004.

[26] M.R. Rieback, B. Crispo, A. Tanenbaum, RFID Guardian: a battery-powered mobile device for RFID privacy management, in: C. Boyd, J.M. González Nieto (Eds.), Australasian Conference on Information Security and Privacy – ACISP 2005, Vol. 3574 of Lecture Notes in Computer Science, Springer-Verlag, 2005, pp. 184–194.

[27] M. Feldhofer, S. Dominikus, J. Wolkerstorfer, Strong authentication for RFID systems using the AES algorithm, in: M. Joye, J.-J. Quisquater (Eds.), Workshop on Cryptographic Hardware and Embedded Systems CHES 04, Vol. 3156 of Lecture Notes in Computer Science, Springer-Verlag, 2004, pp. 357–370.

[28] D. Molnar, D. Wagner, Privacy and security in library RFID: issues, practices, and architectures, in: B. Pfitzmann, P. McDaniel (Eds.), ACM Conference on Communications and Computer Security, ACM Press, 2004, pp. 210–219.

[29] G. Tsudik, YA-TRAP: Yet another trivial RFID authentication protocol, in: Fourth Annual IEEE International Conference on Pervasive Computing and Communications Workshops (PERCOMW'06), 2006, pp. 640–643.

[30] A. Juels, S. Weis, Defining strong privacy for RFID, in: Pervasive Computing and Communications Workshops, 2007.

[31] P. Tuyls, L. Batina, RFID tags for anticounterfeiting, in: D. Pointcheval (Ed.), Topics in Cryptology-CT-RSA 2006, Springer-Verlag, 2006.

[32] L. Batina, J. Guajardo, T. Kerins, N. Mentens, P. Tuyls, I. Verbauwhede, Public-key cryptography for RFID-tags. in: Printed handout of Workshop on RFID Security, RFIDSec06, 2006, pp. 61−76.

[33] T. Okamoto, Provably secure and practical identification schemes and corresponding signature schemes, in: E.F. Brickell (Ed.), Advances in Cryptology | CRYPTO'92, Vol. 740 of LNCS, Springer-Verlag, 1992, pp. 31−53.

[34] A. Shamir, Identity-based cryptosystems and signature scheme, Advances in Cryptology: Proceedings of CRYPTO 84, LNCS, 1984, pp. 47−53.

13

Optical Wireless Security

Scott R. Ellis, EnCE, RCA
kCura Corporation

1. OPTICAL WIRELESS SYSTEMS OVERVIEW

In this section, we examine the origins of using light as a means of communication, and we discuss how, over time, it developed into free space optic (FSO) technology. This section will also cover the use of the technology.

History

The use of light and optics is long standing. The ancient Greeks used their polished shields to send reflected light signals while in battle. In 1880, Alexander Graham Bell and his assistant, Charles Sumner Tainger, jointly created a device they called a photophone, or radiophone. Using it, they could transmit sound on a beam of light. The device was based on the photovoltaic properties of crystalline selenium and worked very similarly to the telephone. Bell did not, however, predict the laser or fiber optics, which needed to predicate any potential success of such a device. World War II saw the use of the invention for secure communication. Early on, its users recognized that clear, targeted, line-of-sight communication, invisible to everyone else, allowed for a high degree of security. FSO technology is inherently secure primarily because of this. It wouldn't be until the 1960s and the invention of lasers that this form of communication would mature into Bell's 1880s vision.

Today

FSO uses optical pulse-modulated signals—light—to transmit data from point to point. The technology is similar to fiber optics, with the exception that instead of being contained in glass fiber, the signal is transmitted through varying degrees of atmospheric conditions.

Each FSO unit consists of an optical transmitter and receiver with full duplex capability. This means it is bidirectional.

Typically, these devices are mounted on buildings. Part of the security of these devices is, of course, ensuring that no harm or damage can come to the device, due to its perceived attractiveness by natural aviary populations (make sure you can keep pigeons off of it). The devices contain an array of optics that is used to signal between the device pair at distances of up to several kilometers.

Because these systems are mounted on buildings and because (conceivably) something could happen that could cause a unit to point or be directed into human (or even pigeon) eyes, there are some safety considerations. FSO systems operate in the infrared range. When discussing these devices, and the range in which they operate, the term *wavelength* is used.

Theory of Operation

It is common knowledge that radio frequency (rf) transmissions are easily intercepted and that the technology of securing the transmissions can, if it is secured at all, usually be circumvented, given enough time and effort. It takes little effort to simply drive around and find an "open" wireless connection, even though Light is both a wave and a particle, but most often is discussed in terms of wavelength. Generally, FSO uses infrared (IR), optical light-emitting diode (LED) laser technology at between 780 and 1550 nm. The higher ranges are thought to be less damaging to the cornea as the beam is absorbed by the cornea and never strikes the retina.

The greatest challenge that faces widespread acceptance of FSO is atmospheric conditions. Factors such as fog, smog, heavy rain, or even clouds of dust raised by construction or in areas near desert locales are detrimental to the optical signal. The greater the distance that the beam attempts to traverse, the greater the likelihood that it will fail. Additionally, scintillation—viewed by human eyes as "heat mirages"—is a perturbation in the homogeneous atmospheric density that can significantly distort the photonic transmission. Units with adaptive power will reduce the power to the laser in clear weather and increase it in inclement conditions. Adaptive power features will also increase the life span of the units. Many units are built with features that will increase the physical security. Features such as the following all contribute to increase the security by significantly reducing overshoot signals:

- Adaptive power—prevents overpowering during clear weather
- High frequency—prevents the use of commercially available optics to detect the signal
- Narrow beamwidth—reduces overshoot footprint
- Higher quality optics—prevents a narrower overshoot footprint

Placement on buildings can determine the amount of security as well as signal degradation due to atmospheric conditions. Higher elevations on buildings may increase the amount of disruption to fog; lower elevations may increase the amount of disruption to construction activities like severe dust. Placement should also ensure that the unit has some sort of backstop that can prevent overshoot footprint.

Finally, as it relates to physical security, the diffraction grating effect of shining a light through a small hole must be considered. As any sophomore physics student knows, the equation of light diffraction through an aperture is:

$$I = I_0 \left(\frac{\sin \beta}{\beta} \right)^2$$

where

$$\beta = \frac{\pi W \sin \theta}{\lambda}$$

W = the size of the aperture.

As can be seen, as the aperture gets larger and the wavelength gets smaller, the central disk of illumination varies inversely with the size of the aperture. An FSO manufacturer that simply assembles parts from various manufacturers without consideration of diffraction grating will be more vulnerable to overspread than a conscientious manufacture that has thoroughly engineered its product.

2. DEPLOYMENT ARCHITECTURES

Deployment of the technology varies. The commonly used variations are mesh, ring, point to multipoint (PMP), and point to point (P2P). Some concern over building movement may be appropriate—there are devices capable of autocorrecting up to a few degrees of range. Most devices are designed with movement-handling capabilities. Building architects may have more information; it would be very disappointing to install a system in July, only to find out, nearly nine months later, that March through May winds cause unacceptable disruptions in service, caused by building sway.

Mesh

In a mesh architecture, every node is connected to every other node in a mesh-like lattice work of connections (see Figure 13.1). An increase in the number of nodes increases the quality of the mesh. Mesh networks offer a high degree of reliability. Mesh and ring architectures are larger scale, metropolitan-style deployments that may be used by large carriers and service providers.

Ring

Large cities, such as Hong Kong, may use ring architecture to deliver quality, high-bandwidth Internet services to the entire city. Ring architecture is a blend of mesh and Point to Point/point-to-point (PTP) (see Figure 13.2). With a broad geographical deployment, the ring itself resides at the center, near or at a large communications trunk, or several. It may or may not link multiple trunk sites for redundancy, which also increases

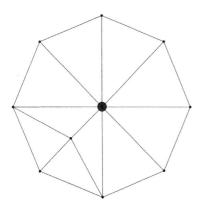

FIGURE 13.1 In a mesh schema, all points are interconnected. This provides a high degree of redundancy.

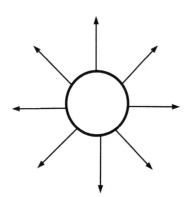

FIGURE 13.2 In a ring schema, a heavy-duty, high-bandwidth ring exists at the center. This provides a high degree of redundancy, as well as pushing the threshold for distance and strength of signal.

the diameter of the ring to extend the range over the area. Communication points are then established as links that radiate outward from the ring, like the spokes of a wheel.

Point to Point

Point-to-point architecture comes in two flavors: PTP and PMP. As the names imply, the only difference lay in the one-to-one relationship versus a one-to-many relationship. This architecture primarily suits smaller deployments, such as an organization that may have multiple office locations or an office that has set up space across the street.

In a PTP network, multiple single connections are chained together, linearly, to increase the range of the network. Perhaps the only connection to be made is across town, or perhaps multiple locations are served along the way. It effectively increases the range of the product or defeats the shortened range that may occur during inclement conditions.

In a PMP schema, all connections to various locations radiate outward from a central location. A single node acts as the source, with a central communications closet in the building serving to link the devices at the central location. For example, by placing the optical wireless devices at all four sides of a single, hub building, you can extend the

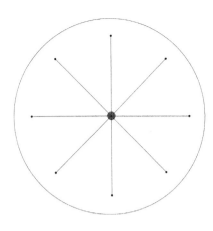

FIGURE 13.3 In a PMP schema, a single, central trunk provides high-bandwidth service to multiple, closely linked optical wireless transmitters. This provides a low-cost solution to providing high-bandwidth network services in a small geographical area, where cost savings is more important than redundancy or high availability.

network to surrounding buildings. Such a deployment would be most suitable for organizations with campus-styled building layouts. Figure 13.3 illustrates the connection points of such an arrangement.

3. HIGH BANDWIDTH

FSO devices boast speeds of up to 10 Gbps in an unhindered atmosphere. Bandwidth decreases in the presence of smog and fog down to complete loss of signal. For this reason, when selecting FSO, it is important to consider the local weather and the distances involved.

4. LOW COST

Security is expensive. The larger the physicality of the surface area, the greater is the area that needs protection from attack. Assuming that line of sight and lease rights are forthcoming and easily procured, setting up a land-based metropolitan network in a city such as Chicago could be very expensive. The price difference of using fiber versus FSO in an installation to connect two offices that are 400 m apart is not just a small percentage. It is several orders of magnitude more expensive to install fiber.

5. IMPLEMENTATION

In theory, FSO has great potential to become far more commonplace and enjoy much greater acceptance in the information technology community than it currently enjoys. At the time of this writing, FSO installations can be found in places such as corporate and educational campuses.

Future use could see the removal of wired communications across long distances in open country, with tall poles housing FSO equipment. It is common knowledge that the technology has already been successfully used in space communications and that Artemis, the European Space Agency Advanced Relay and Technology Mission Satellite, successfully linked with an aircraft at a distance of over 40,000 km. The use of optical boosting equipment could introduce even greater adoption in long-distance (many millions of miles) communications with deep space missions.

High data rates, lightweight equipment, low-energy requirements, little interference, and nearly guaranteed clear and unobstructed paths between space platforms makes space the ideal environment for FSO networks. They would also be somewhat tap proof, though it is conceivable that an enemy satellite could interpose and successfully relay the signal, undetected, the whole while recording and transmitting it back to Wreaking Havoc headquarters (HQ).

6. SURFACE AREA

Microwave and radio frequency (RF) antennas that are typically used to interconnect remote stations have a radial dispersion of 5 to 25 degrees. The actual wavelength of light for optical wireless is in the near-infrared range of 800—1500 nm.

Narrow beams are usually less than 0.5 degrees. By using the diagram and formula given in Figure 13.4, the approximate spread of the beam can be calculated providing the distance is known.

Generally speaking, optical wireless devices operate at the same wavelength as fiber-optic networks. Thus, a small wavelength creates frequencies in the several hundred tera-hertz (THz) range. This is much higher than commercial microwave communications. The lower power and tighter beam of the wireless optics prevent wide angles of reflection, which can be intercepted in an attack (see checklist: An Agenda for Action When Implementing the Security of FSO). Government organizations were among the first to recognize that the greater ability to control the wireless beam inherently meant a higher degree of freedom. The 128 and 256 advanced encryption standard is frequently used in microwave transmissions; while this is all well and good, many are concerned that it can be broken.

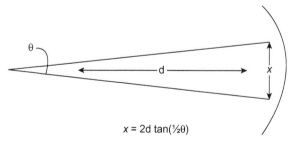

FIGURE 13.4 The width of the broadcast at x distance can be calculated using simple trigonometry. Different manufacturers boast different theta and use this formula to calculate the spread based on equipment specifications.

$$x = 2d \tan(\tfrac{1}{2}\theta)$$

AN AGENDA FOR ACTION WHEN IMPLEMENTING THE SECURITY OF FSO

The five items in this checklist are, in the author's experience; the most important and critical things to address (and they are listed in order of priority) in any project that aspires to achieve true security of the physical infrastructure. The easiest way to gain access to classified access is always the first way that will be attempted by those who wish to gain unauthorized access. So, assuming that data access prevention through traditional hacking attacks is in place, the key to security of FSO lies in the following (check all tasks completed):

_____1. *Intrusion alerts*: When a signal is lost or disrupted, make sure your management software is capable of pinpointing when and where the interruption occurred.

_____2. *Entrusted access:* Make sure that, either real or verified, the people working with the data are not selling it out the back door—that they are incorruptible.

_____3. *Physical security of hardware:* Prevent actual physical access by unauthorized personnel.

_____4. *Eavesdropping on transmissions*: Make sure that any mechanism that collects the data in transit is thwarted.

_____5. *Data security*: Make sure that the data is encrypted, so that should it be intercepted it cannot be understood.

To intercept an optical wireless system, the hacker must know the location of either the origin or the target. The intruder must also have unhindered access to a location where he can set up his electronic equipment without being caught or disturbed. Since this location is usually a commercial location, at an elevation well above ground, the ability to insert becomes tremendously more challenging. FSO devices also employ multiplex, bidirectional signals. If the insertion is occlusive, then the units *know* when the signal has been disrupted. They will not continue to broadcast without the reverse bias feedback that indicates a successful connection. The interloper will only intercept connections establishing signals.

Additionally, the very high installations that are typical of optical wireless present additional challenges. But what about light scattered from rain, fog, dust, aerosol, or the like? Optical wireless transmissions use extremely low power levels, but the main reason for discounting this possible attack is the scattering of light in many different directions from the transmitted path.

The amount of radiation that can be collected with a detector capable of processing the signal is well beneath the range of what most detectors would consider noise. Because the beam is a laser, once the beam is scattered, the scattered photons still maintain their cohesion. However, being lasers, they tend to move in a very straight line with little incoherence. Capturing enough of the scattered light would require a collector that encapsulates the entire beam, and even then, it may not be enough. Ultimately, though, if the fog is such that one can see the actual beam (imagine a laser pen shining through fog), then it is conceivable that a collector could be designed that would be able to read the signal and translate its longitudinal section. The most likely scenario is that such an intercept device would only capture useless noise and would be so large as to make it extremely noticeable and unwieldy.

Lastly, a hacker could conceivably parachute onto the roof of a building and set his or her intercept device down on top of or next to the network FSO he or she wished to crack. For this reason, take the following precautions:

- FSOs should have backstops to prevent overshoot to neighboring office windows or rooftops.
- They should be mounted in difficult to reach places.
- They should have physical security such as keycard and/or biometric access.
- They should be protected by motion detection systems and motion-activated video surveillance.

7. SUMMARY

The advantages of FSO technology are easily summarized. Its security is achieved primarily through the difficulty in interception of the signal. Additional security can easily be introduced in the form of traffic encryption, though this will subtract from the overall, available bandwidth. Deployment of the technology is easy because large areas can be quickly spanned with the installation of just two devices. Additionally, the technology is unaffected by electromagnetic interference, and it has low rates of error in the transmission, which means higher overall bandwidth. It also has no licensing fees, unlike microwave transmissions, and with a range of 2 KM, this is a very attractive feature.

While it does face its challenges, such as fog and very dense weather, in such areas where this is common, it could serve to offer a layer of Disaster Recovery (DR) protection. If land links are compromised due to earthquake, flood, or hurricane, FSO can offer a way of bringing signal in to an area quickly from an unaffected area.

Regardless of the configuration used, and its strengths and weaknesses, FSO is a technology that should be examined and considered as a potentially essential element in any large-area communications architecture. In the end, it is important to realize that security is never a *one-step* task. It has multiple dimensions, and every product has its security weaknesses and strengths. The most important aspect is to choose a technology that, in the existing enterprise, meshes well with existing security features, or is capable of being adapted easily and quickly to them.

The most attractive feature of FSO systems is the tremendous transmission security provided by the very narrow width of the beam used. Lasers can be aimed with a great deal of precision, and considering that the aperture of a laser beam that is very much larger than the actual wavelength of the laser, diffraction interference is minimal. This prevents even further scattering that could potentially be used to even detect that laser transmissions are occurring. The combination of keeping the location of the transceivers secret, the lack of distortion scattering, and the narrow beamwidth offers a high level of security in that the beam is virtually undetectable.

Finally, let's move on to the real interactive part of this chapter: review questions/exercises, hands-on projects, case projects, and optional team case project. The answers and/or solutions by chapter can be found in the Online Instructor's Solution Manual.

CHAPTER REVIEW QUESTIONS/EXERCISES

True/False

1. True or False? FSO uses optical pulse-modulated signals—light—to transmit data from point to point.
2. True or False? It is not common knowledge that radio frequency transmissions are easily intercepted and that the technology of securing the transmissions can, if it is secured at all, usually be circumvented, given enough time and effort.
3. True or False? Most devices are not designed with movement-handling capabilities.
4. True or False? In a mesh architecture, every other node is connected to every other node in a mesh-like lattice work of connections.
5. True or False? Ring architecture is a blend of mesh and PTP.

Multiple Choice

1. What architecture comes in two flavors: PTP and PMP?
   A. Spoofing.
   B. Point-to-point.
   C. Application programming interfaces.
   D. Network areas.
   E. Extensible Authentication Protocol (EAP) framework.
2. What devices boast speeds of up to 10 Gbps in an unhindered atmosphere?
   A. SSO.
   B. RSO.
   C. FSO.
   D. OSO.
   E. TSO.
3. The larger the physicality of the surface area, the greater is the area that needs protection from:
   A. attack.
   B. high expenses.
   C. price differences.
   D. lease rights.
   E. All of the above.
4. In theory, what has great potential to become far more commonplace and enjoy much greater acceptance in the information technology community than is currently the case?
   A. Splicing.
   B. Accessing.

C. Bending.

D. FSO.

E. Cabling.

5. Microwave and RF antennas that are typically used to interconnect remote stations have a radial dispersion of:

A. 5–20 degrees.

B. 5–30 degrees.

C. 5–35 degrees.

D. 5–40 degrees.

E. 5–25 degrees.

EXERCISE

Problem

Are wireless fiber-optic networks more secure than standard wiring or airwaves?

Hands-On Projects

Project

How would you set up a fiber tap?

Case Projects

Problem

After homing in on the target and gaining access to the fiber-optic cable itself, what is the next step to extract light and, ultimately, data from the fiber-optic cable?

Optional Team Case Project

Problem

Can a light shield actually be created?

Index